Story & Art by
Julietta Suzuki

CHARACTERS

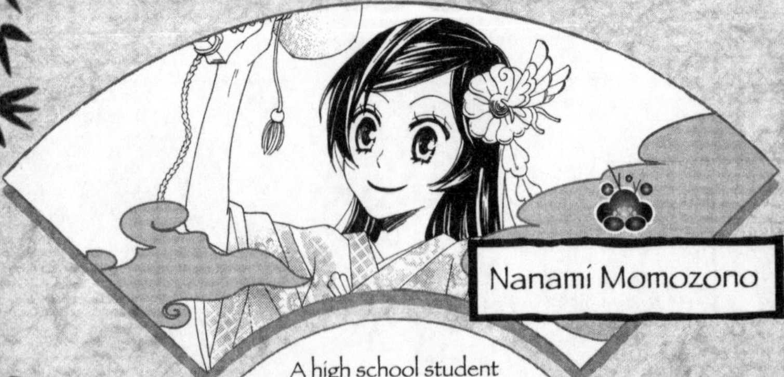
Nanami Momozono

A high school student who was turned into a kamisama by the tochigami Mikage.

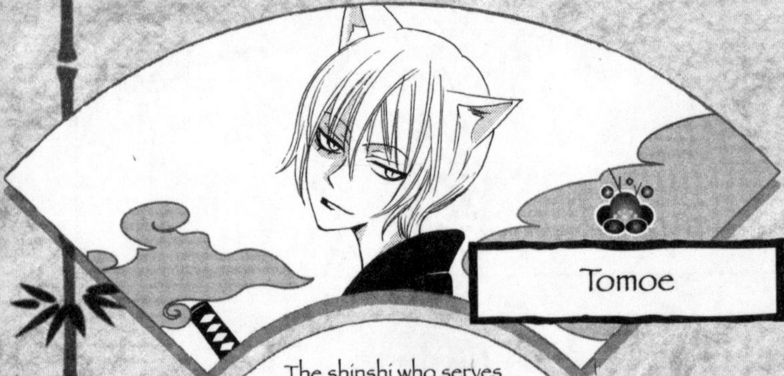
Tomoe

The shinshi who serves Nanami now that she's the new tochigami. Originally a wild fox ayakashi.

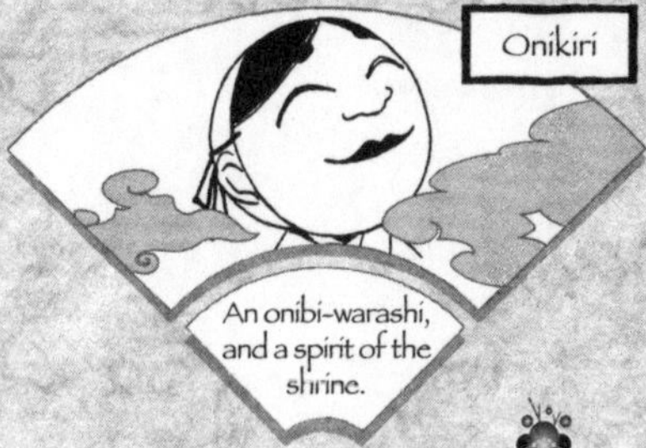
Onikiri
An onibi-warashi, and a spirit of the shrine.

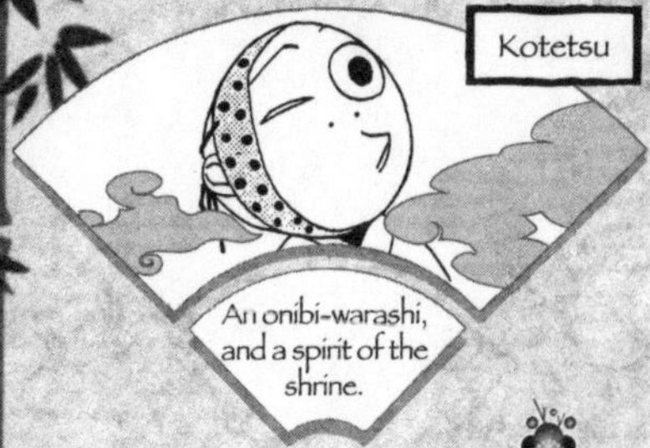
Kotetsu
An onibi-warashi, and a spirit of the shrine.

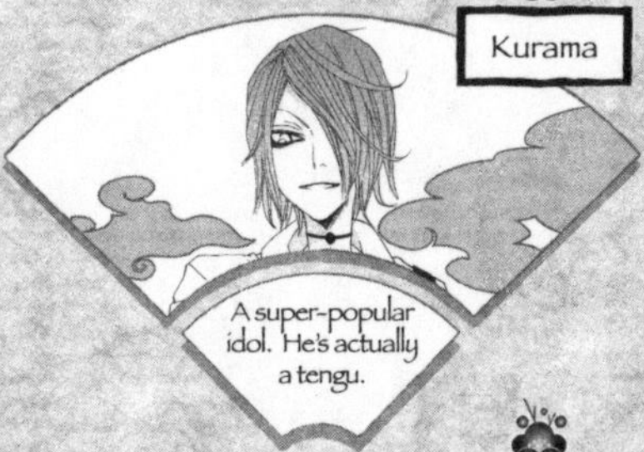
Kurama
A super-popular idol. He's actually a tengu.

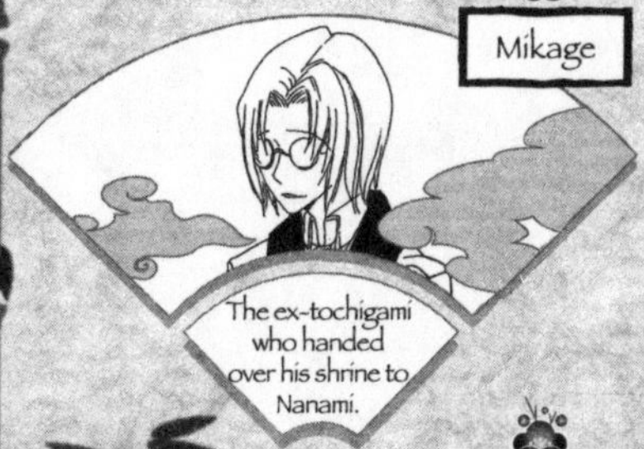
Mikage
The ex-tochigami who handed over his shrine to Nanami.

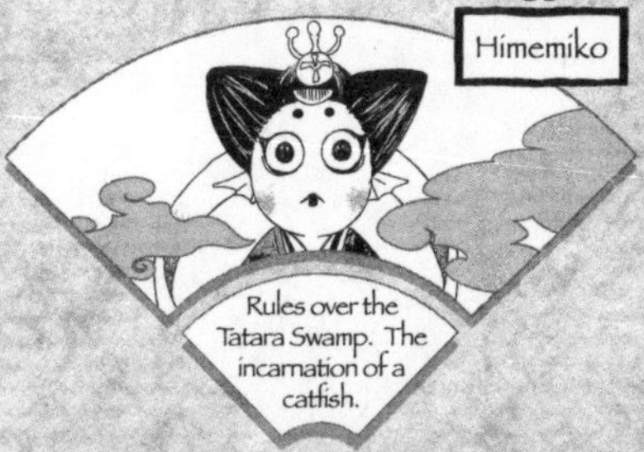
Himemiko
Rules over the Tatara Swamp. The incarnation of a catfish.

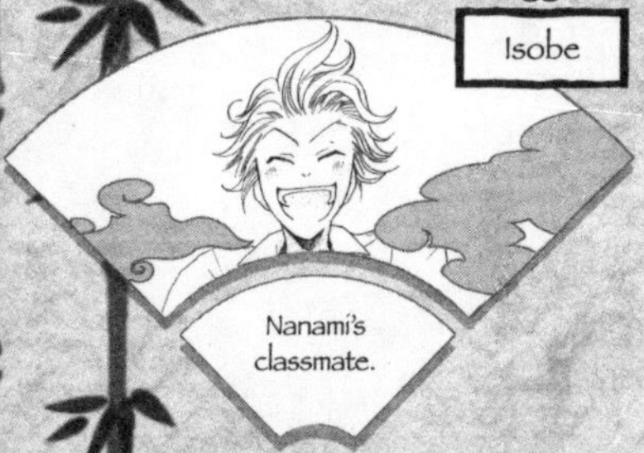
Isobe
Nanami's classmate.

Story so far

Nanami Momozono is a high school student who was evicted from her home when her dad skipped town.

She rescued a strange man in a park, and in thanks he offered her his home. But when she got there, it turned out to be a ruined shrine. The man she rescued was the tochigami Mikage, who ran away from his shrine.

Now Nanami must fulfill the shrine duties of the kamisama. She spends her days with Tomoe (her shinshi) and with Onikiri and Kotetsu (the onibi-warashi spirits of the shrine).

Nanami grants the prayers of those who come to her shrine. Less pleasantly, she's also attacked by supernatural creatures that want to become the kamisama themselves. She can't catch a break...

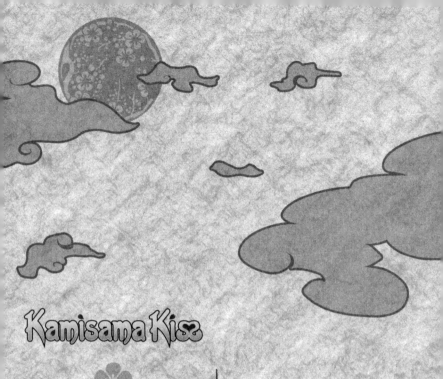

Kamisama Kiss

Volume 3
CONTENTS

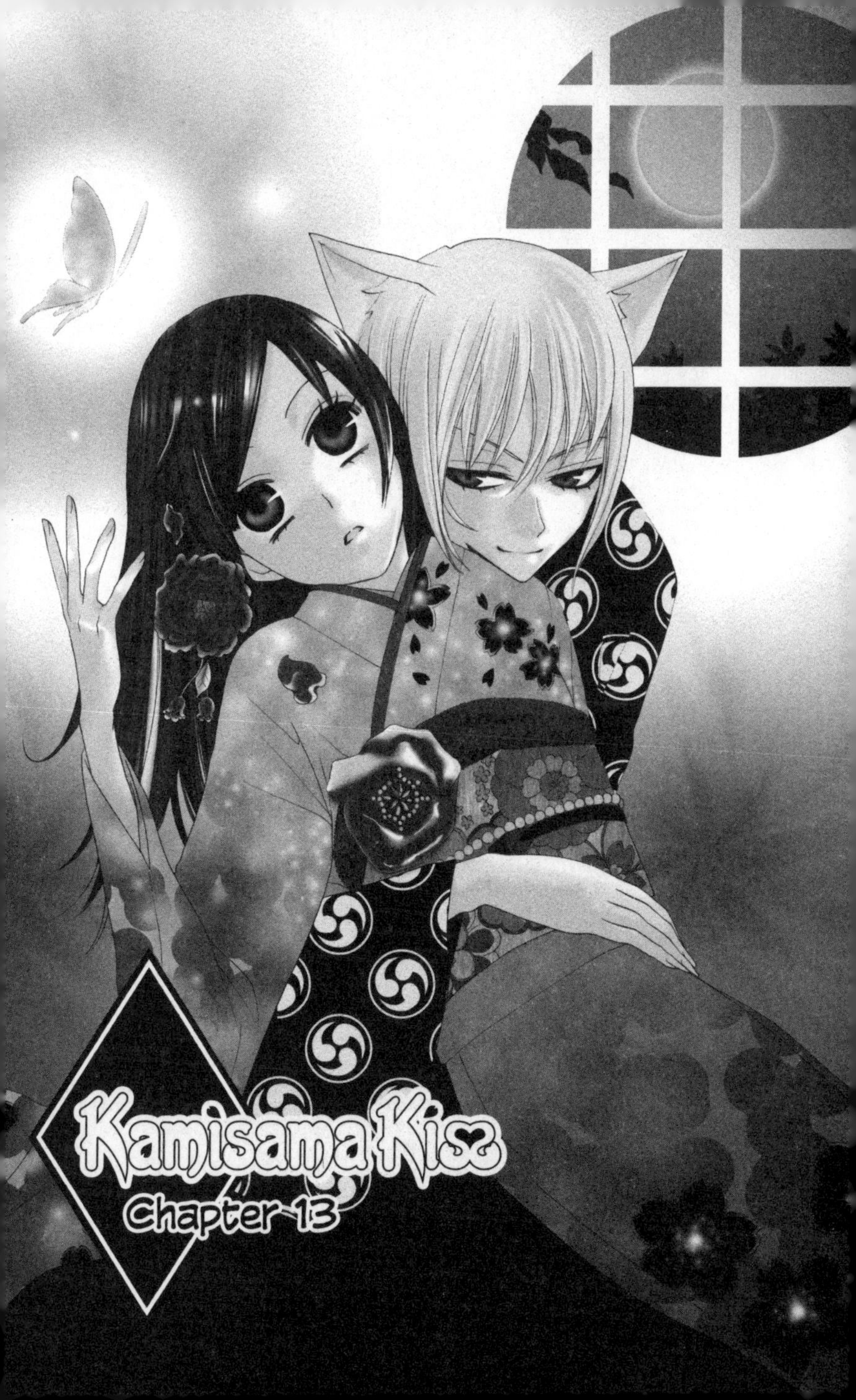
Kamisama Kiss
Chapter 13

Tomoe's
Ennui Blog

Month ◯, Day ✗

I saw a tengu this morning.
Maybe something will happen today.

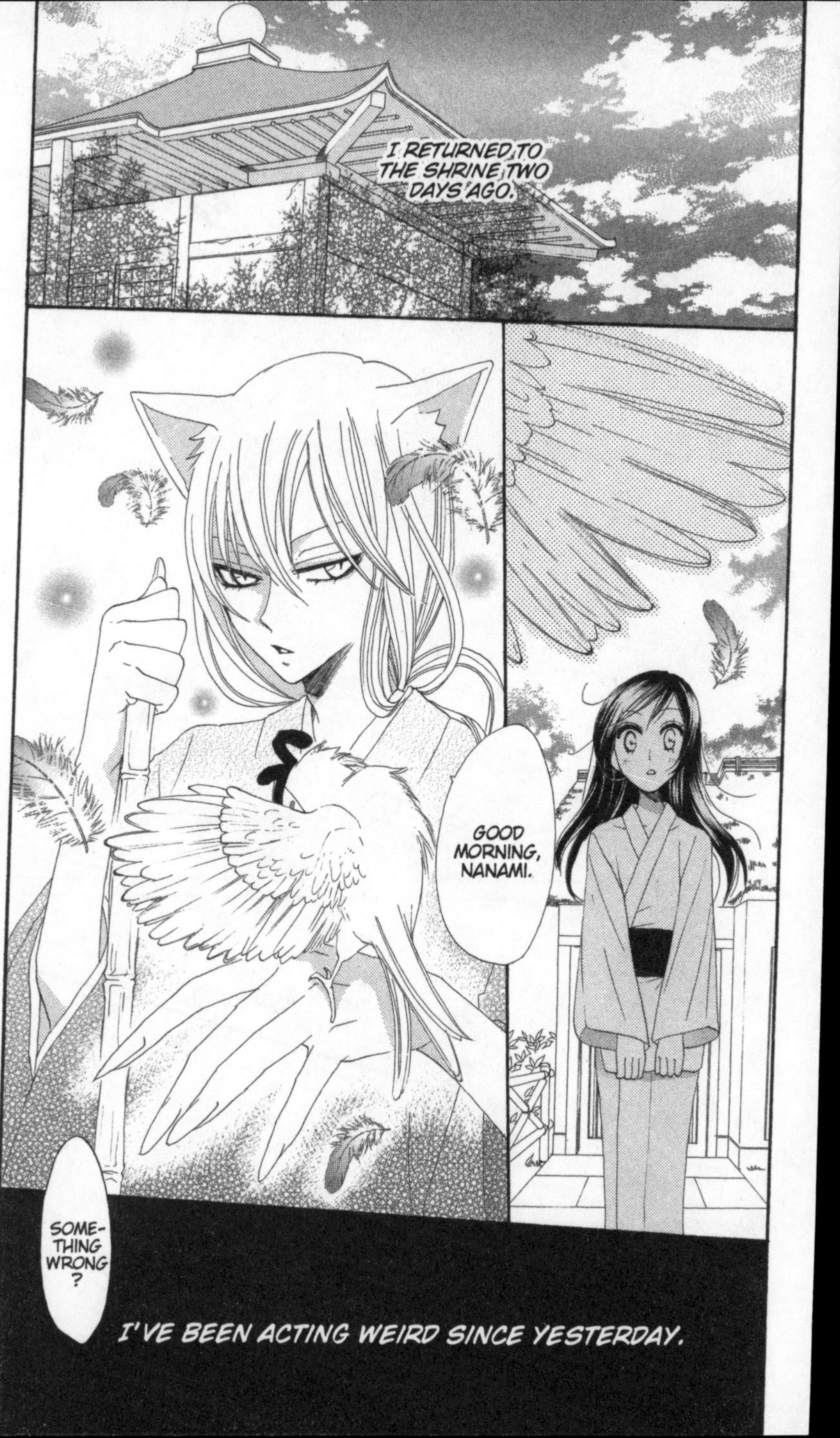
I RETURNED TO THE SHRINE TWO DAYS AGO.
GOOD MORNING, NANAMI.
SOME-THING WRONG?
I'VE BEEN ACTING WEIRD SINCE YESTERDAY.

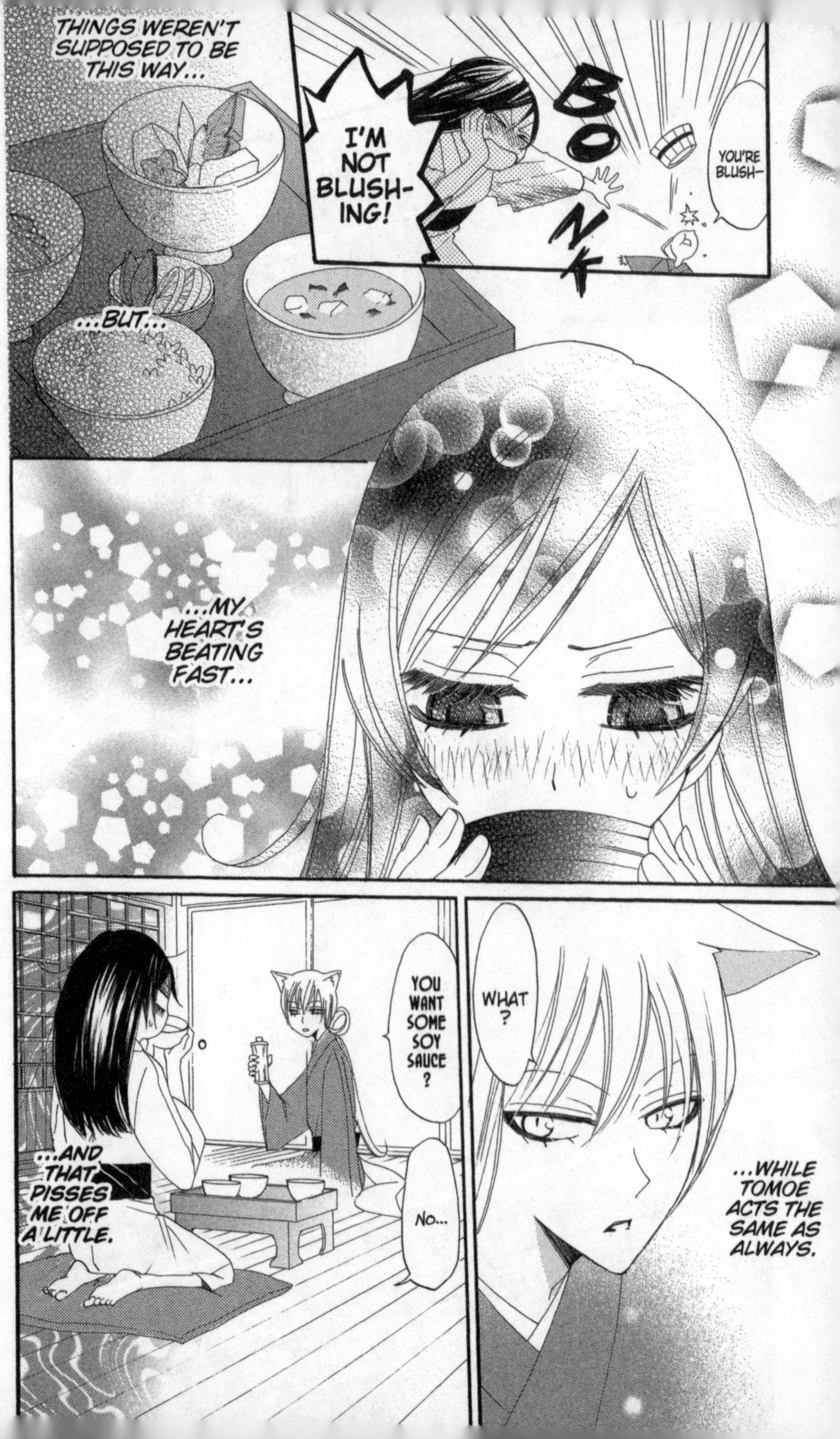
YOU'RE BLUSH—
BONK
I'M NOT BLUSHING!
THINGS WEREN'T SUPPOSED TO BE THIS WAY...
...BUT...
...MY HEART'S BEATING FAST...
...WHILE TOMOE ACTS THE SAME AS ALWAYS.
WHAT?
No...
YOU WANT SOME SOY SAUCE?
...AND THAT PISSES ME OFF A LITTLE.

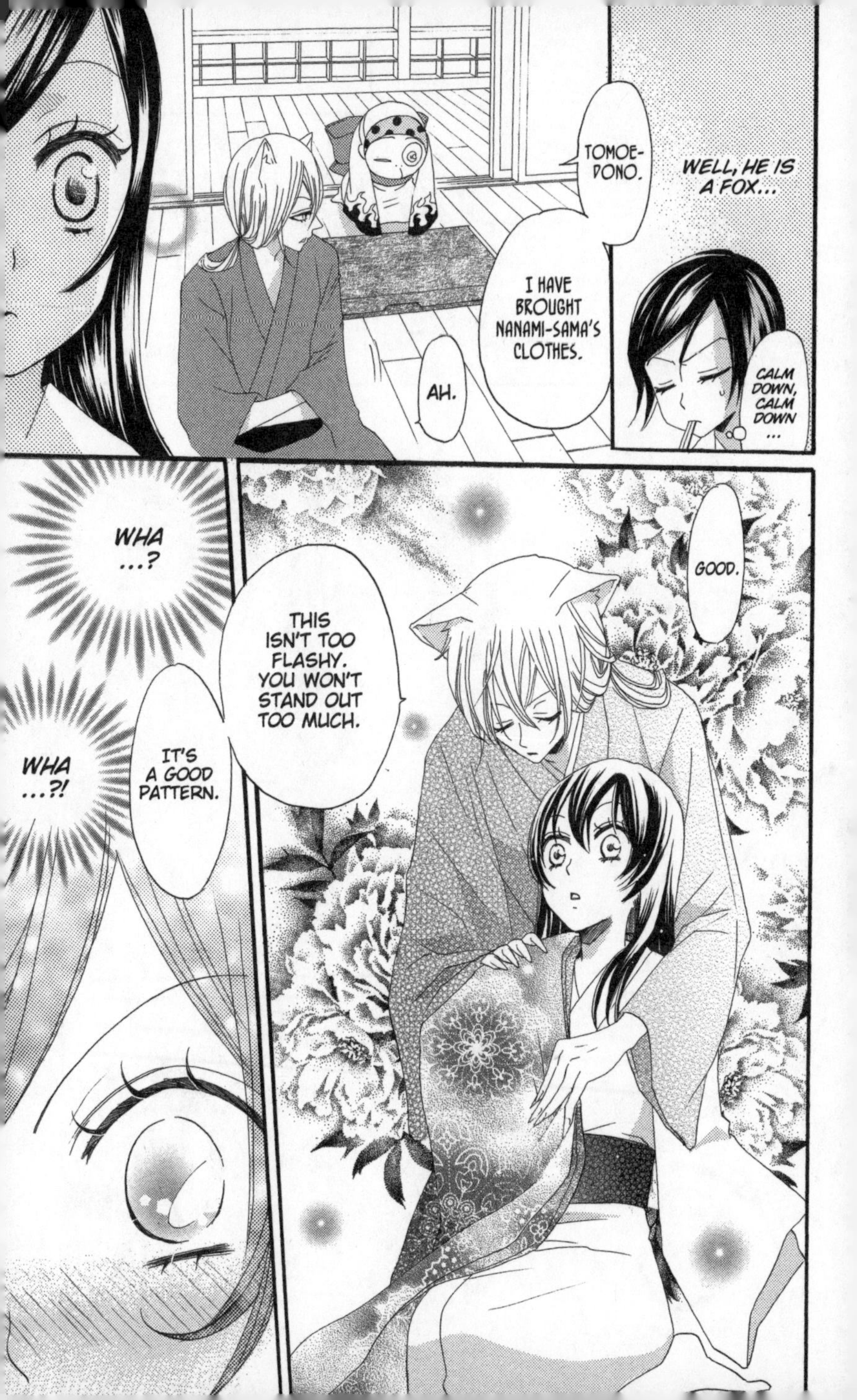
WELL, HE IS A FOX...
CALM DOWN, CALM DOWN ...
TOMOE-DONO.
I HAVE BROUGHT NANAMI-SAMA'S CLOTHES.
AH.
GOOD.
THIS ISN'T TOO FLASHY. YOU WON'T STAND OUT TOO MUCH.
IT'S A GOOD PATTERN.
WHA ...?
WHA ...?!

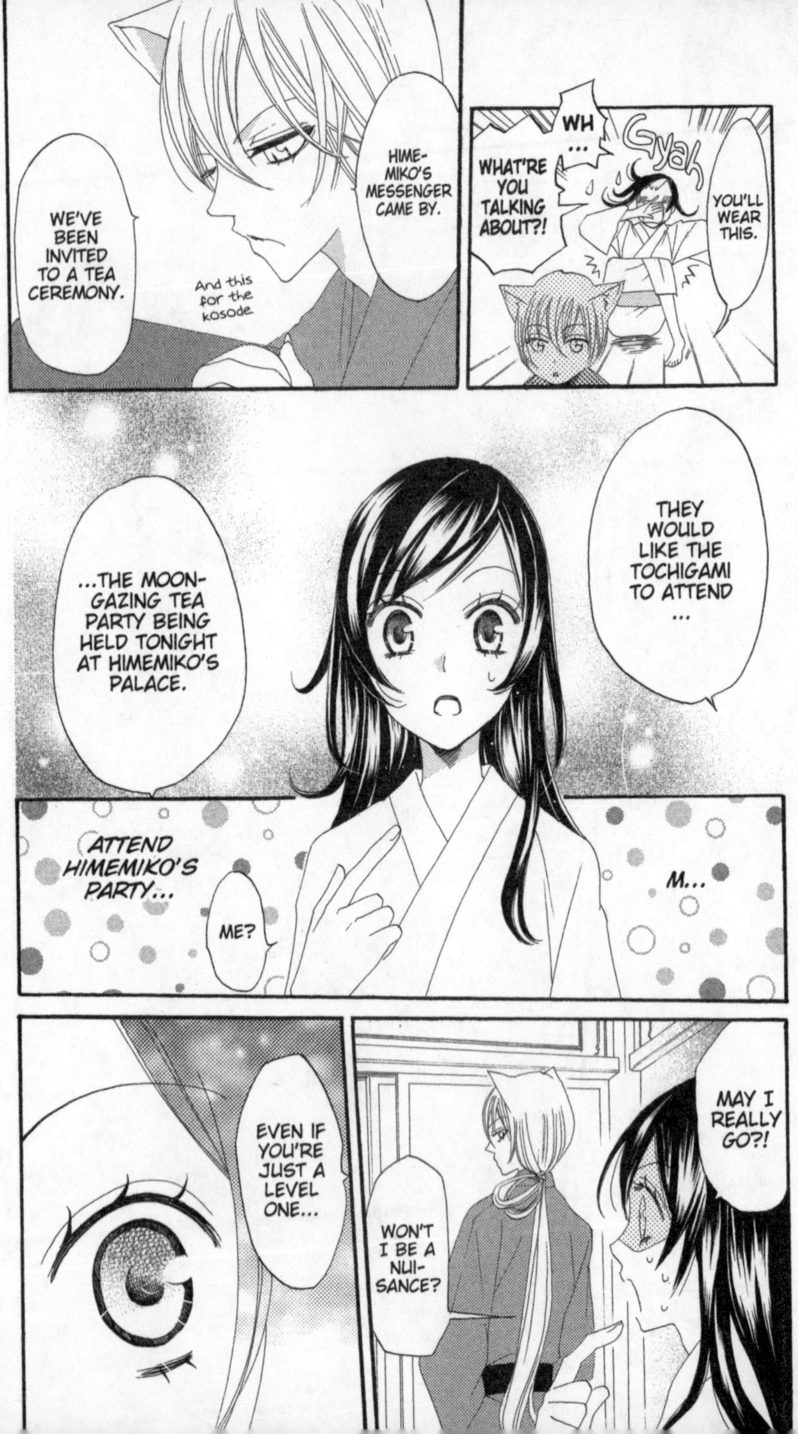
YOU'LL WEAR THIS.
Gyah
WH...
WHAT'RE YOU TALKING ABOUT?!
HIME-MIKO'S MESSENGER CAME BY.
And this for the kosode.
WE'VE BEEN INVITED TO A TEA CEREMONY.
THEY WOULD LIKE THE TOCHIGAMI TO ATTEND...
...THE MOON-GAZING TEA PARTY BEING HELD TONIGHT AT HIMEMIKO'S PALACE.
M...
ME?
ATTEND HIMEMIKO'S PARTY...
MAY I REALLY GO?!
WON'T I BE A NUI-SANCE?
EVEN IF YOU'RE JUST A LEVEL ONE...

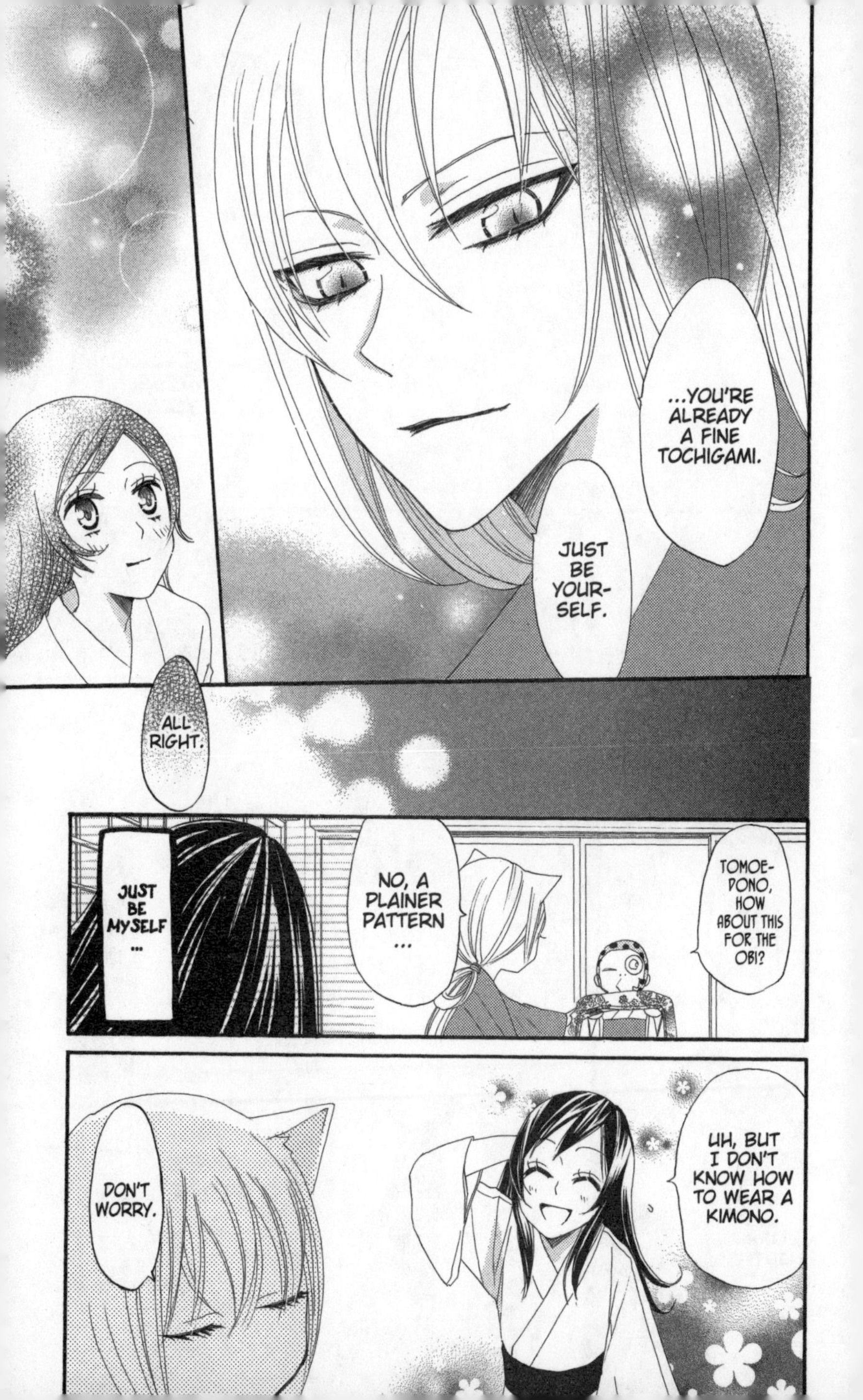
...YOU'RE ALREADY A FINE TOCHIGAMI.
JUST BE YOURSELF.
ALL RIGHT.
TOMOE-DONO, HOW ABOUT THIS FOR THE OBI?
NO, A PLAINER PATTERN ...
JUST BE MYSELF ...
UH, BUT I DON'T KNOW HOW TO WEAR A KIMONO.
DON'T WORRY.

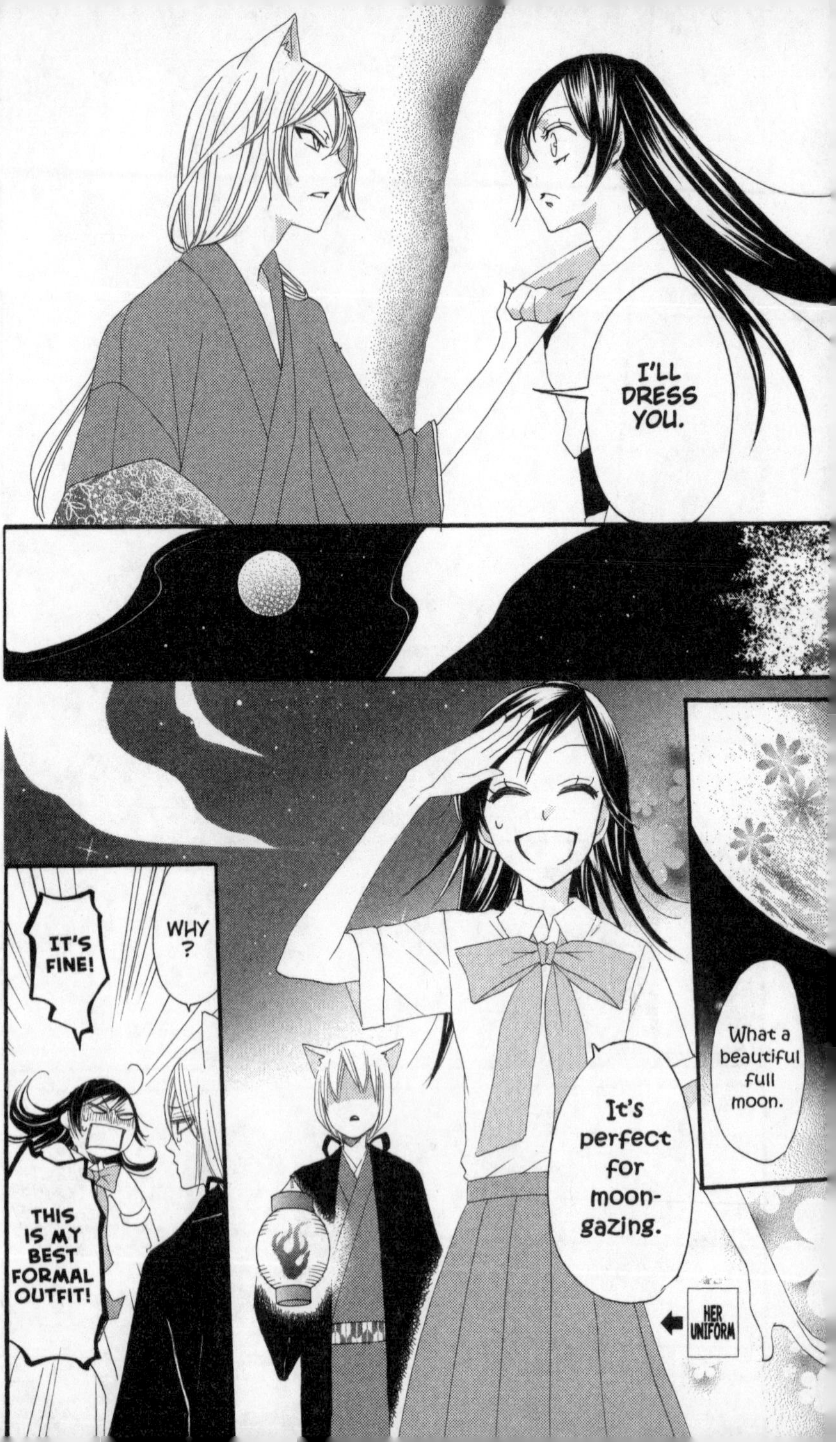
I'LL DRESS YOU.
What a beautiful full moon.
It's perfect for moon-gazing.
HER UNIFORM
WHY?
IT'S FINE!
THIS IS MY BEST FORMAL OUTFIT!

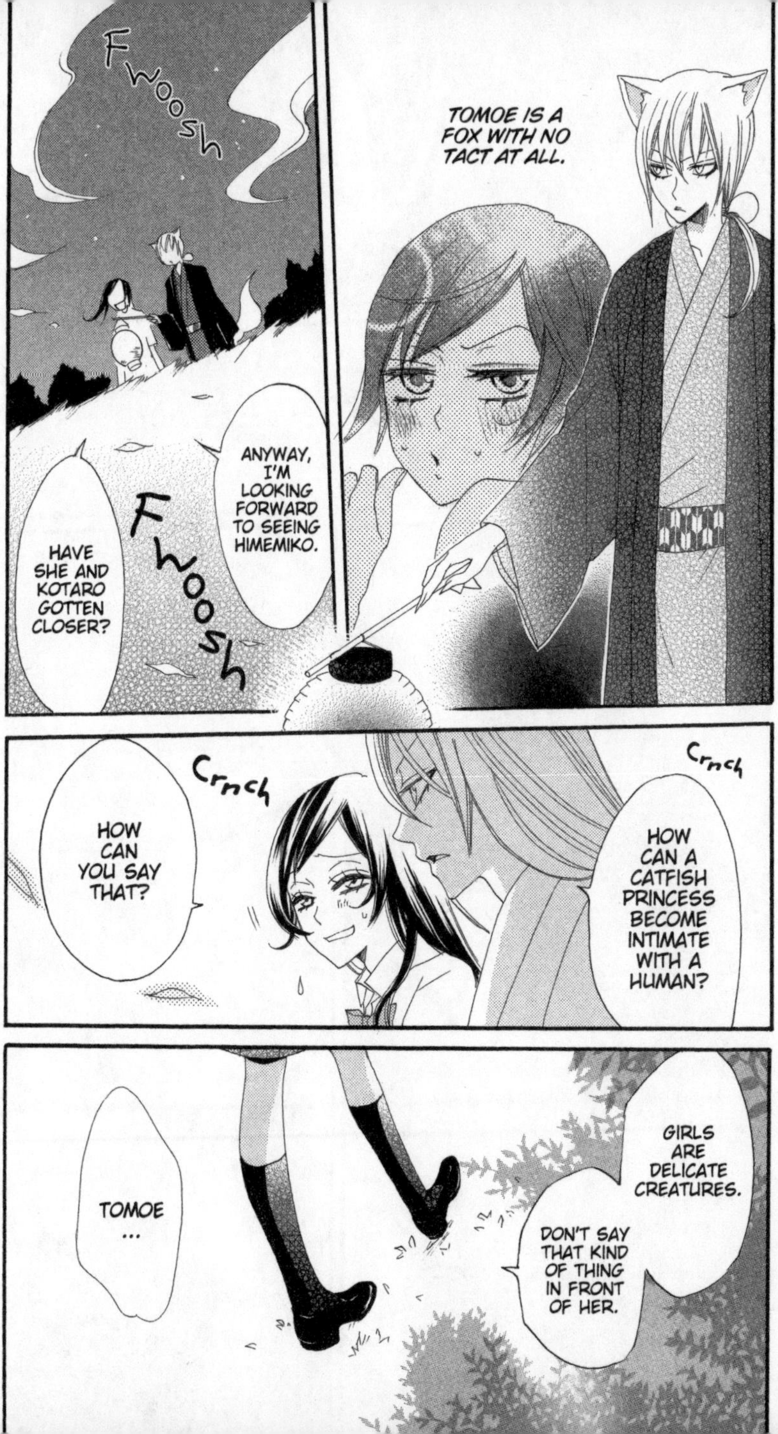
TOMOE IS A FOX WITH NO TACT AT ALL.
Fwoosh
ANYWAY, I'M LOOKING FORWARD TO SEEING HIMEMIKO.
Fwoosh
HAVE SHE AND KOTARO GOTTEN CLOSER?
Crnch
HOW CAN A CATFISH PRINCESS BECOME INTIMATE WITH A HUMAN?
Crnch
HOW CAN YOU SAY THAT?
GIRLS ARE DELICATE CREATURES.
DON'T SAY THAT KIND OF THING IN FRONT OF HER.
TOMOE ...

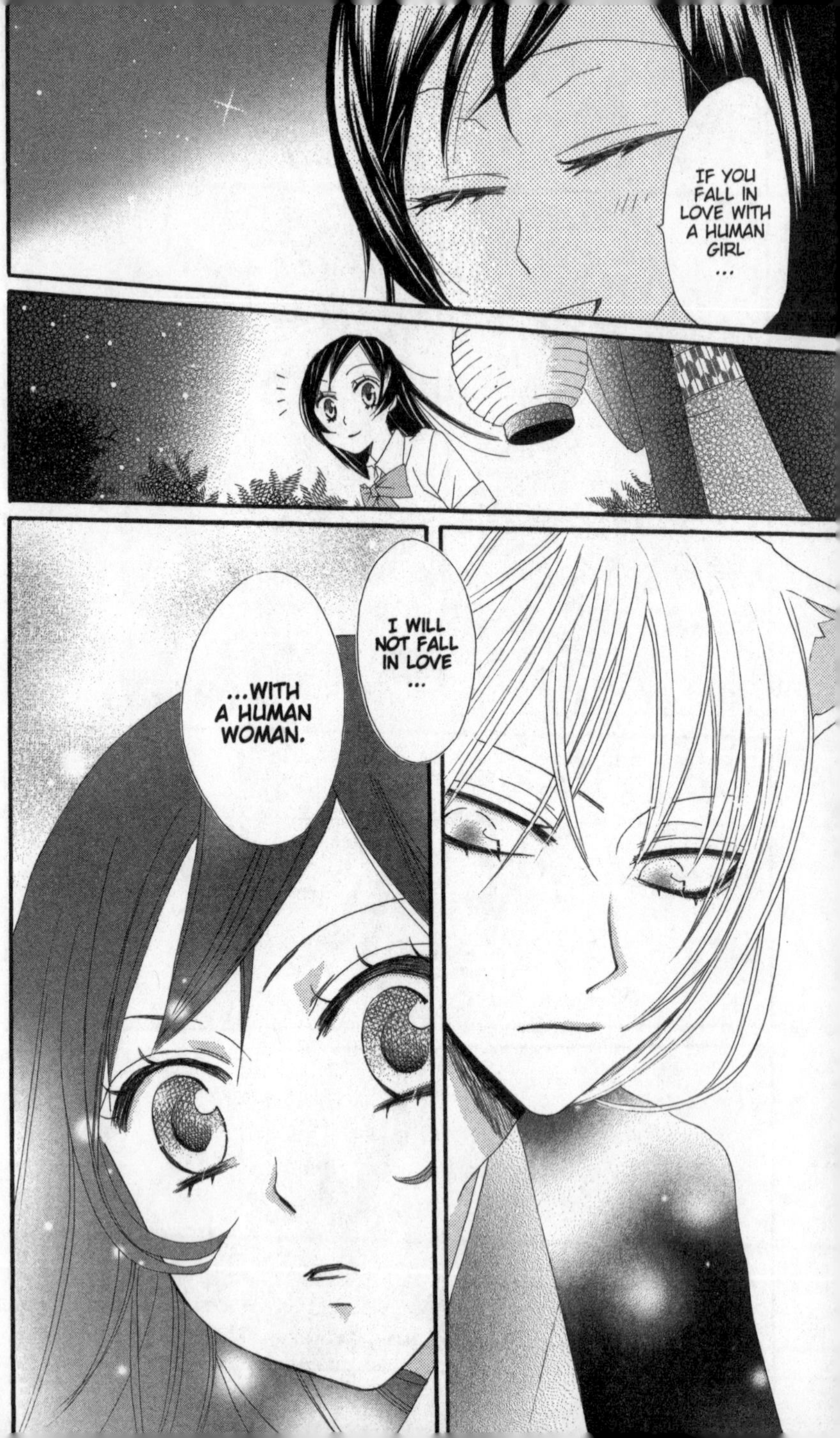
IF YOU FALL IN LOVE WITH A HUMAN GIRL ...
I WILL NOT FALL IN LOVE ...
...WITH A HUMAN WOMAN.

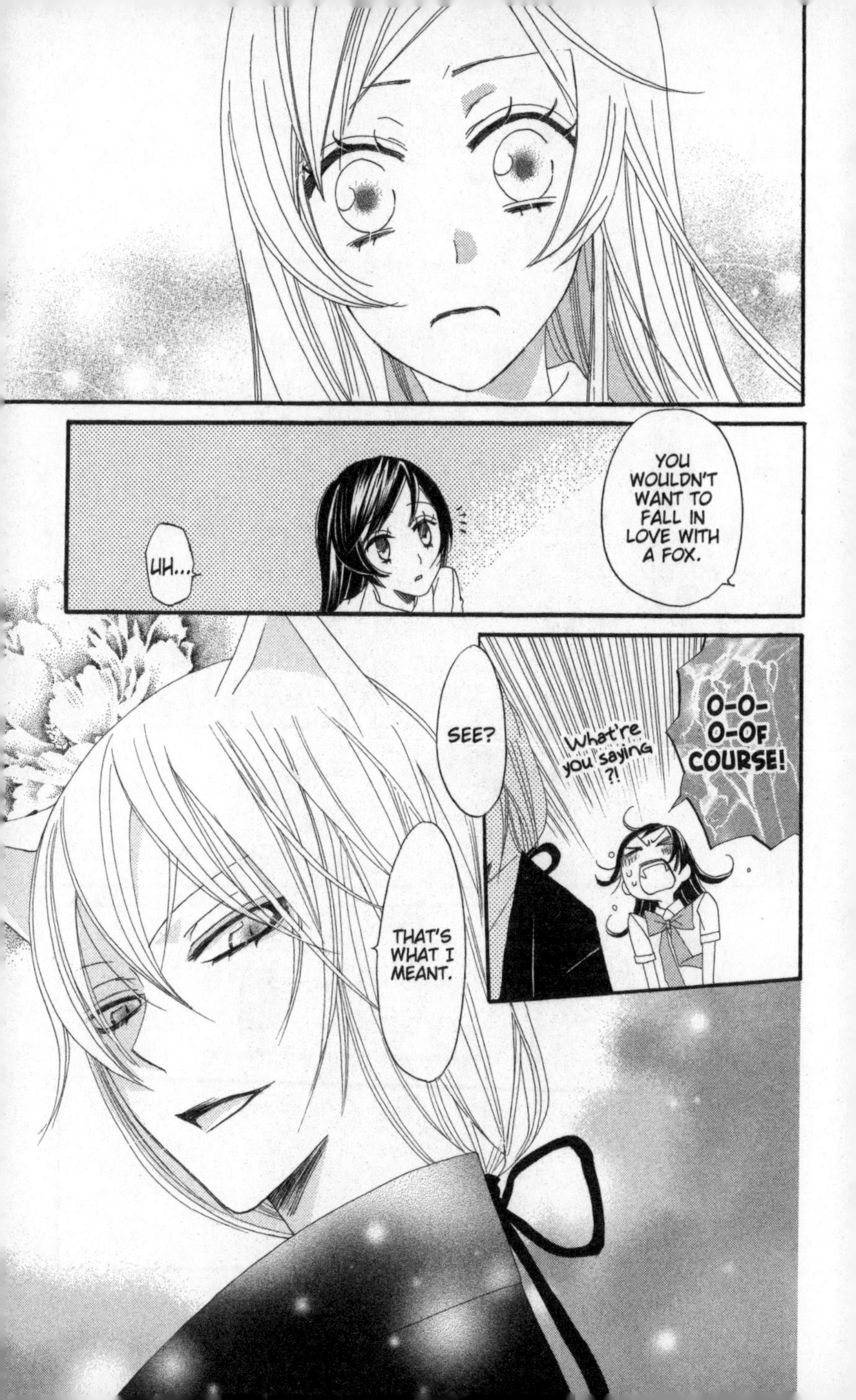
YOU WOULDN'T WANT TO FALL IN LOVE WITH A FOX.
UH...
O-O-O-OF COURSE!
What're you saying ?!
SEE?
THAT'S WHAT I MEANT.

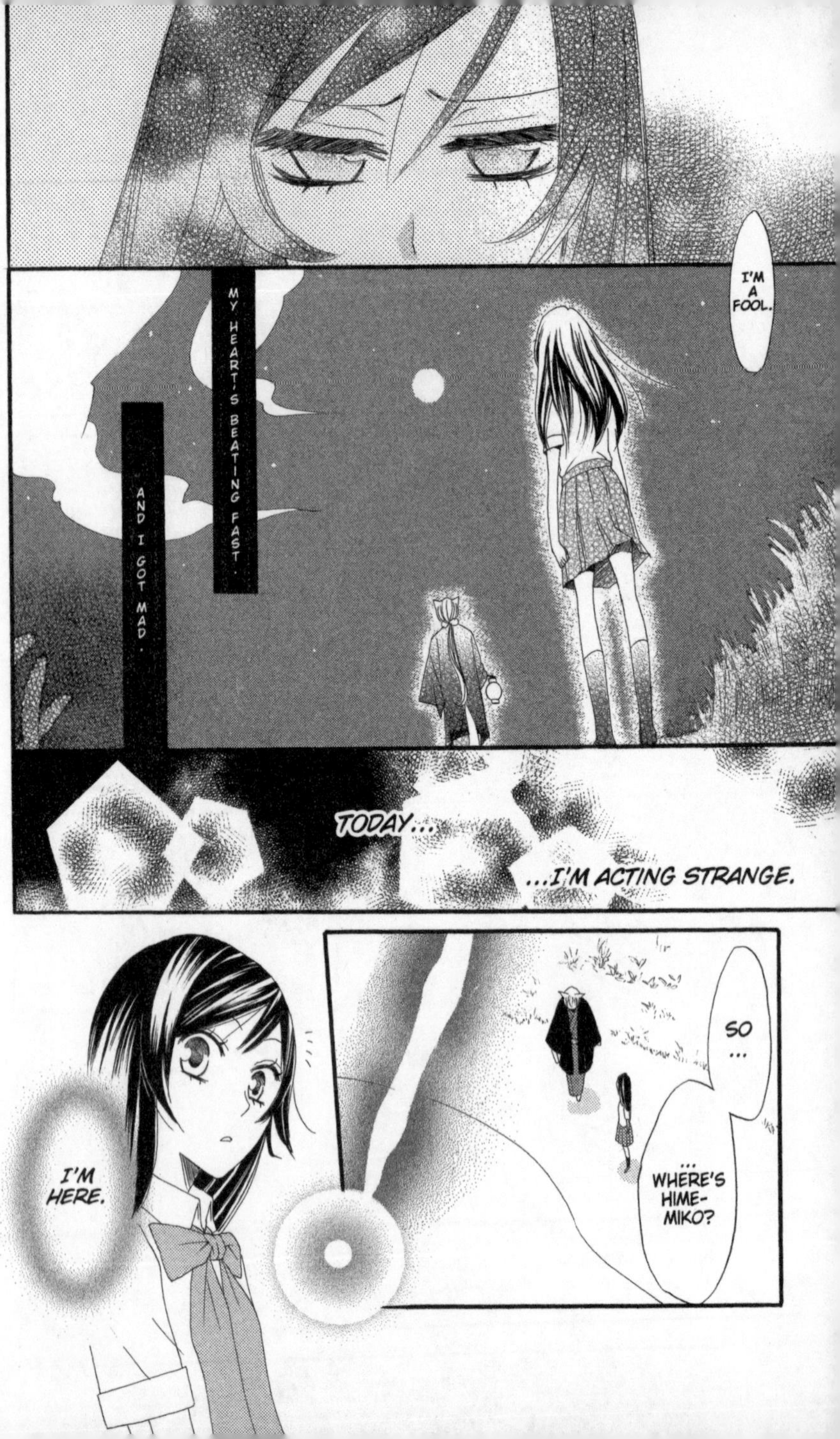
I'M A FOOL.
MY HEART'S BEATING FAST.
AND I GOT MAD.
TODAY...
...I'M ACTING STRANGE.
SO ...
... WHERE'S HIME-MIKO?
I'M HERE.

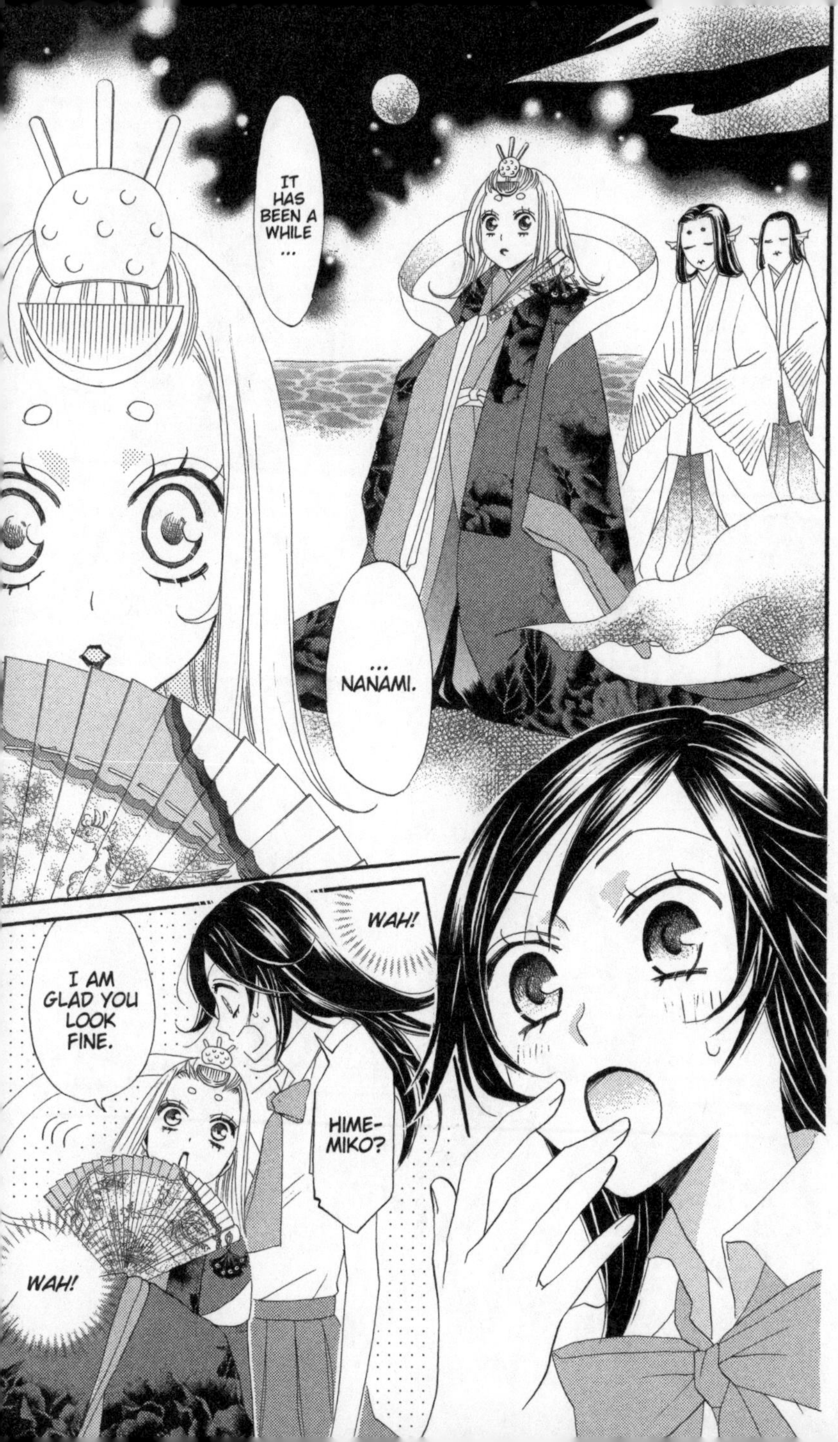
IT HAS BEEN A WHILE ...
... NANAMI.
WAH!
I AM GLAD YOU LOOK FINE.
HIME-MIKO?
WAH!

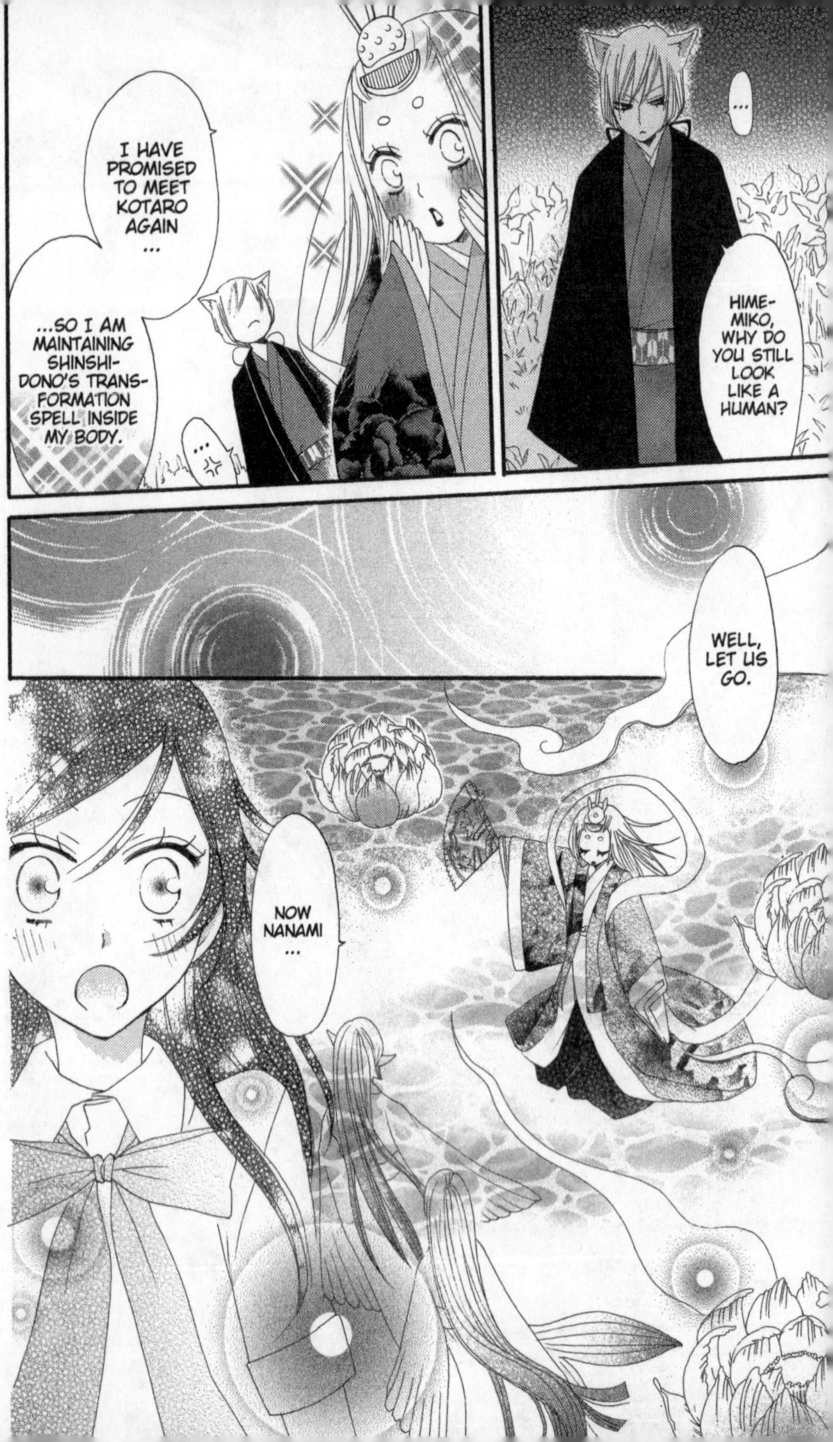
...
HIME-MIKO, WHY DO YOU STILL LOOK LIKE A HUMAN?
I HAVE PROMISED TO MEET KOTARO AGAIN ...
...SO I AM MAINTAINING SHINSHI-DONO'S TRANS-FORMATION SPELL INSIDE MY BODY.
...
WELL, LET US GO.
NOW NANAMI ...

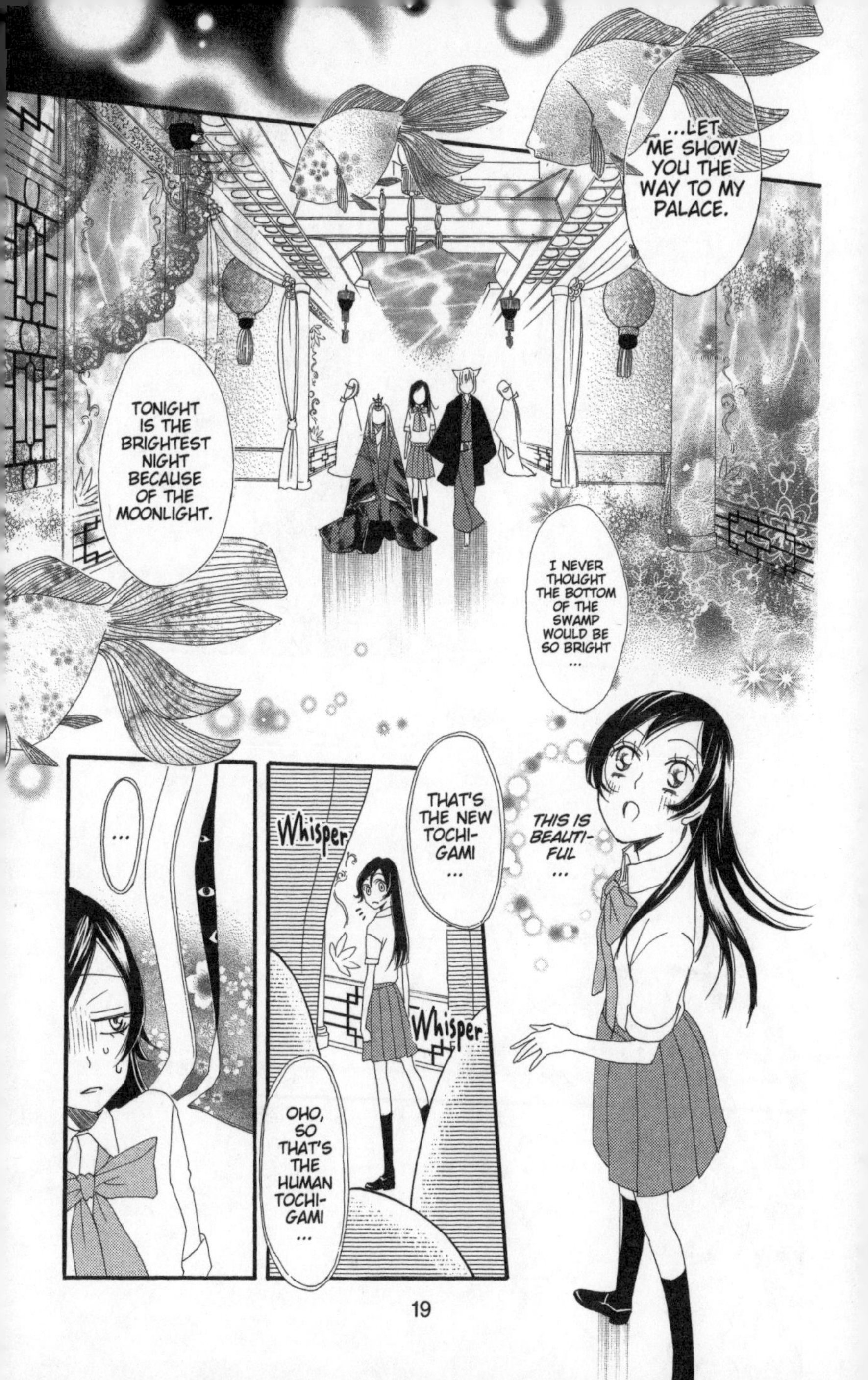
...LET ME SHOW YOU THE WAY TO MY PALACE.
TONIGHT IS THE BRIGHTEST NIGHT BECAUSE OF THE MOONLIGHT.
I NEVER THOUGHT THE BOTTOM OF THE SWAMP WOULD BE SO BRIGHT ...
THIS IS BEAUTI-FUL ...
THAT'S THE NEW TOCHI-GAMI ...
Whisper
Whisper
OHO, SO THAT'S THE HUMAN TOCHI-GAMI ...
...

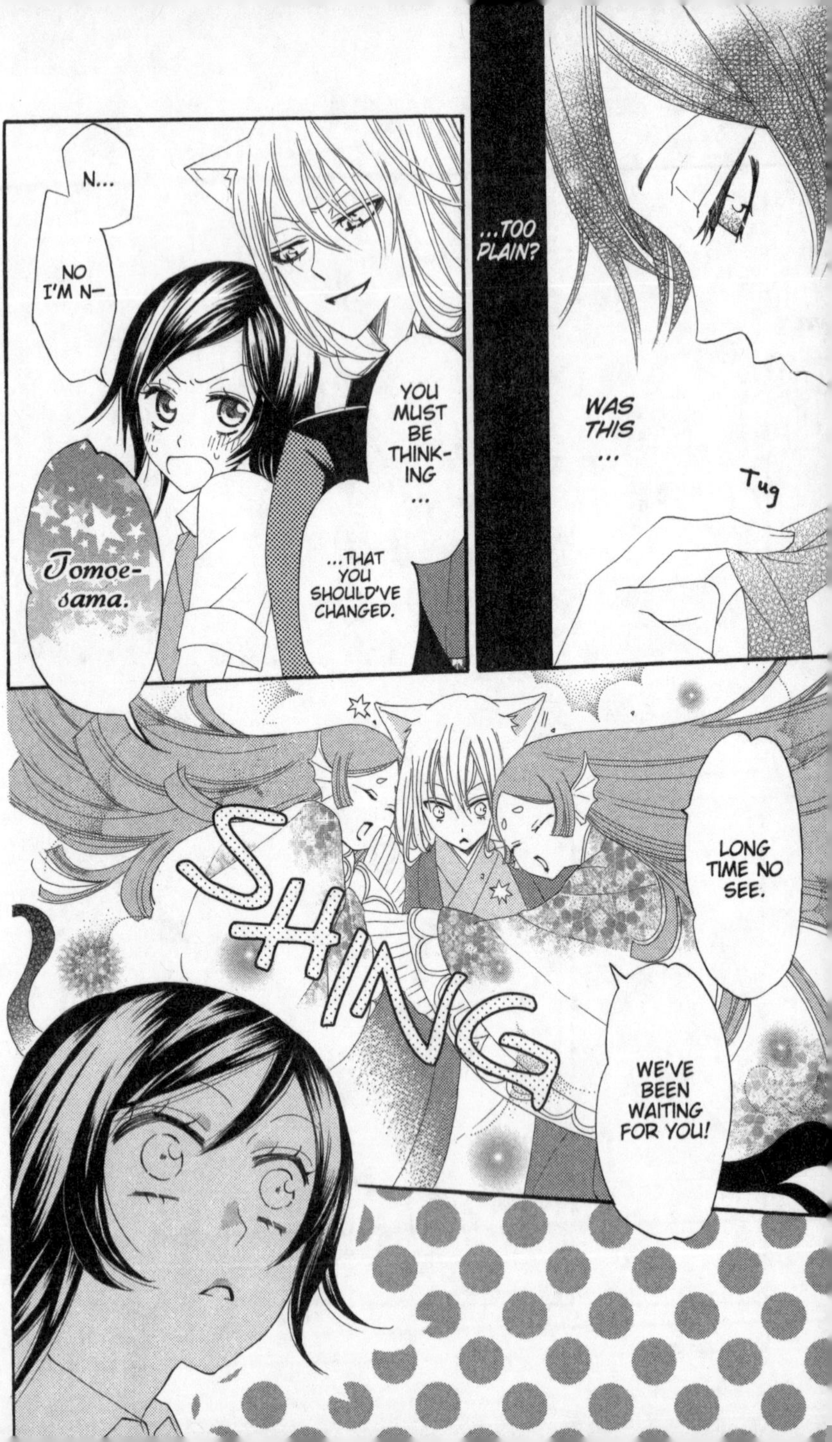
WAS THIS ...
Tug
...TOO PLAIN?
YOU MUST BE THINKING ...
...THAT YOU SHOULD'VE CHANGED.
N...
NO I'M N—
Tomoe-sama.
LONG TIME NO SEE.
WE'VE BEEN WAITING FOR YOU!
SHING

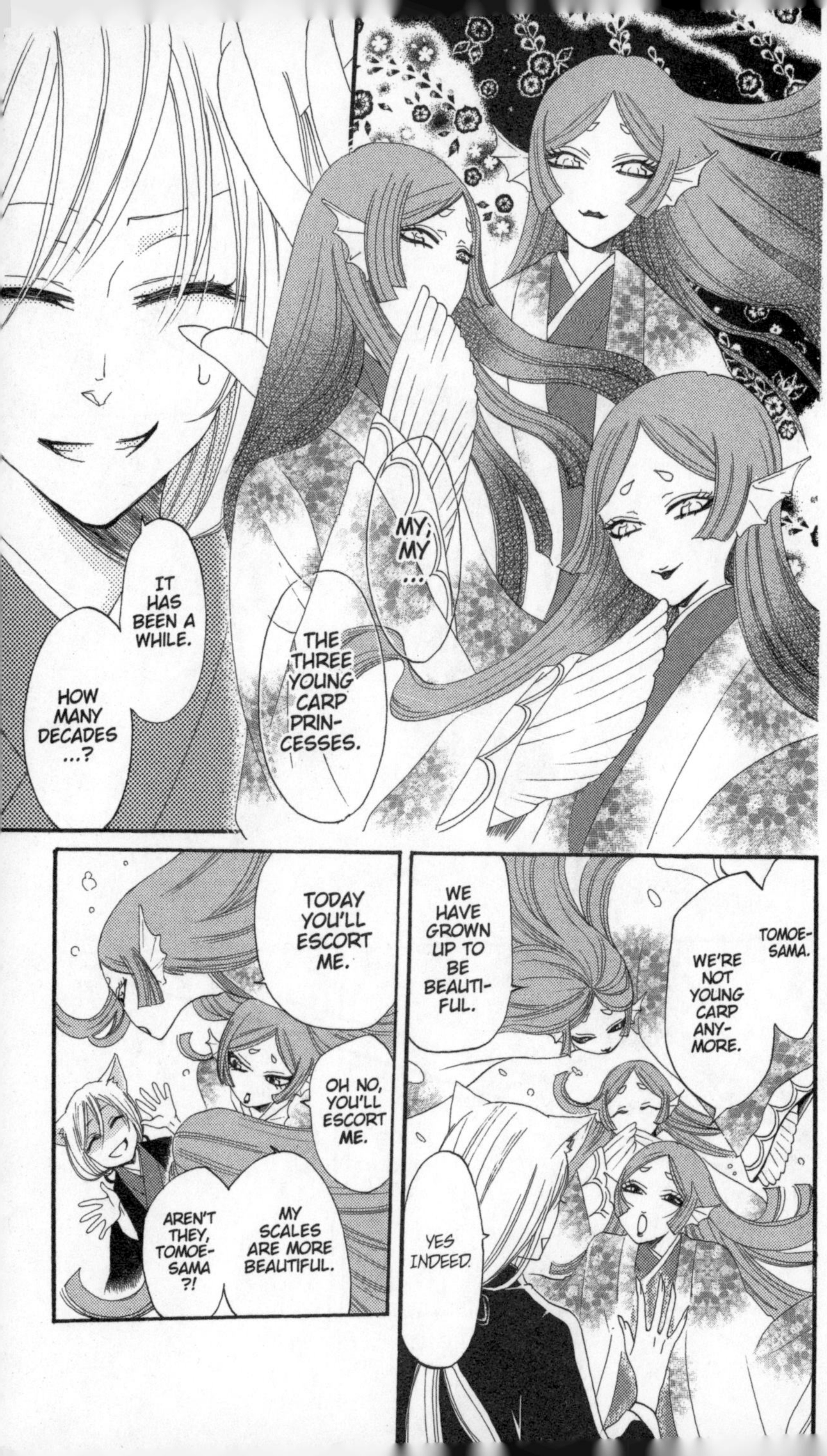
MY, MY...
THE THREE YOUNG CARP PRINCESSES.
IT HAS BEEN A WHILE.
HOW MANY DECADES...?
TOMOE-SAMA.
WE'RE NOT YOUNG CARP ANYMORE.
WE HAVE GROWN UP TO BE BEAUTIFUL.
YES INDEED.
TODAY YOU'LL ESCORT ME.
OH NO, YOU'LL ESCORT ME.
MY SCALES ARE MORE BEAUTIFUL.
AREN'T THEY, TOMOE-SAMA?!

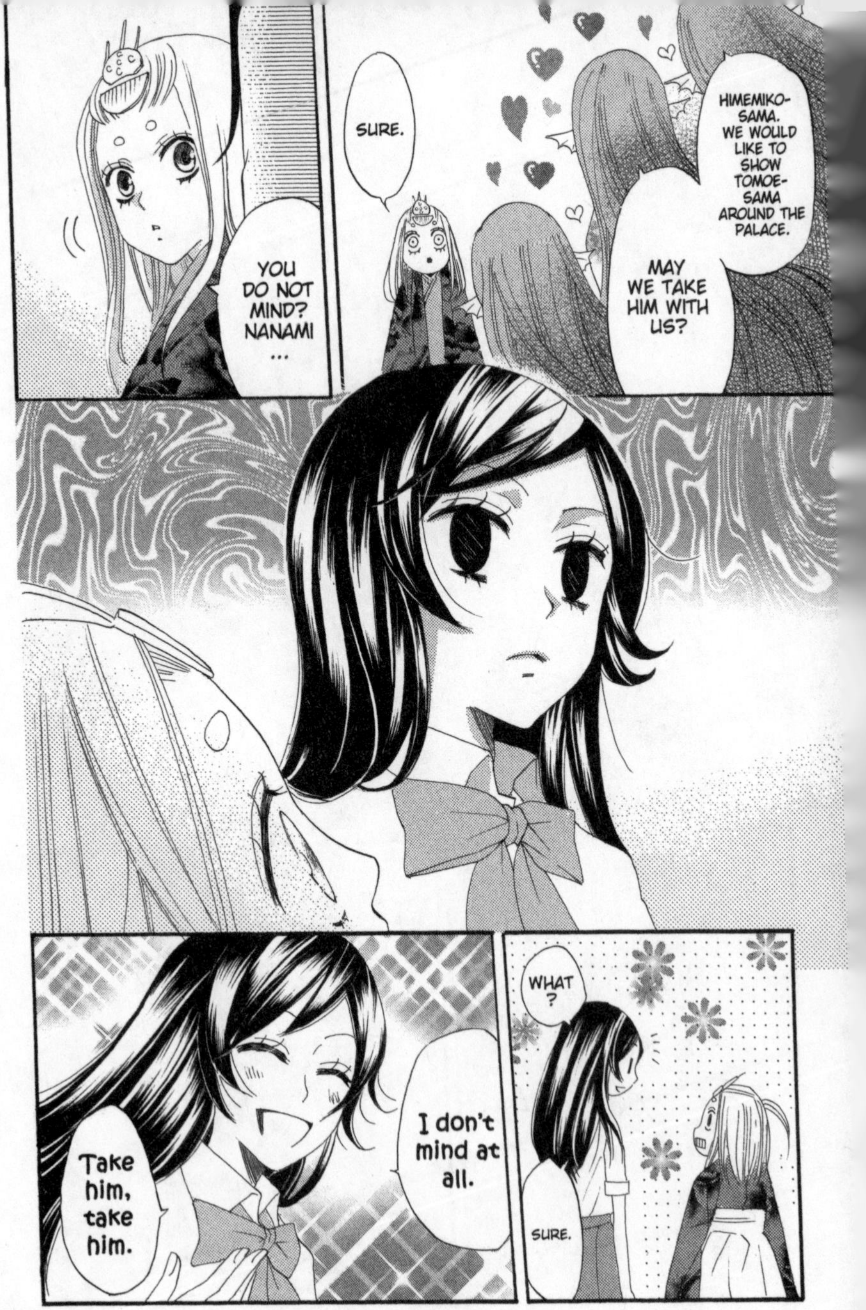

HIMEMIKO-SAMA. WE WOULD LIKE TO SHOW TOMOE-SAMA AROUND THE PALACE.
MAY WE TAKE HIM WITH US?
SURE.
YOU DO NOT MIND? NANAMI ...
WHAT?
SURE.
I don't mind at all.
Take him, take him.

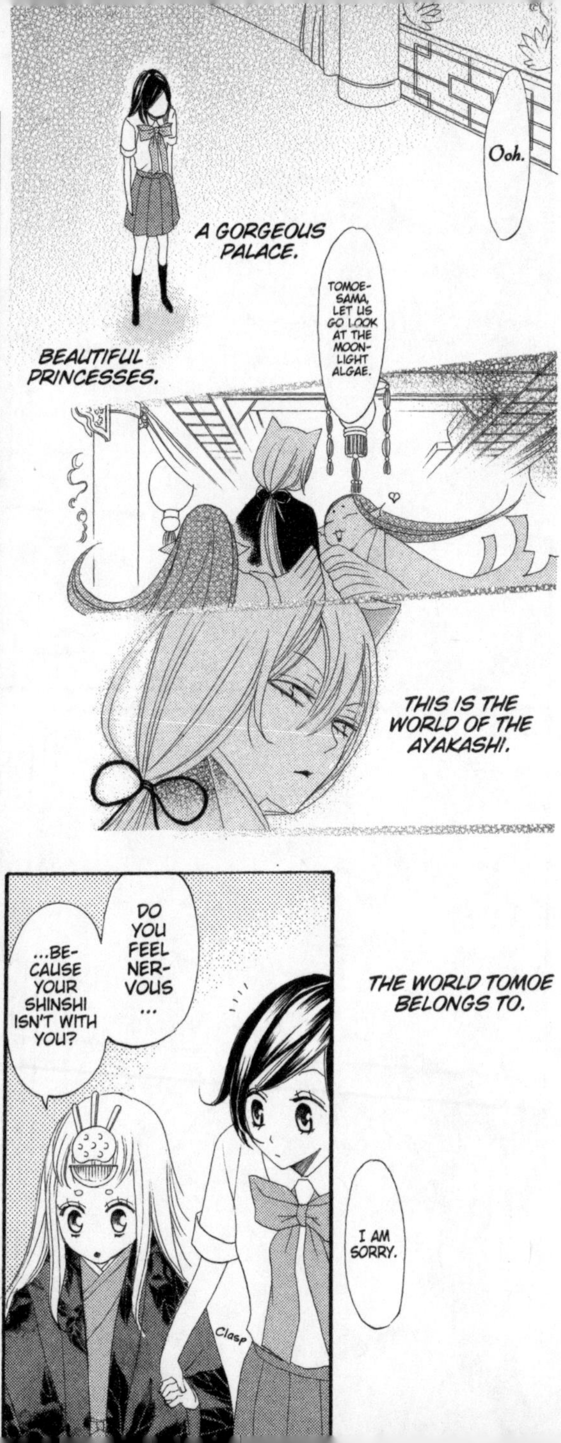
Ooh.
A GORGEOUS PALACE.
TOMOE-SAMA, LET US GO LOOK AT THE MOONLIGHT ALGAE.
BEAUTIFUL PRINCESSES.
THIS IS THE WORLD OF THE AYAKASHI.
THE WORLD TOMOE BELONGS TO.
DO YOU FEEL NERVOUS...
...BECAUSE YOUR SHINSHI ISN'T WITH YOU?
I AM SORRY.
Clasp

One

Hello.

I'm Julietta Suzuki. Thank you for reading vol. 3 of Kamisama Kiss! I'm happy if you enjoy reading it.★

The other day, I went to Takachiho in Miyazaki Prefecture. This was a trip to relax (the main objective) with friends who were worn out from work. It was a good trip... I'd heard that a day would be enough to see everything, but it was impossible. We visited many shrines, and then the day was over.

There were many famous places mentioned in Japanese myths. The surroundings were beautiful. And the food was so, so delicious!

In Kyoto, you feel the history of humans, but in Takachiho, I felt the history of those not human. I was able to really relax and I'm full of energy again.

If you're thinking about traveling to Kyushu, please do go to Takachiho. I'd like to go visit again. I'd also like to go to Izumo (which I have been talking about with my editor) and Ise, which I haven't gone to yet. And Nikko. (I was able to go to Hakone. It was good).

There're no afterword pages in this volume, but please read the sidebars and extras.

See you.

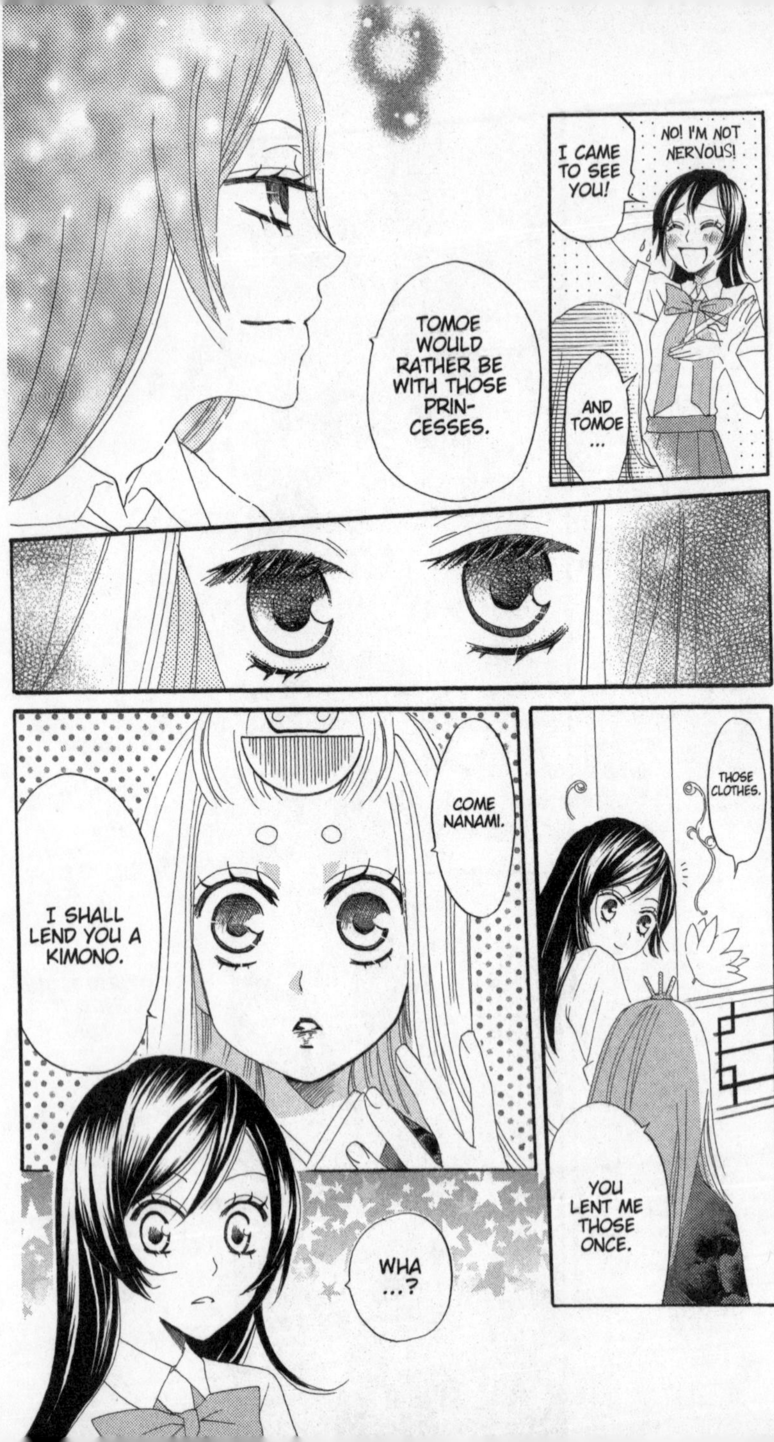
NO! I'M NOT NERVOUS!
I CAME TO SEE YOU!
AND TOMOE ...
TOMOE WOULD RATHER BE WITH THOSE PRIN-CESSES.
THOSE CLOTHES.
YOU LENT ME THOSE ONCE.
COME NANAMI.
I SHALL LEND YOU A KIMONO.
WHA ...?

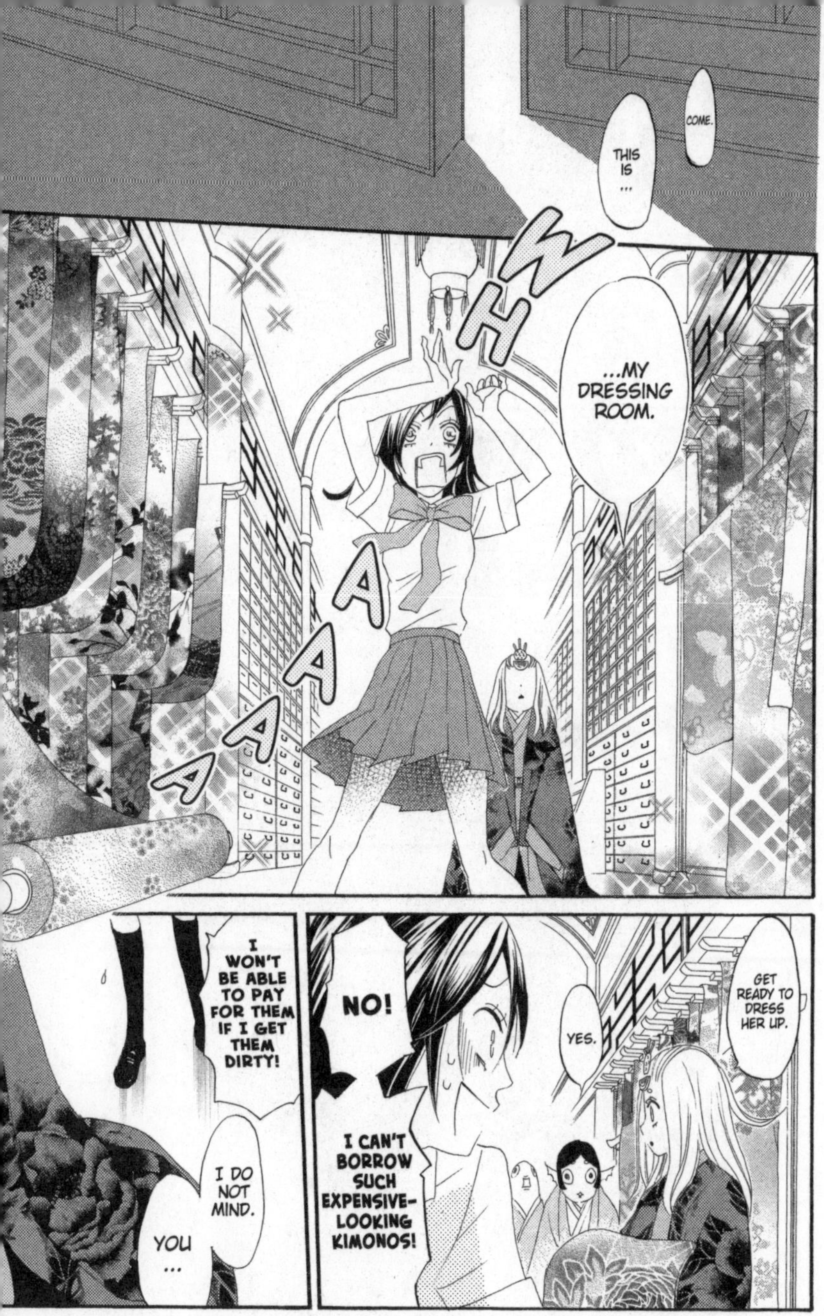

COME.
THIS IS ...
...MY DRESSING ROOM.
WHAAAA
GET READY TO DRESS HER UP.
YES.
NO!
I CAN'T BORROW SUCH EXPENSIVE-LOOKING KIMONOS!
I WON'T BE ABLE TO PAY FOR THEM IF I GET THEM DIRTY!
I DO NOT MIND.
YOU ...

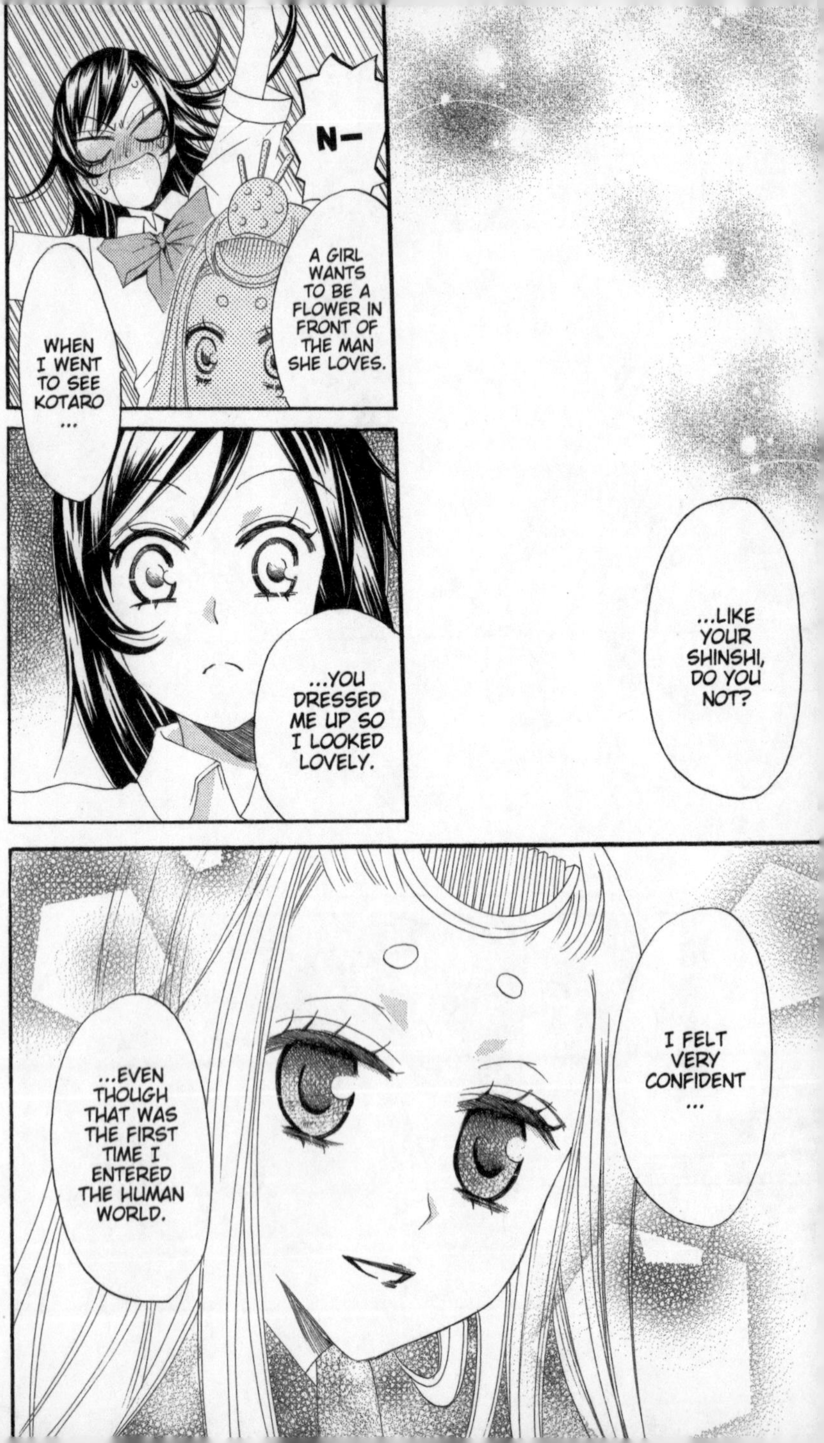
...LIKE YOUR SHINSHI, DO YOU NOT?
N-
A GIRL WANTS TO BE A FLOWER IN FRONT OF THE MAN SHE LOVES.
WHEN I WENT TO SEE KOTARO ...
...YOU DRESSED ME UP SO I LOOKED LOVELY.
I FELT VERY CONFIDENT ...
...EVEN THOUGH THAT WAS THE FIRST TIME I ENTERED THE HUMAN WORLD.

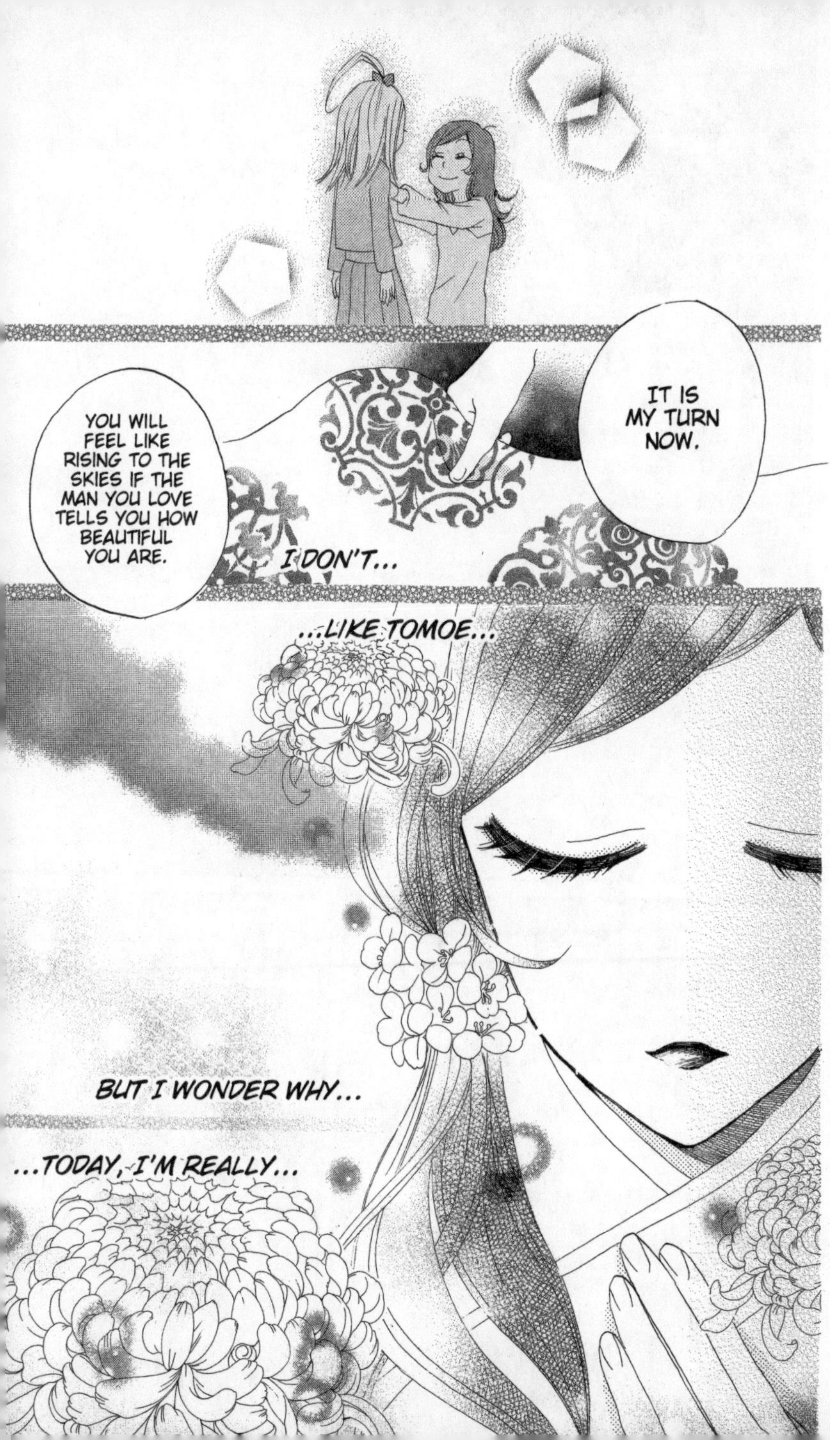
IT IS MY TURN NOW.
YOU WILL FEEL LIKE RISING TO THE SKIES IF THE MAN YOU LOVE TELLS YOU HOW BEAUTIFUL YOU ARE.
I DON'T...
...LIKE TOMOE...
BUT I WONDER WHY...
...TODAY, I'M REALLY...

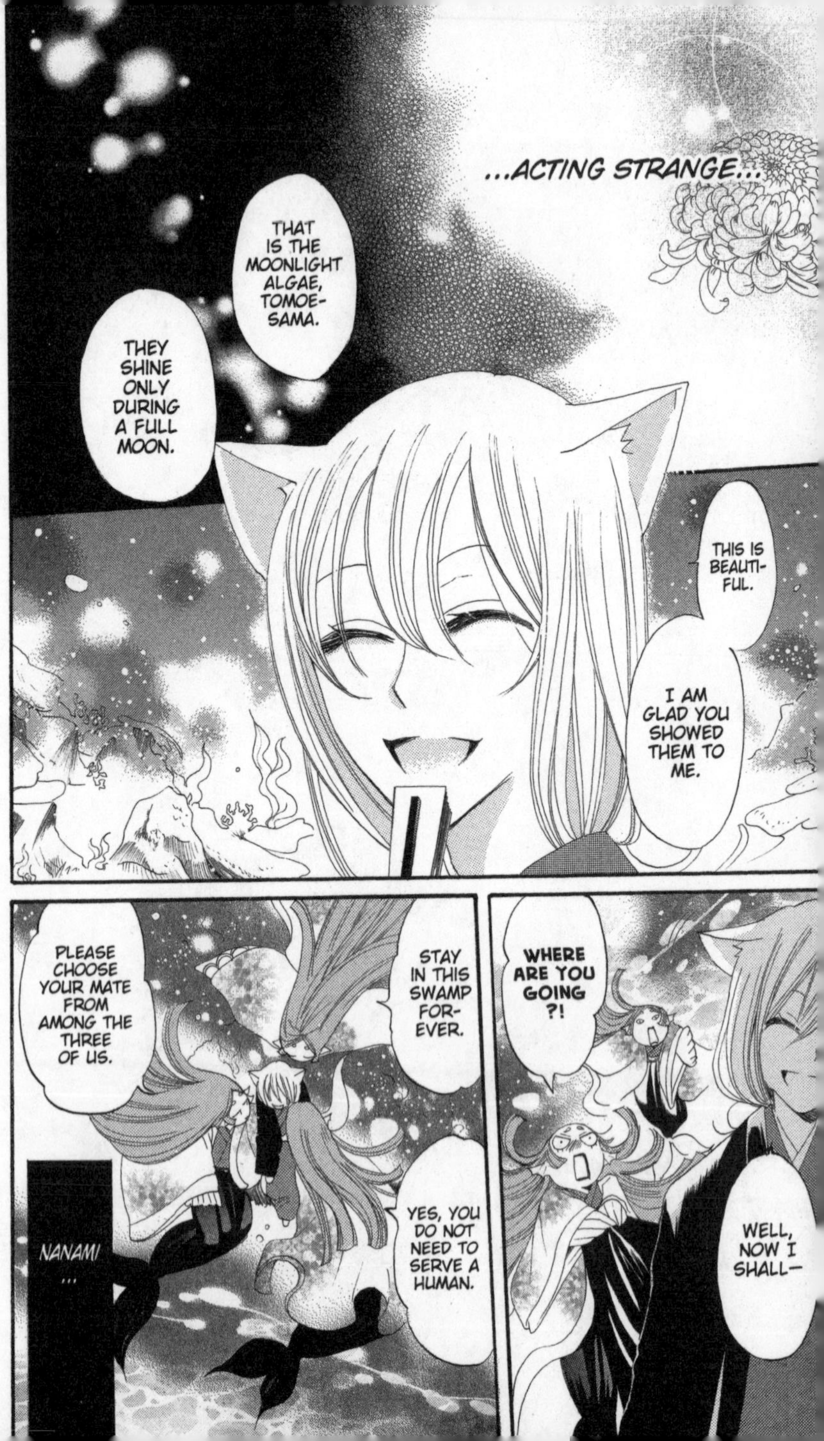

...ACTING STRANGE...
THAT IS THE MOONLIGHT ALGAE, TOMOE-SAMA.
THEY SHINE ONLY DURING A FULL MOON.
THIS IS BEAUTI-FUL.
I AM GLAD YOU SHOWED THEM TO ME.
WELL, NOW I SHALL—
WHERE ARE YOU GOING?!
STAY IN THIS SWAMP FOR-EVER.
PLEASE CHOOSE YOUR MATE FROM AMONG THE THREE OF US.
YES, YOU DO NOT NEED TO SERVE A HUMAN.
NANAMI...

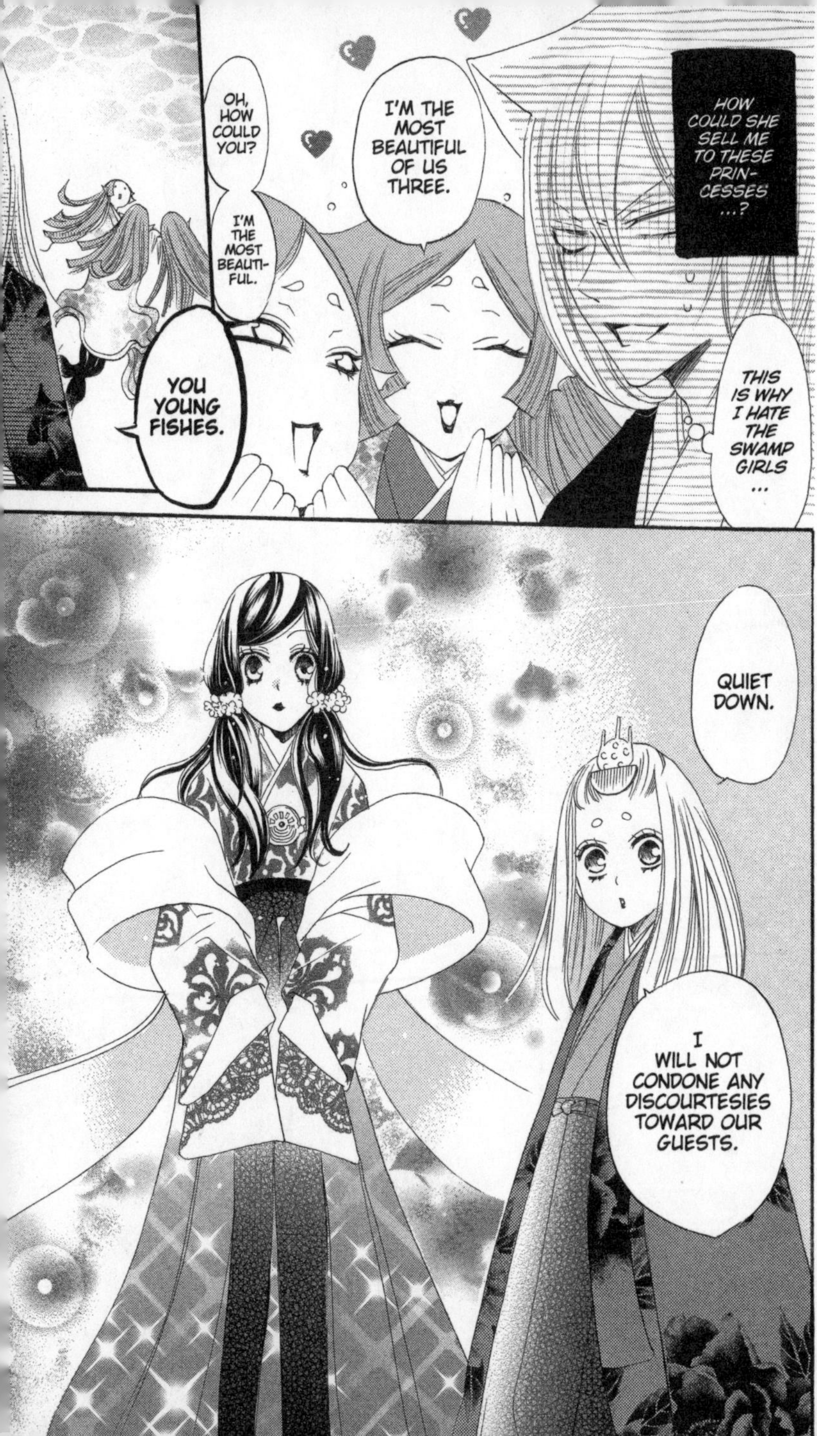
HOW COULD SHE SELL ME TO THESE PRIN-CESSES ...?
I'M THE MOST BEAUTIFUL OF US THREE.
OH, HOW COULD YOU?
I'M THE MOST BEAUTI-FUL.
THIS IS WHY I HATE THE SWAMP GIRLS ...
YOU YOUNG FISHES.
QUIET DOWN.
I WILL NOT CONDONE ANY DISCOURTESIES TOWARD OUR GUESTS.

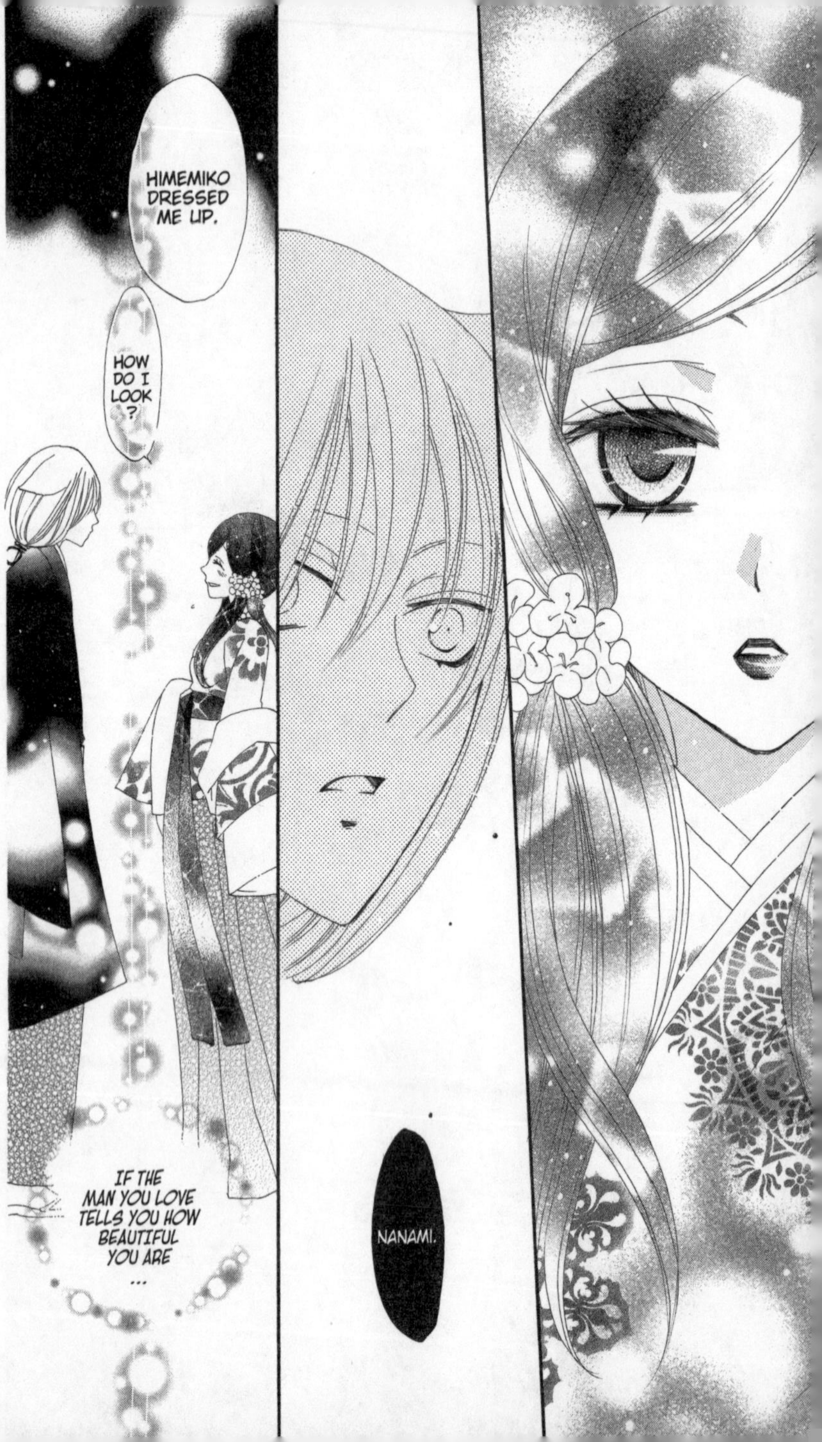
NANAMI.
HIMEMIKO DRESSED ME UP.
HOW DO I LOOK?
IF THE MAN YOU LOVE TELLS YOU HOW BEAUTIFUL YOU ARE ...

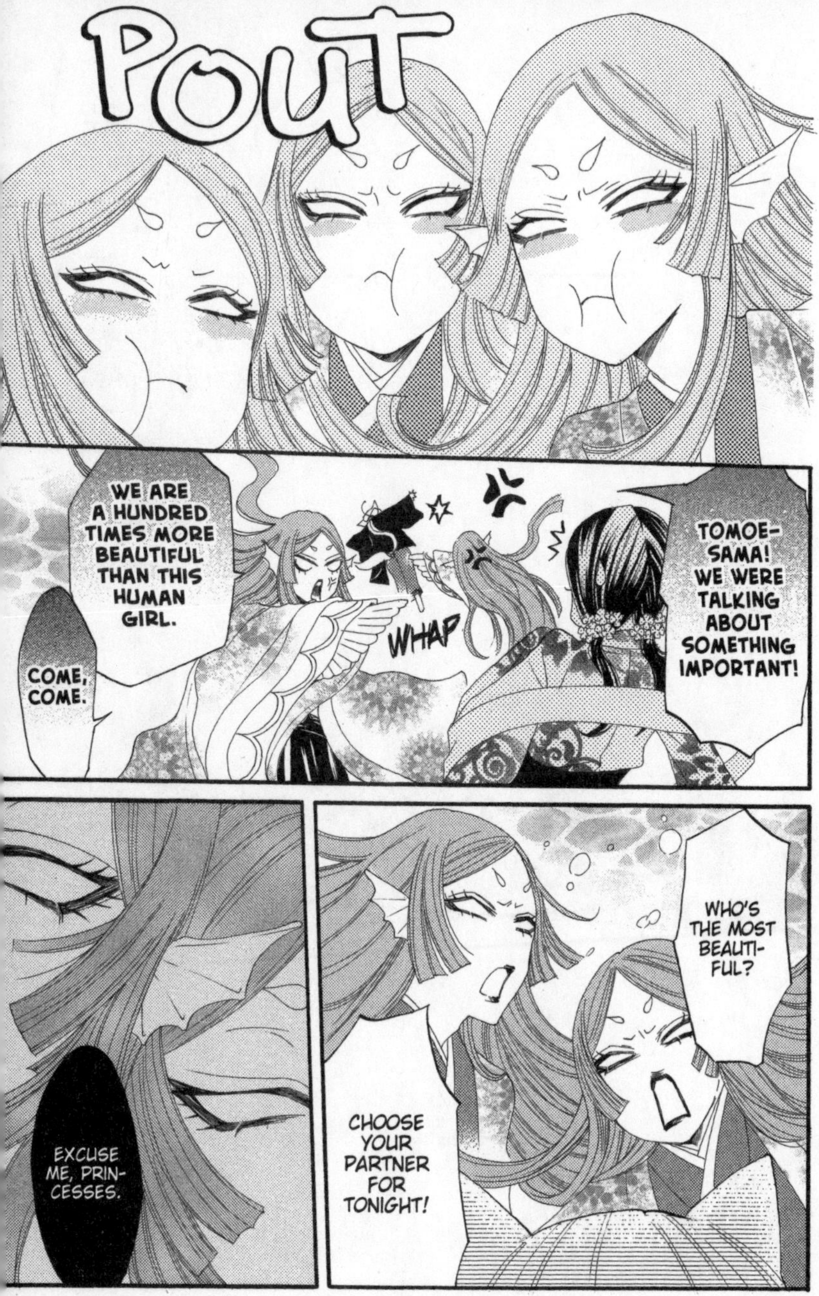
POUT
TOMOE-SAMA! WE WERE TALKING ABOUT SOMETHING IMPORTANT!
WE ARE A HUNDRED TIMES MORE BEAUTIFUL THAN THIS HUMAN GIRL.
WHAP
COME, COME.
WHO'S THE MOST BEAUTI-FUL?
CHOOSE YOUR PARTNER FOR TONIGHT!
EXCUSE ME, PRIN-CESSES.

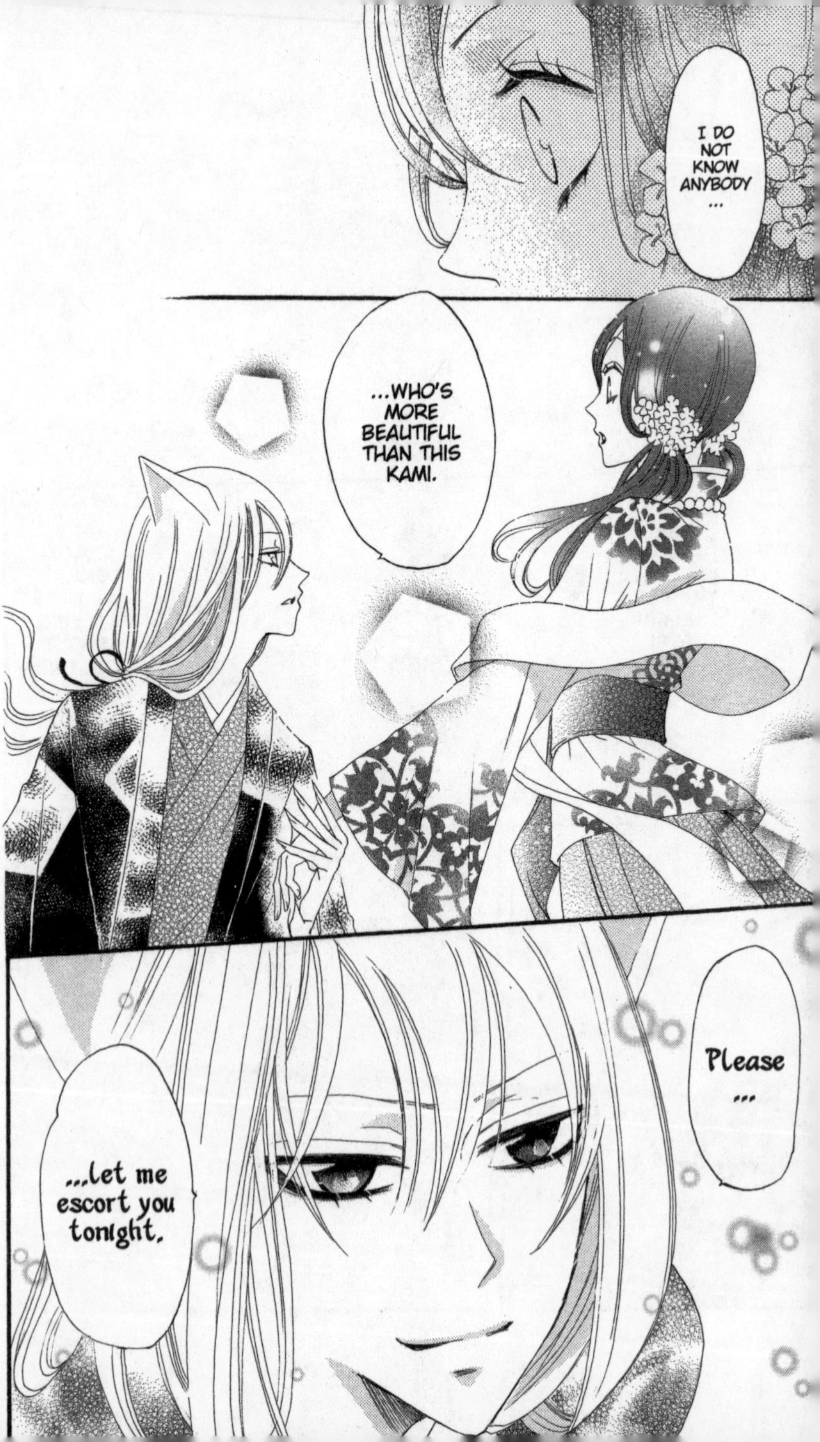
I DO NOT KNOW ANYBODY ...
...WHO'S MORE BEAUTIFUL THAN THIS KAMI.
Please ...
...let me escort you tonight.

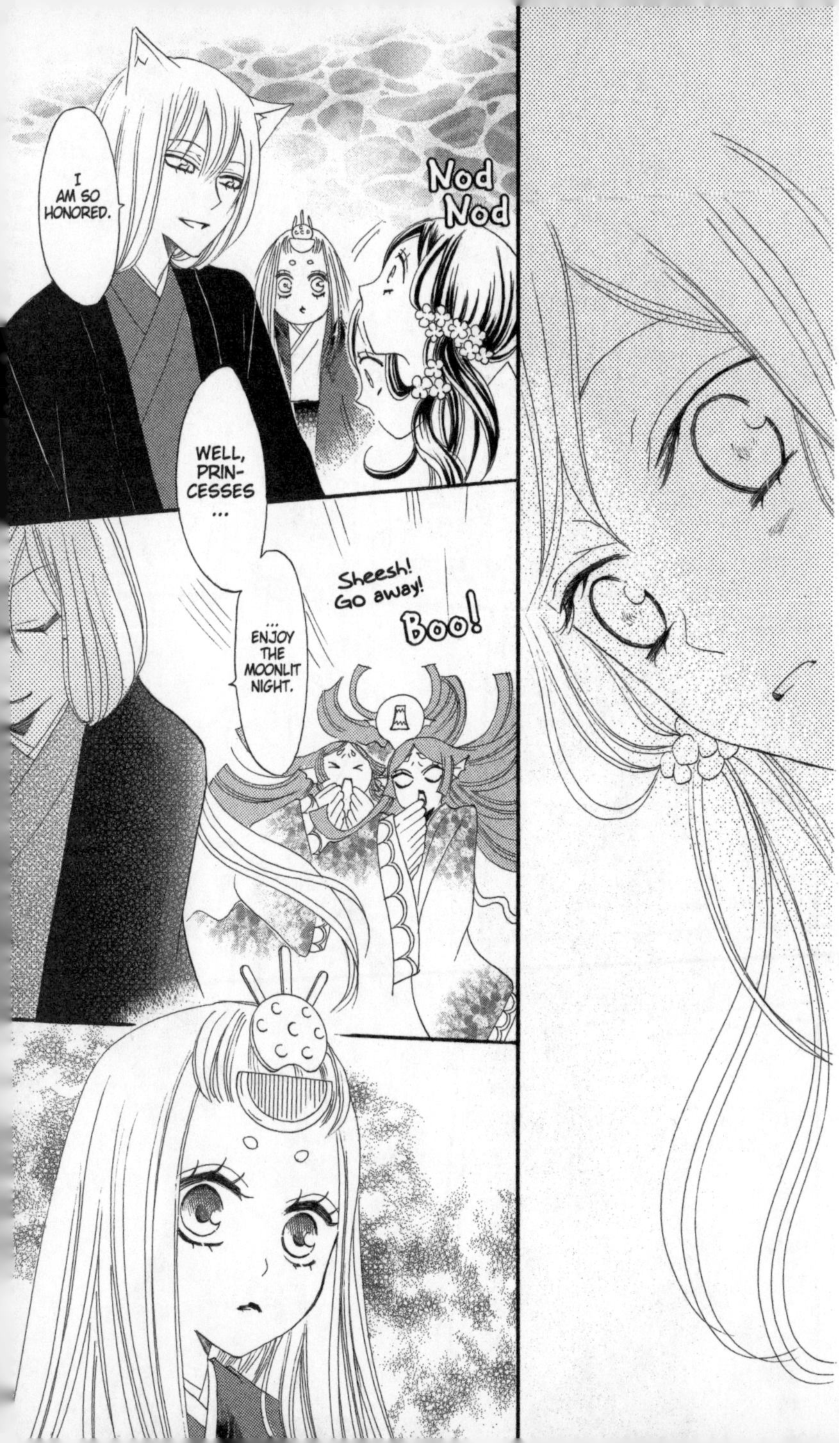
Nod Nod
I AM SO HONORED.
WELL, PRINCESSES ...
... ENJOY THE MOONLIT NIGHT.
Sheesh! Go away!
Boo!

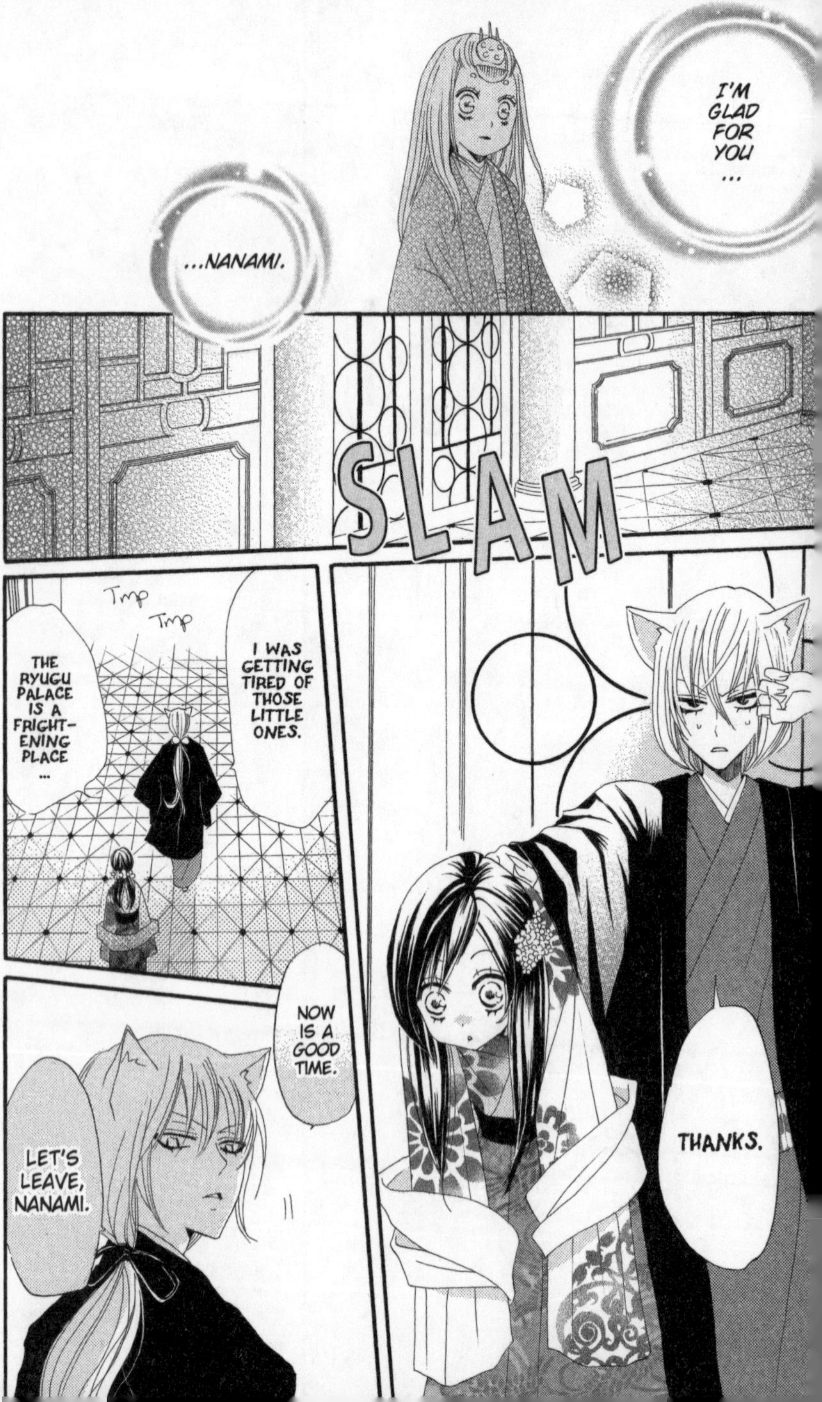
I'M GLAD FOR YOU...
...NANAMI.
SLAM
THANKS.
Tmp Tmp
I WAS GETTING TIRED OF THOSE LITTLE ONES.
THE RYUGU PALACE IS A FRIGHTENING PLACE...
NOW IS A GOOD TIME.
LET'S LEAVE, NANAMI.

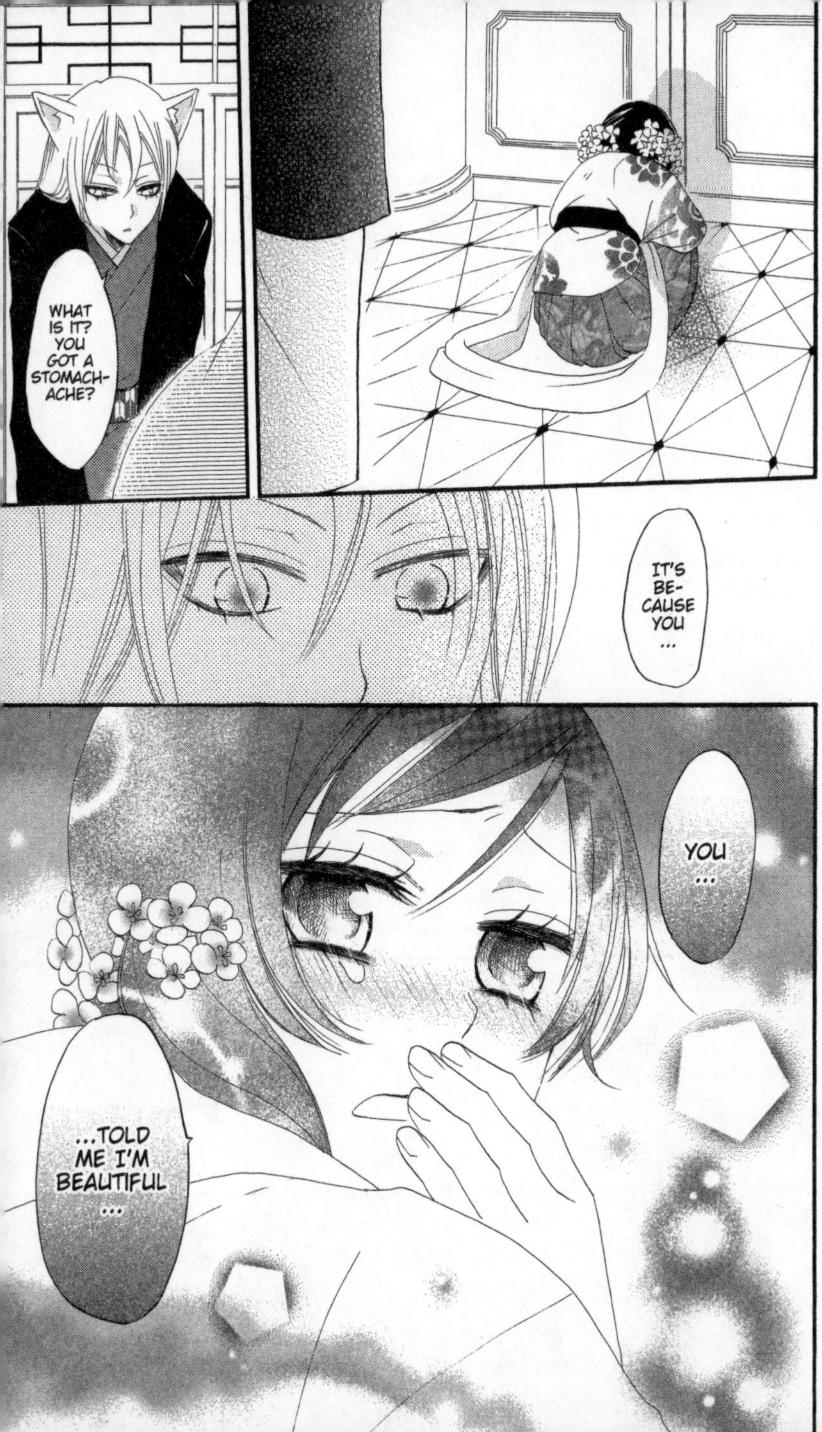
WHAT IS IT? YOU GOT A STOMACH-ACHE?
IT'S BE-CAUSE YOU ...
YOU ...
...TOLD ME I'M BEAUTIFUL ...

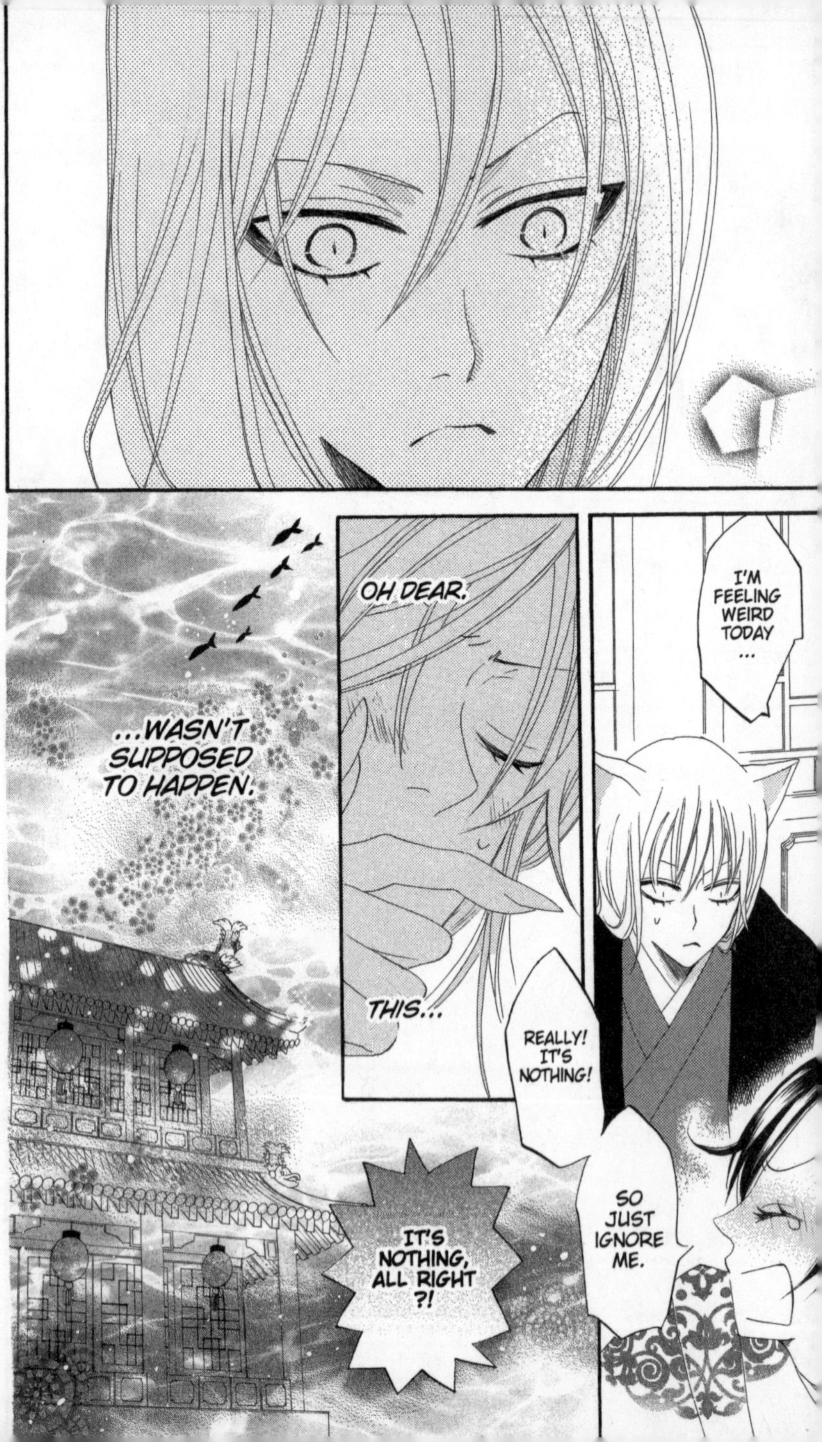
I'M FEELING WEIRD TODAY...
REALLY! IT'S NOTHING!
SO JUST IGNORE ME.
IT'S NOTHING, ALL RIGHT?!
OH DEAR.
THIS...
...WASN'T SUPPOSED TO HAPPEN.

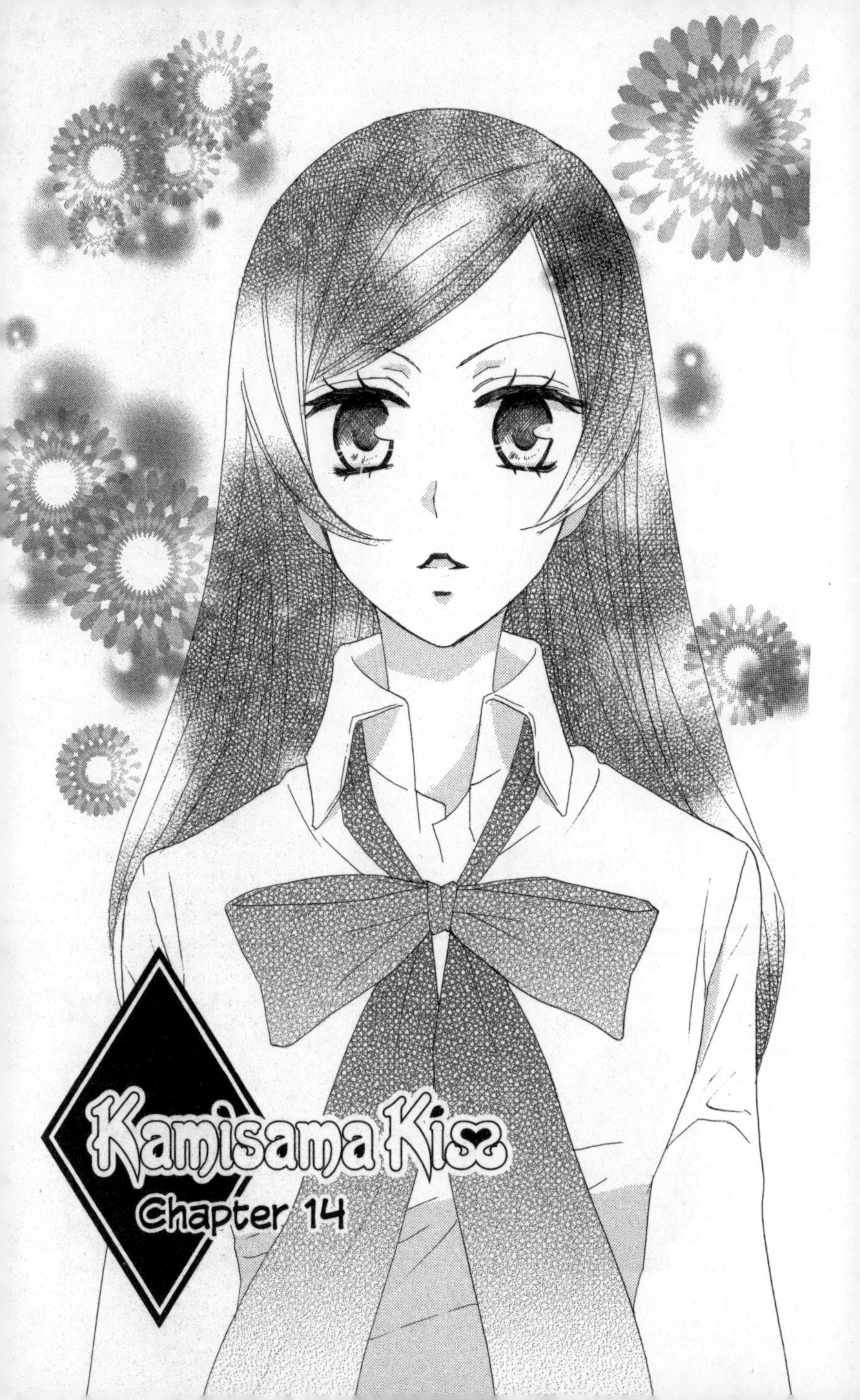
Kamisama Kiss
Chapter 14

IT'S RAINING A LOT ...

KShhh

KYAH!

HEY, LOOK.

A SNAKE, A SNAKE!

Himemiko of the Swamp

Rules over the Tatara Swamp.

Owns lots of clothes.

Loves Kotaro.

Recently suffering from dry eyes.

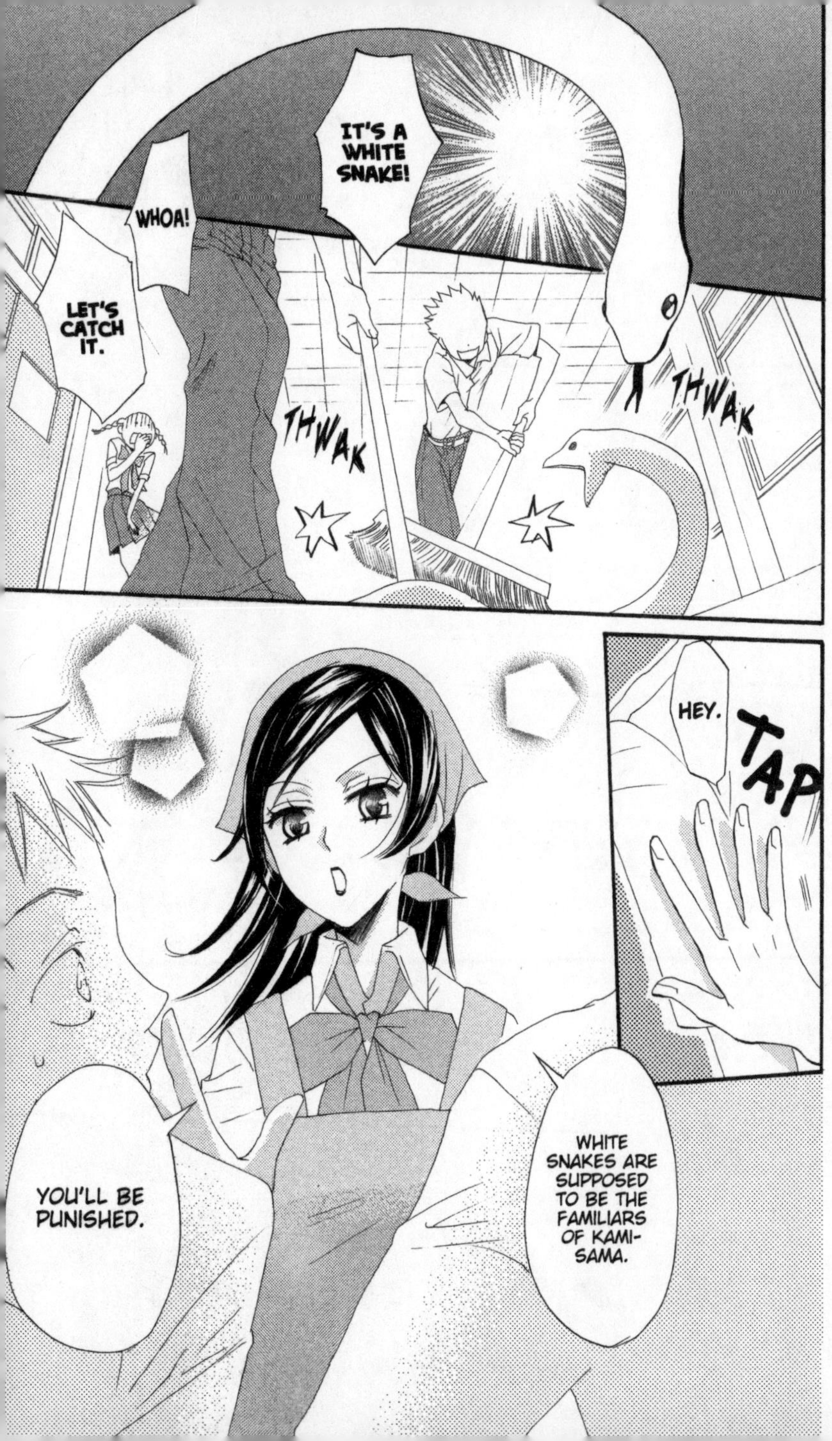
IT'S A WHITE SNAKE!
WHOA!
LET'S CATCH IT.
THWAK
THWAK
HEY.
TAP
WHITE SNAKES ARE SUPPOSED TO BE THE FAMILIARS OF KAMI-SAMA.
YOU'LL BE PUNISHED.

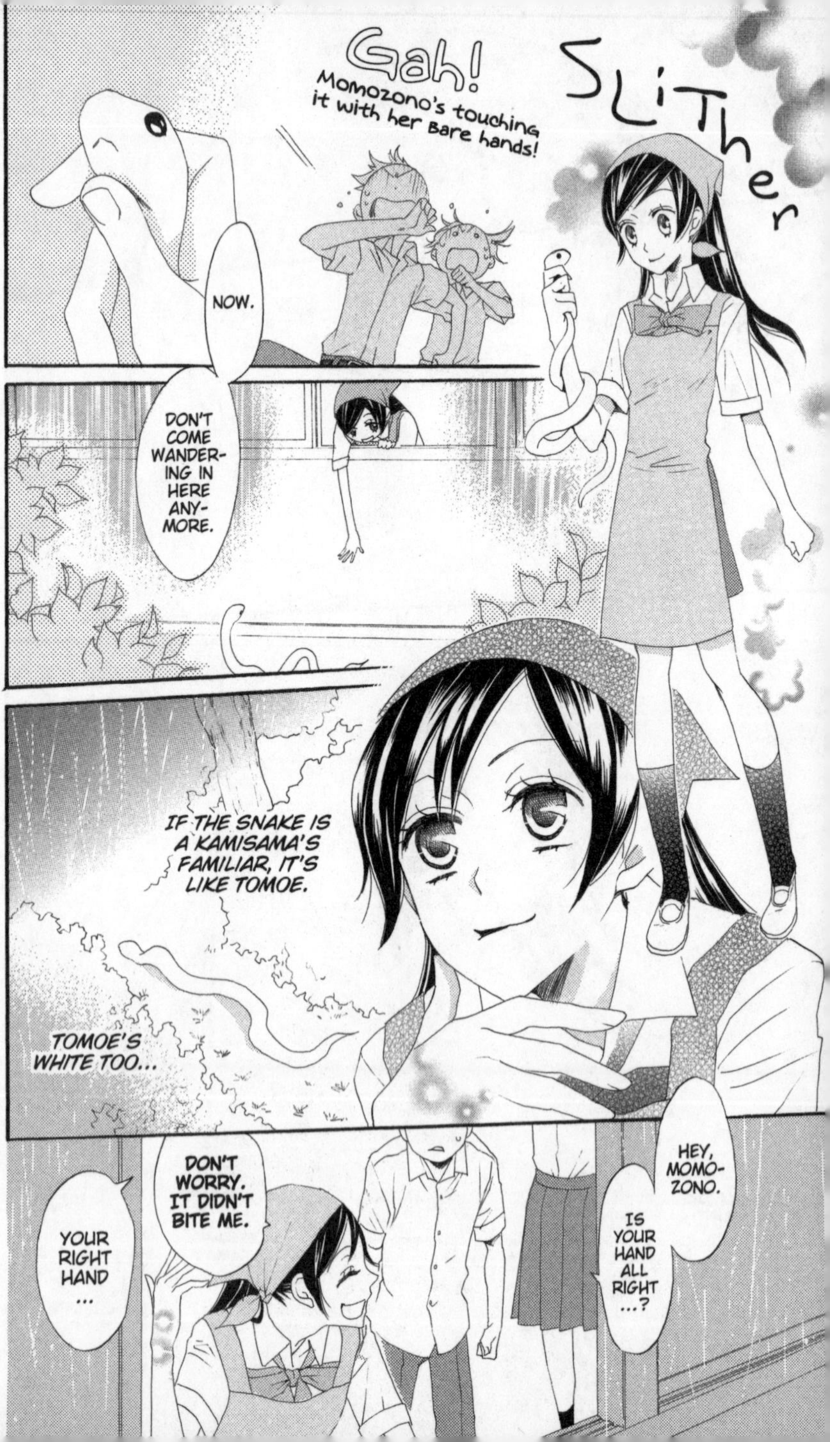
SLiTher
Gah!
Momozono's touching it with her bare hands!
NOW.
DON'T COME WANDERING IN HERE ANYMORE.
IF THE SNAKE IS A KAMISAMA'S FAMILIAR, IT'S LIKE TOMOE.
TOMOE'S WHITE TOO...
HEY, MOMOZONO.
IS YOUR HAND ALL RIGHT...?
DON'T WORRY. IT DIDN'T BITE ME.
YOUR RIGHT HAND ...

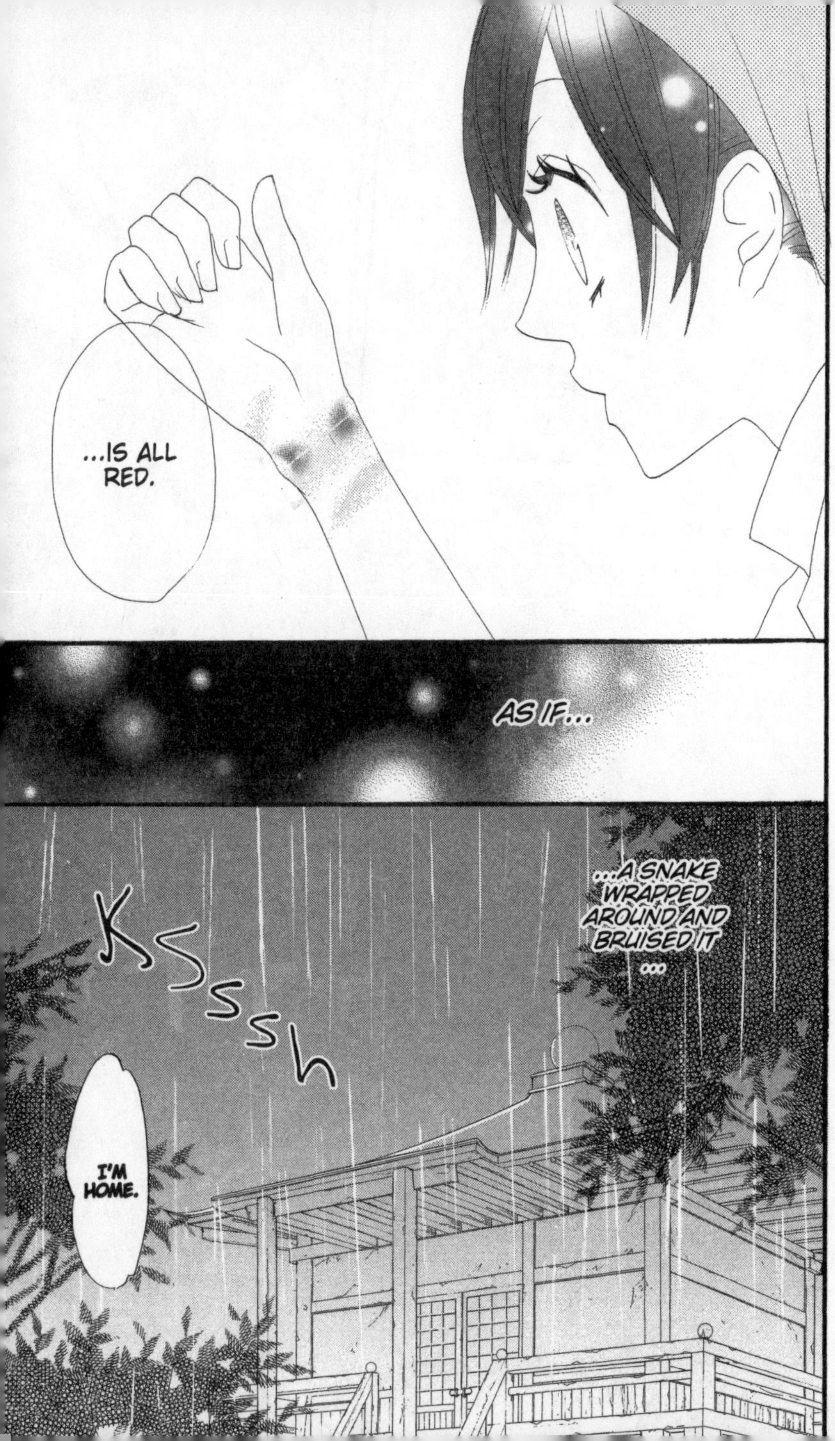
...IS ALL RED.
AS IF...
...A SNAKE WRAPPED AROUND AND BRUISED IT...
KSSSH
I'M HOME.

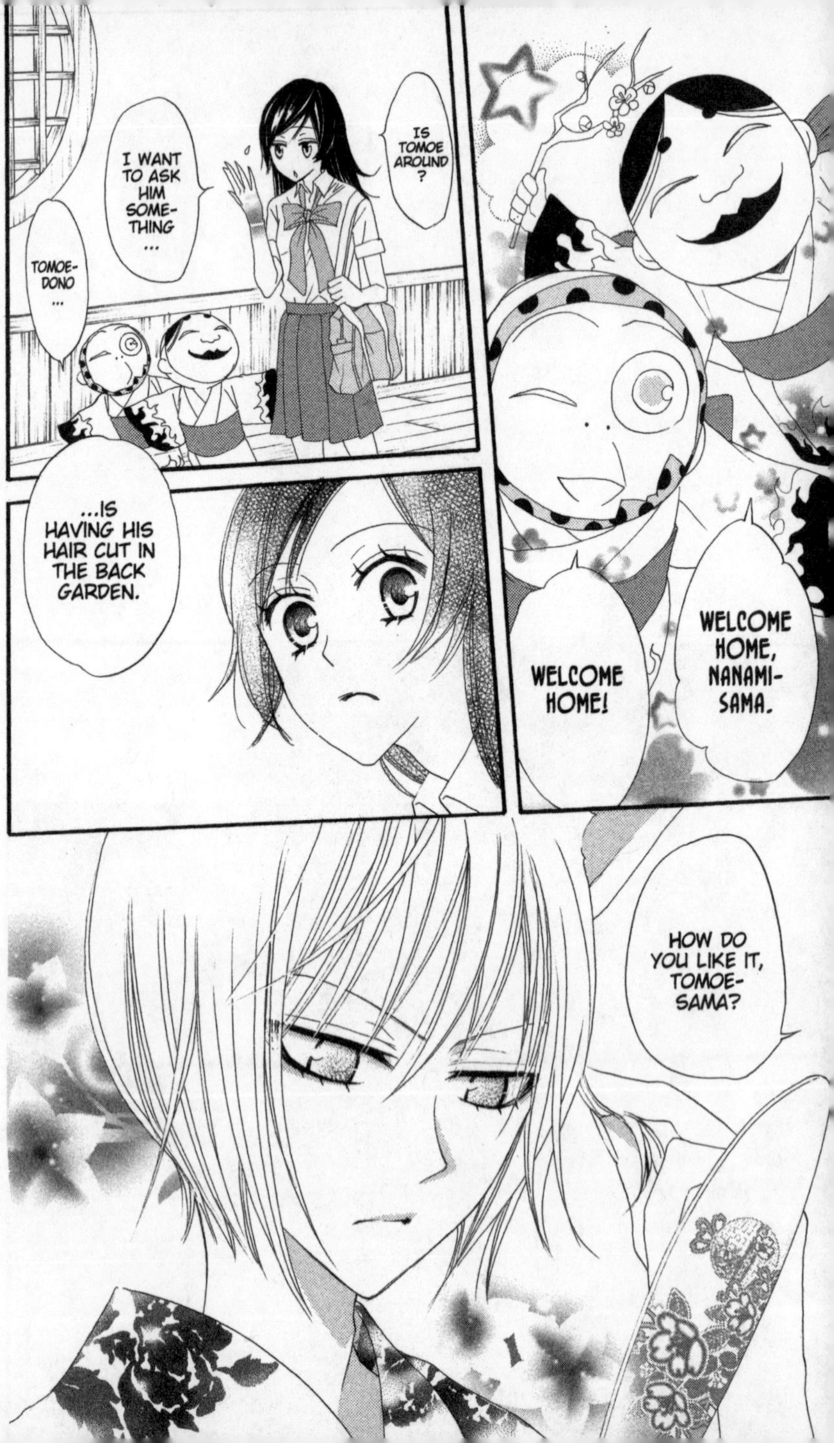
WELCOME HOME, NANAMI-SAMA.
WELCOME HOME!
IS TOMOE AROUND?
I WANT TO ASK HIM SOMETHING...
TOMOE-DONO...
...IS HAVING HIS HAIR CUT IN THE BACK GARDEN.
HOW DO YOU LIKE IT, TOMOE-SAMA?

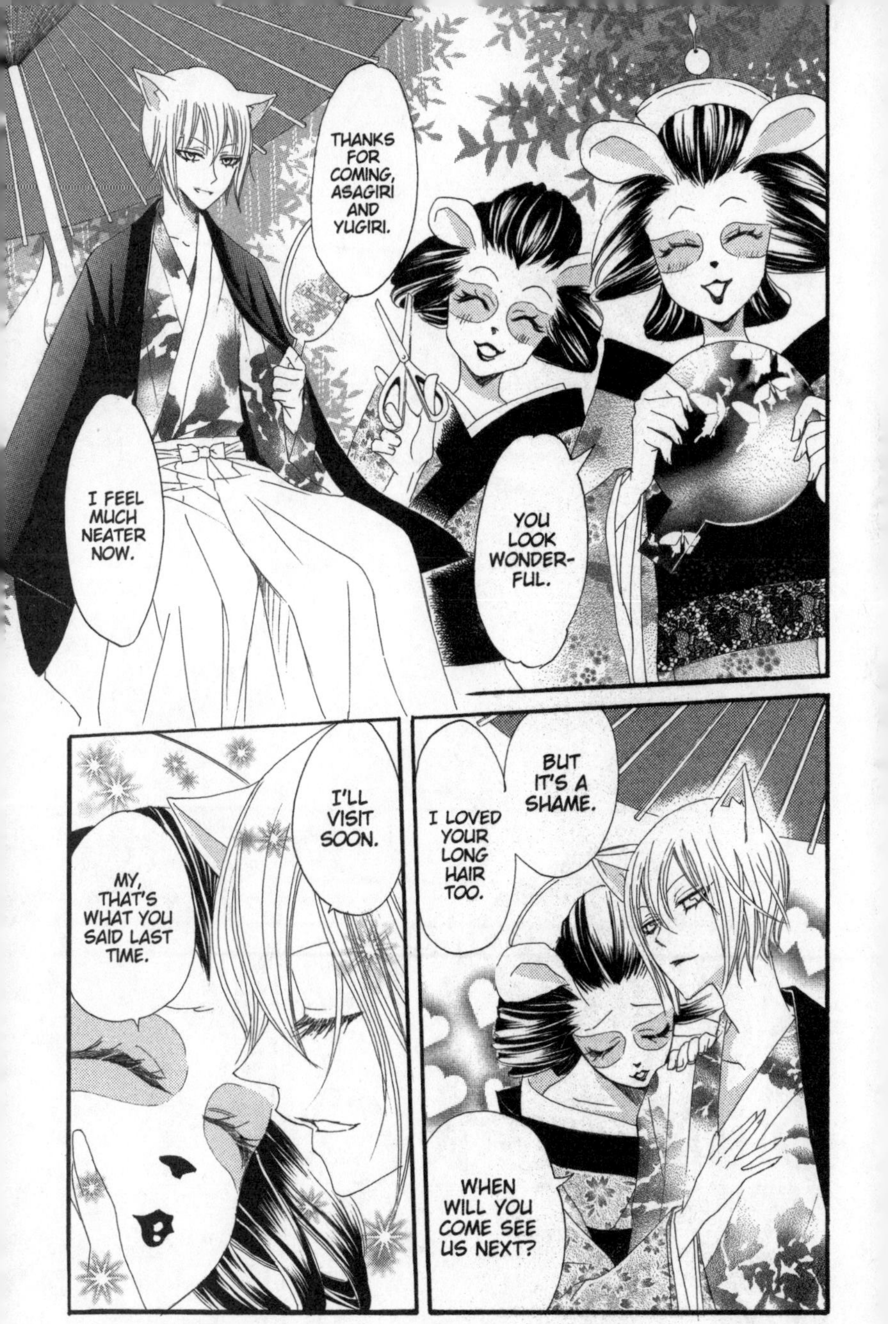
THANKS FOR COMING, ASAGIRI AND YUGIRI.
YOU LOOK WONDER-FUL.
I FEEL MUCH NEATER NOW.
BUT IT'S A SHAME.
I LOVED YOUR LONG HAIR TOO.
WHEN WILL YOU COME SEE US NEXT?
I'LL VISIT SOON.
MY, THAT'S WHAT YOU SAID LAST TIME.

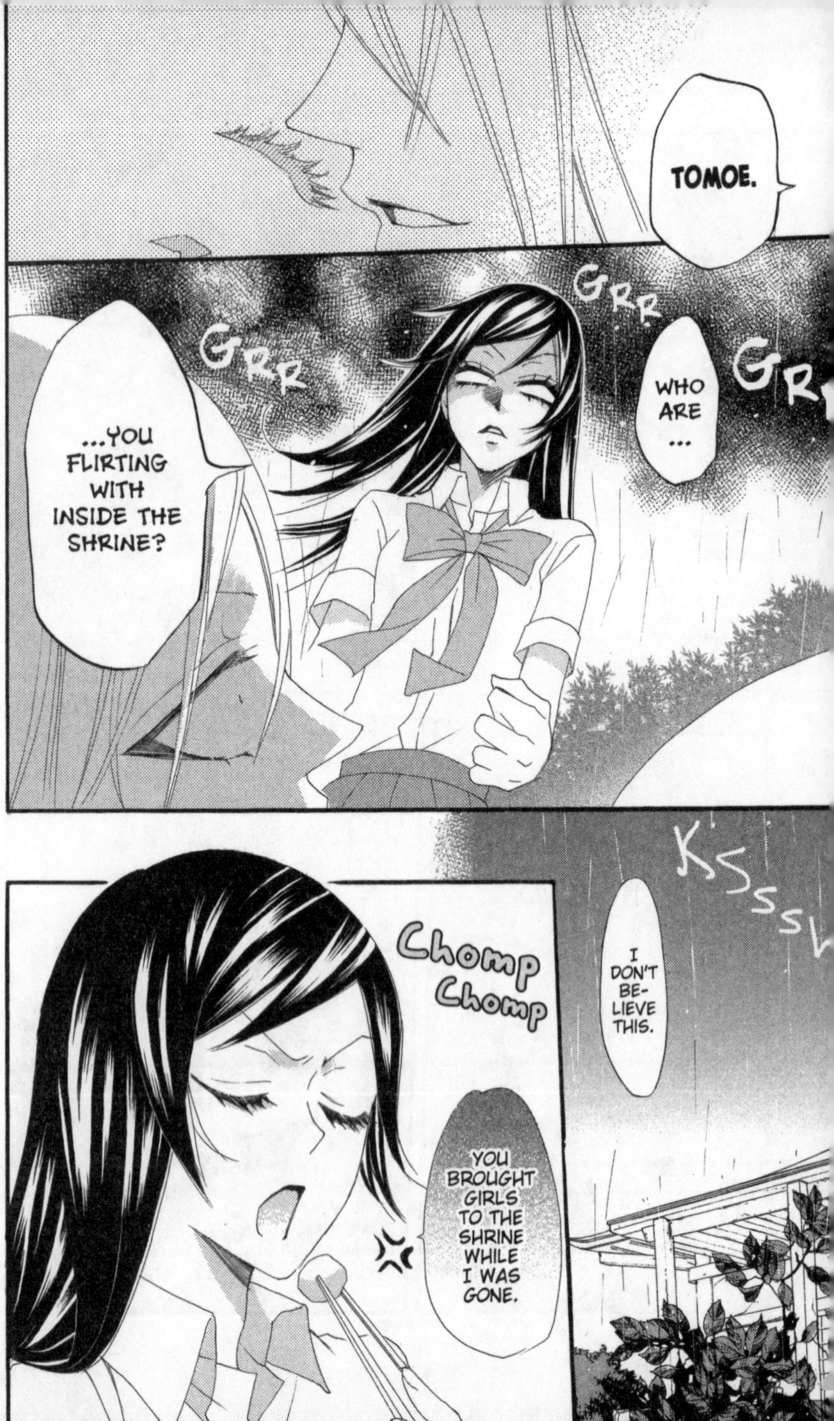
TOMOE.
GRR
WHO ARE ...
GRR
...YOU FLIRTING WITH INSIDE THE SHRINE?
I DON'T BE-LIEVE THIS.
Chomp Chomp
YOU BROUGHT GIRLS TO THE SHRINE WHILE I WAS GONE.

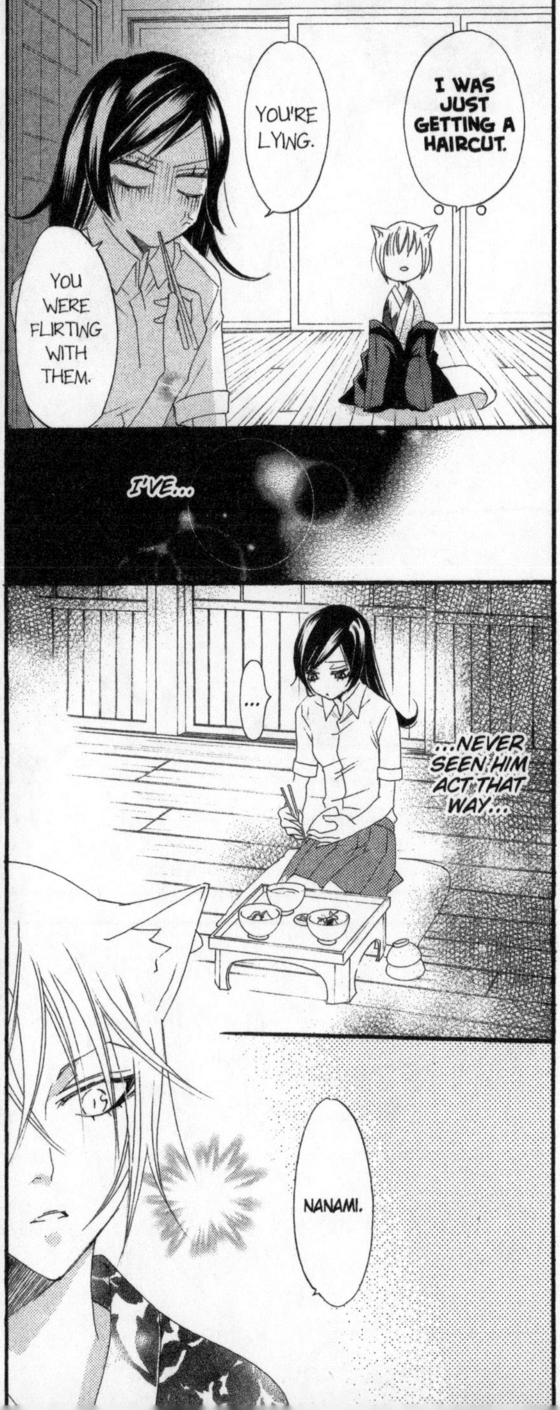
I WAS JUST GETTING A HAIRCUT.
YOU'RE LYING.
YOU WERE FLIRTING WITH THEM.
I'VE...
...NEVER SEEN HIM ACT THAT WAY...
...
NANAMI.

Two

For this volume, I had Shun and Kaga-san draw a sidebar each. They always help out with my work. Wah, thanks! They drew Kurama and Nanami.

I really enjoy having other people draw my characters. Work is always a pleasure thanks to these two. Thank you!

Kaga-san can see the color of people's auras. When I have a chance, I ask, "What's my color now??" I ask thinking "I must be a calm pastel green now." Then I hear "vermilion" and feel gah.

The other day I asked, "What color is Chiro (the cat)?" and the result was "I can't tell because of the fur." Colors are interesting.

Shun can see the color of her own aura as well as other people's aura. The two both came up with the same color when I asked them. Wow. I cannot see auras. My eyesight is so poor, I cannot even see road signs. It would be fun if I could see more things.

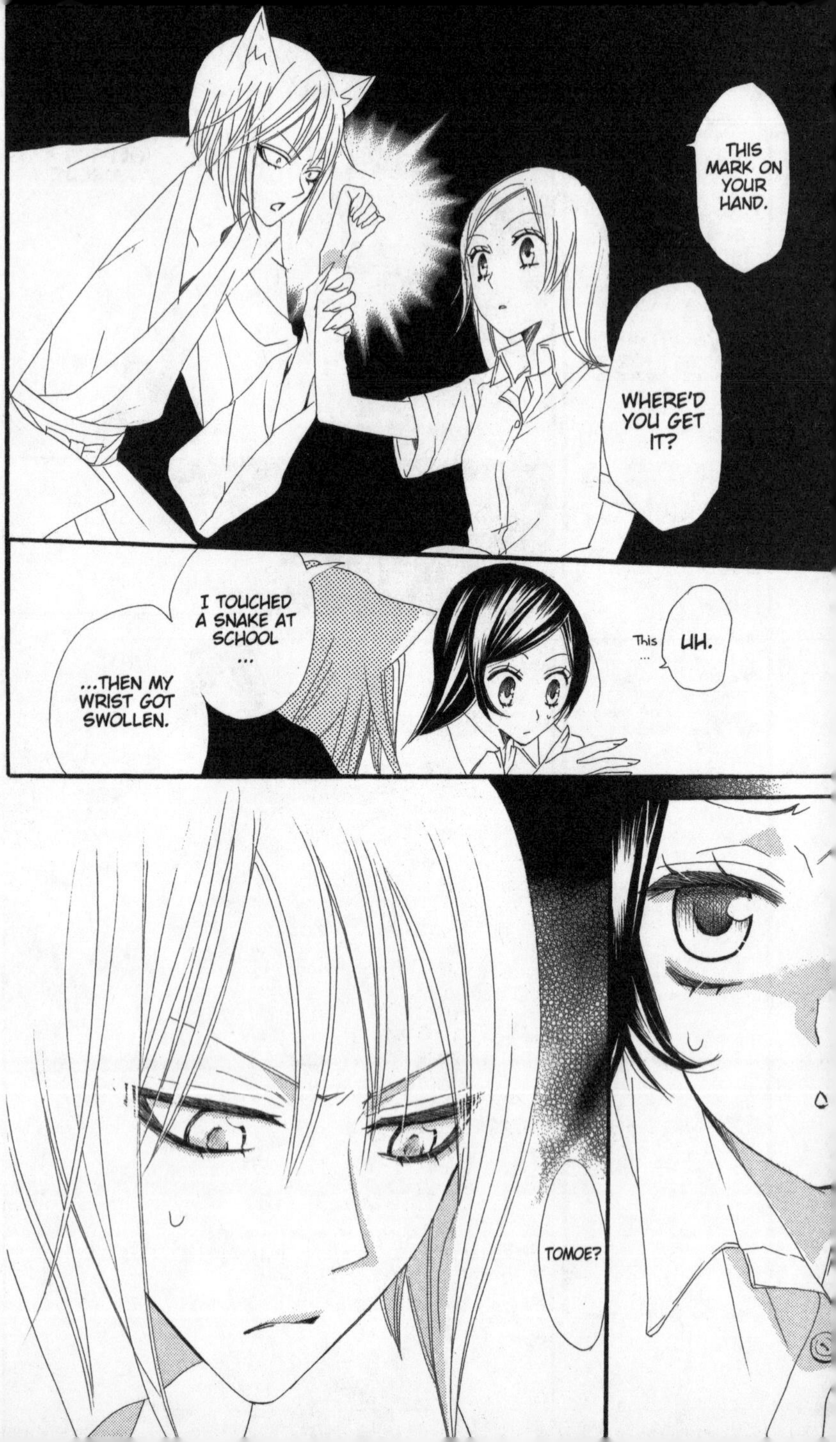
THIS MARK ON YOUR HAND.
WHERE'D YOU GET IT?
This ...
UH.
I TOUCHED A SNAKE AT SCHOOL ...
...THEN MY WRIST GOT SWOLLEN.
TOMOE?

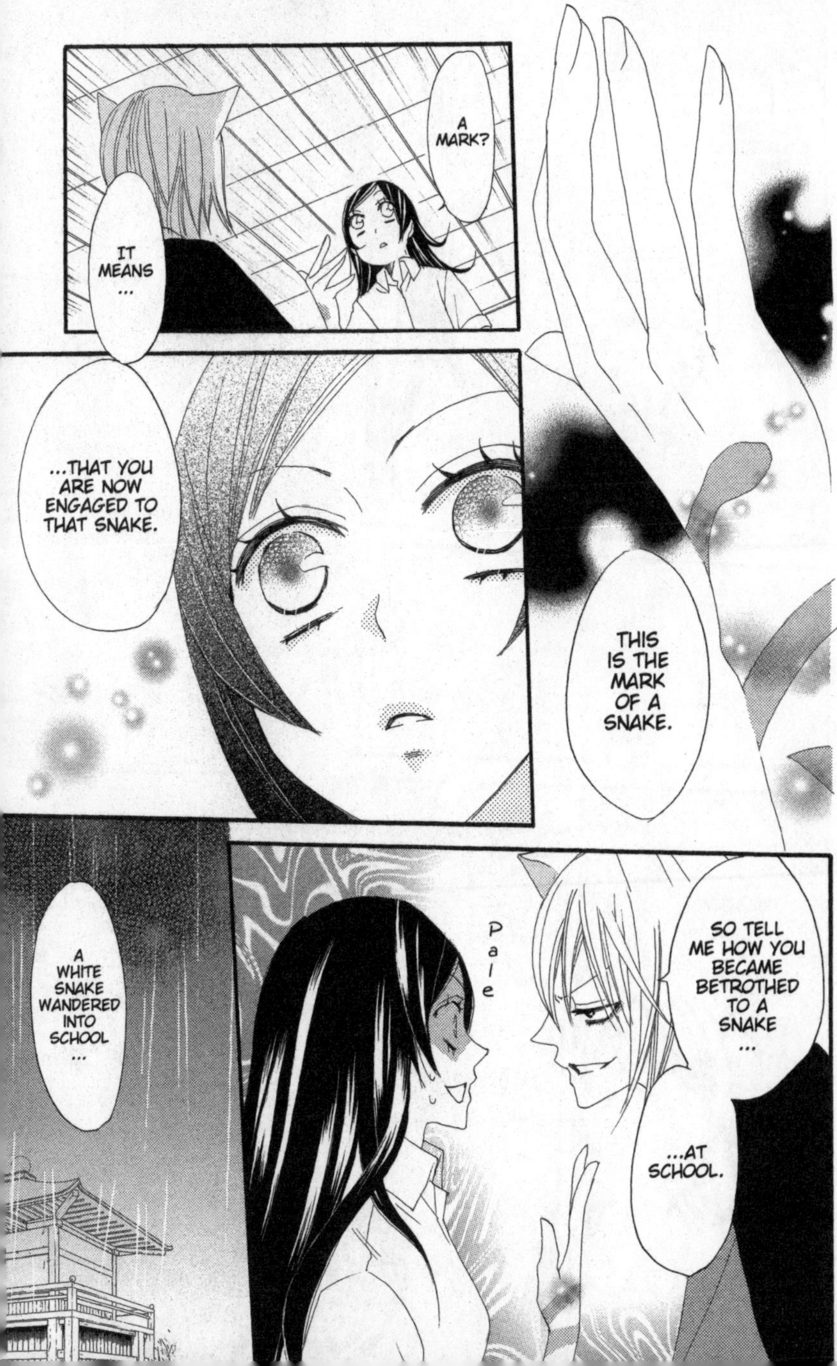
THIS IS THE MARK OF A SNAKE.
A MARK?
IT MEANS ...
...THAT YOU ARE NOW ENGAGED TO THAT SNAKE.
Pale
SO TELL ME HOW YOU BECAME BETROTHED TO A SNAKE ...
...AT SCHOOL.
A WHITE SNAKE WANDERED INTO SCHOOL ...

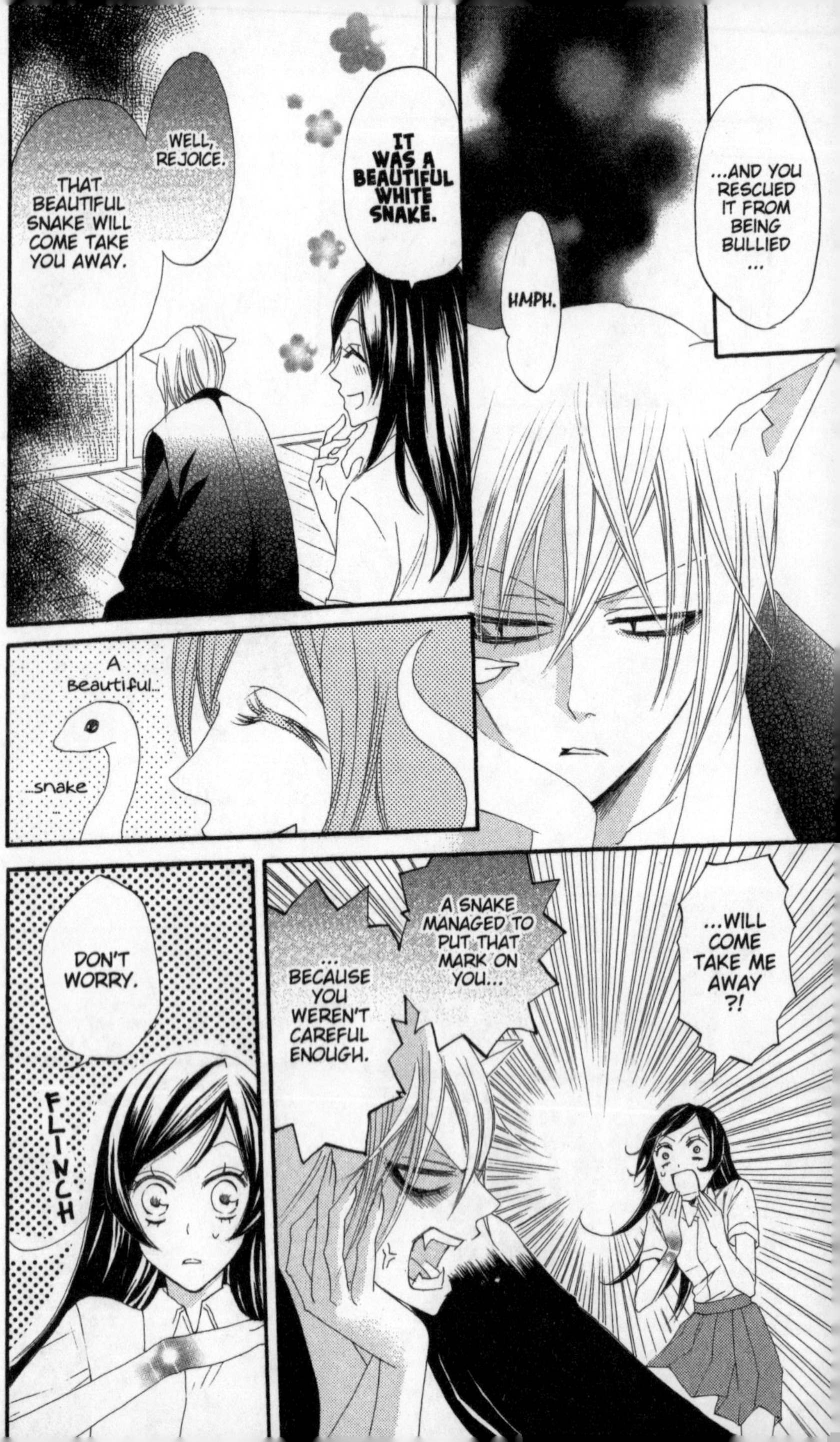
...AND YOU RESCUED IT FROM BEING BULLIED...
HMPH.
IT WAS A BEAUTIFUL WHITE SNAKE.
WELL, REJOICE.
THAT BEAUTIFUL SNAKE WILL COME TAKE YOU AWAY.
A beautiful...
...snake...
...WILL COME TAKE ME AWAY?!
A SNAKE MANAGED TO PUT THAT MARK ON YOU...
...BECAUSE YOU WEREN'T CAREFUL ENOUGH.
DON'T WORRY.
FLINCH

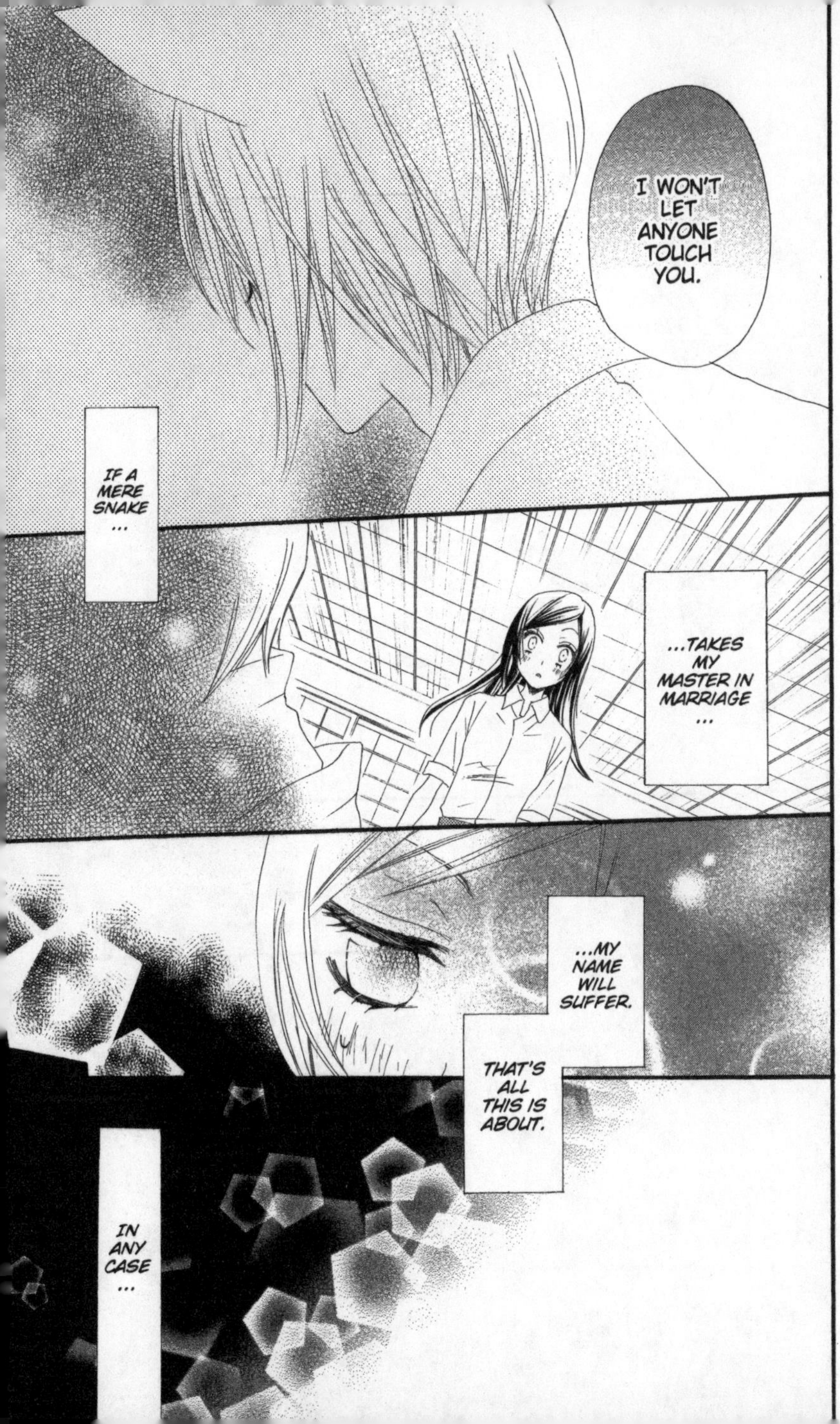
I WON'T LET ANYONE TOUCH YOU.
IF A MERE SNAKE...
...TAKES MY MASTER IN MARRIAGE...
...MY NAME WILL SUFFER.
THAT'S ALL THIS IS ABOUT.
IN ANY CASE...

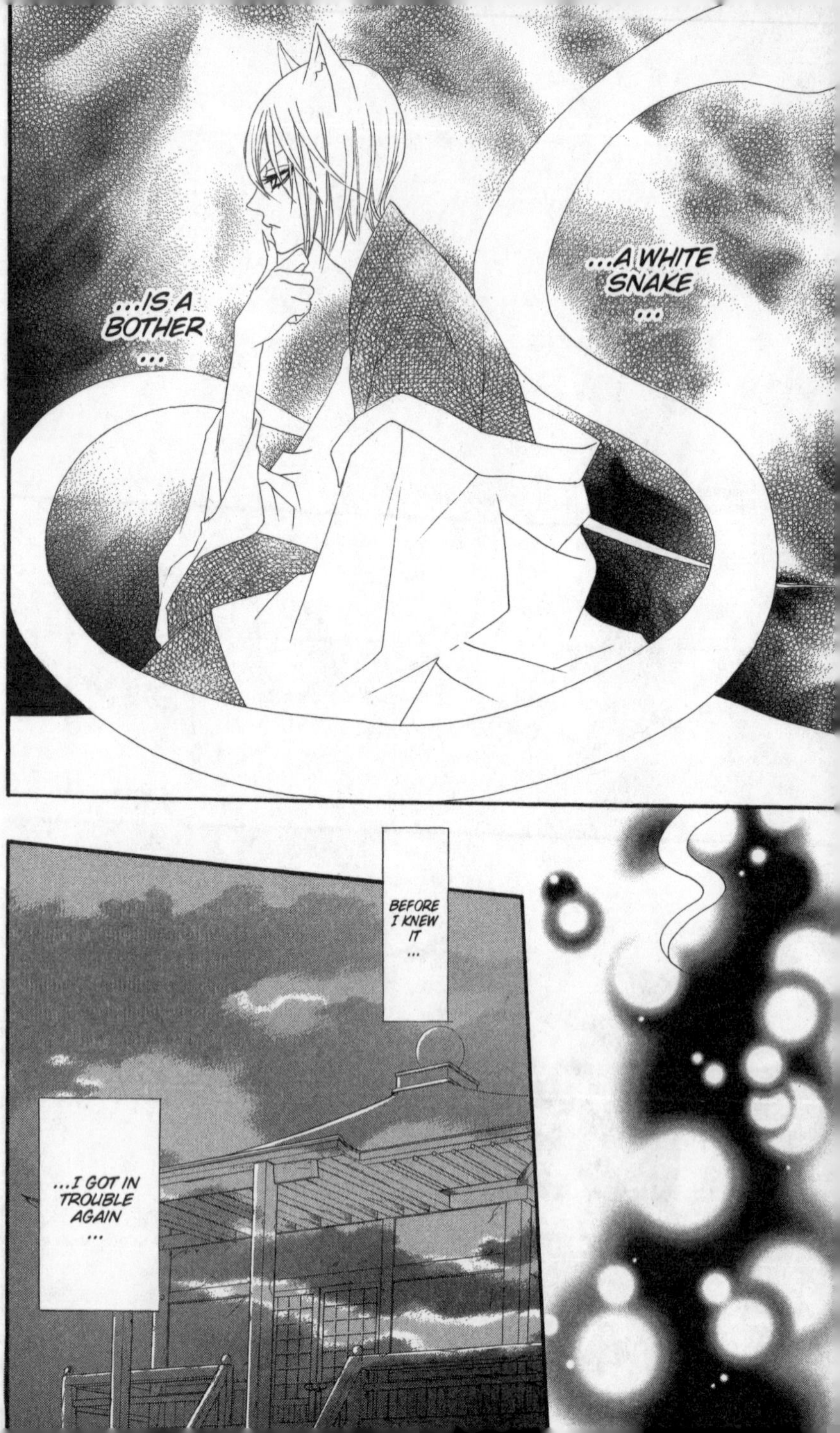
...A WHITE SNAKE ...
...IS A BOTHER ...
BEFORE I KNEW IT ...
...I GOT IN TROUBLE AGAIN ...

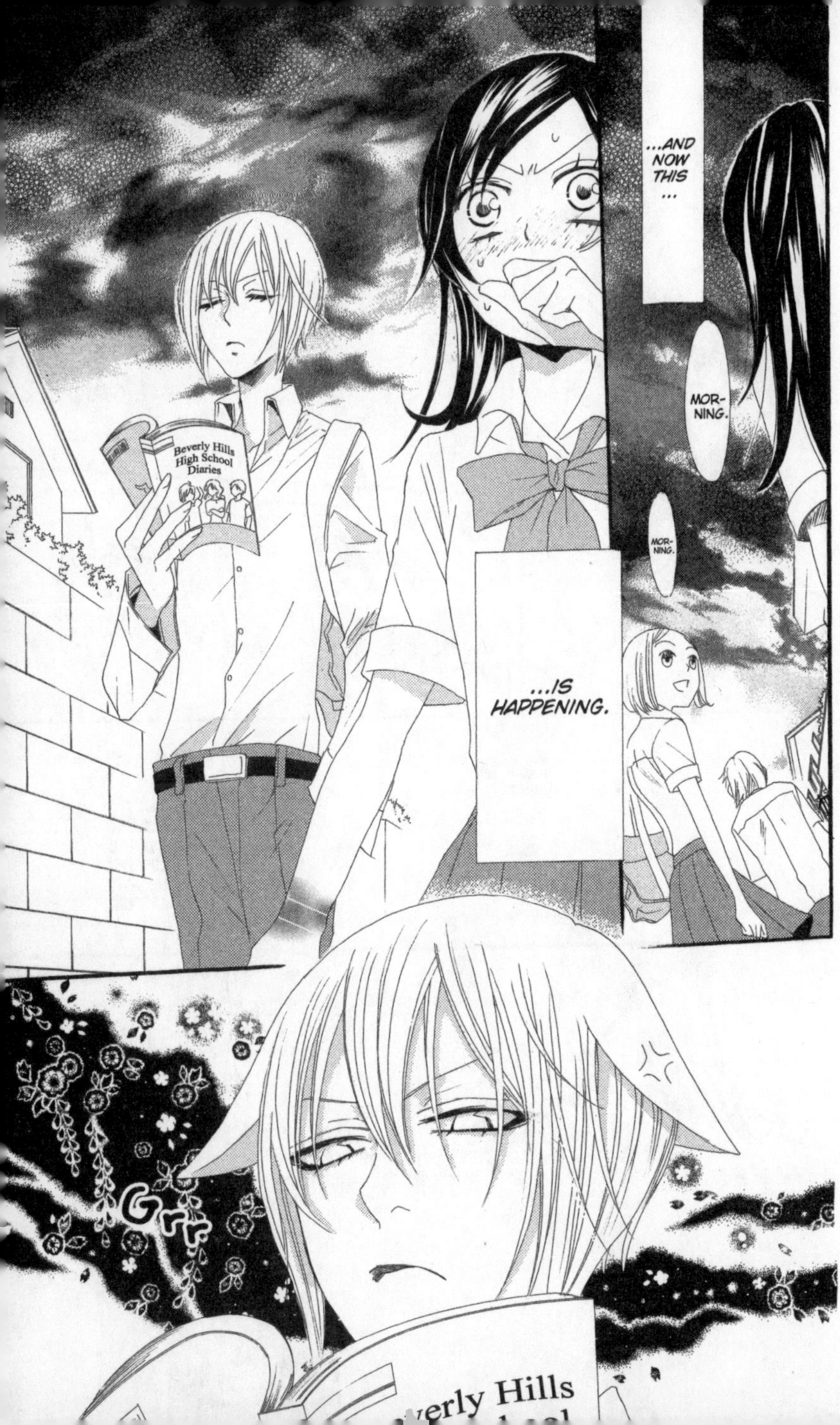
...AND NOW THIS ...
MOR-NING.
MOR-NING.
...IS HAPPENING.
Beverly Hills High School Diaries
Grr

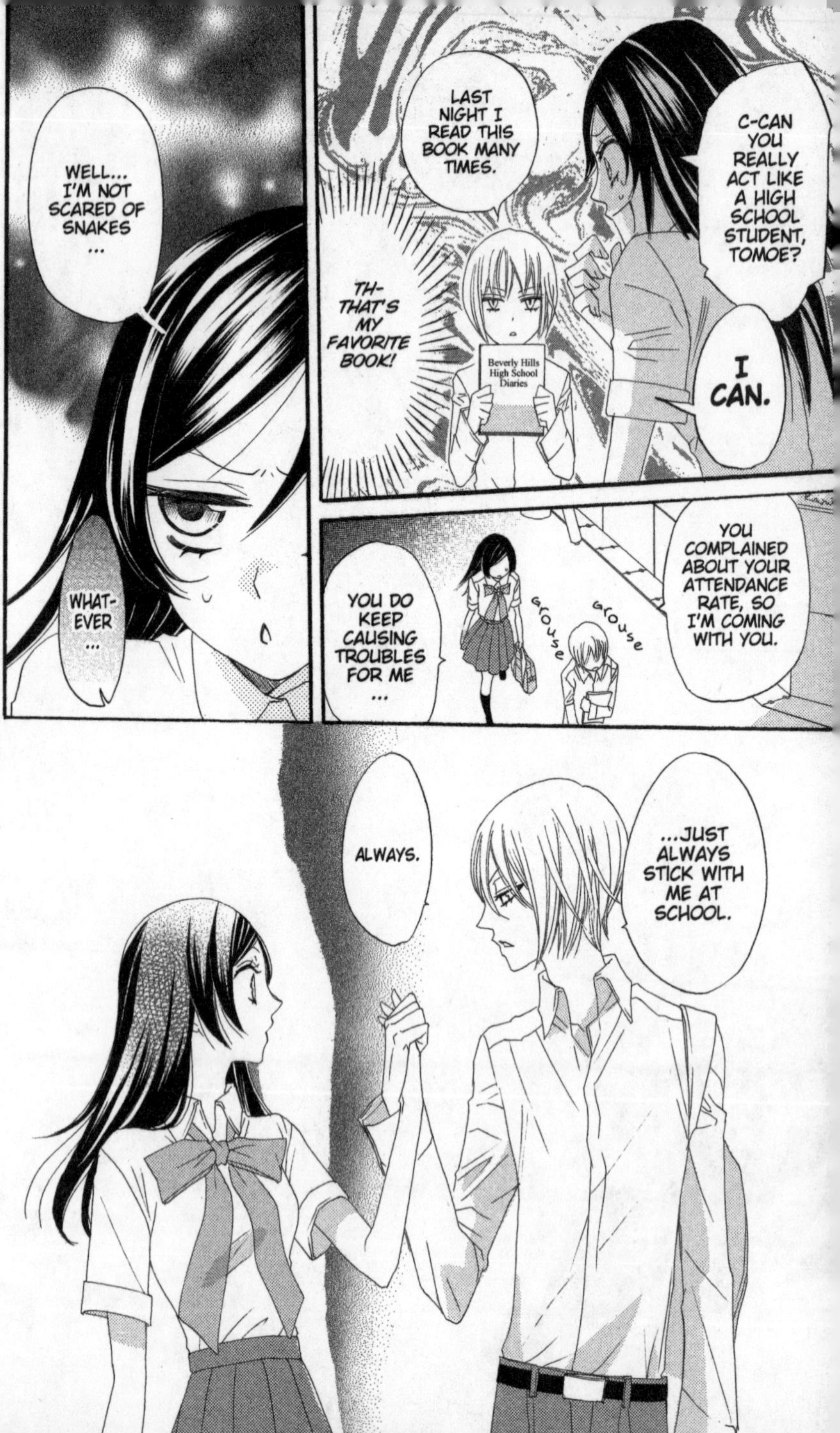
C-CAN YOU REALLY ACT LIKE A HIGH SCHOOL STUDENT, TOMOE?
I CAN.
LAST NIGHT I READ THIS BOOK MANY TIMES.
Beverly Hills High School Diaries
TH-THAT'S MY FAVORITE BOOK!
YOU COMPLAINED ABOUT YOUR ATTENDANCE RATE, SO I'M COMING WITH YOU.
Grouse
Grouse
YOU DO KEEP CAUSING TROUBLES FOR ME ...
WELL... I'M NOT SCARED OF SNAKES ...
WHAT-EVER ...
...JUST ALWAYS STICK WITH ME AT SCHOOL.
ALWAYS.

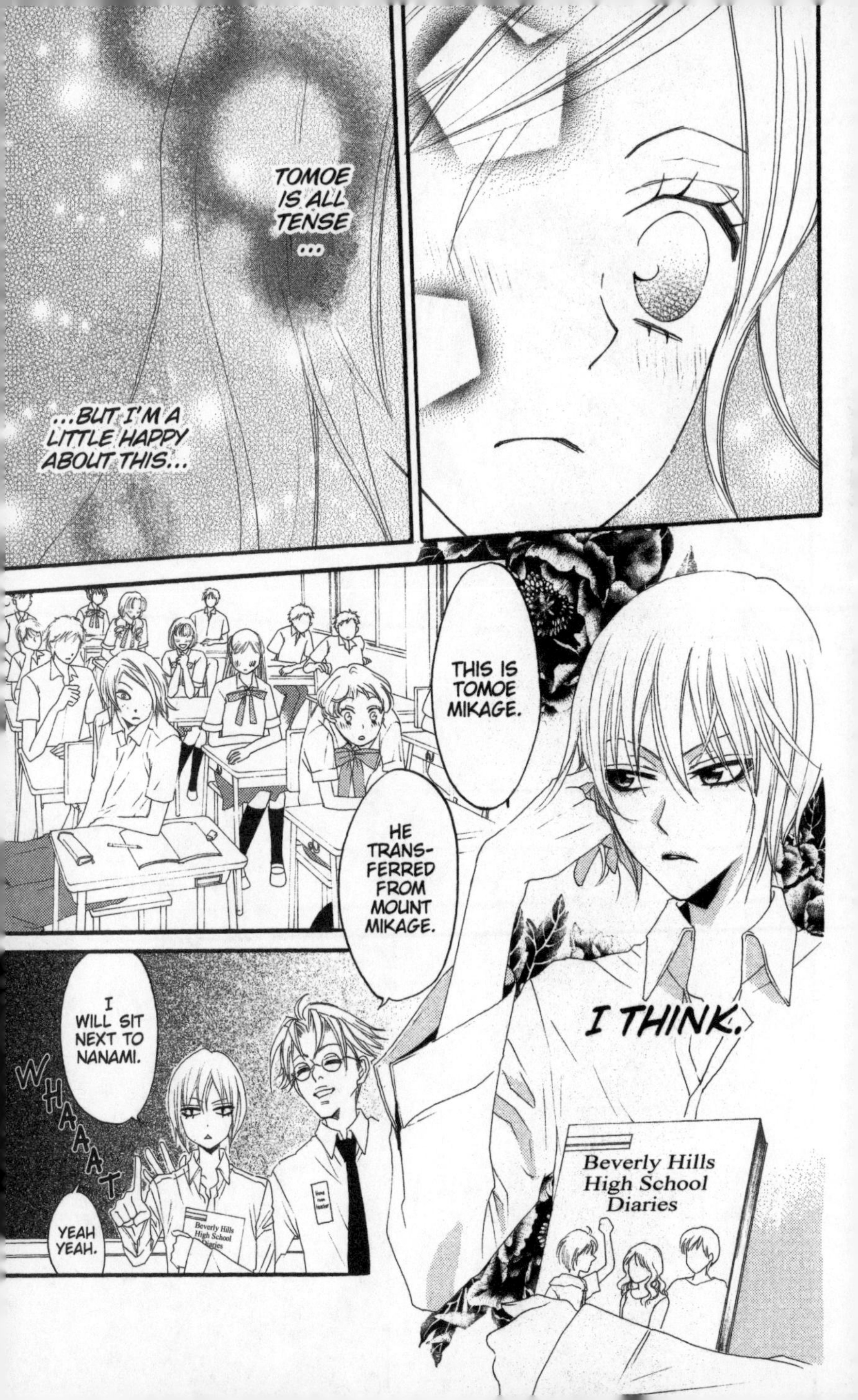

TOMOE IS ALL TENSE ...
...BUT I'M A LITTLE HAPPY ABOUT THIS...
I THINK.
Beverly Hills High School Diaries
THIS IS TOMOE MIKAGE.
HE TRANS-FERRED FROM MOUNT MIKAGE.
I WILL SIT NEXT TO NANAMI.
WHAAAAT
YEAH YEAH.
Beverly Hills High School Diaries

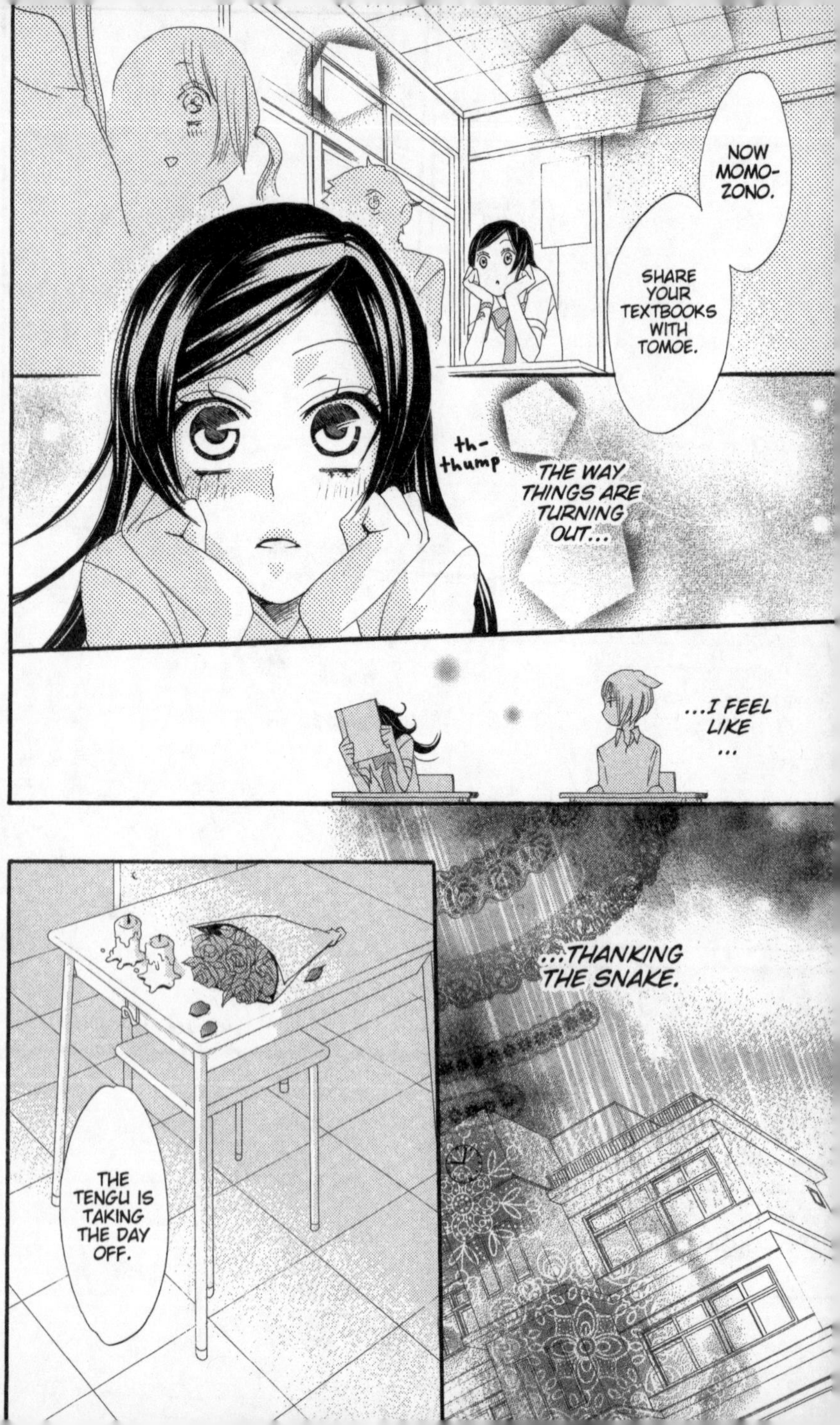
NOW MOMO-ZONO.
SHARE YOUR TEXTBOOKS WITH TOMOE.
th-thump
THE WAY THINGS ARE TURNING OUT...
...I FEEL LIKE ...
...THANKING THE SNAKE.
THE TENGU IS TAKING THE DAY OFF.

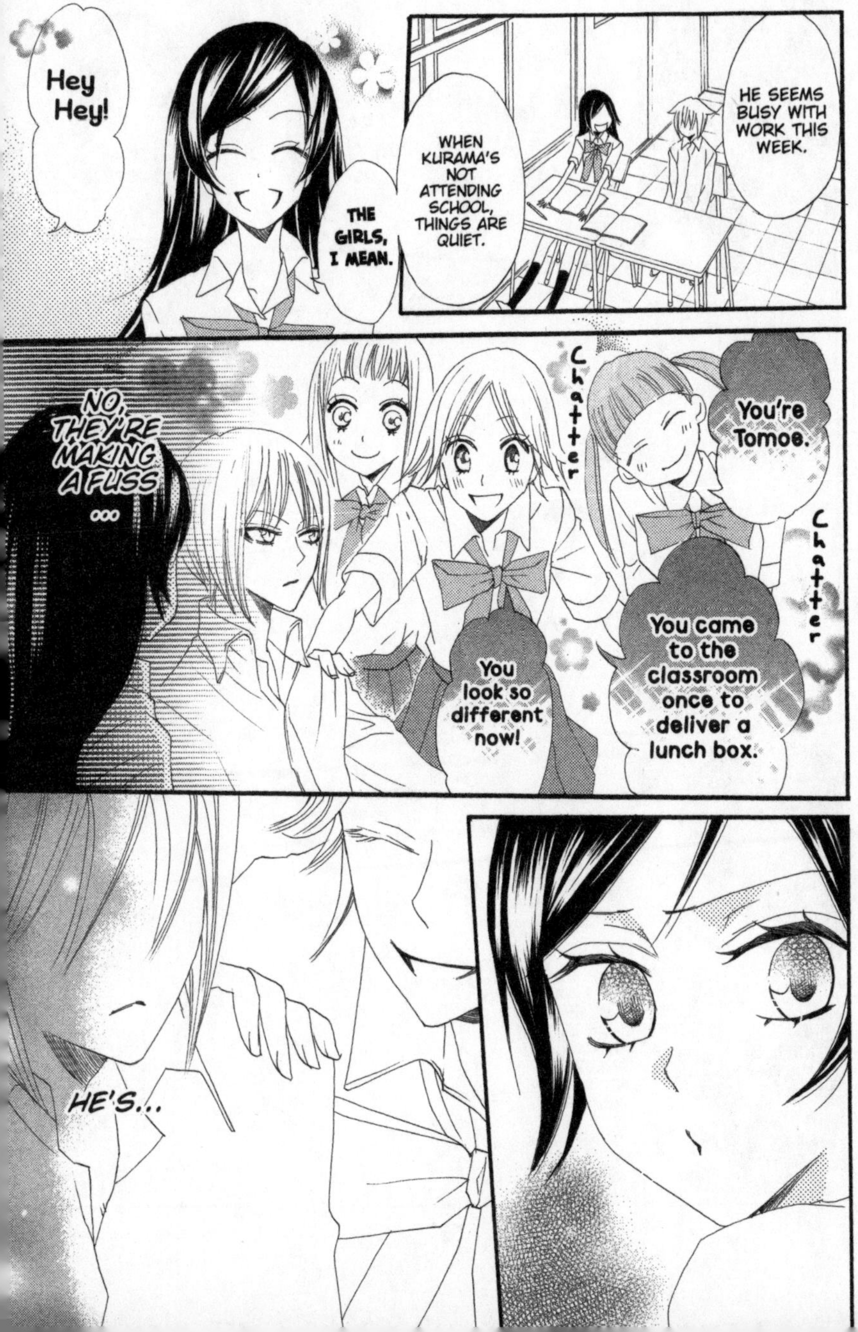
HE SEEMS BUSY WITH WORK THIS WEEK.
WHEN KURAMA'S NOT ATTENDING SCHOOL, THINGS ARE QUIET.
THE GIRLS, I MEAN.
Hey Hey!
Chatter
You're Tomoe.
Chatter
You came to the classroom once to deliver a lunch box.
You look so different now!
NO, THEY'RE MAKING A FUSS...
HE'S...

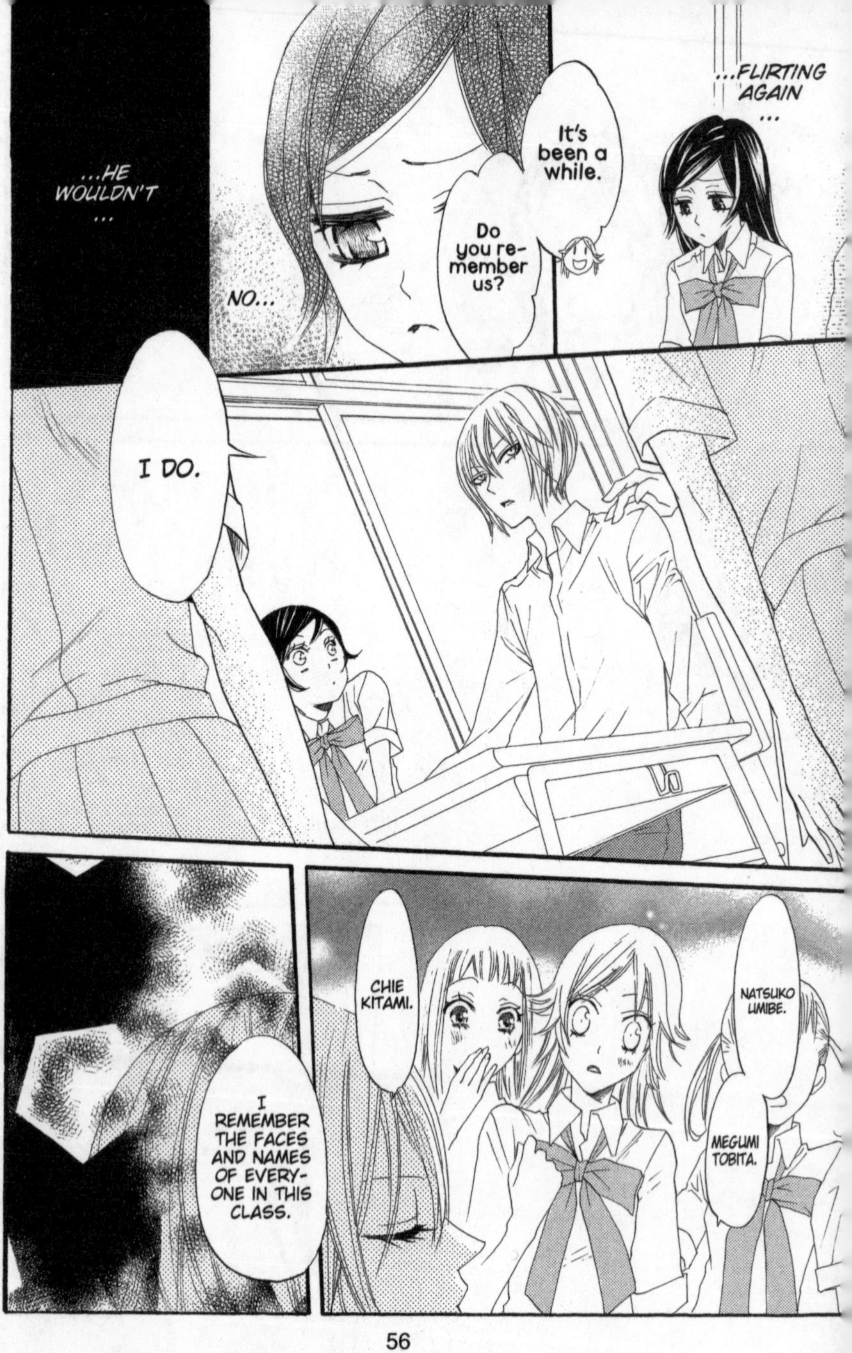
...FLIRTING AGAIN ...
It's been a while.
Do you remember us?
NO...
...HE WOULDN'T ...
I DO.
NATSUKO UMIBE.
MEGUMI TOBITA.
CHIE KITAMI.
I REMEMBER THE FACES AND NAMES OF EVERY-ONE IN THIS CLASS.

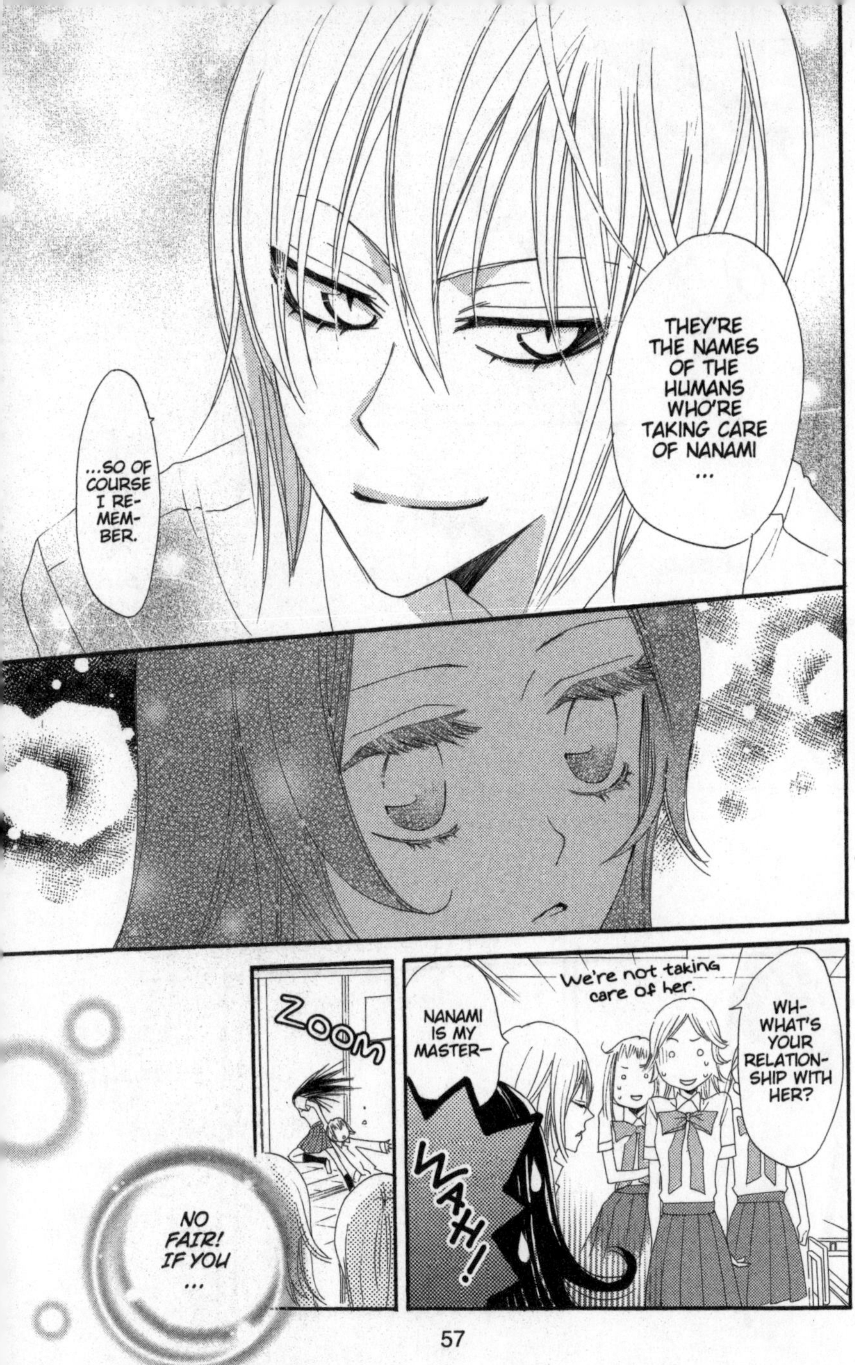
THEY'RE THE NAMES OF THE HUMANS WHO'RE TAKING CARE OF NANAMI ...
...SO OF COURSE I RE-MEM-BER.
WH- WHAT'S YOUR RELATION-SHIP WITH HER?
We're not taking care of her.
NANAMI IS MY MASTER—
WAH!
ZOOM
NO FAIR! IF YOU ...

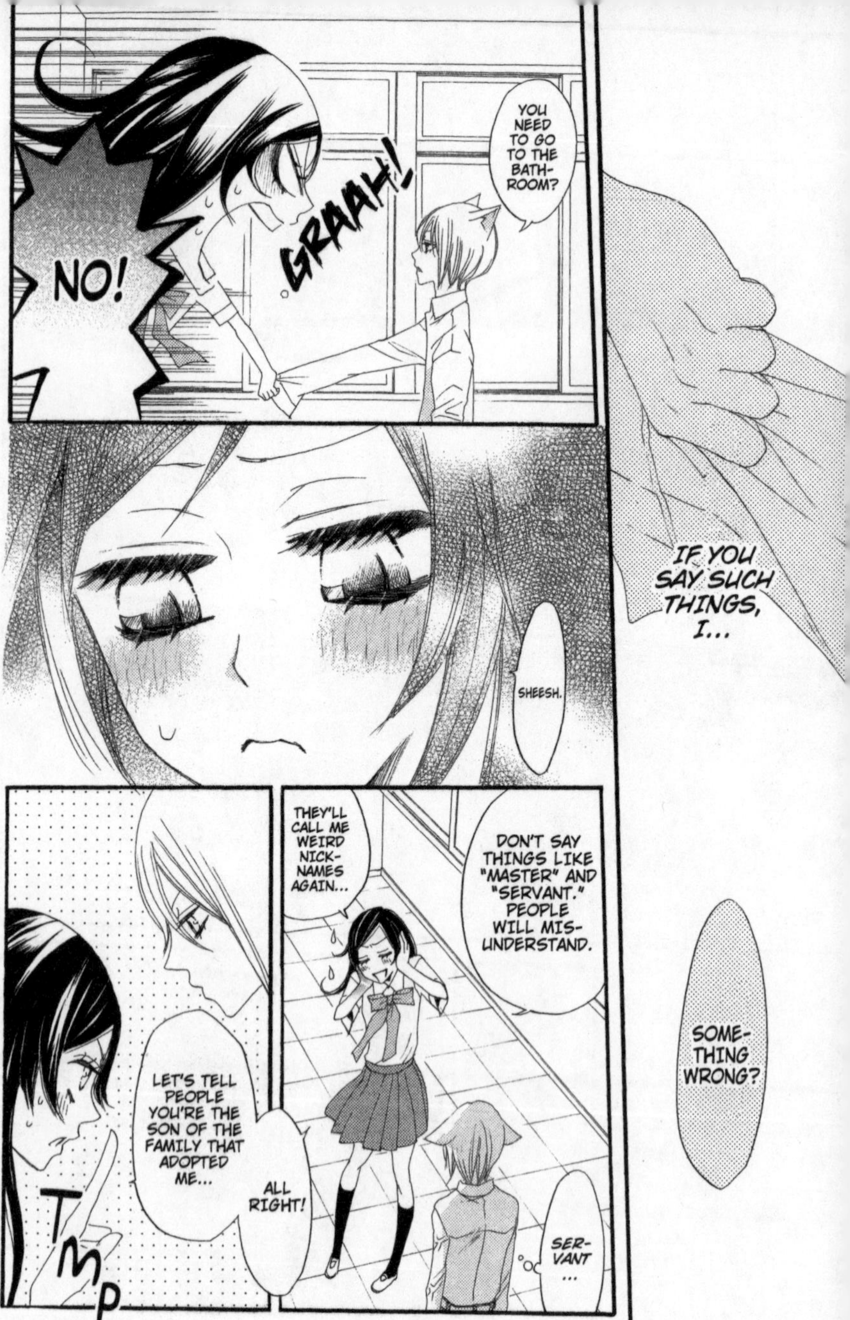
IF YOU SAY SUCH THINGS, I...
SOMETHING WRONG?
YOU NEED TO GO TO THE BATHROOM?
GRAAH!
NO!
SHEESH.
DON'T SAY THINGS LIKE "MASTER" AND "SERVANT." PEOPLE WILL MISUNDERSTAND.
THEY'LL CALL ME WEIRD NICKNAMES AGAIN...
SERVANT...
LET'S TELL PEOPLE YOU'RE THE SON OF THE FAMILY THAT ADOPTED ME...
ALL RIGHT!
TMP

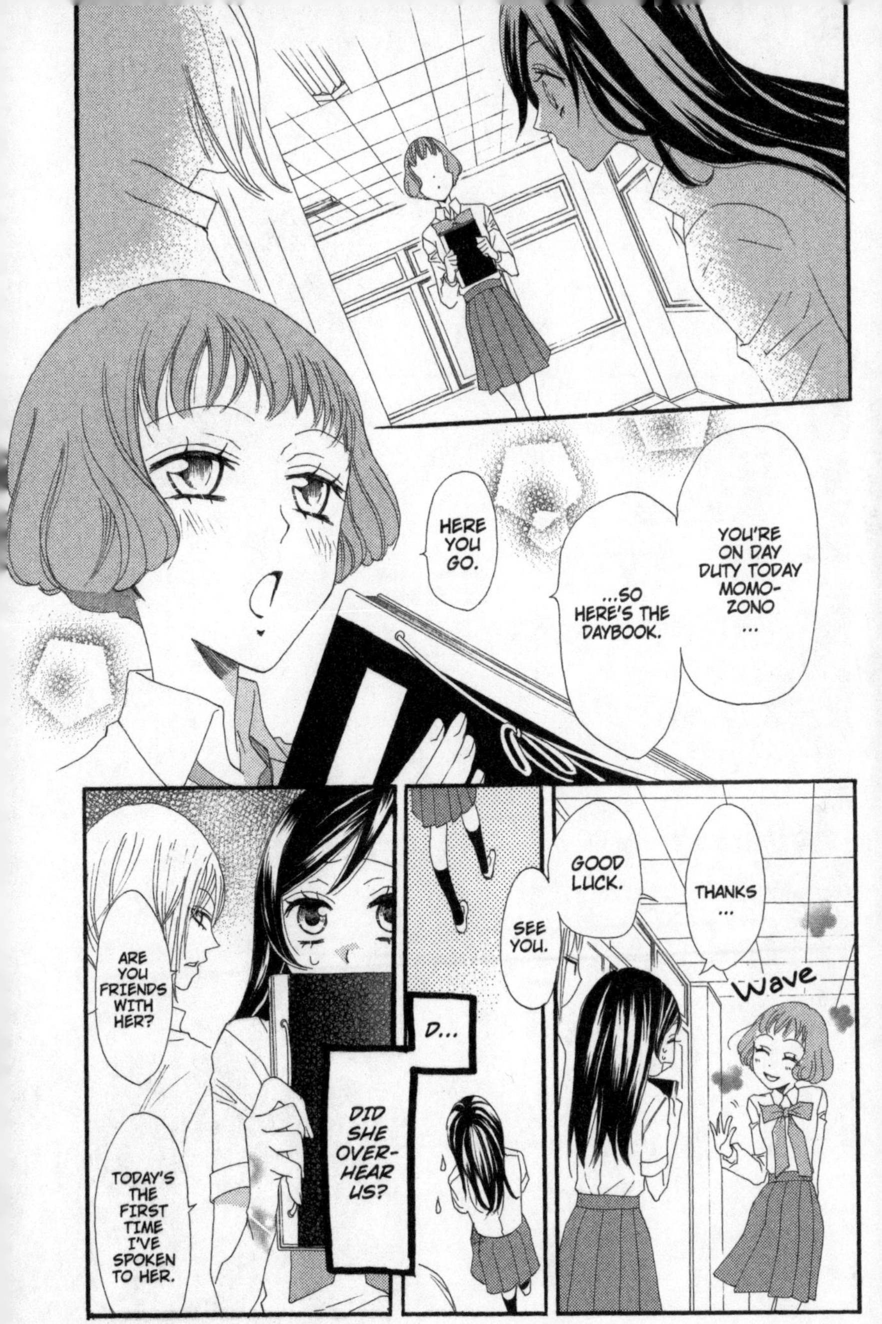
YOU'RE ON DAY DUTY TODAY MOMO-ZONO ...
...SO HERE'S THE DAYBOOK.
HERE YOU GO.
THANKS ...
GOOD LUCK.
SEE YOU.
Wave
D...
DID SHE OVER-HEAR US?
ARE YOU FRIENDS WITH HER?
TODAY'S THE FIRST TIME I'VE SPOKEN TO HER.

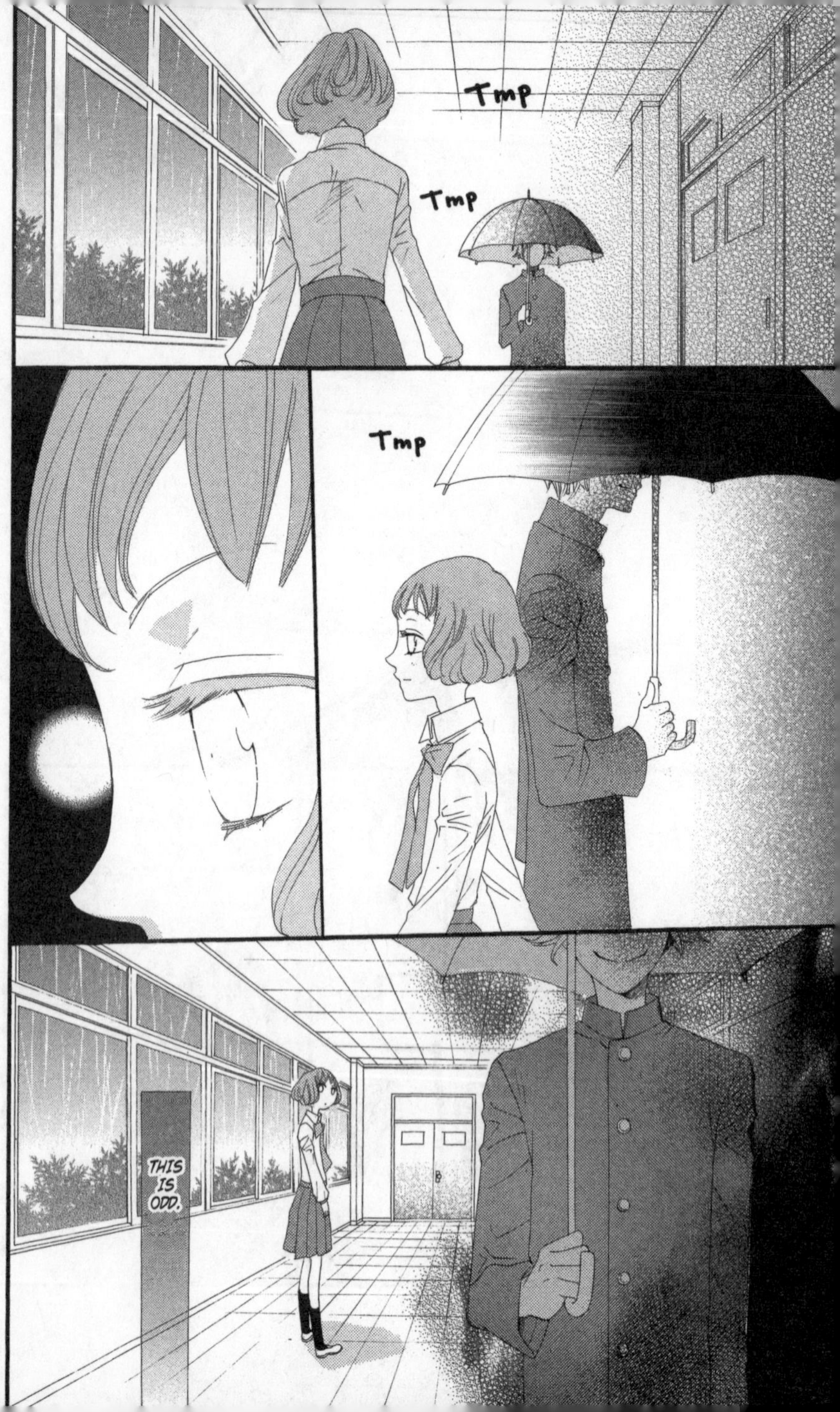
Tmp
Tmp
Tmp
THIS IS ODD.

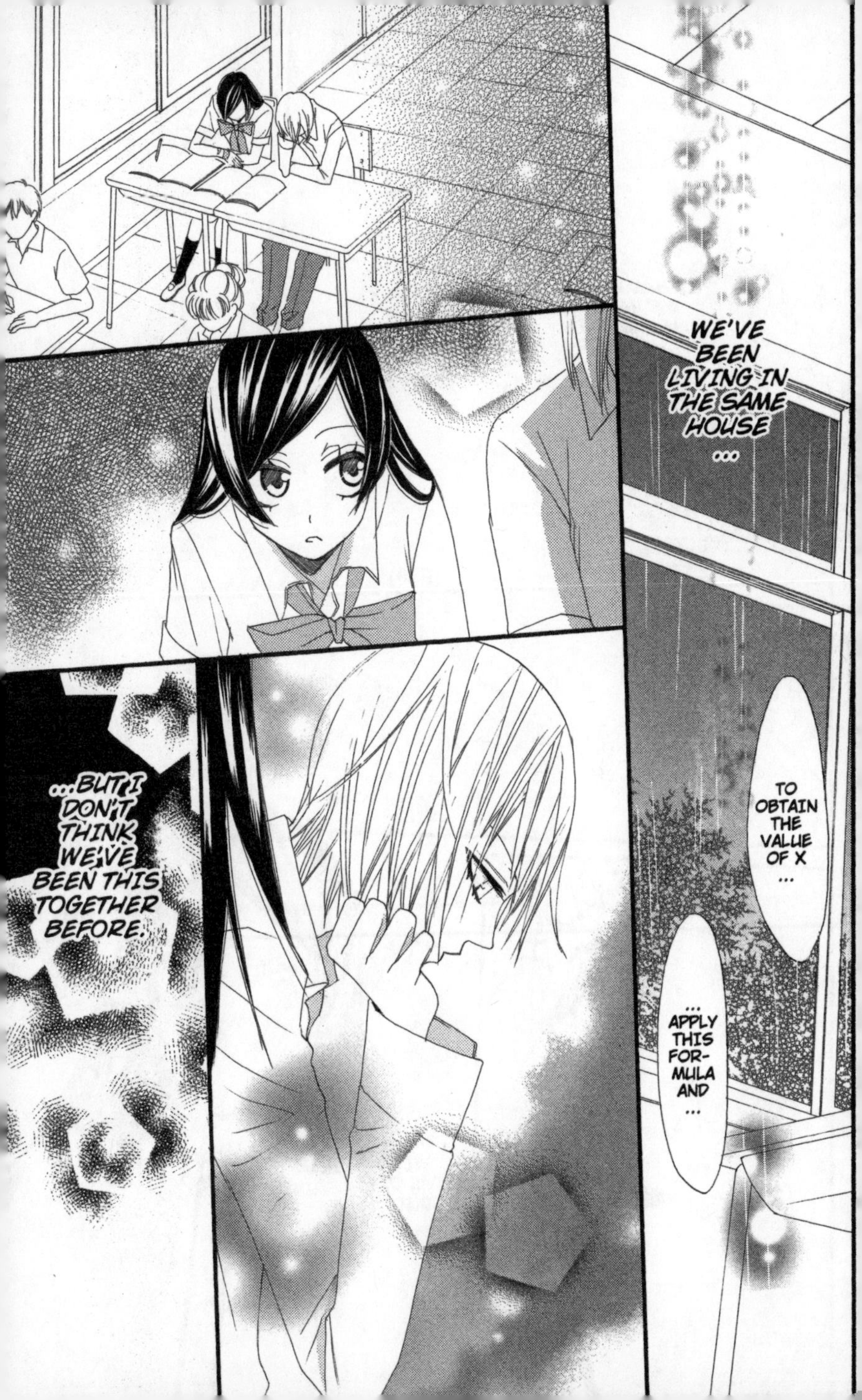
WE'VE BEEN LIVING IN THE SAME HOUSE...
TO OBTAIN THE VALUE OF X...
...APPLY THIS FOR-MULA AND...
...BUT I DON'T THINK WE'VE BEEN THIS TOGETHER BEFORE.

...MUCH MORE...

...THAN WHEN WE'RE AT THE SHRINE.

I FEEL CLOSE TO TOMOE.

	period	5th period		SCIENCE

Everyone was very... too.

...from the teacher...

THERE.

SORRY TO KEEP YOU WAITING, TOMOE.

CLATTER

WHAP

LET'S GO TO THE FACULTY LOUNGE.

I'M DONE WITH THE DAY DUTY.

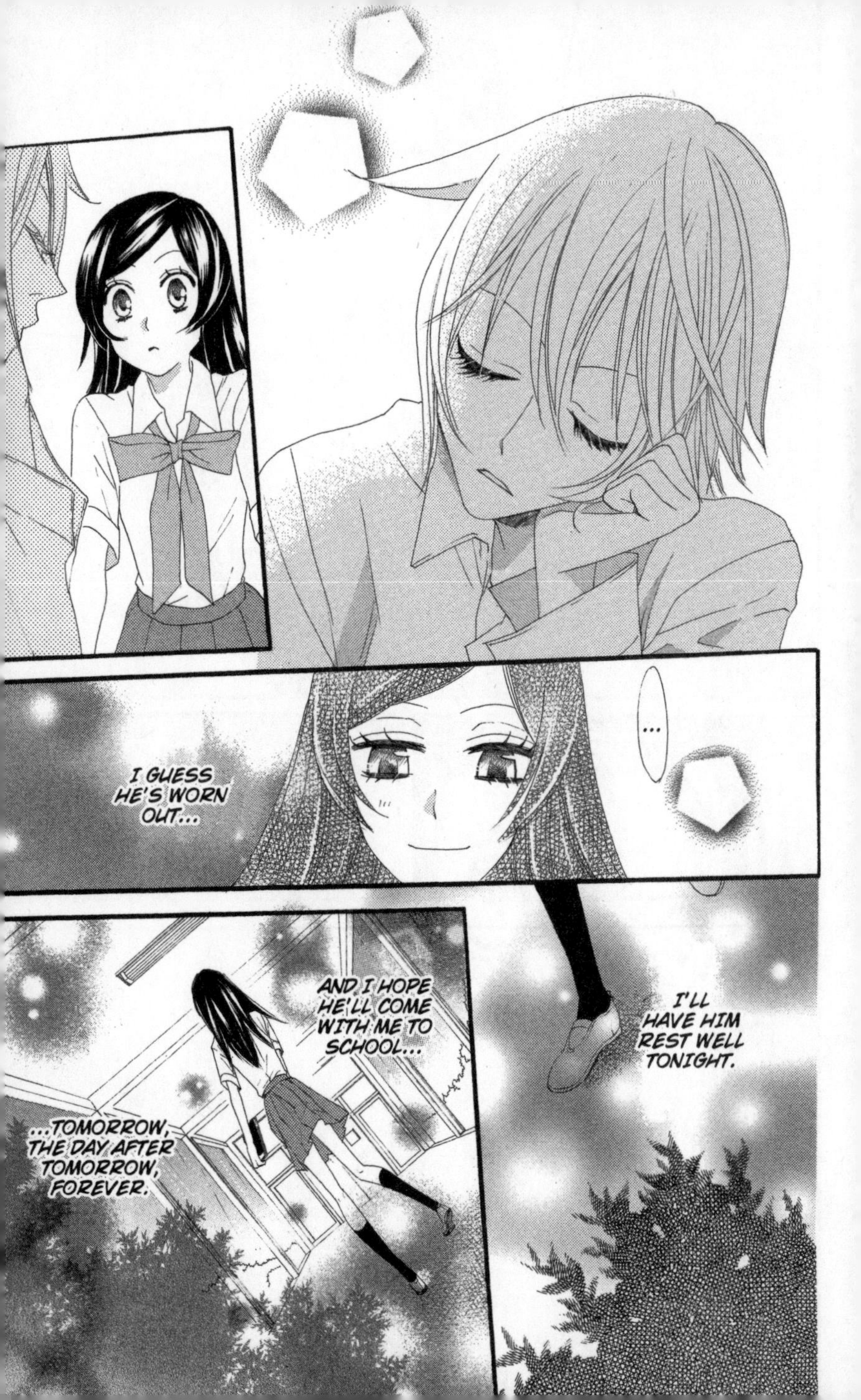
...
I GUESS HE'S WORN OUT...
I'LL HAVE HIM REST WELL TONIGHT.
AND I HOPE HE'LL COME WITH ME TO SCHOOL...
...TOMORROW, THE DAY AFTER TOMORROW, FOREVER.

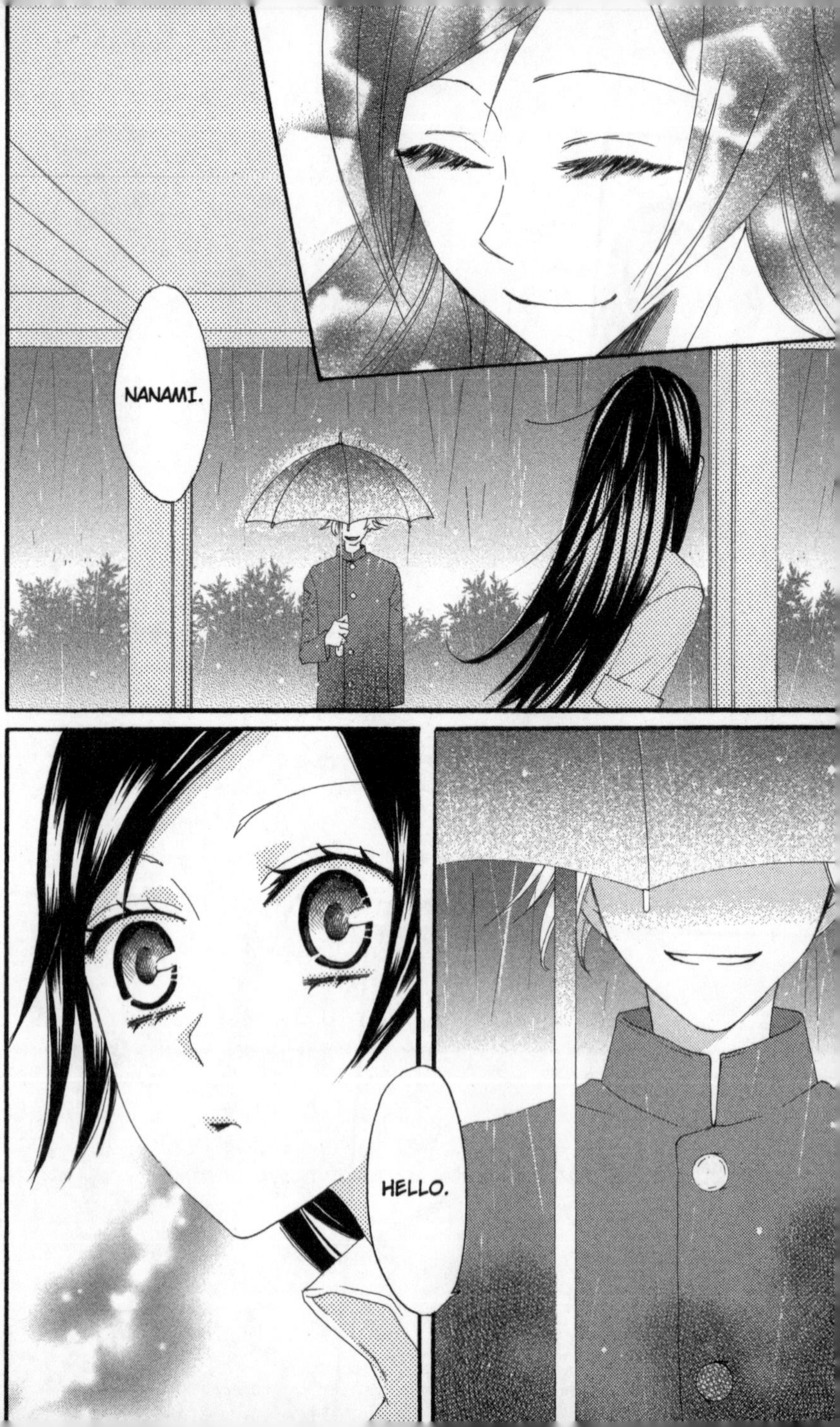
NANAMI.
HELLO.

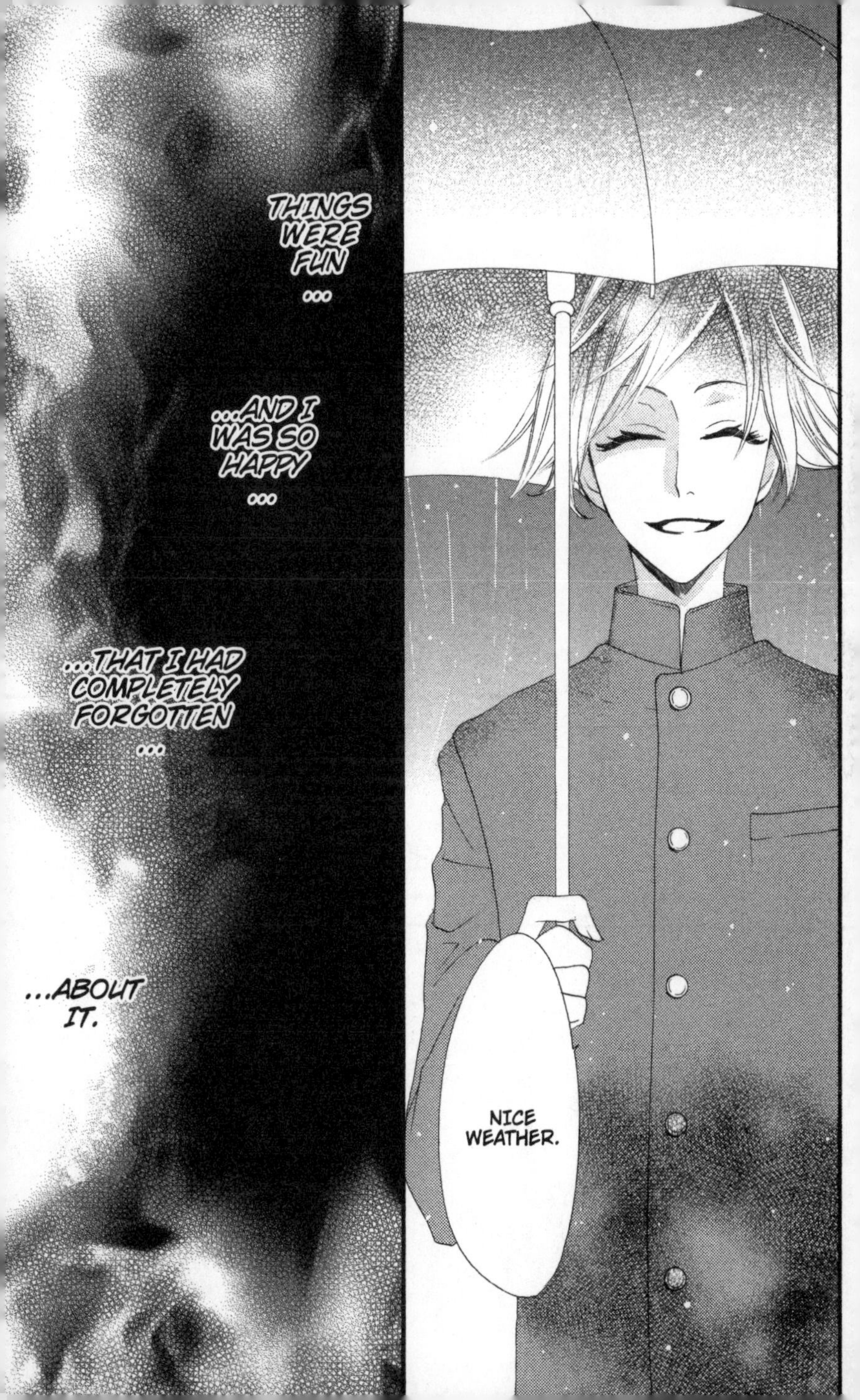
NICE WEATHER.
THINGS WERE FUN ...
...AND I WAS SO HAPPY ...
...THAT I HAD COMPLETELY FORGOTTEN ...
...ABOUT IT.

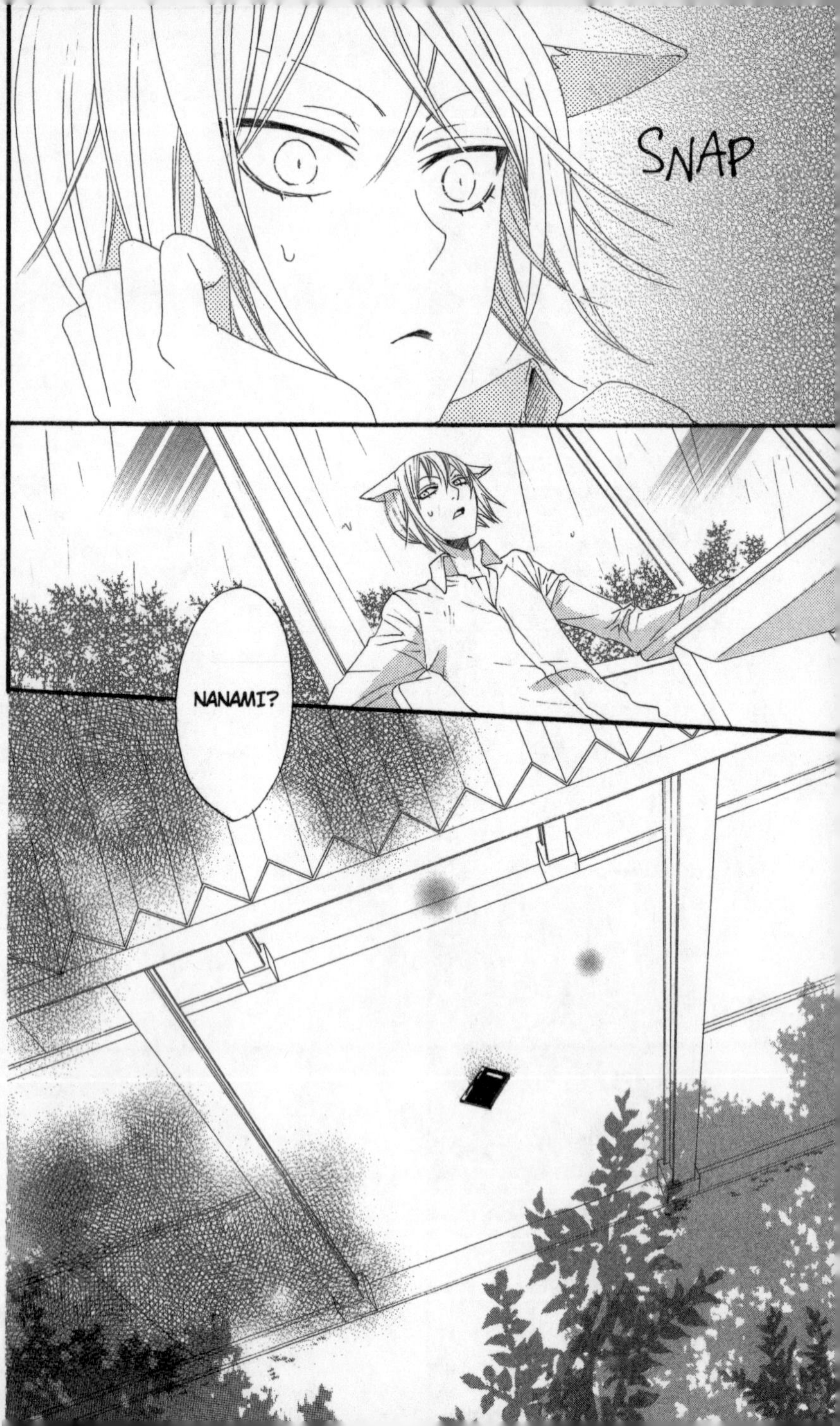
SNAP
NANAMI?

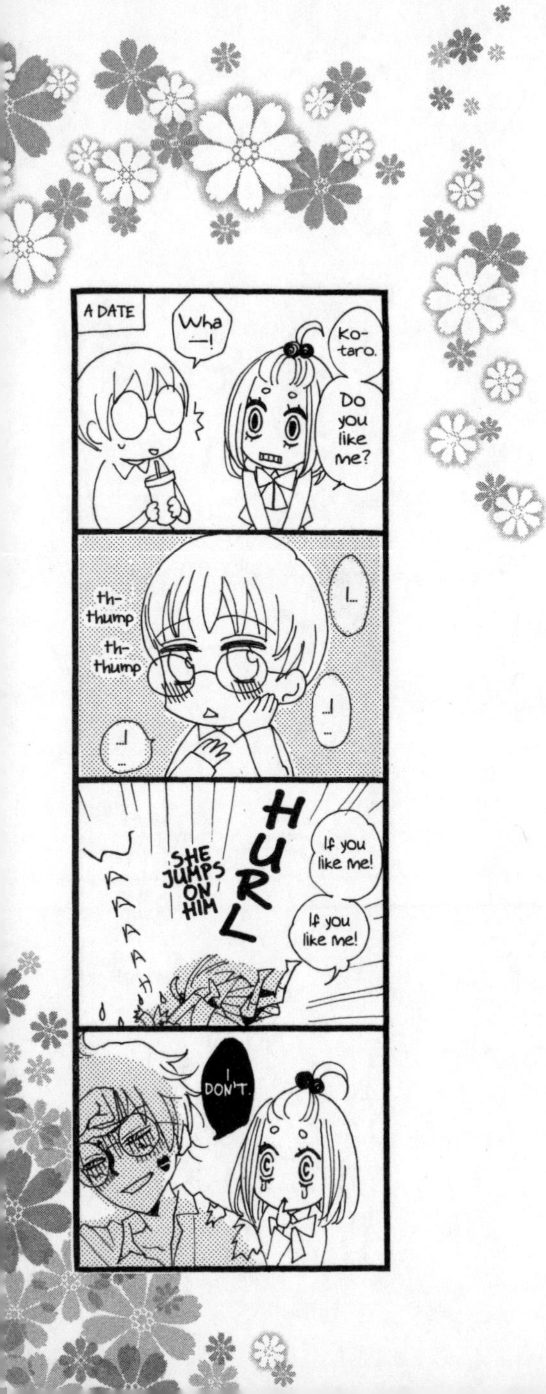
A DATE
Ko-taro.
Do you like me?
Wha—!
I...
...I
th-thump th-thump
...I
If you like me!
If you like me!
HURL
SHE JUMPS ON HIM
WAAAAAH
I DON'T.

What should we do today?
Do you want to go some-place?
FWIP
PIA
A DATE
I WOULD LOVE TO GO TO THE BOTTOM OF THE SWAMP.
I WANT TO DRIFT AT THE BOTTOM OF THE SWAMP, JUST KOTARO AND ME.
I cannot tell him that.
AH HA HA HA

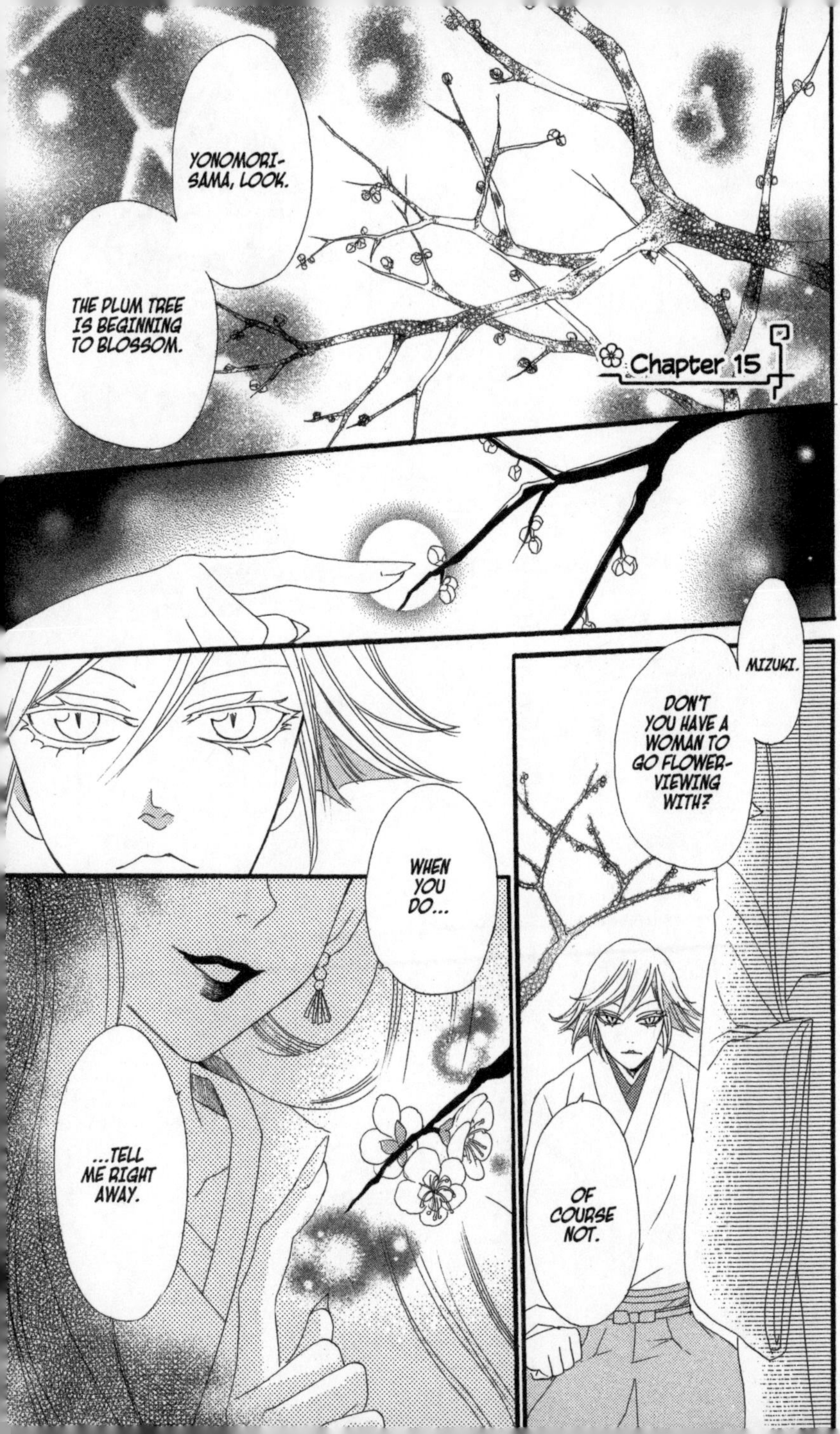
YONOMORI-SAMA, LOOK.
THE PLUM TREE IS BEGINNING TO BLOSSOM.
Chapter 15
MIZUKI.
DON'T YOU HAVE A WOMAN TO GO FLOWER-VIEWING WITH?
OF COURSE NOT.
WHEN YOU DO...
...TELL ME RIGHT AWAY.

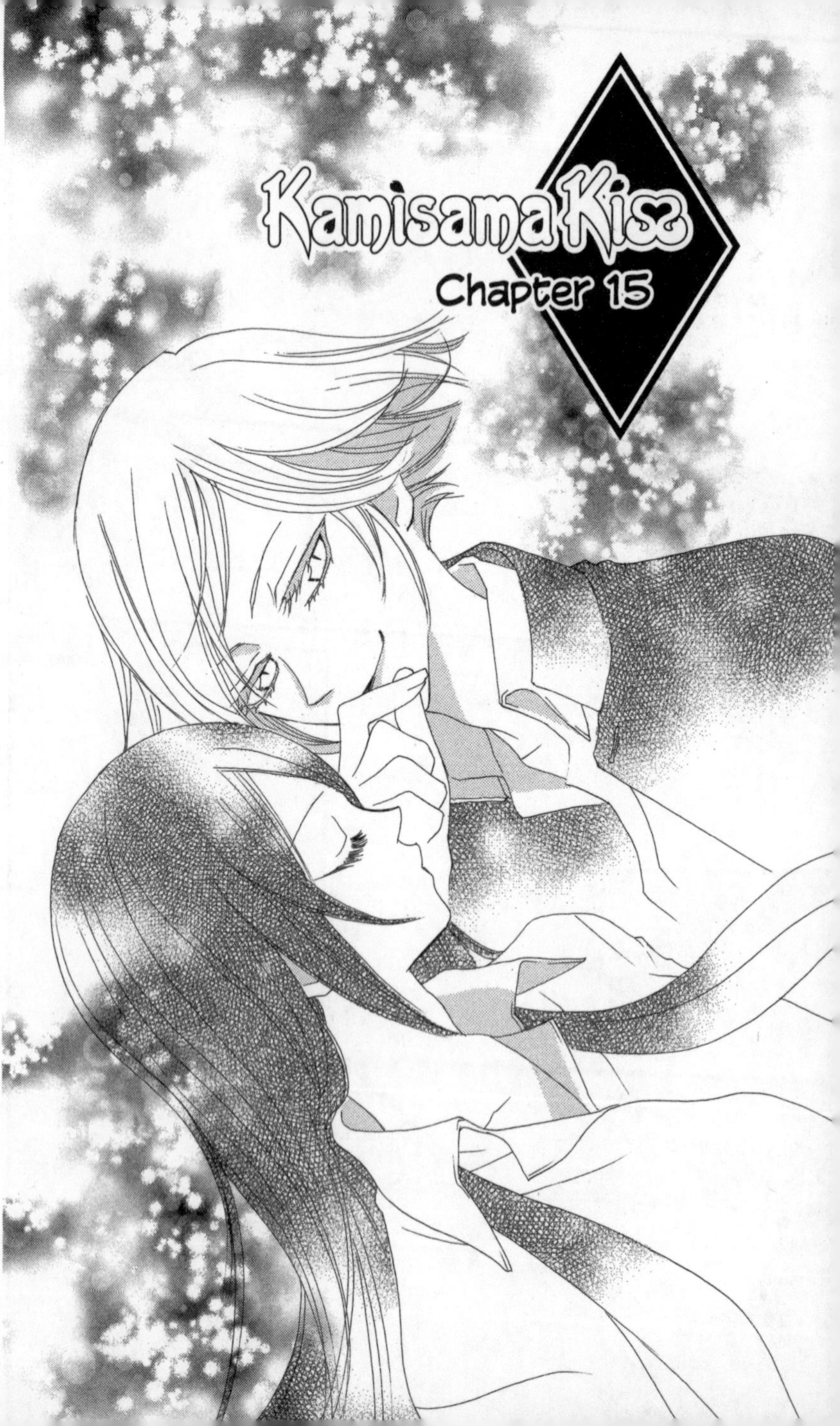
Kamisama Kiss
Chapter 15

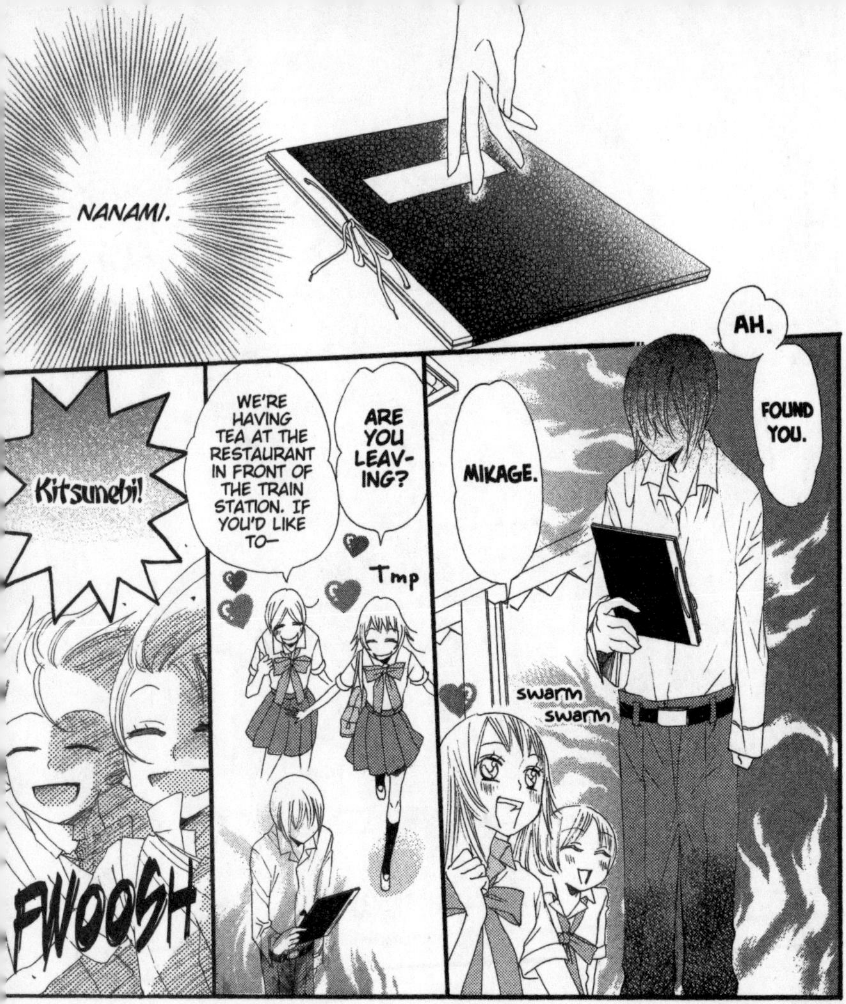
NANAMI.
AH.
FOUND YOU.
MIKAGE.
swarm swarm
ARE YOU LEAV-ING?
WE'RE HAVING TEA AT THE RESTAURANT IN FRONT OF THE TRAIN STATION. IF YOU'D LIKE TO—
Tmp
Kitsunebi!
FWOOSH

Ami Nekota

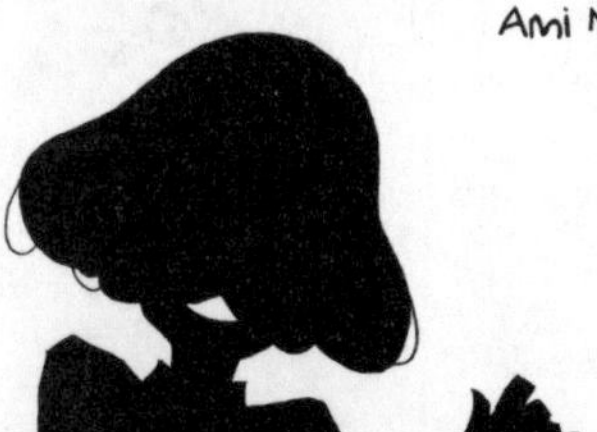

A female student in Year 2, Class 2

She drinks milk every morning, but she's stopped growing.

She puts sugar in soy-flavored omelets.

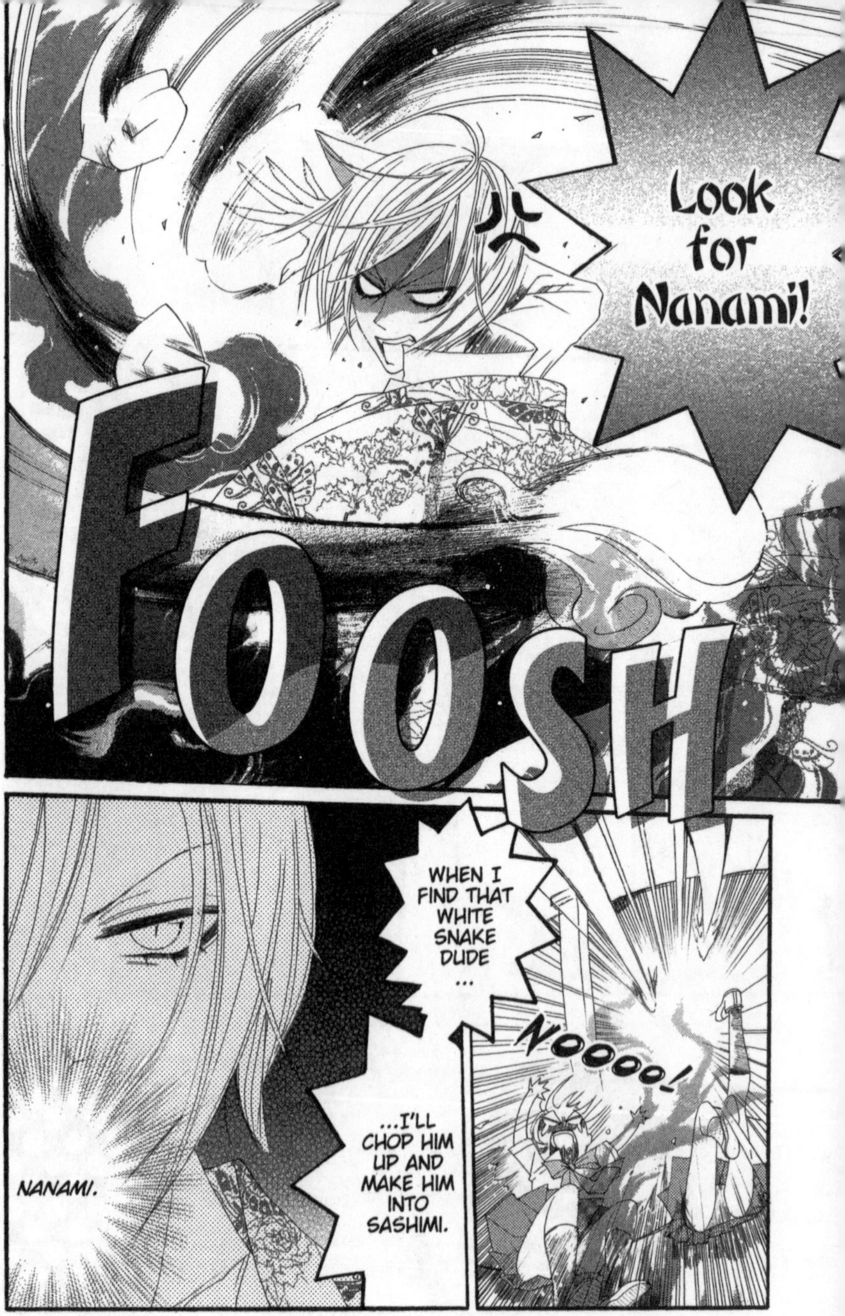
Look for Nanami!
FOOSH
WHEN I FIND THAT WHITE SNAKE DUDE...
...I'LL CHOP HIM UP AND MAKE HIM INTO SASHIMI.
NOOOO!
NANAMI.

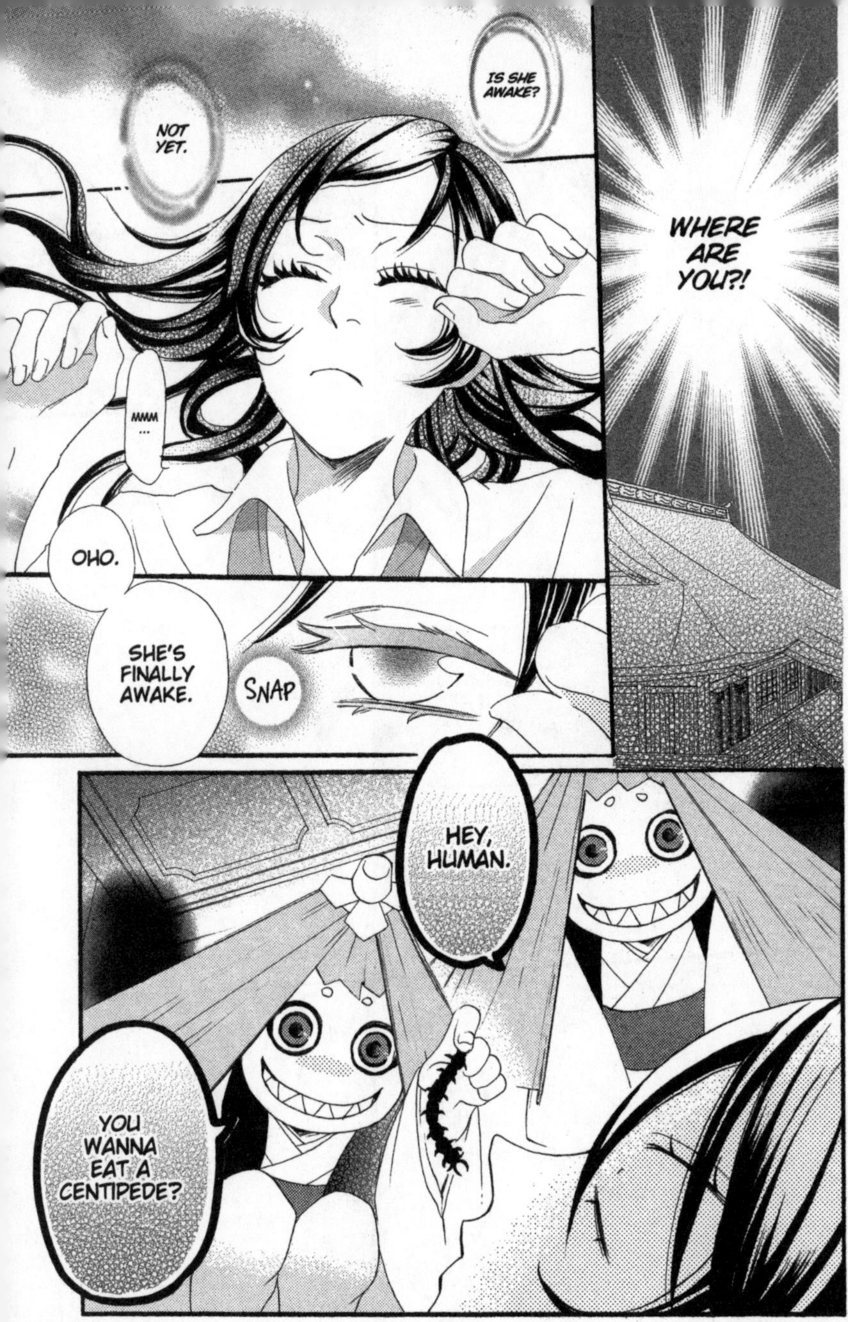
WHERE ARE YOU?!
IS SHE AWAKE?
NOT YET.
MMM...
OHO.
SHE'S FINALLY AWAKE.
SNAP
HEY, HUMAN.
YOU WANNA EAT A CENTIPEDE?

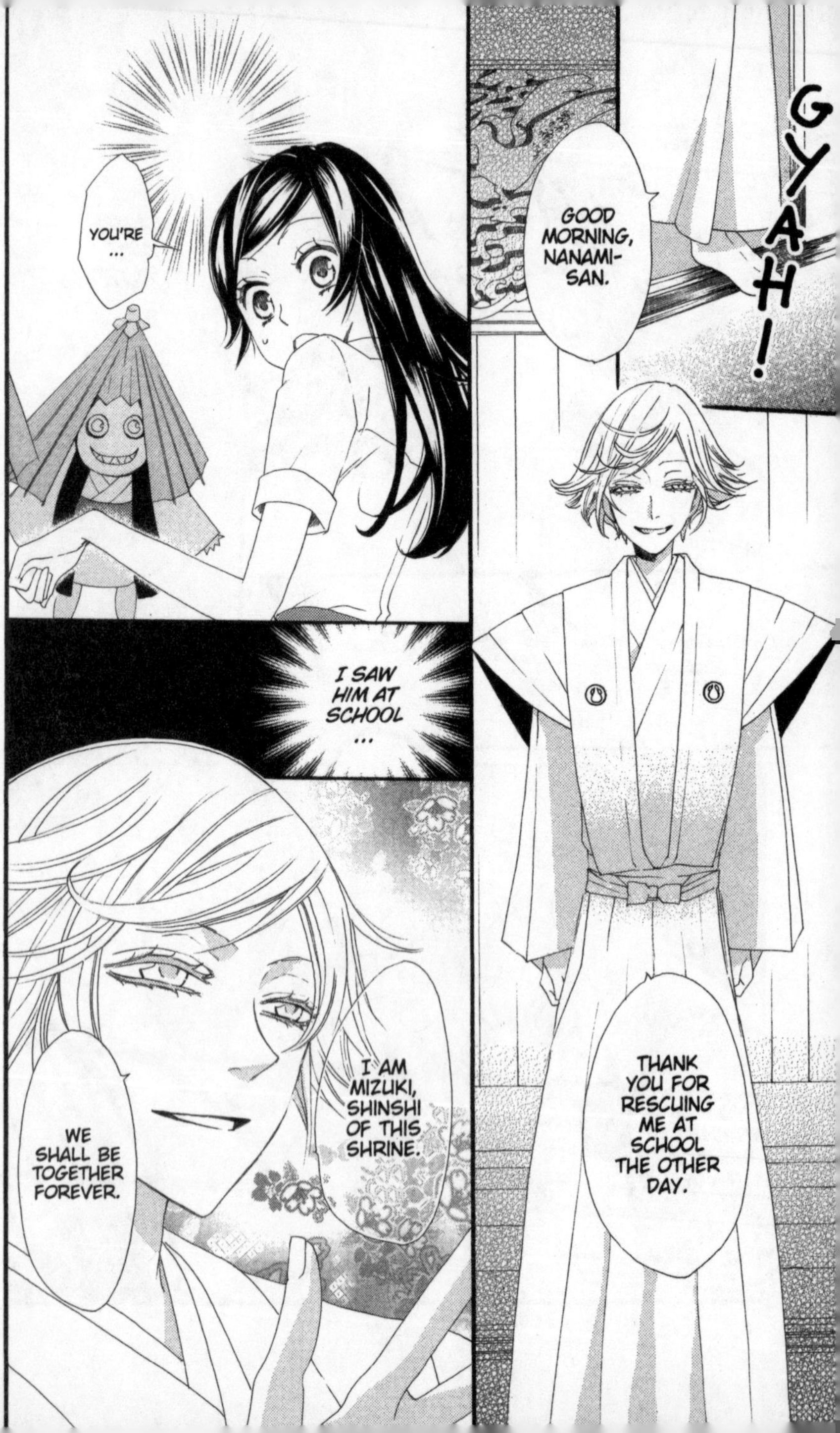
GYAH!
GOOD MORNING, NANAMI-SAN.
THANK YOU FOR RESCUING ME AT SCHOOL THE OTHER DAY.
YOU'RE ...
I SAW HIM AT SCHOOL ...
I AM MIZUKI, SHINSHI OF THIS SHRINE.
WE SHALL BE TOGETHER FOREVER.

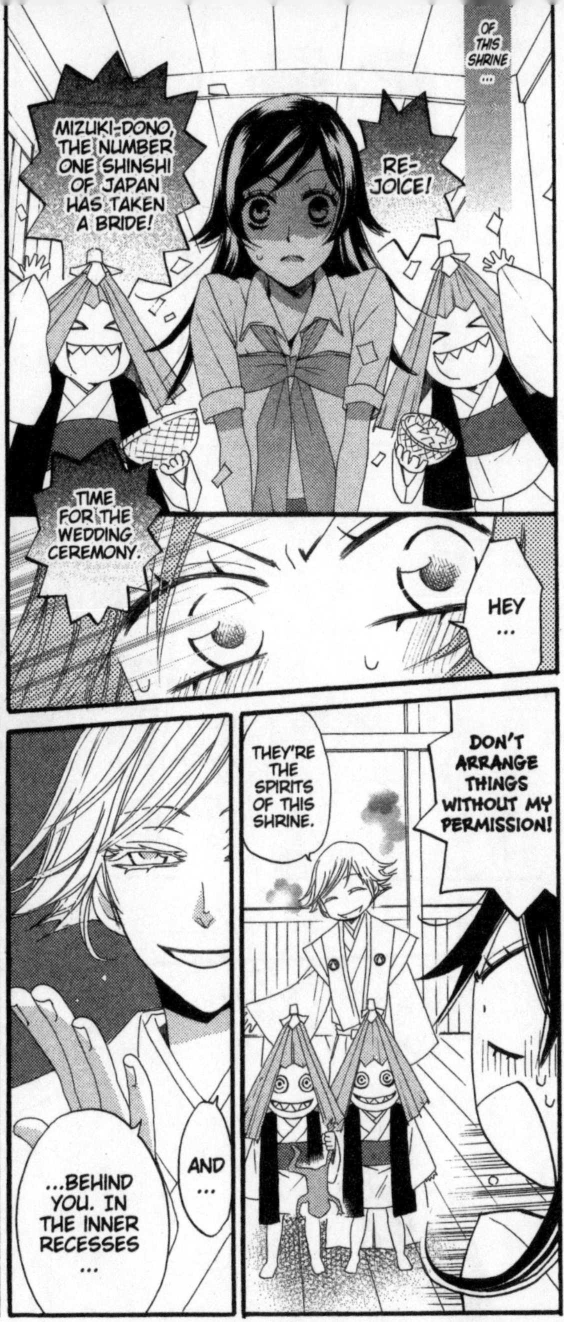
OF THIS SHRINE ...
RE-JOICE!
MIZUKI-DONO, THE NUMBER ONE SHINSHI OF JAPAN HAS TAKEN A BRIDE!
TIME FOR THE WEDDING CEREMONY.
HEY ...
DON'T ARRANGE THINGS WITHOUT MY PERMISSION!
THEY'RE THE SPIRITS OF THIS SHRINE.
AND ...
...BEHIND YOU. IN THE INNER RECESSES ...

Three

The other day, the magazine *Kikan S-sama* printed my interview as part of their mythology special. I talked a lot about the manga, so I'd be happy if you read it. This was my first interview, and I was very nervous. Thank you so much!

I've been writing a blog for a couple years, but the other day it was shut down. Uh, I lost it. So I'm telling everyone here. Thanks to everyone who used to read it!

I bought a new pinky ring. I wore my old one for about five, six years. I guess I'll be wearing this one for five, six years too.

Speaking of fingers—because of the way I hold my pencil, I haven't gotten a writer's callous, but I finally have one on my little finger. Because the callous is on my little finger, it really stands out and I feel depressed... Won't this go away? I think I'll put a bandaid around my little finger next time I draw.

When I was in high school, I used to do kendo, and the callous that formed then is still on the sole of my foot...I guess it's not gonna go away... (depressed)

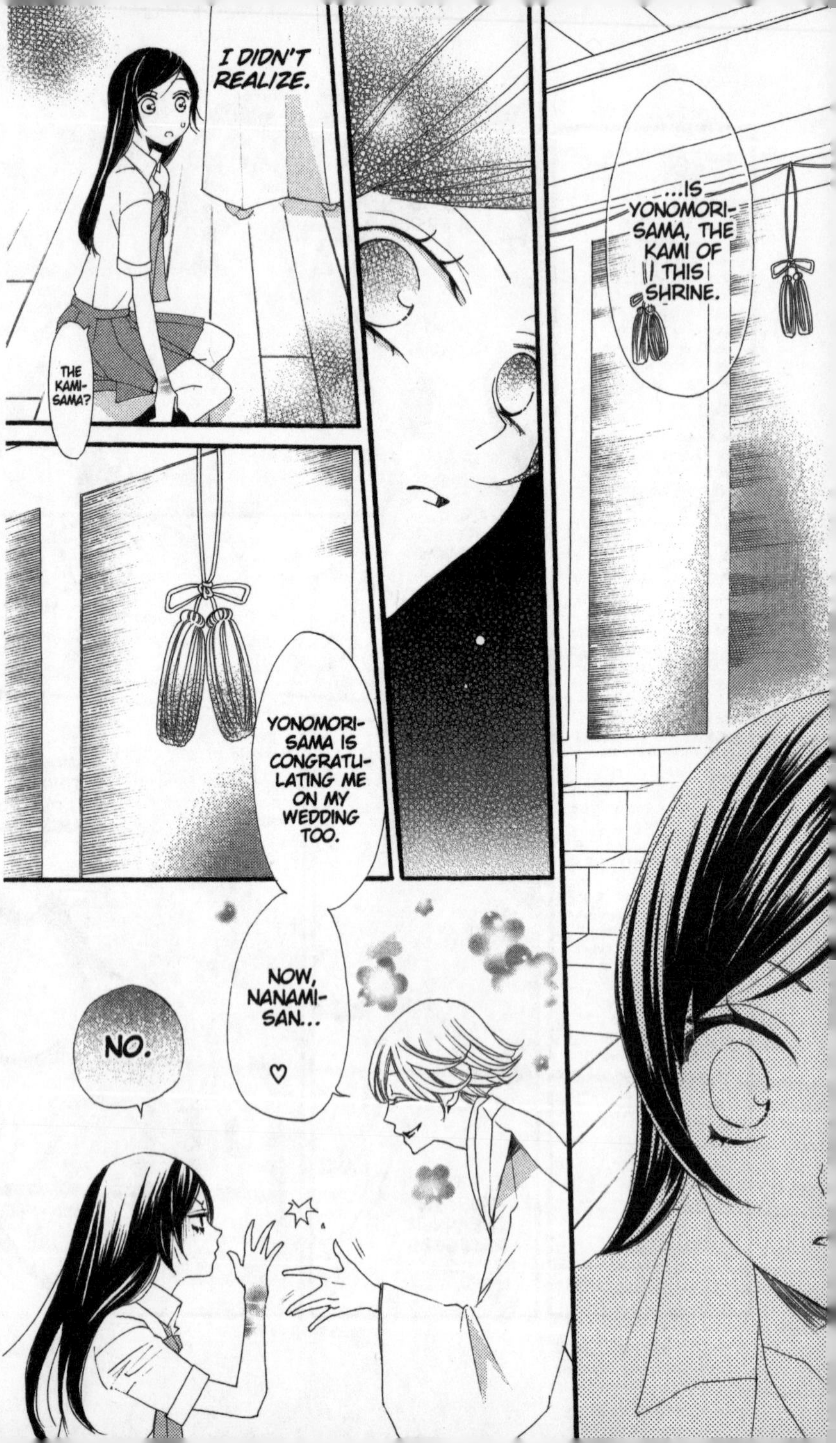
...IS YONOMORI-SAMA, THE KAMI OF THIS SHRINE.
I DIDN'T REALIZE.
THE KAMI-SAMA?
YONOMORI-SAMA IS CONGRATULATING ME ON MY WEDDING TOO.
NOW, NANAMI-SAN... ♡
NO.

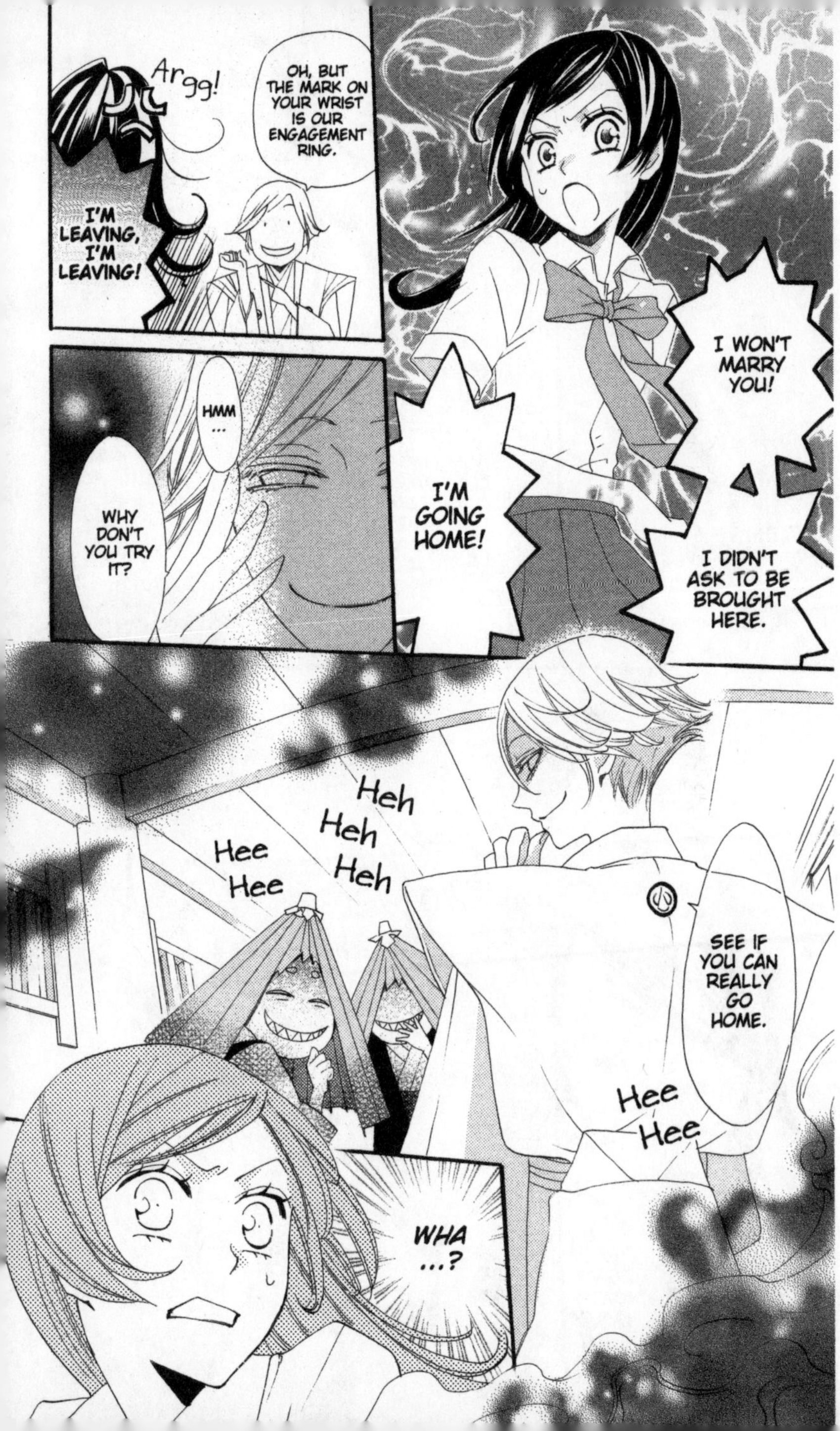
I WON'T MARRY YOU!
I DIDN'T ASK TO BE BROUGHT HERE.
I'M GOING HOME!
OH, BUT THE MARK ON YOUR WRIST IS OUR ENGAGEMENT RING.
Argg!
I'M LEAVING, I'M LEAVING!
HMM ...
WHY DON'T YOU TRY IT?
SEE IF YOU CAN REALLY GO HOME.
Heh Heh Heh
Hee Hee
Hee Hee
WHA ...?

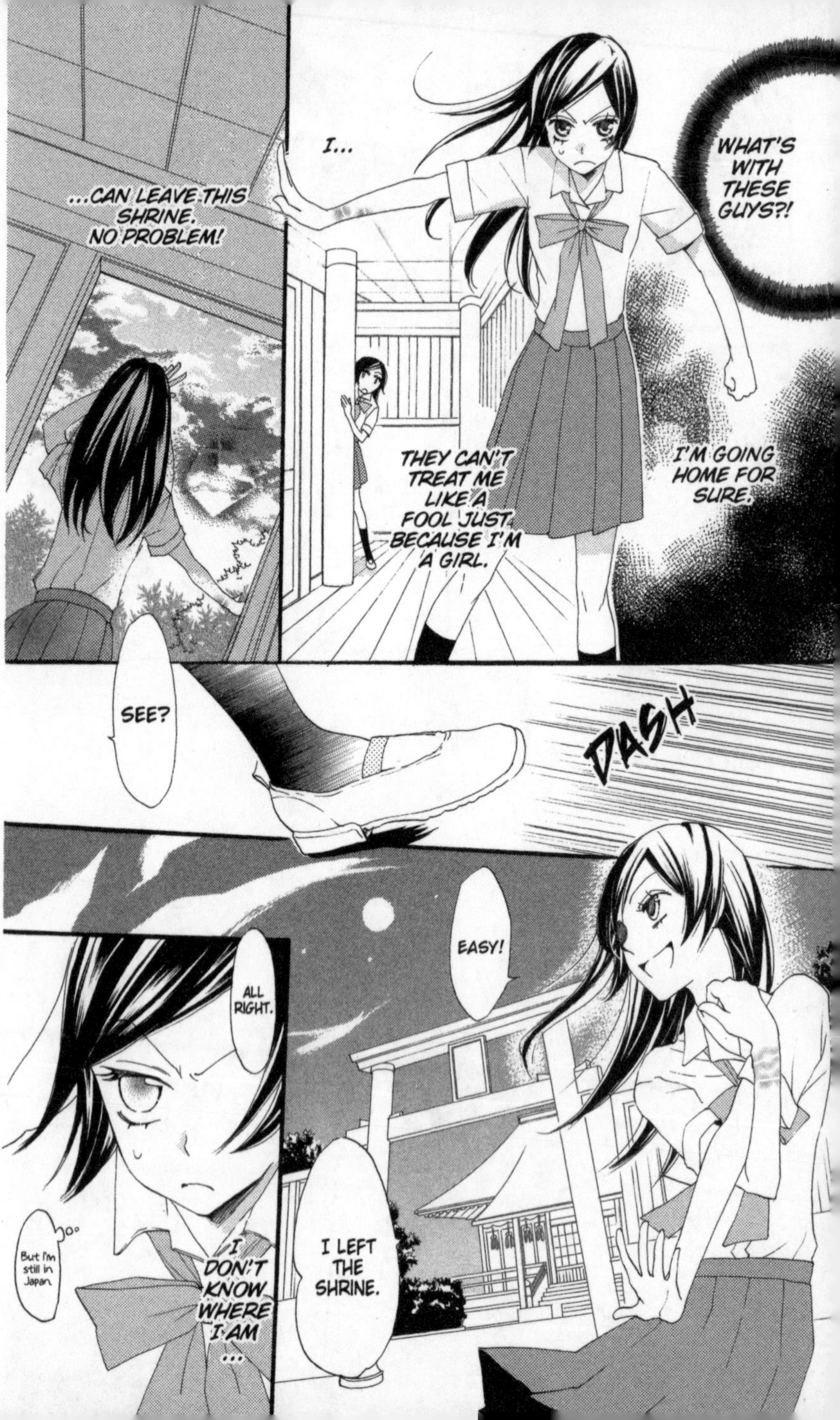

WHAT'S WITH THESE GUYS?!
I...
I'M GOING HOME FOR SURE.
THEY CAN'T TREAT ME LIKE A FOOL JUST BECAUSE I'M A GIRL.
...CAN LEAVE THIS SHRINE. NO PROBLEM!
DASH
SEE?
EASY!
I LEFT THE SHRINE.
ALL RIGHT.
I DON'T KNOW WHERE I AM...
But I'm still in Japan.

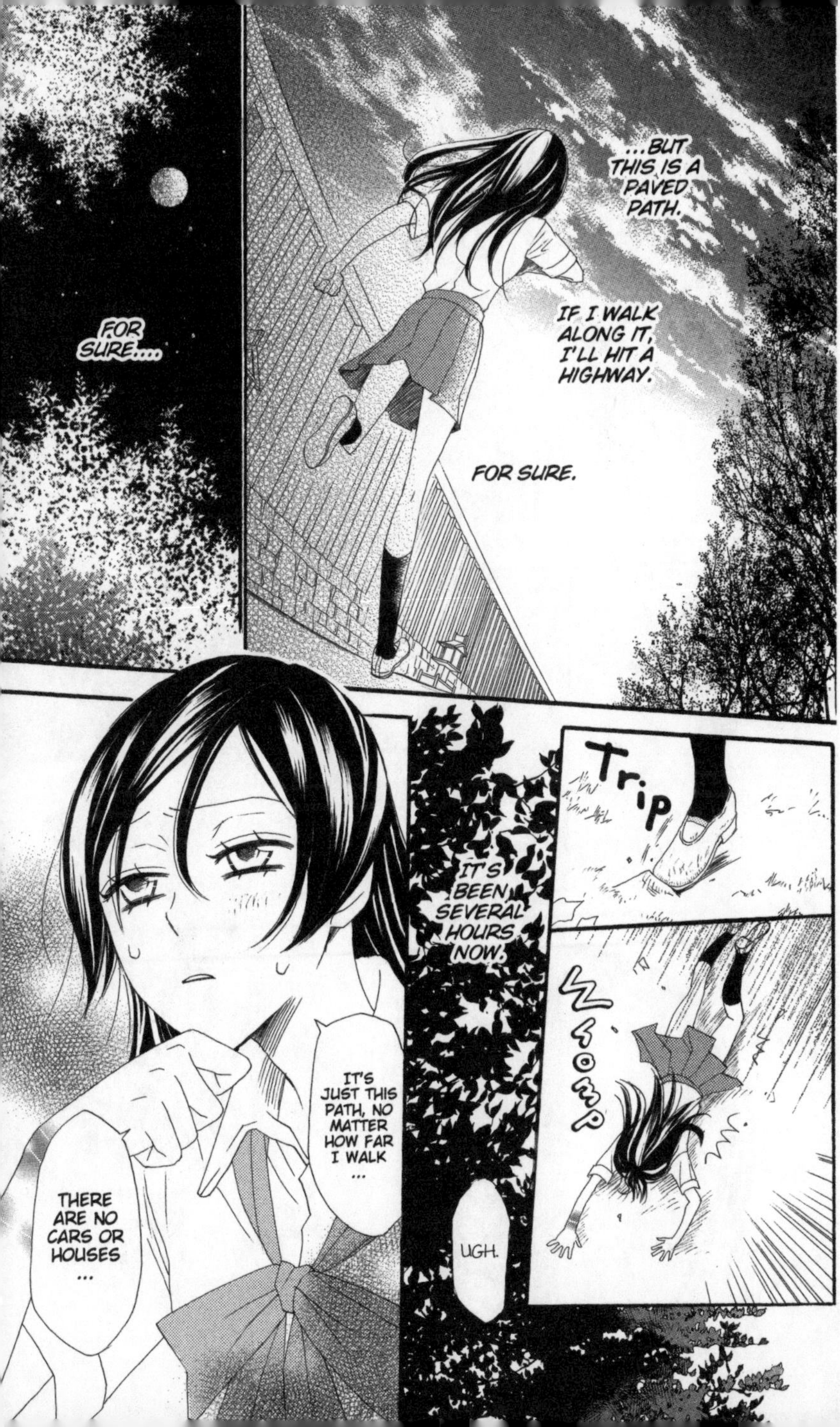
...BUT THIS IS A PAVED PATH.
IF I WALK ALONG IT, I'LL HIT A HIGHWAY.
FOR SURE.
FOR SURE....
Trip
Womp
IT'S BEEN SEVERAL HOURS NOW.
UGH.
IT'S JUST THIS PATH, NO MATTER HOW FAR I WALK ...
THERE ARE NO CARS OR HOUSES ...

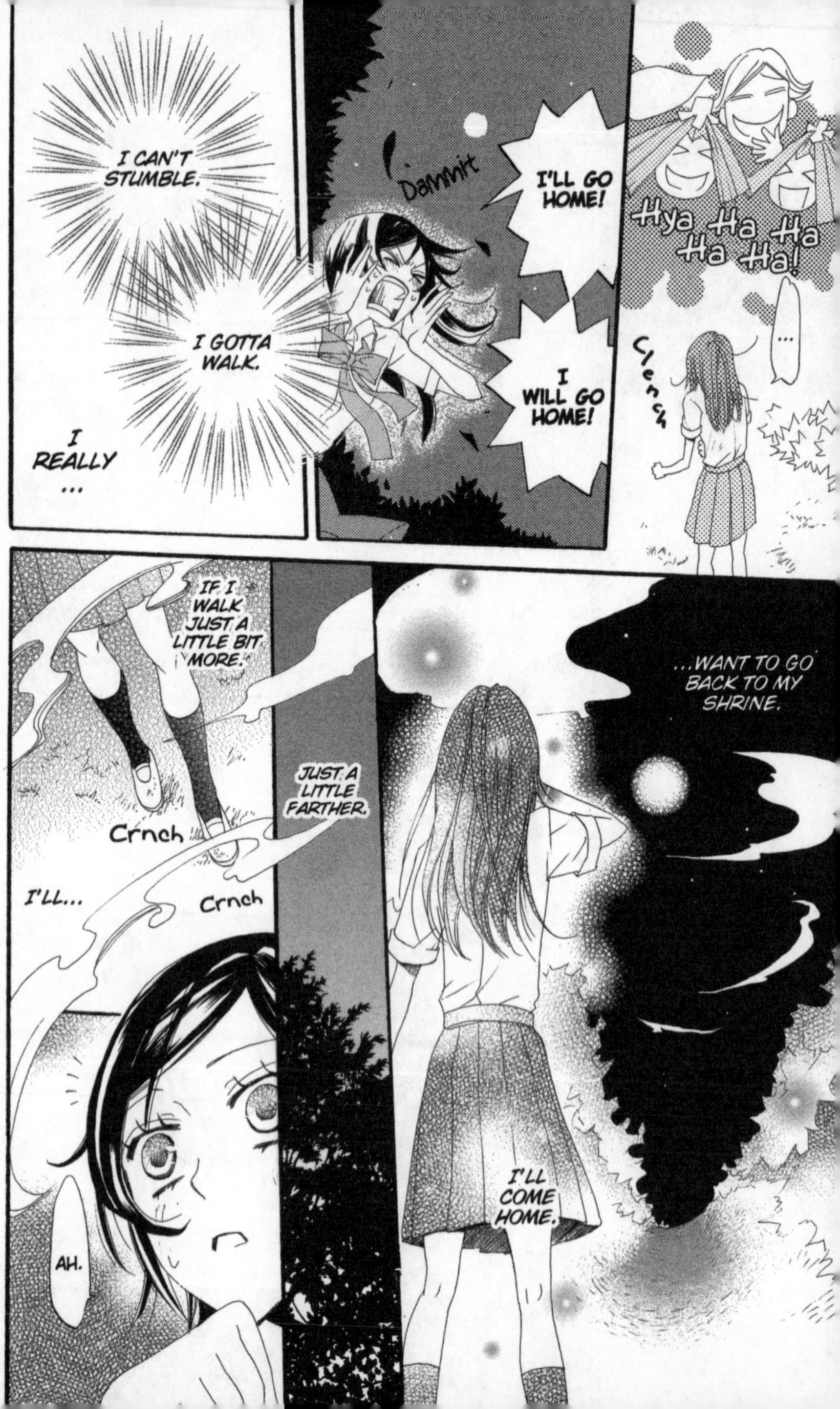

Hya Ha Ha Ha Ha!
...
Clench
Dammit
I'LL GO HOME!
I WILL GO HOME!
I CAN'T STUMBLE.
I GOTTA WALK.
I REALLY ...
...WANT TO GO BACK TO MY SHRINE.
I'LL COME HOME.
JUST A LITTLE FARTHER.
IF I WALK JUST A LITTLE BIT MORE.
Crnch
I'LL...
Crnch
AH.

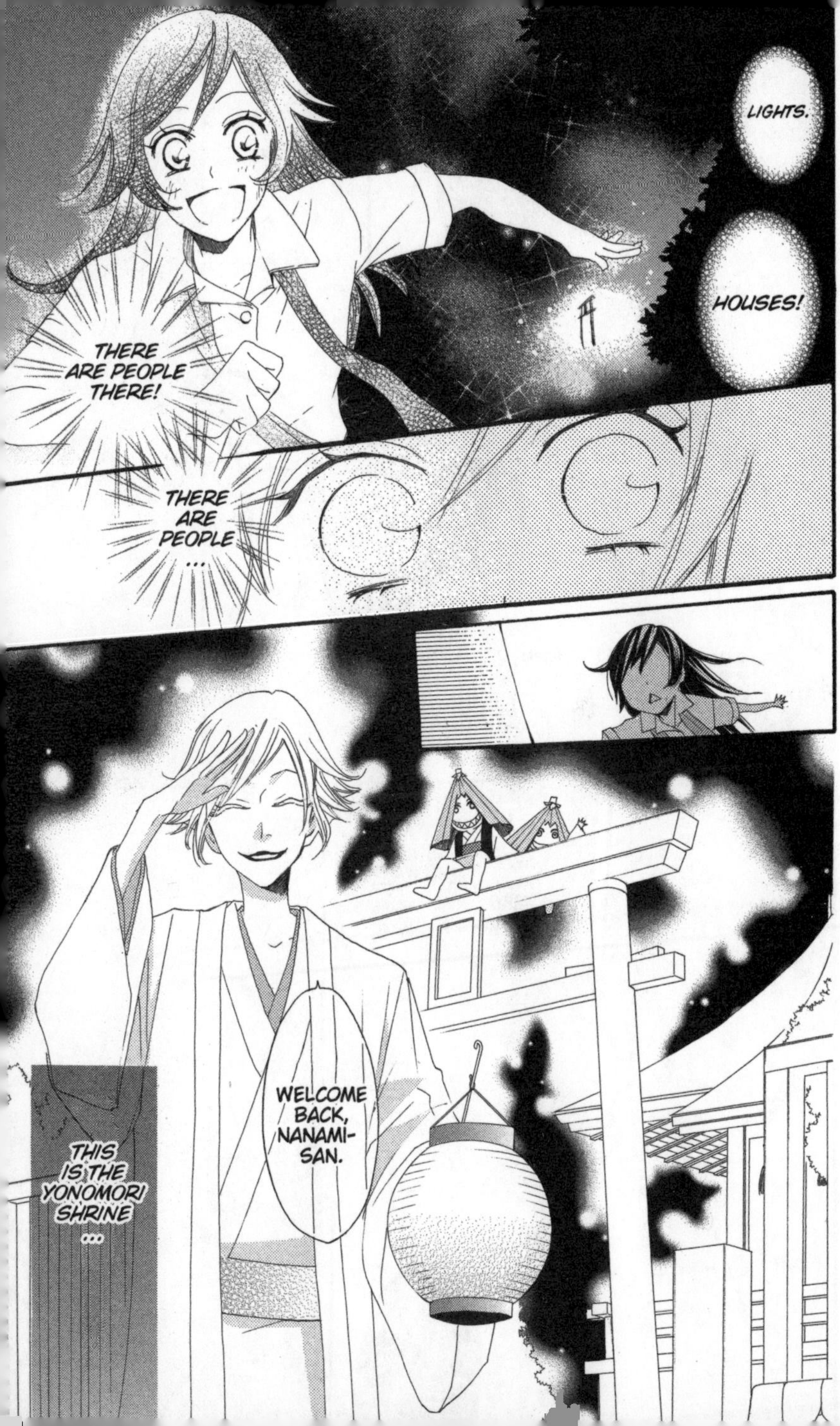
LIGHTS.
HOUSES!
THERE ARE PEOPLE THERE!
THERE ARE PEOPLE ...
WELCOME BACK, NANAMI-SAN.
THIS IS THE YONOMORI SHRINE ...

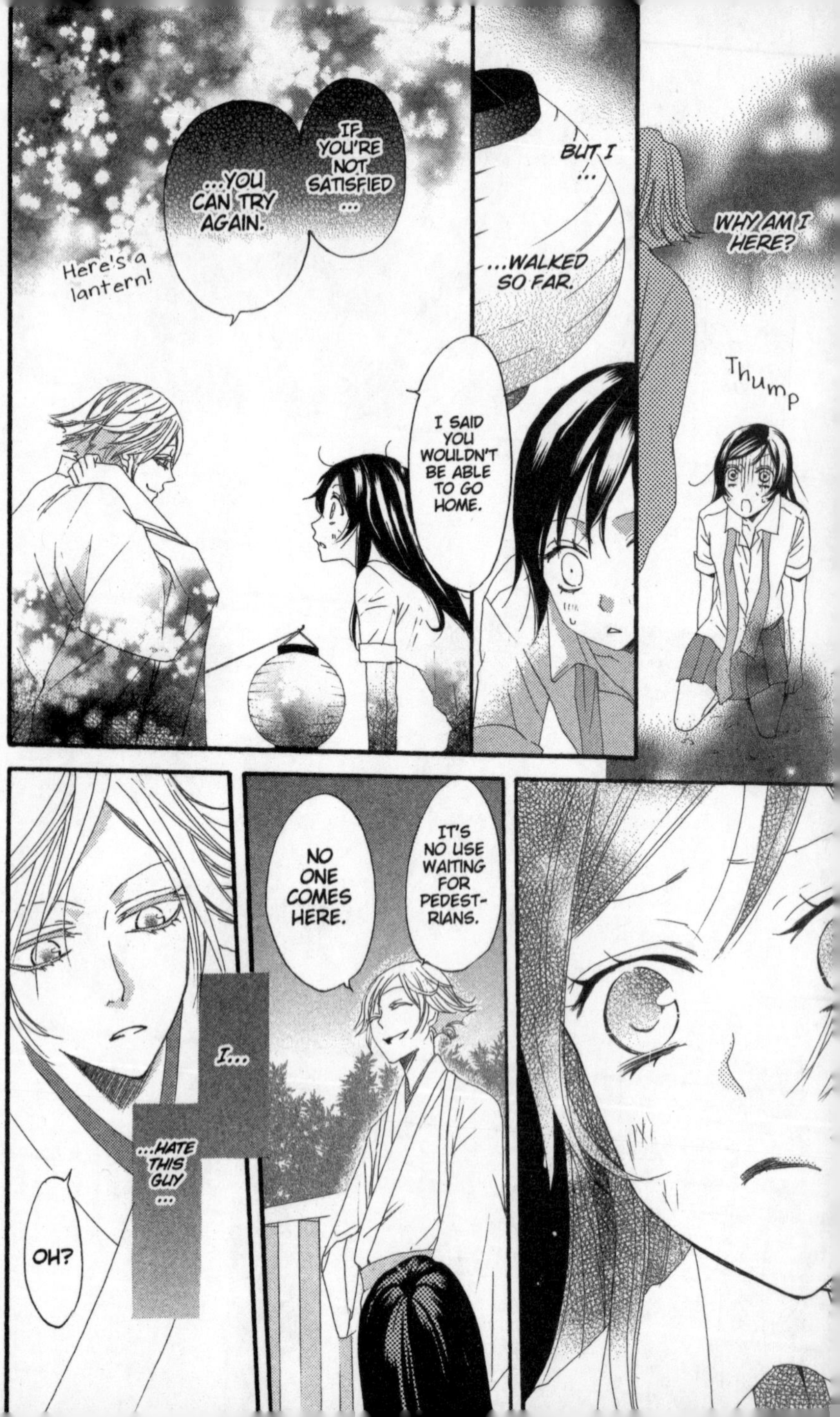
WHY AM I HERE?
Thump
BUT I ...
...WALKED SO FAR.
I SAID YOU WOULDN'T BE ABLE TO GO HOME.
IF YOU'RE NOT SATISFIED ...
...YOU CAN TRY AGAIN.
Here's a lantern!
IT'S NO USE WAITING FOR PEDEST-RIANS.
NO ONE COMES HERE.
I...
...HATE THIS GUY ...
OH?

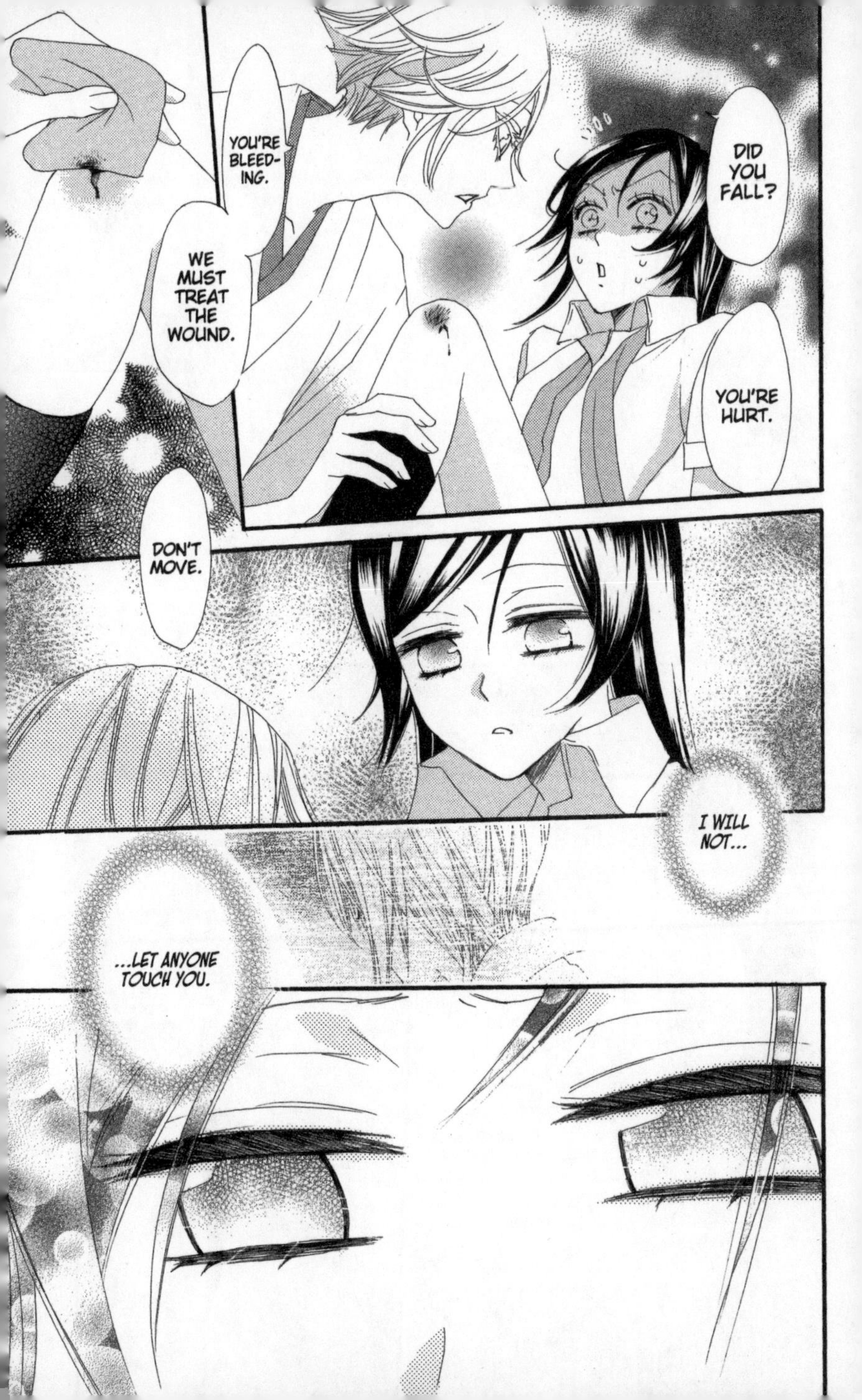
DID YOU FALL?
YOU'RE HURT.
YOU'RE BLEED-ING.
WE MUST TREAT THE WOUND.
DON'T MOVE.
I WILL NOT...
...LET ANYONE TOUCH YOU.

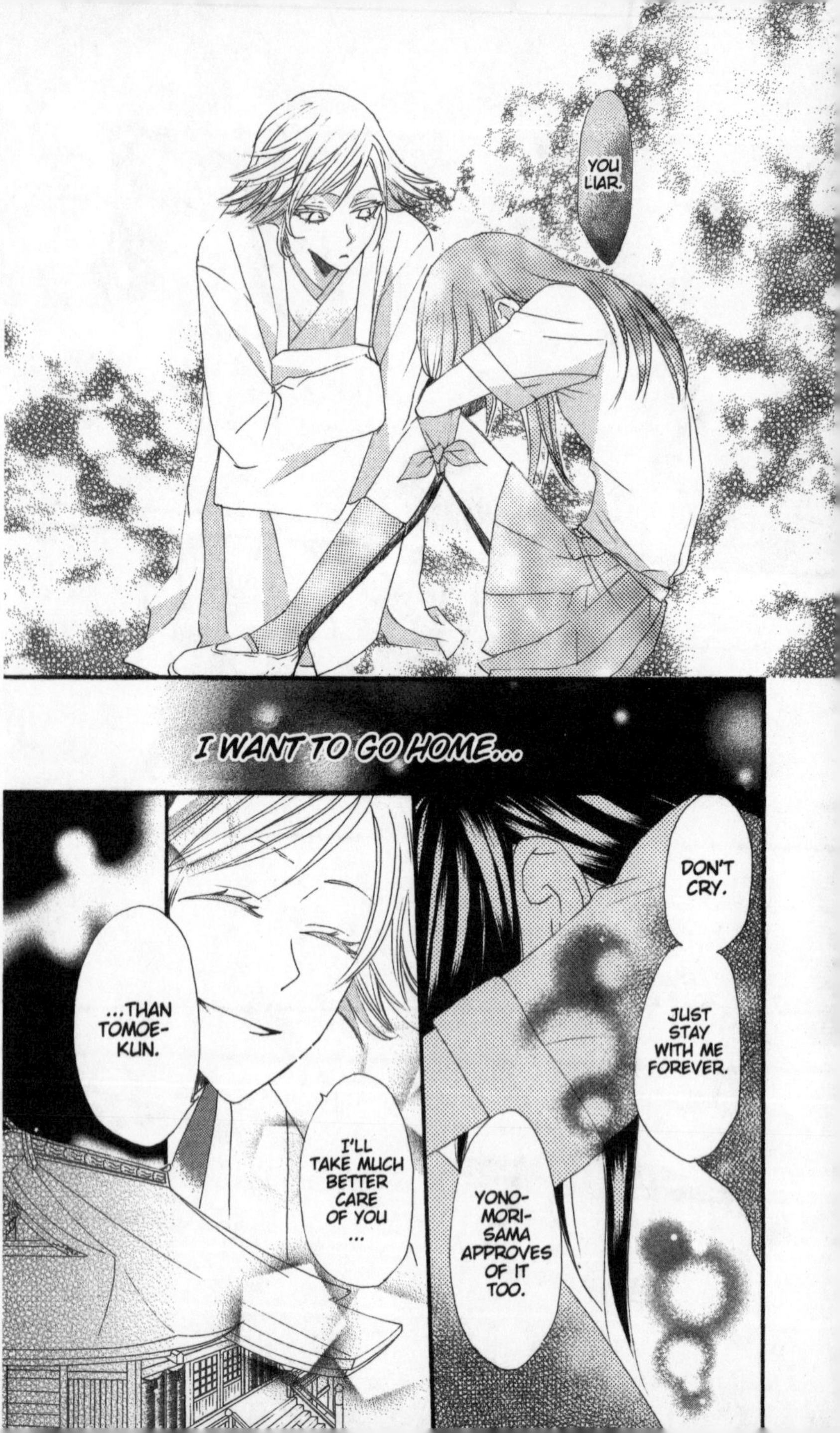
YOU LIAR.
I WANT TO GO HOME...
DON'T CRY.
JUST STAY WITH ME FOREVER.
YONO-MORI-SAMA APPROVES OF IT TOO.
I'LL TAKE MUCH BETTER CARE OF YOU ...
...THAN TOMOE-KUN.

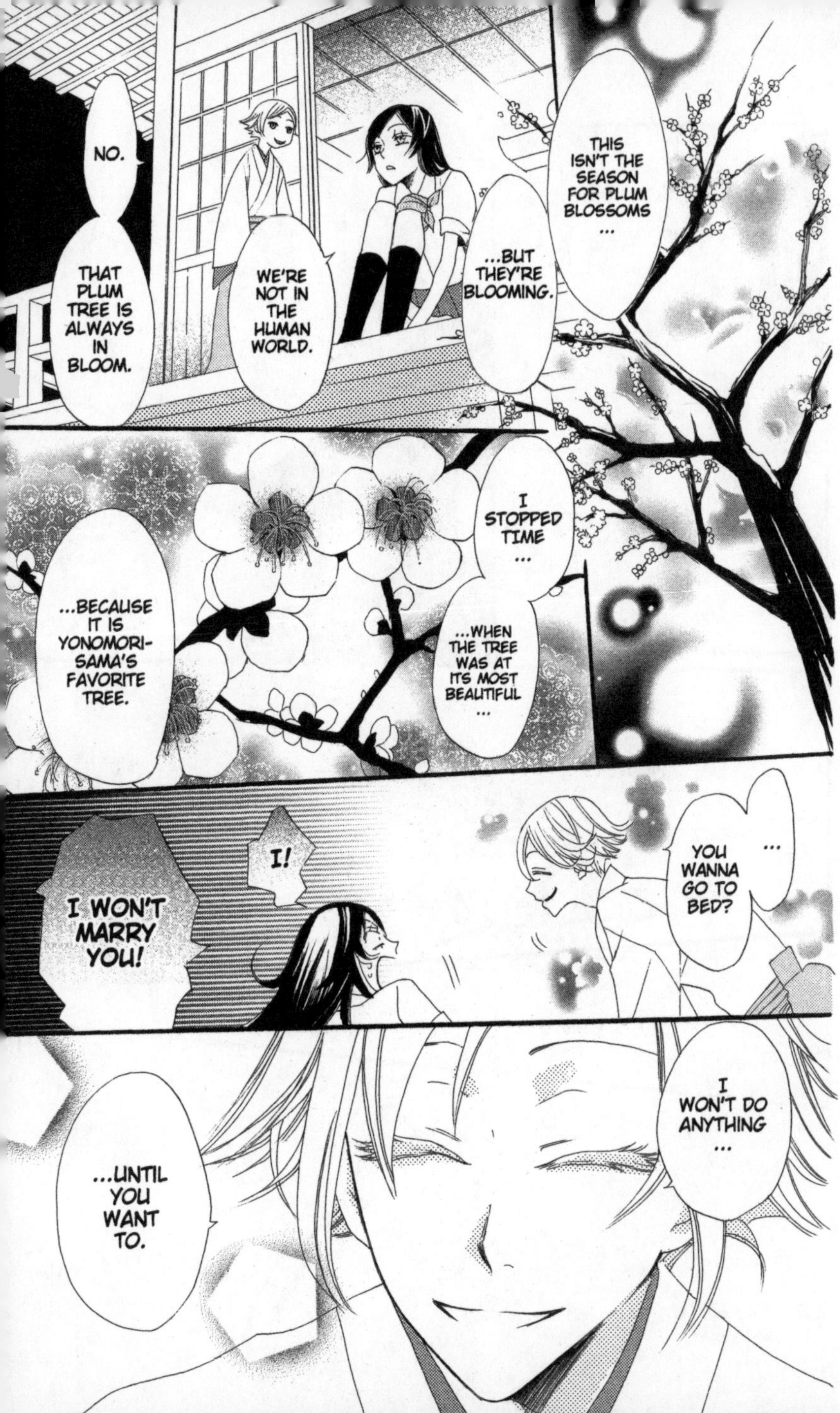
THIS ISN'T THE SEASON FOR PLUM BLOSSOMS ...
...BUT THEY'RE BLOOMING.
WE'RE NOT IN THE HUMAN WORLD.
NO.
THAT PLUM TREE IS ALWAYS IN BLOOM.
I STOPPED TIME ...
...WHEN THE TREE WAS AT ITS MOST BEAUTIFUL ...
...BECAUSE IT IS YONOMORI-SAMA'S FAVORITE TREE.
...
YOU WANNA GO TO BED?
I!
I WON'T MARRY YOU!
I WON'T DO ANYTHING ...
...UNTIL YOU WANT TO.

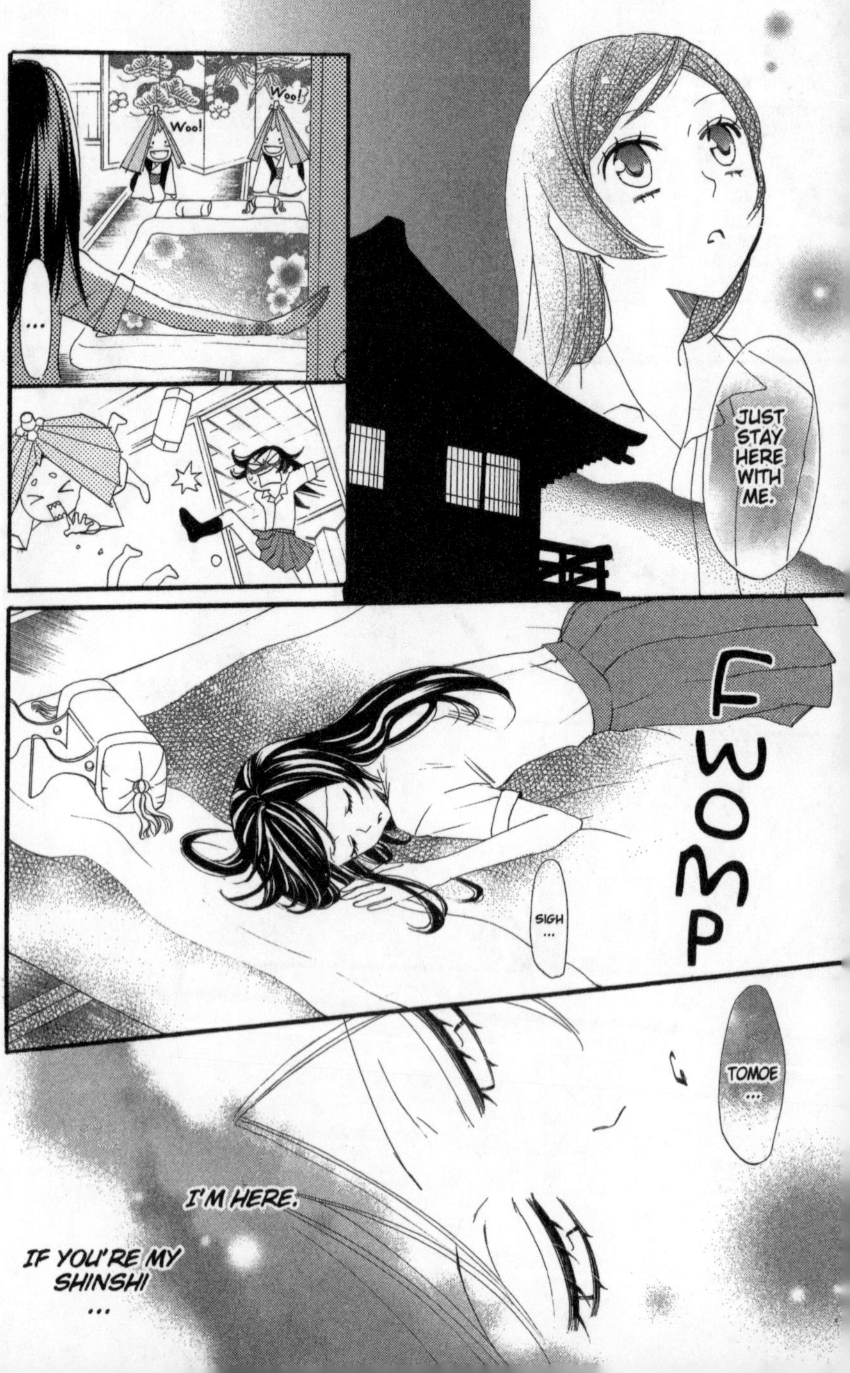
JUST STAY HERE WITH ME.
Woo!
Woo!
...
FWOMP
SIGH ...
TOMOE ...
I'M HERE.
IF YOU'RE MY SHINSHI ...

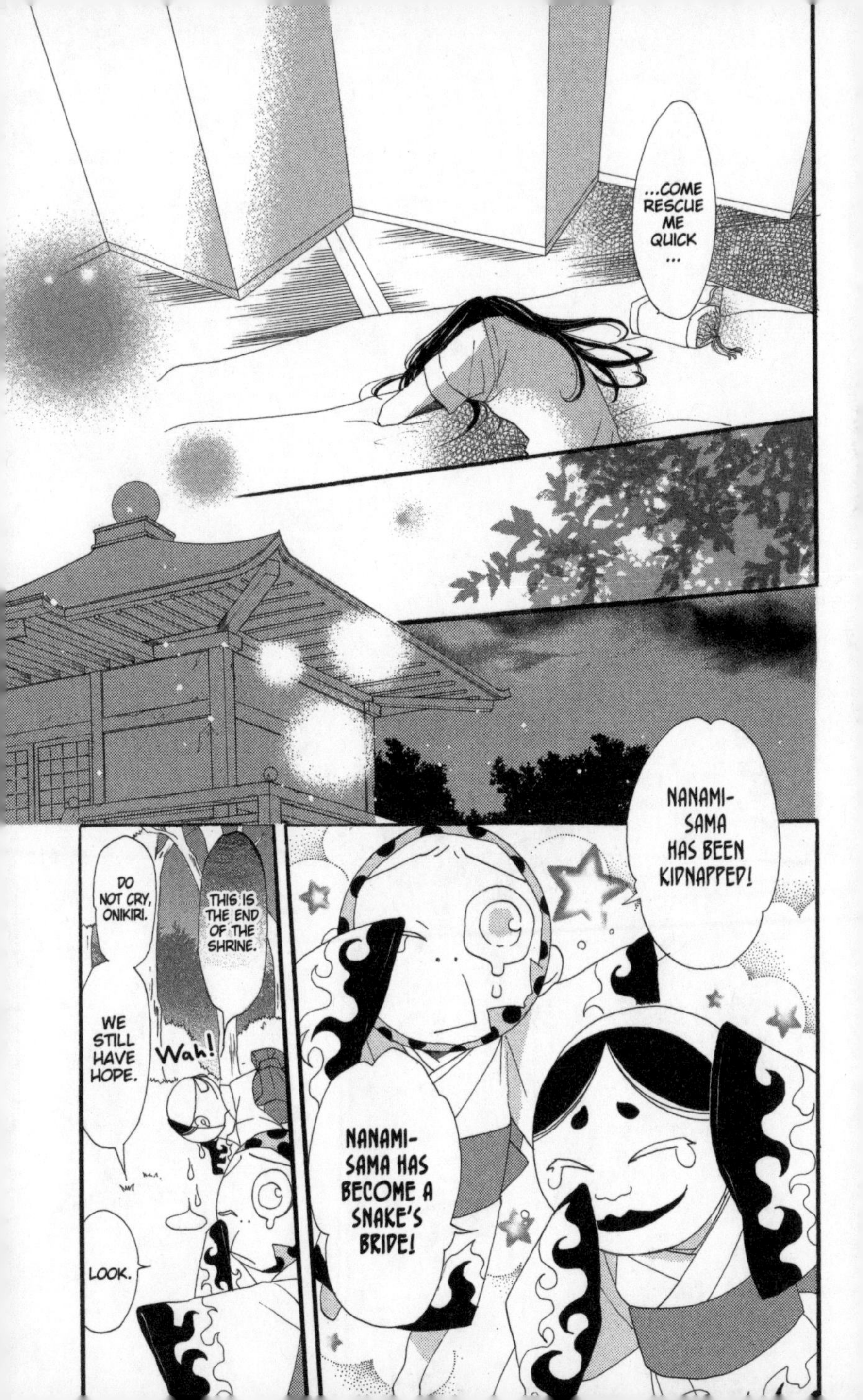
...COME RESCUE ME QUICK ...
NANAMI-SAMA HAS BEEN KIDNAPPED!
NANAMI-SAMA HAS BECOME A SNAKE'S BRIDE!
THIS IS THE END OF THE SHRINE.
Wah!
DO NOT CRY, ONIKIRI.
WE STILL HAVE HOPE.
LOOK.

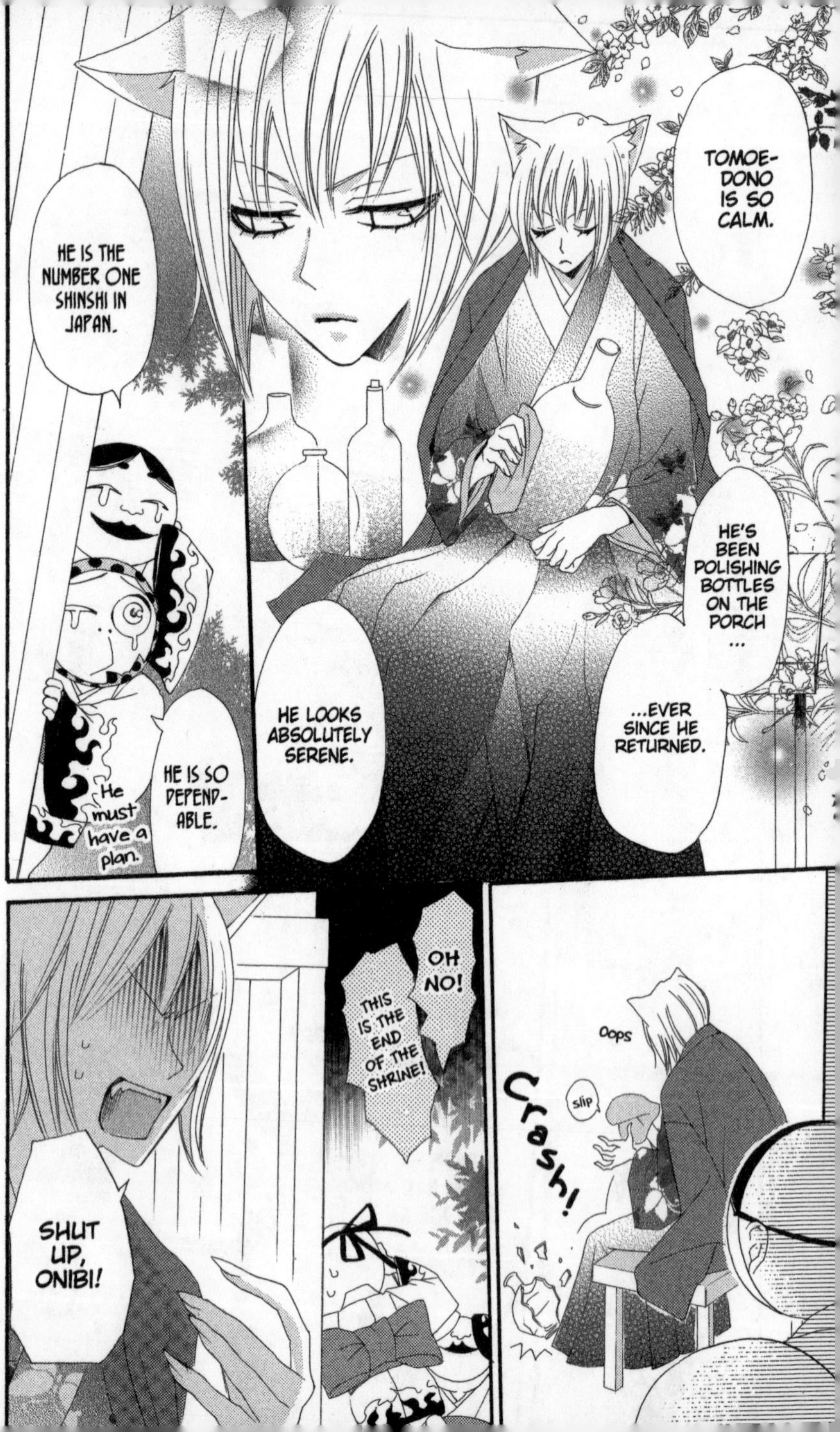
TOMOE-DONO IS SO CALM.
HE IS THE NUMBER ONE SHINSHI IN JAPAN.
HE'S BEEN POLISHING BOTTLES ON THE PORCH ...
...EVER SINCE HE RETURNED.
HE LOOKS ABSOLUTELY SERENE.
HE IS SO DEPENDABLE.
He must have a plan.
Oops
slip
Crash!
OH NO!
THIS IS THE END OF THE SHRINE!
SHUT UP, ONIBI!

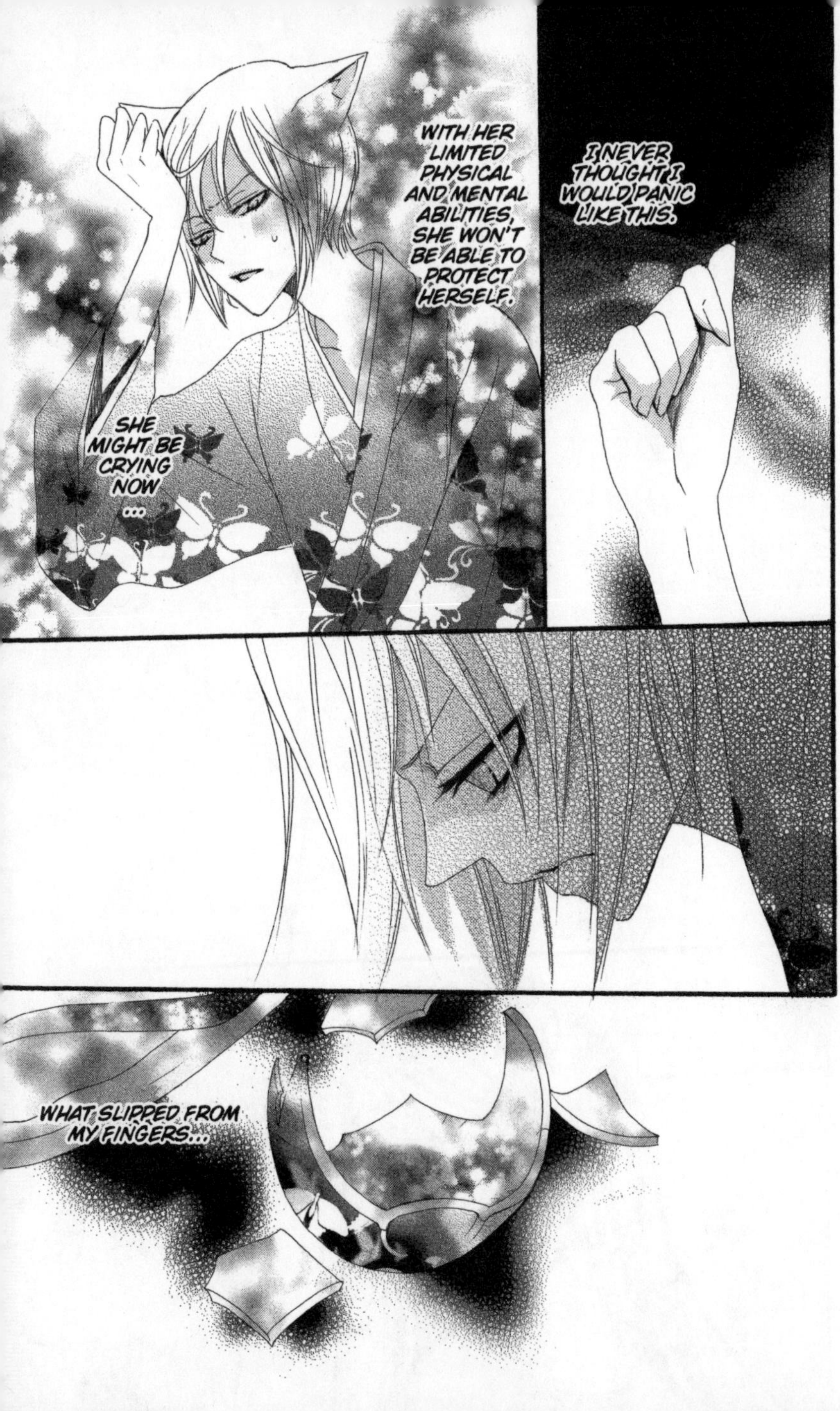
I NEVER THOUGHT I WOULD PANIC LIKE THIS.
WITH HER LIMITED PHYSICAL AND MENTAL ABILITIES, SHE WON'T BE ABLE TO PROTECT HERSELF.
SHE MIGHT BE CRYING NOW...
WHAT SLIPPED FROM MY FINGERS...

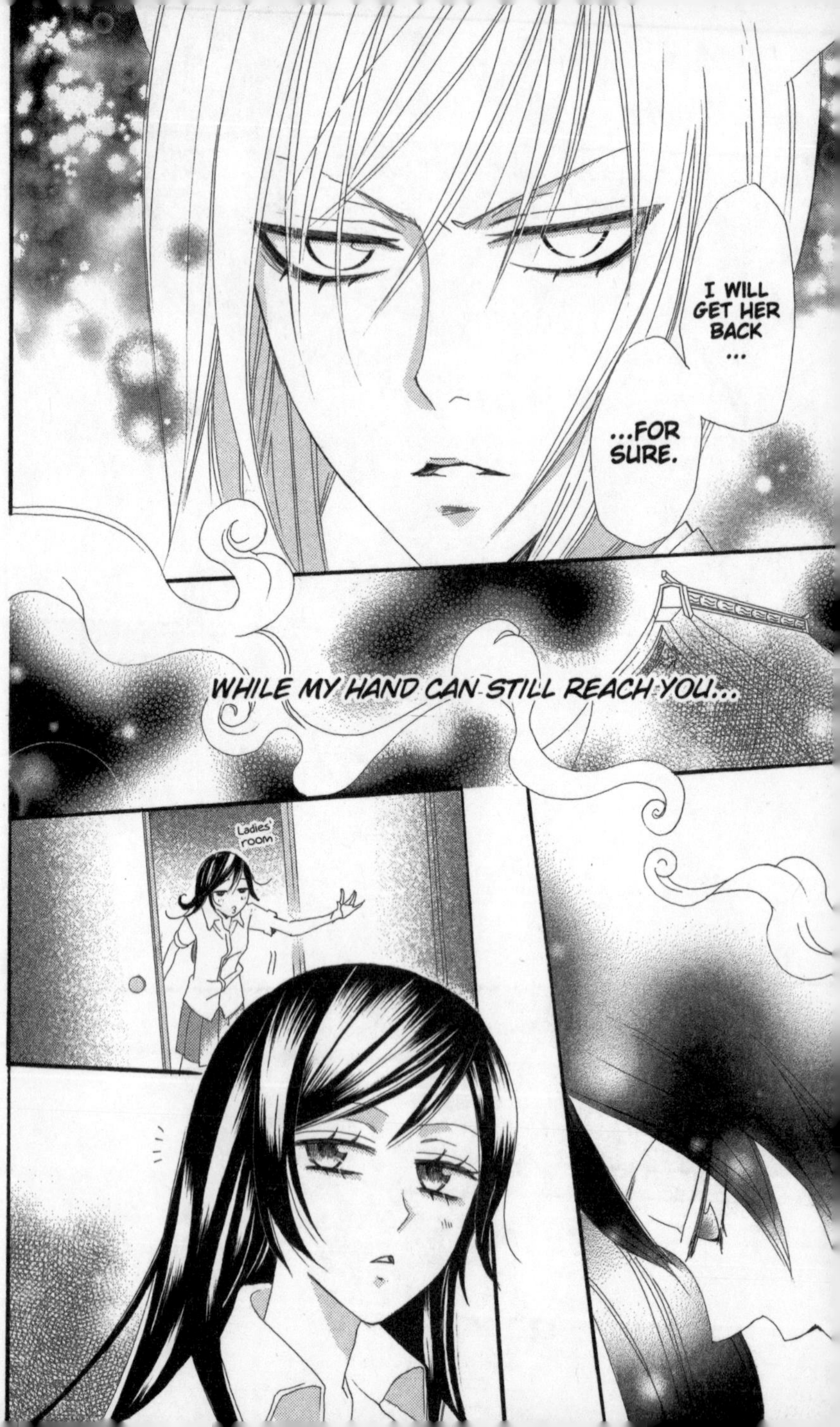
I WILL GET HER BACK ...
...FOR SURE.
WHILE MY HAND CAN STILL REACH YOU...
Ladies' room

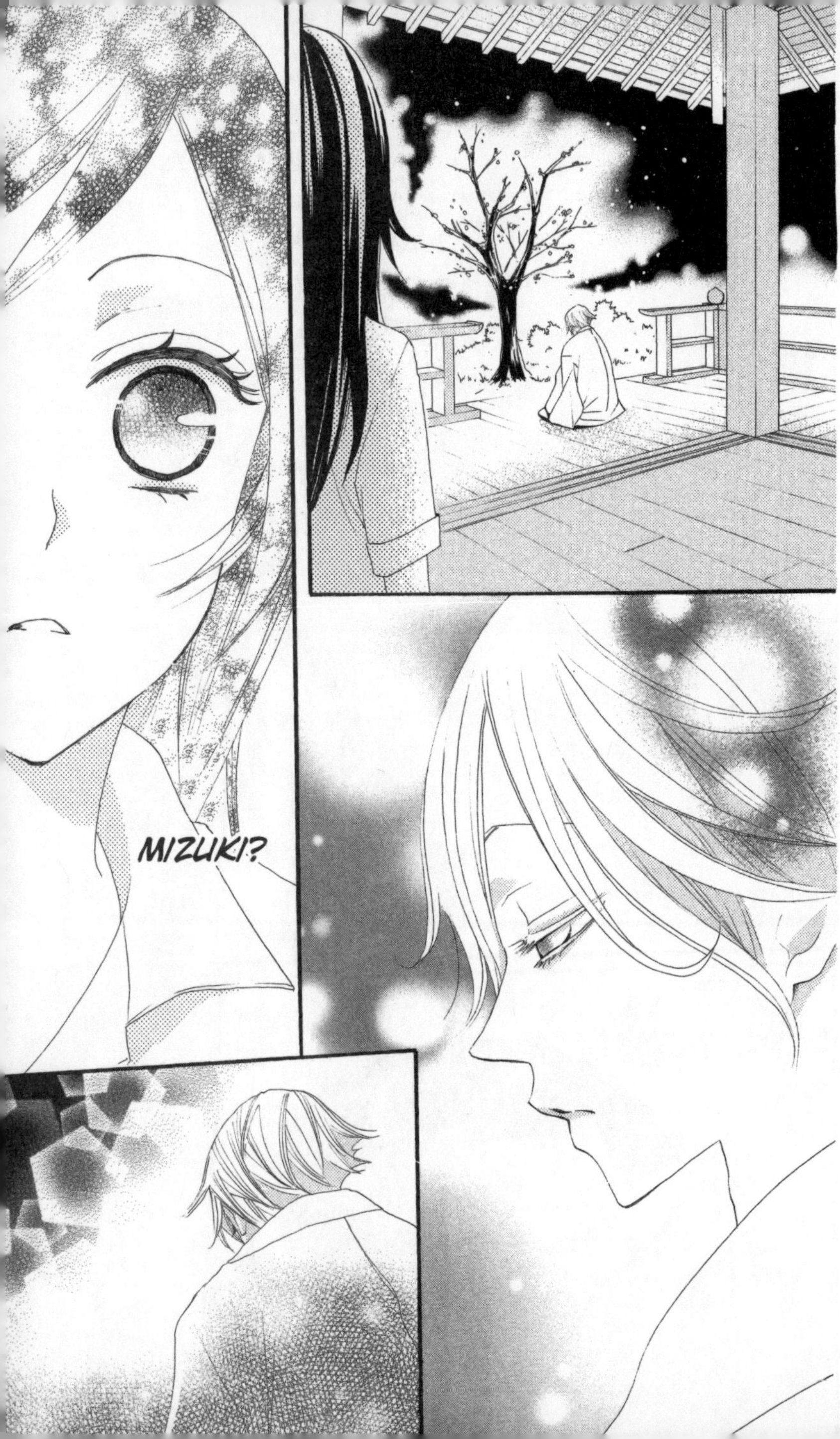
MIZUKI?

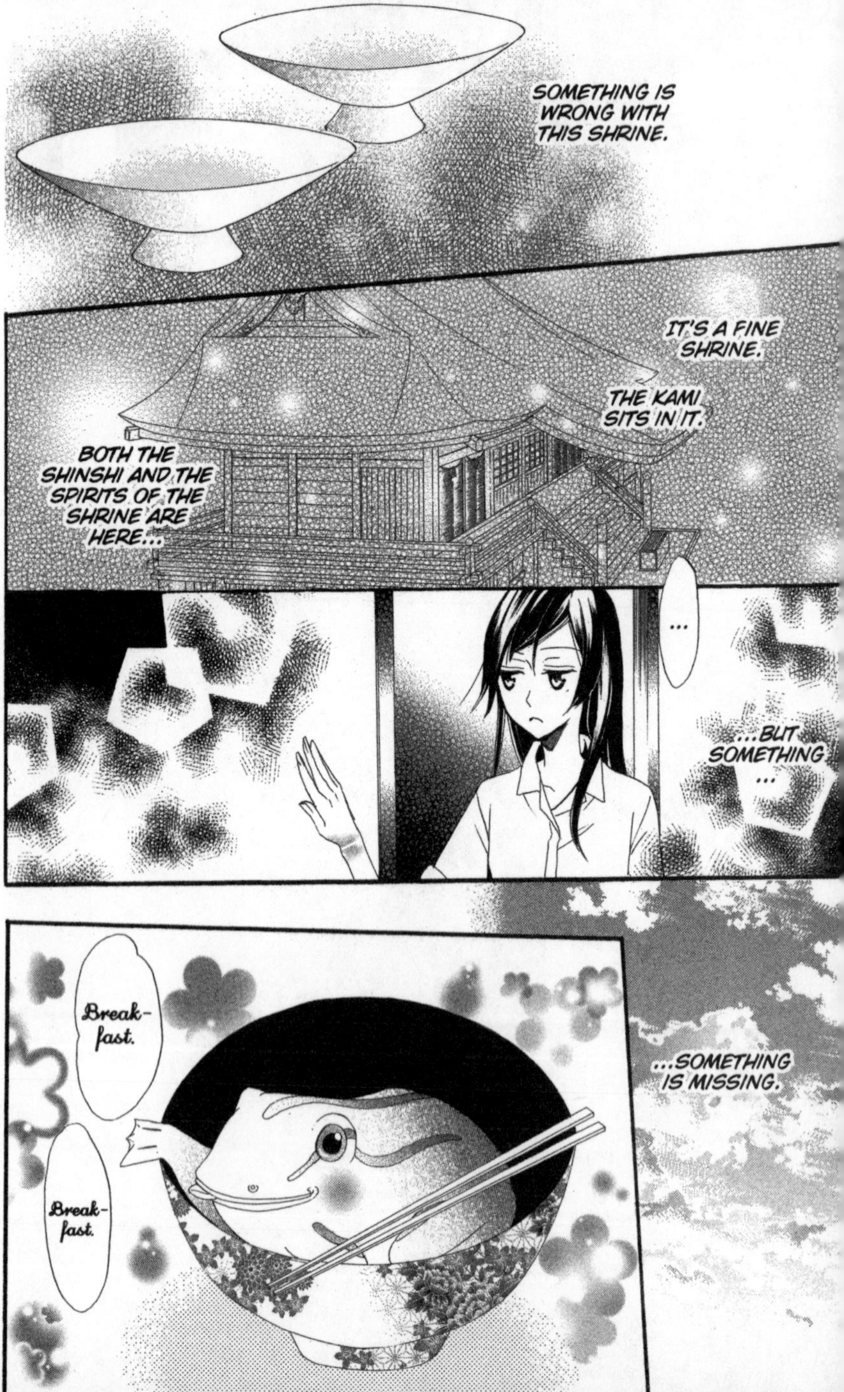
SOMETHING IS WRONG WITH THIS SHRINE.
IT'S A FINE SHRINE.
THE KAMI SITS IN IT.
BOTH THE SHINSHI AND THE SPIRITS OF THE SHRINE ARE HERE...
...
...BUT SOMETHING ...
...SOMETHING IS MISSING.
Break-fast.
Break-fast.

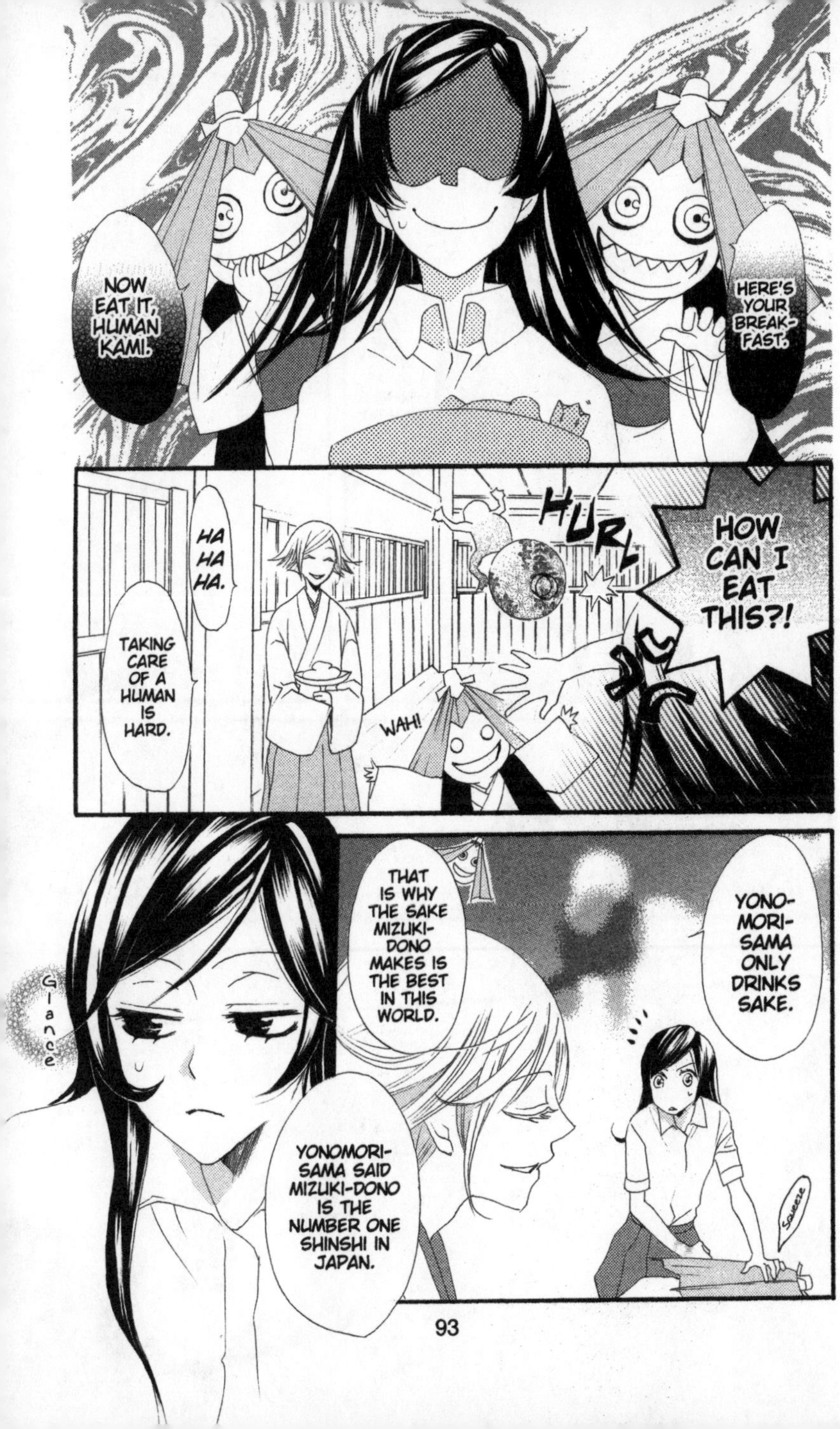
HERE'S YOUR BREAK-FAST.
NOW EAT IT, HUMAN KAMI.
HOW CAN I EAT THIS?!
HURL
WAH!
HA HA HA.
TAKING CARE OF A HUMAN IS HARD.
YONO-MORI-SAMA ONLY DRINKS SAKE.
Squeeze
THAT IS WHY THE SAKE MIZUKI-DONO MAKES IS THE BEST IN THIS WORLD.
YONOMORI-SAMA SAID MIZUKI-DONO IS THE NUMBER ONE SHINSHI IN JAPAN.
Glance

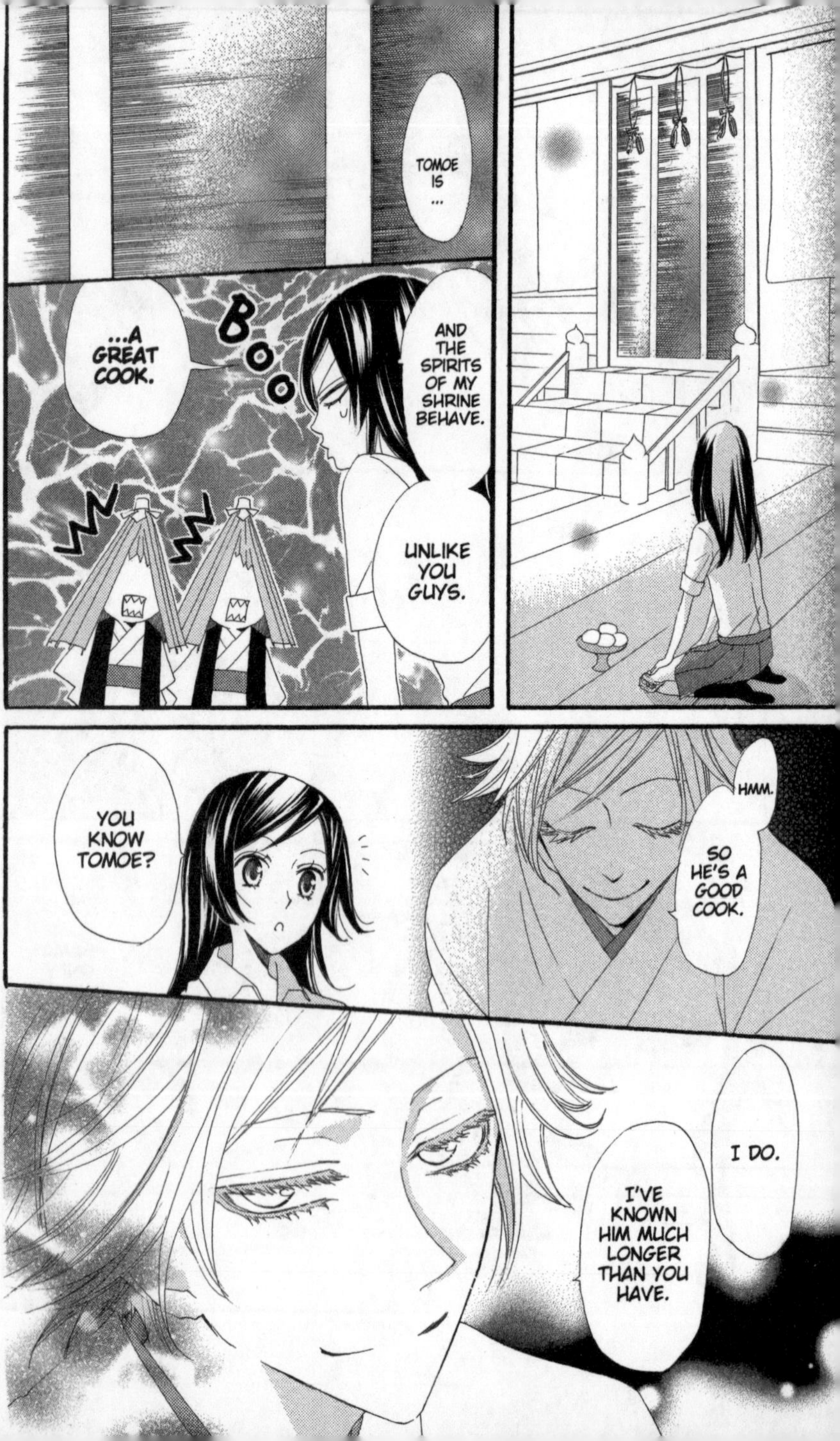
TOMOE IS ...
...A GREAT COOK.
AND THE SPIRITS OF MY SHRINE BEHAVE.
UNLIKE YOU GUYS.
BOO
HMM.
SO HE'S A GOOD COOK.
YOU KNOW TOMOE?
I DO.
I'VE KNOWN HIM MUCH LONGER THAN YOU HAVE.

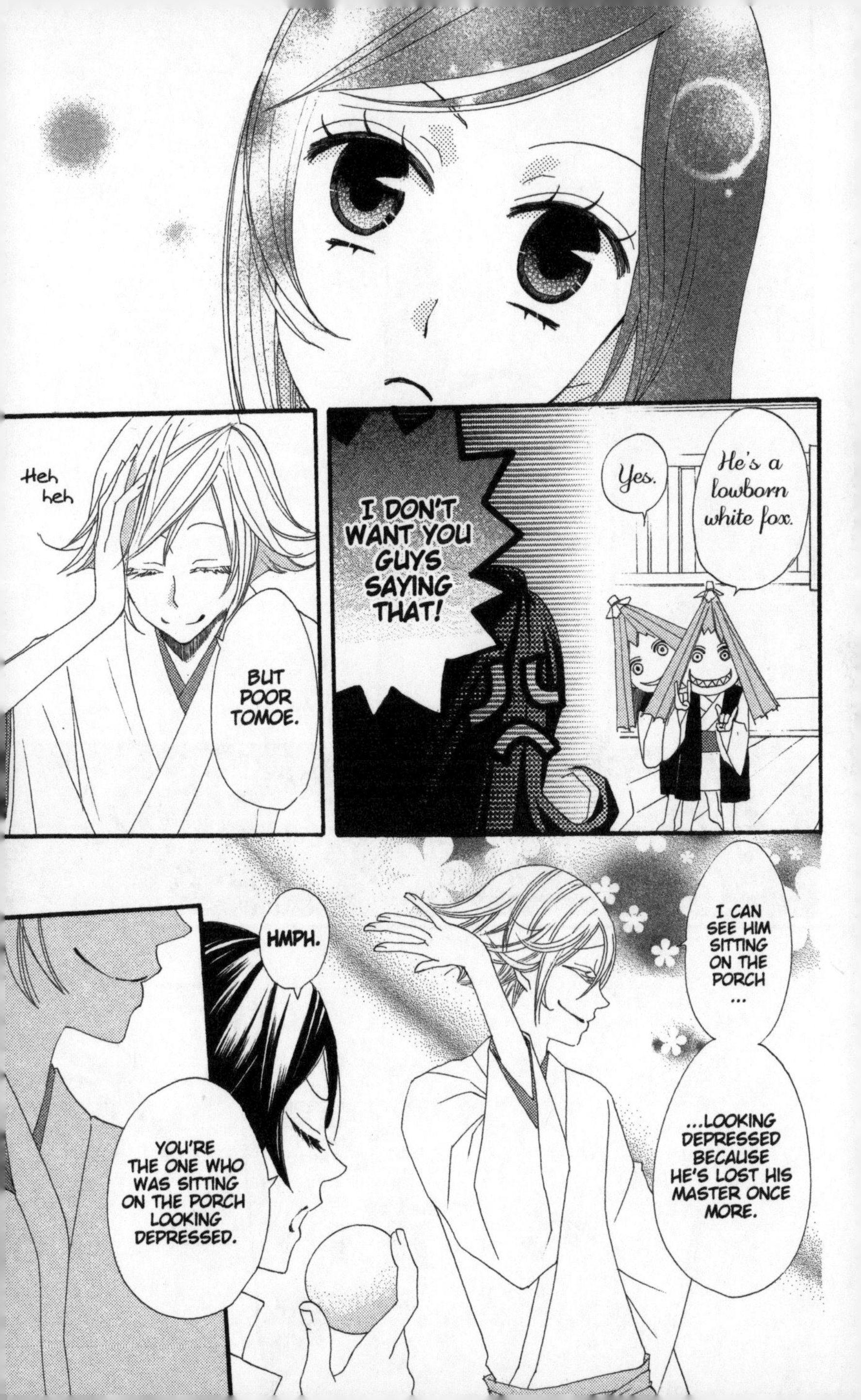
He's a lowborn white fox.
Yes.
I DON'T WANT YOU GUYS SAYING THAT!
Heh heh
BUT POOR TOMOE.
I CAN SEE HIM SITTING ON THE PORCH ...
...LOOKING DEPRESSED BECAUSE HE'S LOST HIS MASTER ONCE MORE.
HMPH.
YOU'RE THE ONE WHO WAS SITTING ON THE PORCH LOOKING DEPRESSED.

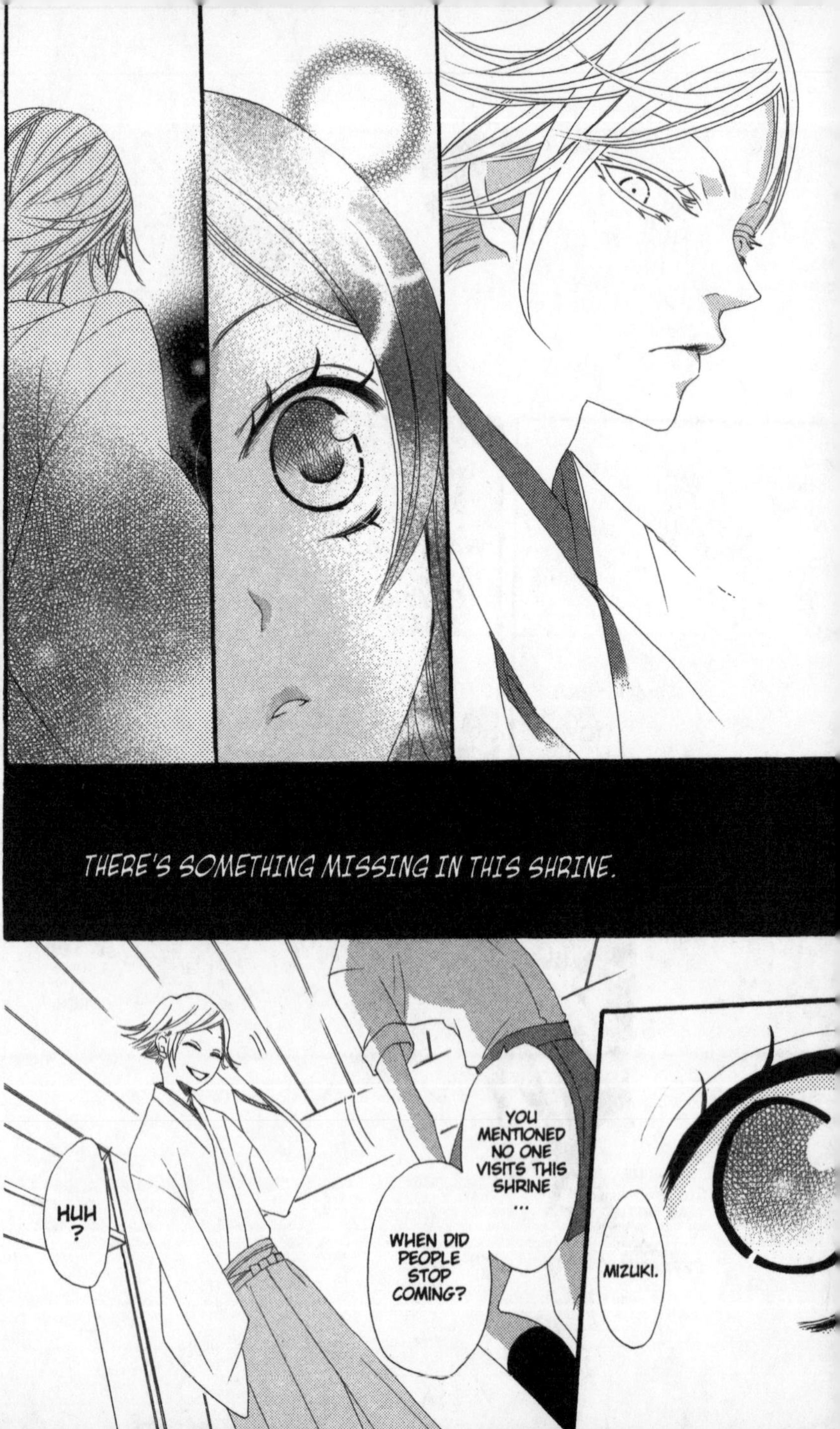
THERE'S SOMETHING MISSING IN THIS SHRINE.
MIZUKI.
YOU MENTIONED NO ONE VISITS THIS SHRINE...
WHEN DID PEOPLE STOP COMING?
HUH?

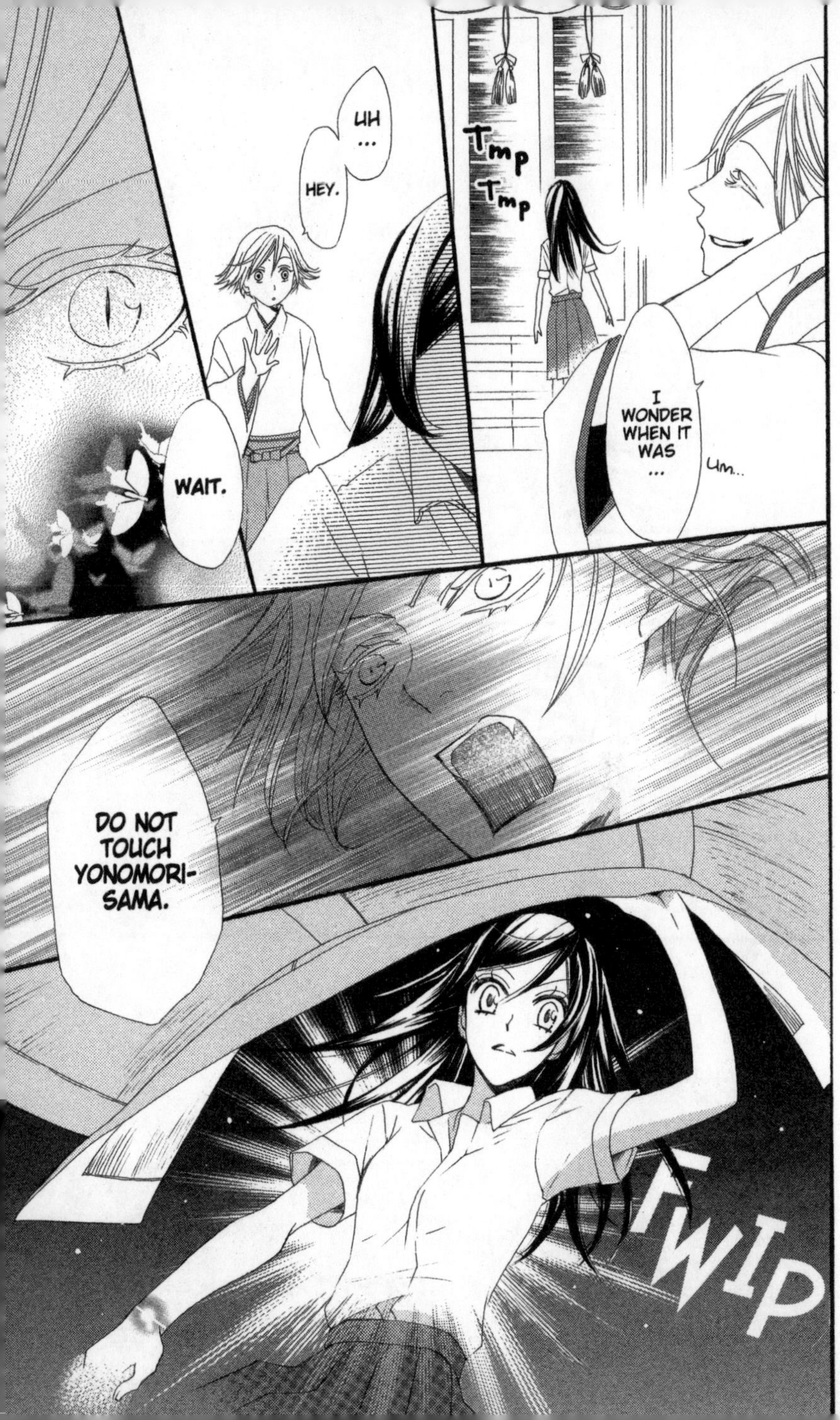
Tmp Tmp
I WONDER WHEN IT WAS ...
Um..
UH ...
HEY.
WAIT.
DO NOT TOUCH YONOMORI-SAMA.
FWIP

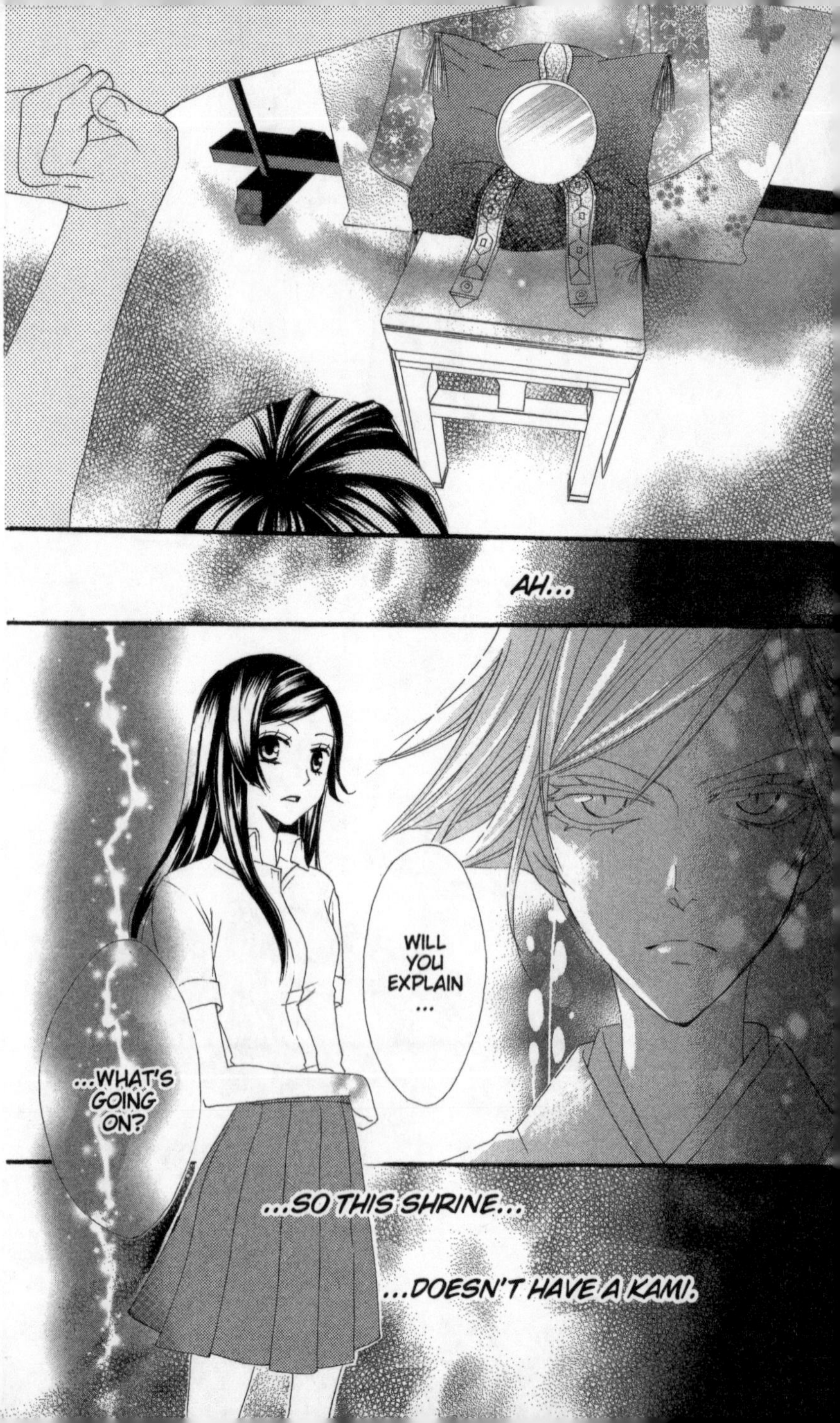
AH...
WILL YOU EXPLAIN ...
...WHAT'S GOING ON?
...SO THIS SHRINE...
...DOESN'T HAVE A KAMI.

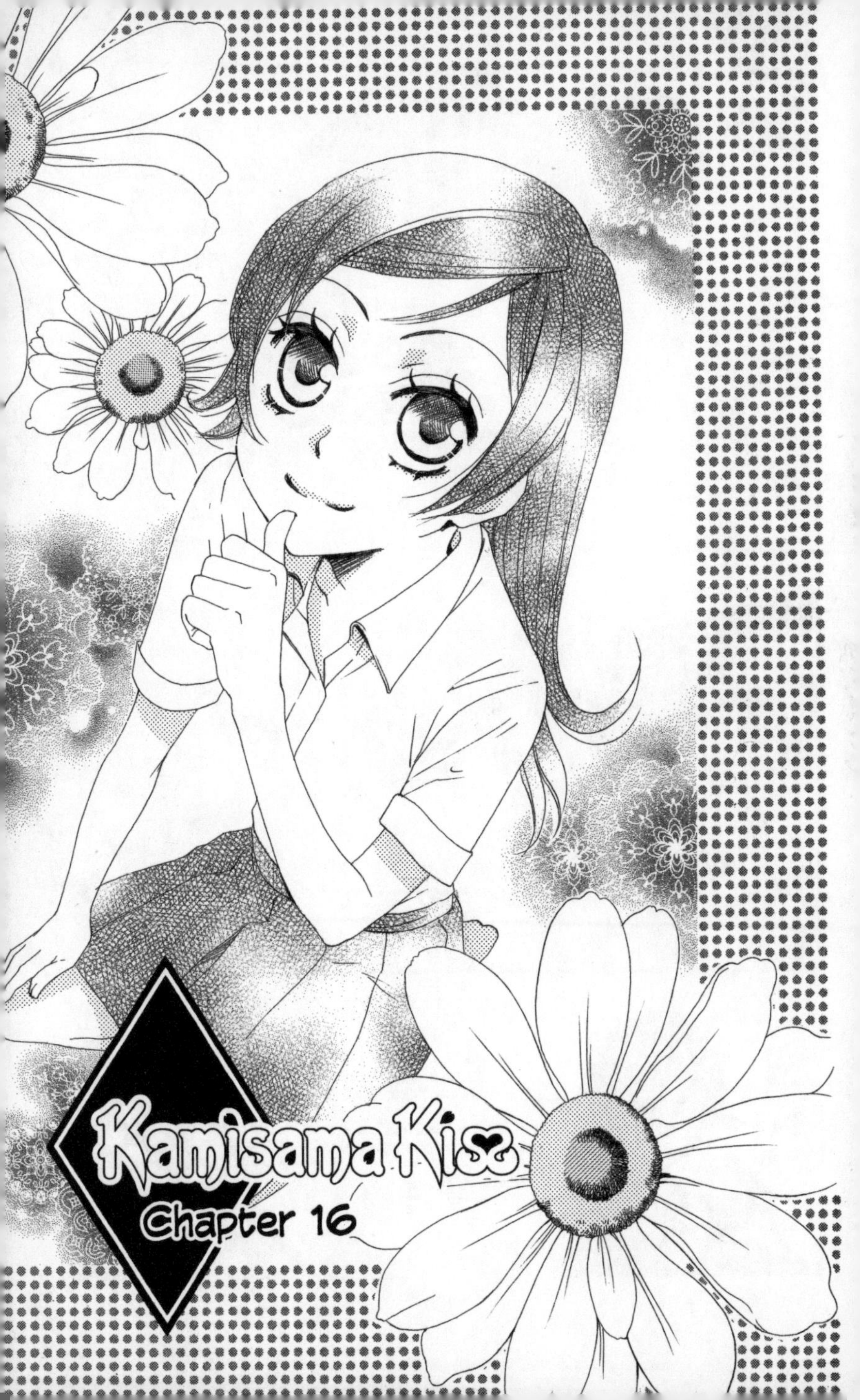
Kamisama Kiss
Chapter 16

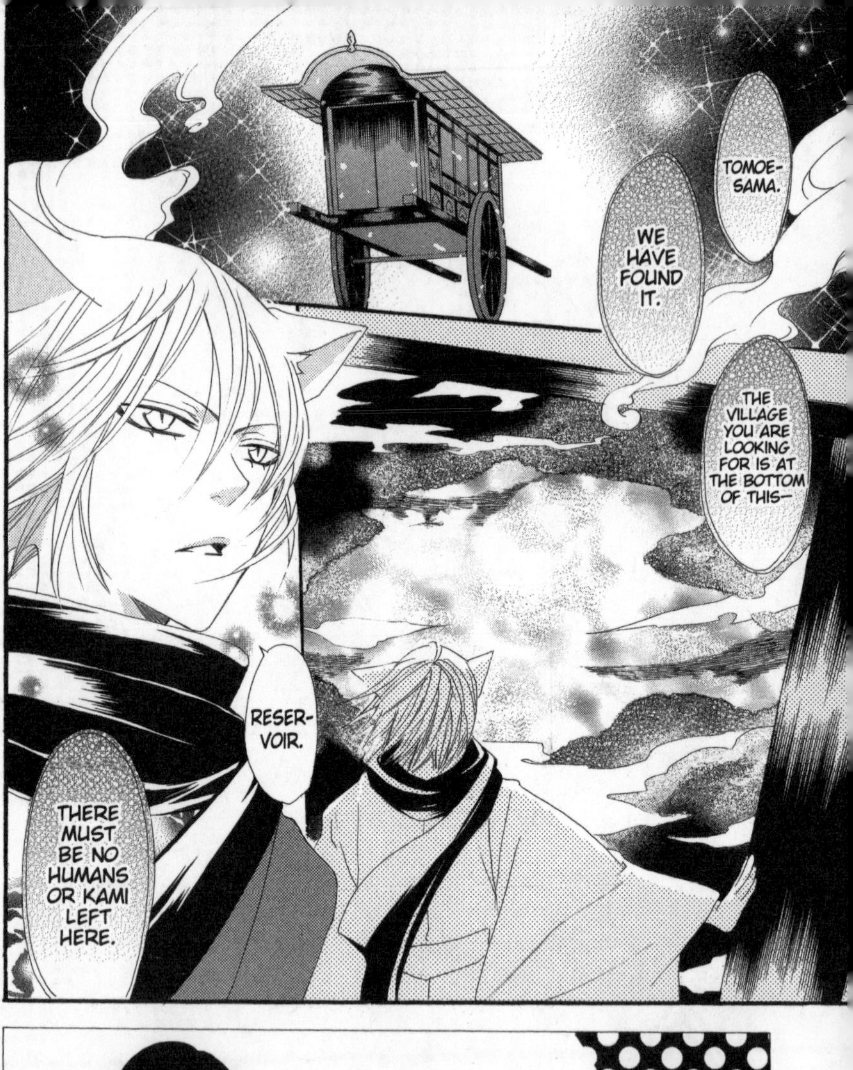
TOMOE-SAMA.
WE HAVE FOUND IT.
THE VILLAGE YOU ARE LOOKING FOR IS AT THE BOTTOM OF THIS—
RESERVOIR.
THERE MUST BE NO HUMANS OR KAMI LEFT HERE.

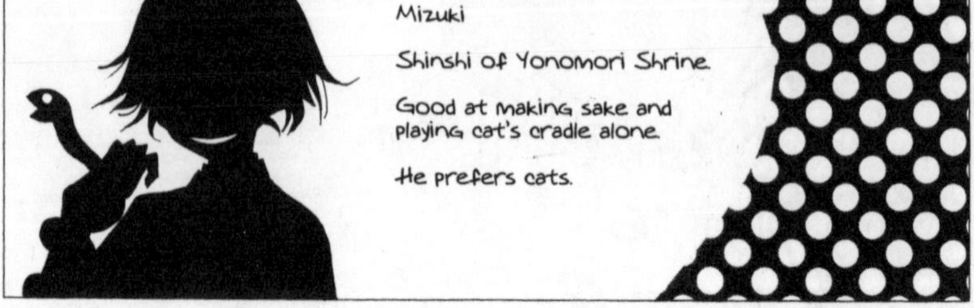
Mizuki
Shinshi of Yonomori Shrine.
Good at making sake and playing cat's cradle alone.
He prefers cats.

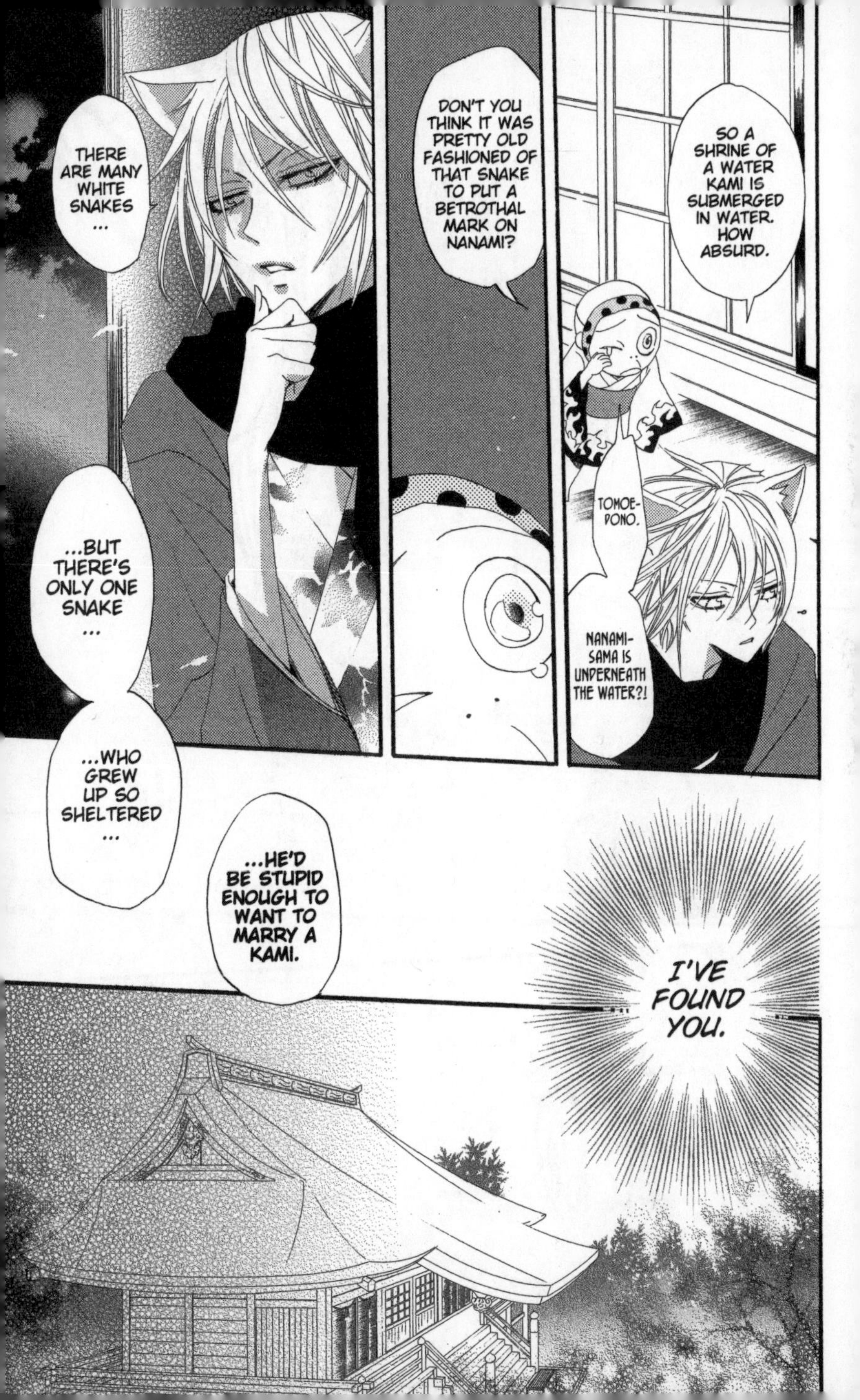
SO A SHRINE OF A WATER KAMI IS SUBMERGED IN WATER. HOW ABSURD.
TOMOE-DONO.
NANAMI-SAMA IS UNDERNEATH THE WATER?!
DON'T YOU THINK IT WAS PRETTY OLD FASHIONED OF THAT SNAKE TO PUT A BETROTHAL MARK ON NANAMI?
THERE ARE MANY WHITE SNAKES ...
...BUT THERE'S ONLY ONE SNAKE ...
...WHO GREW UP SO SHELTERED ...
...HE'D BE STUPID ENOUGH TO WANT TO MARRY A KAMI.
I'VE FOUND YOU.

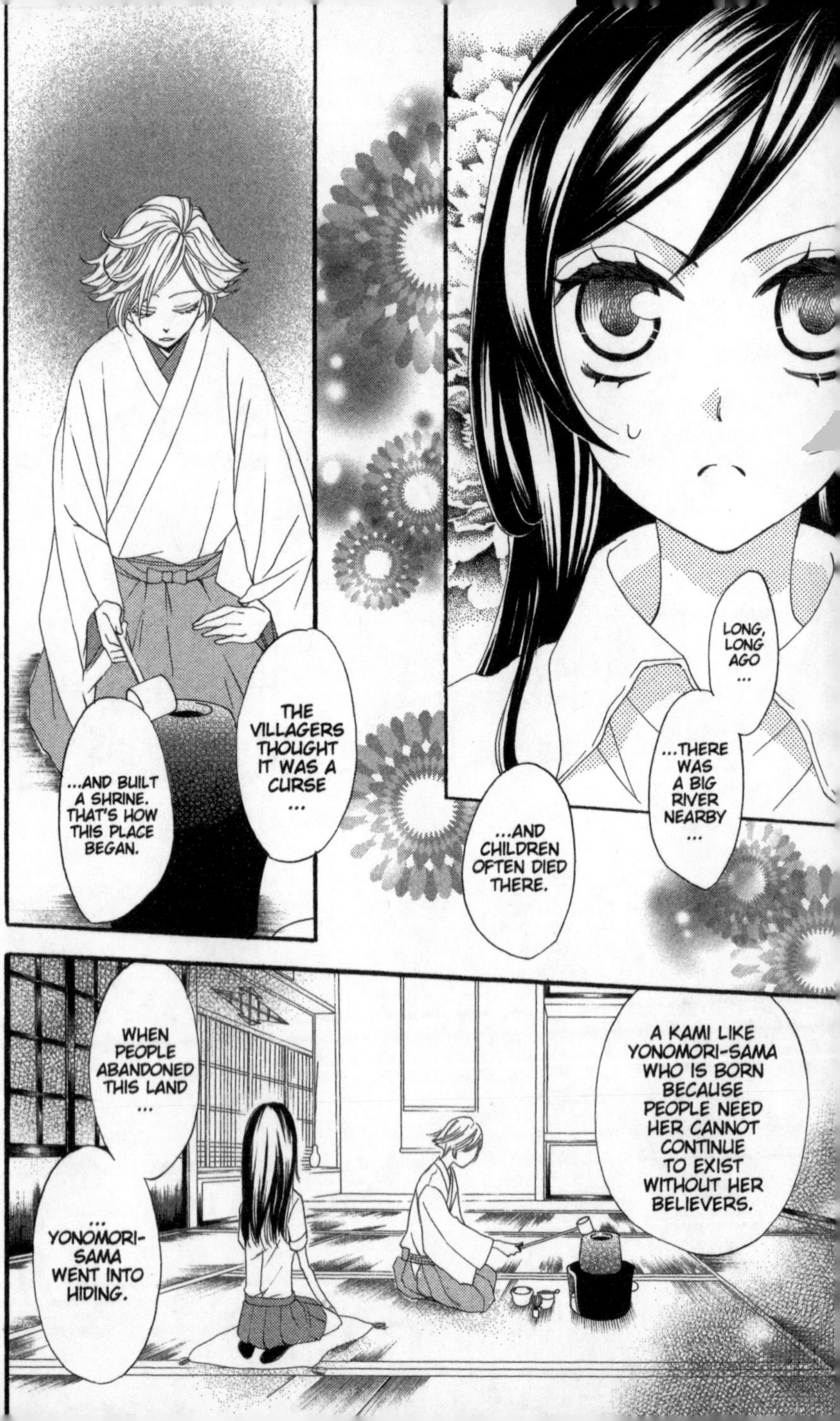
LONG, LONG AGO ...
...THERE WAS A BIG RIVER NEARBY ...
...AND CHILDREN OFTEN DIED THERE.
THE VILLAGERS THOUGHT IT WAS A CURSE ...
...AND BUILT A SHRINE. THAT'S HOW THIS PLACE BEGAN.
A KAMI LIKE YONOMORI-SAMA WHO IS BORN BECAUSE PEOPLE NEED HER CANNOT CONTINUE TO EXIST WITHOUT HER BELIEVERS.
WHEN PEOPLE ABANDONED THIS LAND ...
... YONOMORI-SAMA WENT INTO HIDING.

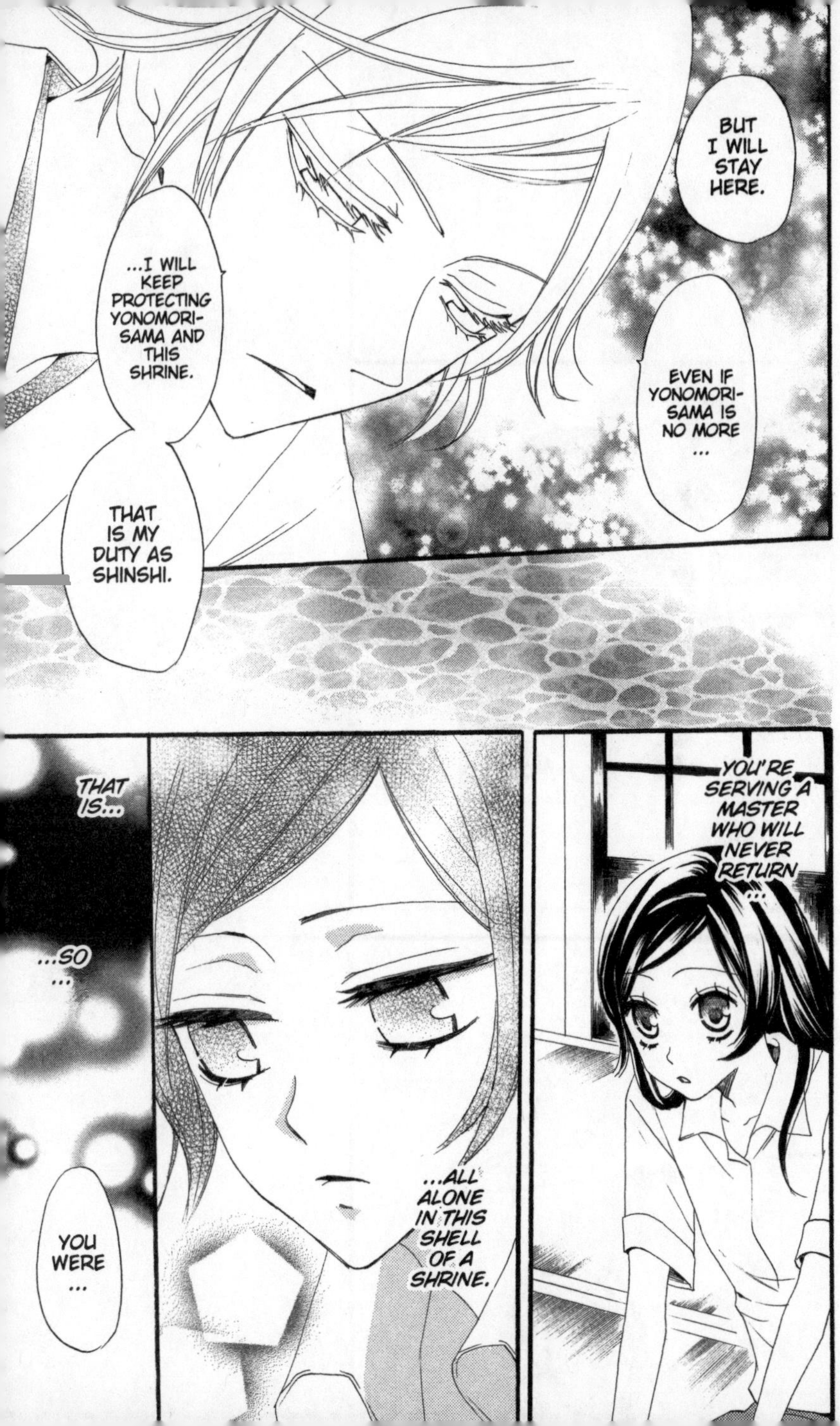
BUT I WILL STAY HERE.
EVEN IF YONOMORI-SAMA IS NO MORE ...
...I WILL KEEP PROTECTING YONOMORI-SAMA AND THIS SHRINE.
THAT IS MY DUTY AS SHINSHI.
YOU'RE SERVING A MASTER WHO WILL NEVER RETURN ...
THAT IS...
...SO ...
YOU WERE ...
...ALL ALONE IN THIS SHELL OF A SHRINE.

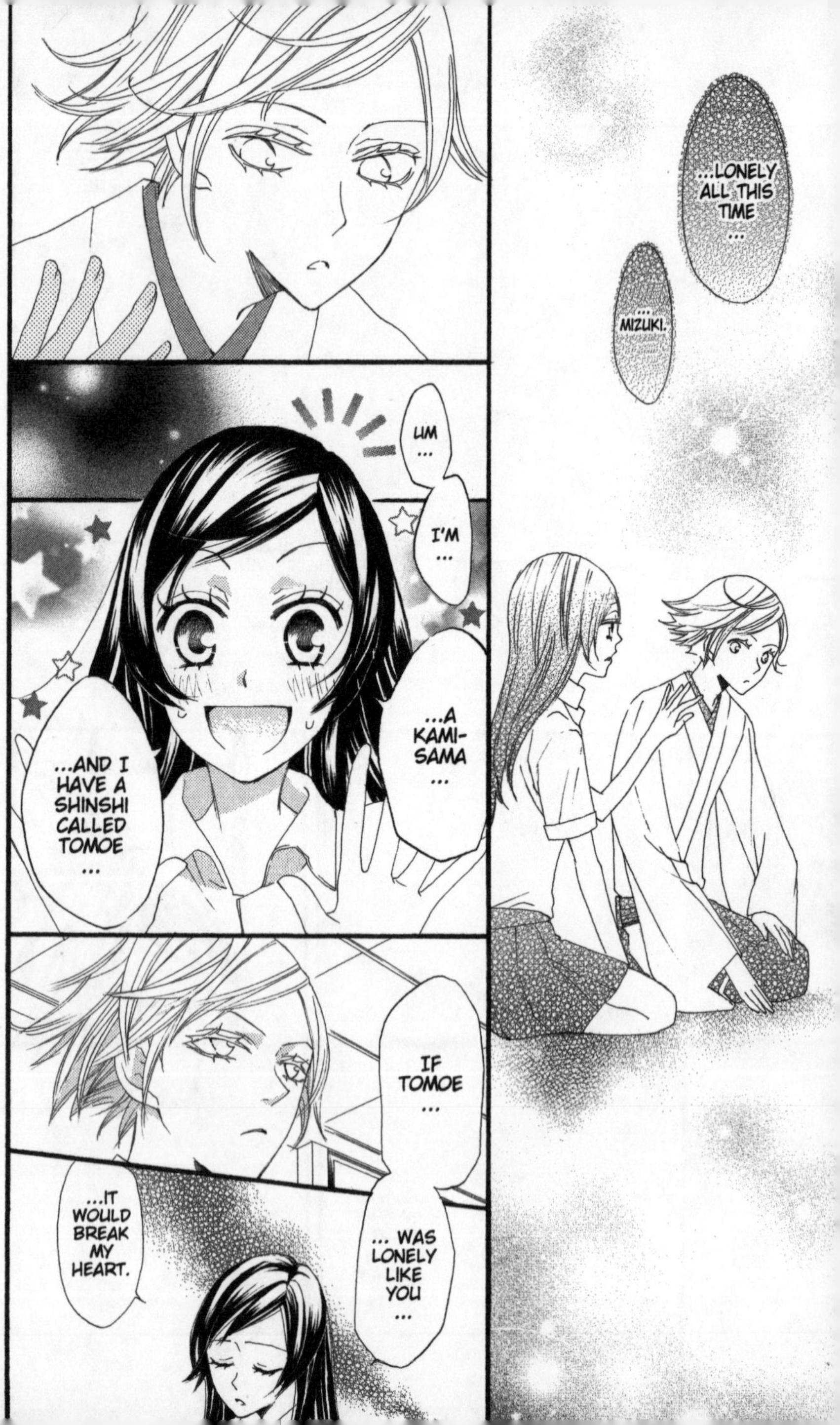
...LONELY ALL THIS TIME ...
... MIZUKI.
UM ...
I'M ...
...A KAMI-SAMA ...
...AND I HAVE A SHINSHI CALLED TOMOE ...
IF TOMOE ...
... WAS LONELY LIKE YOU ...
...IT WOULD BREAK MY HEART.

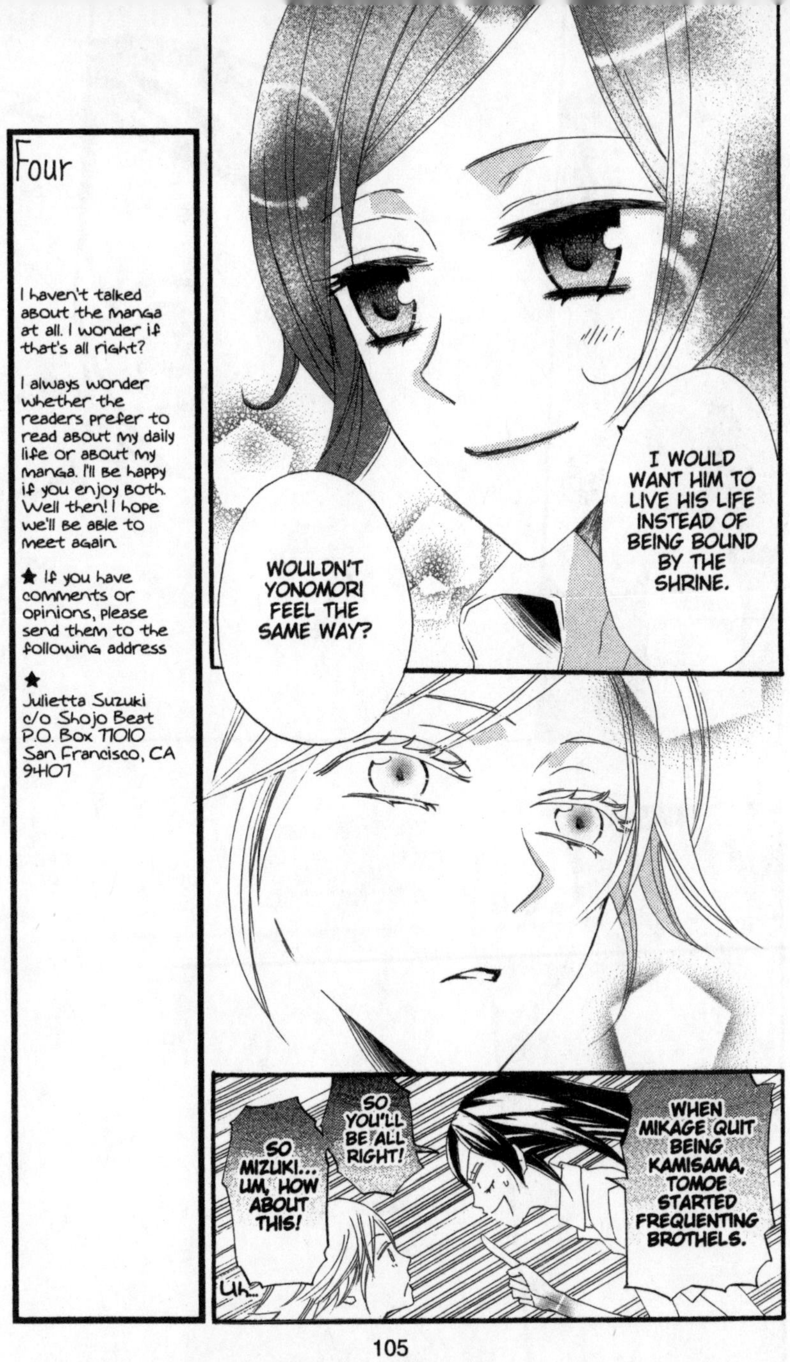
I WOULD WANT HIM TO LIVE HIS LIFE INSTEAD OF BEING BOUND BY THE SHRINE.
WOULDN'T YONOMORI FEEL THE SAME WAY?
WHEN MIKAGE QUIT BEING KAMISAMA, TOMOE STARTED FREQUENTING BROTHELS.
SO YOU'LL BE ALL RIGHT!
SO MIZUKI... UM, HOW ABOUT THIS!
Uh...

Four

I haven't talked about the manga at all. I wonder if that's all right?

I always wonder whether the readers prefer to read about my daily life or about my manga. I'll be happy if you enjoy both. Well then! I hope we'll be able to meet again.

★ If you have comments or opinions, please send them to the following address

★

Julietta Suzuki
c/o Shojo Beat
P.O. Box 77010
San Francisco, CA
94107

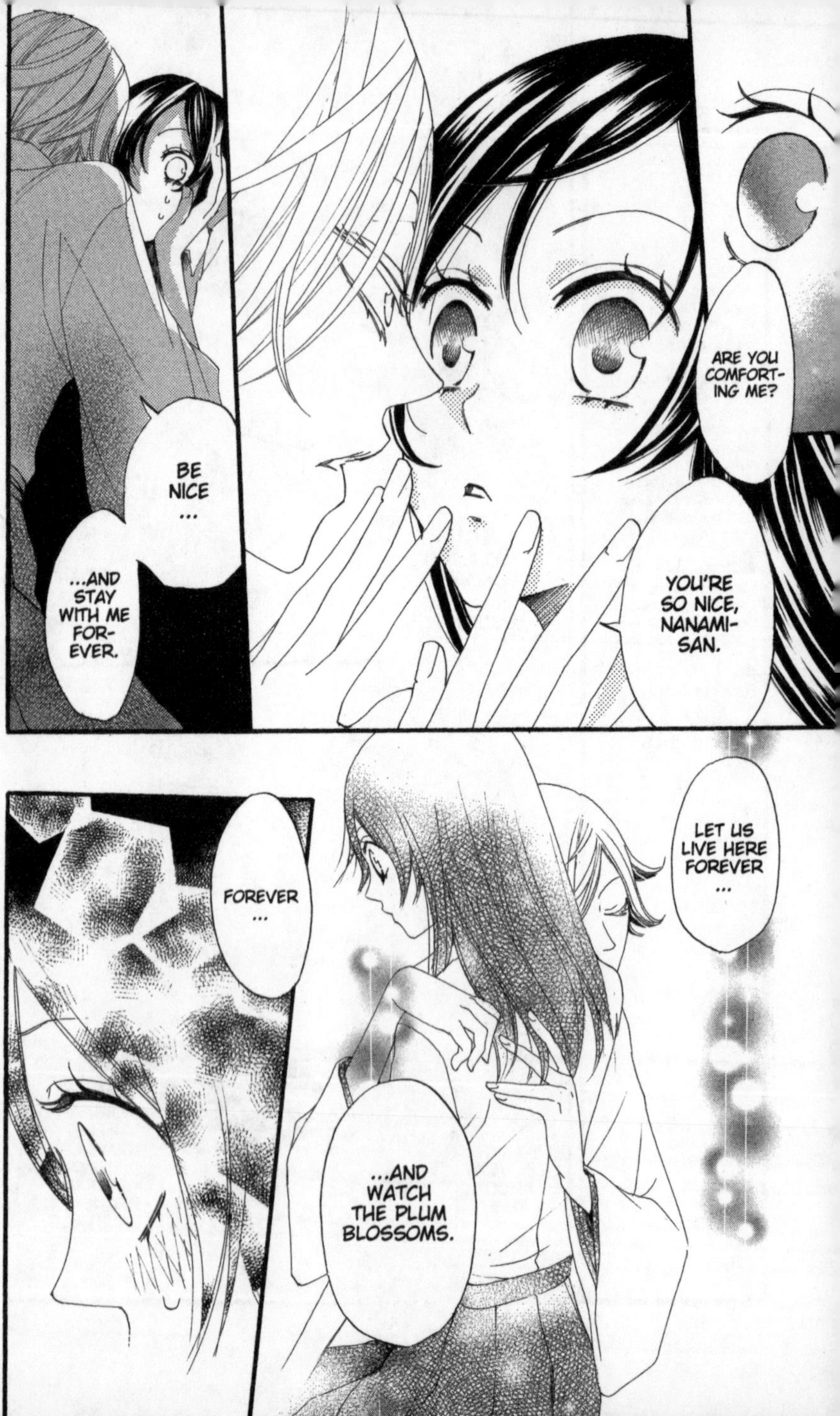
ARE YOU COMFORTING ME?
YOU'RE SO NICE, NANAMI-SAN.
BE NICE ...
...AND STAY WITH ME FOREVER.
LET US LIVE HERE FOREVER ...
...AND WATCH THE PLUM BLOSSOMS.
FOREVER ...

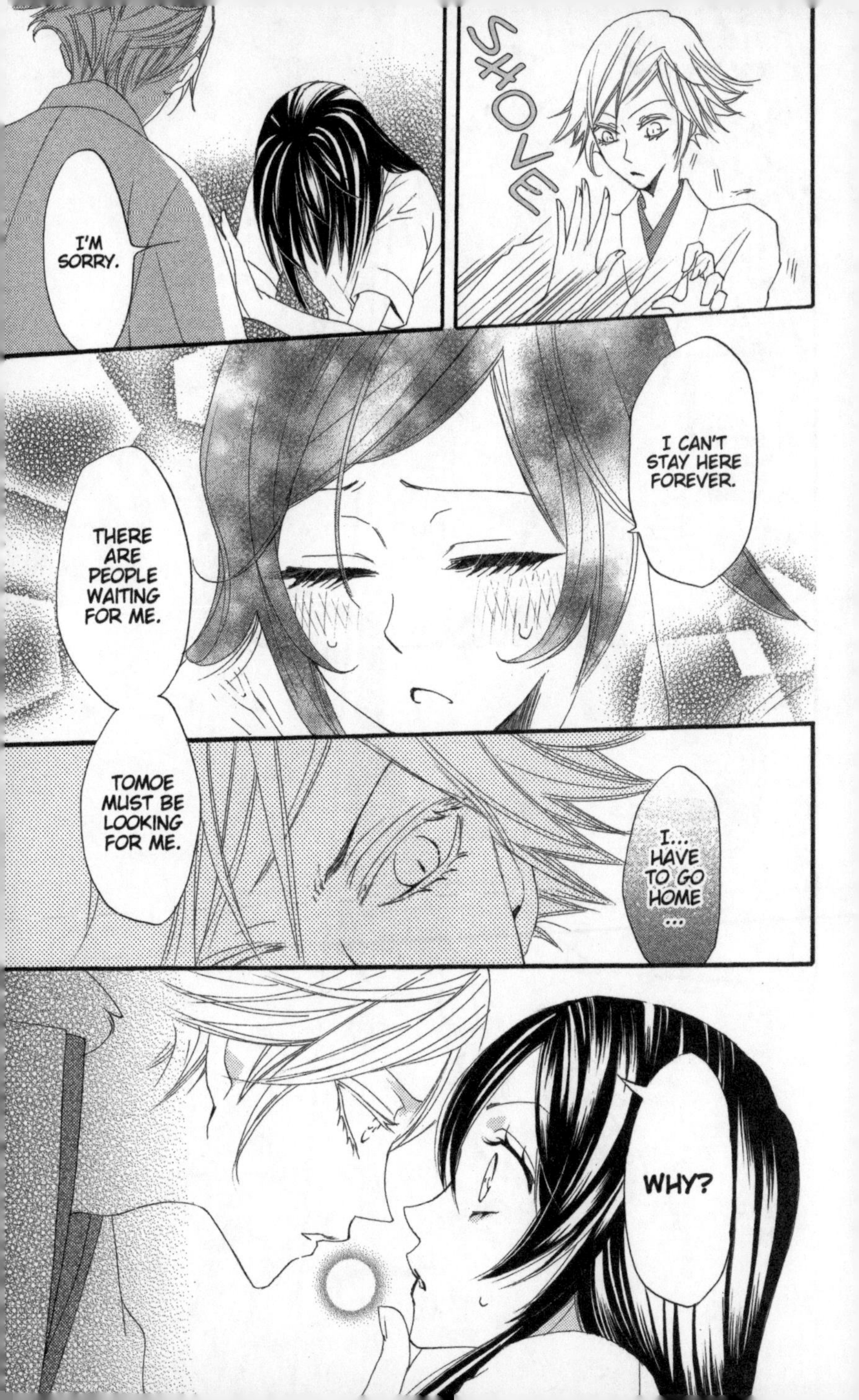
SHOVE
I'M SORRY.
I CAN'T STAY HERE FOREVER.
THERE ARE PEOPLE WAITING FOR ME.
I... HAVE TO GO HOME...
TOMOE MUST BE LOOKING FOR ME.
WHY?

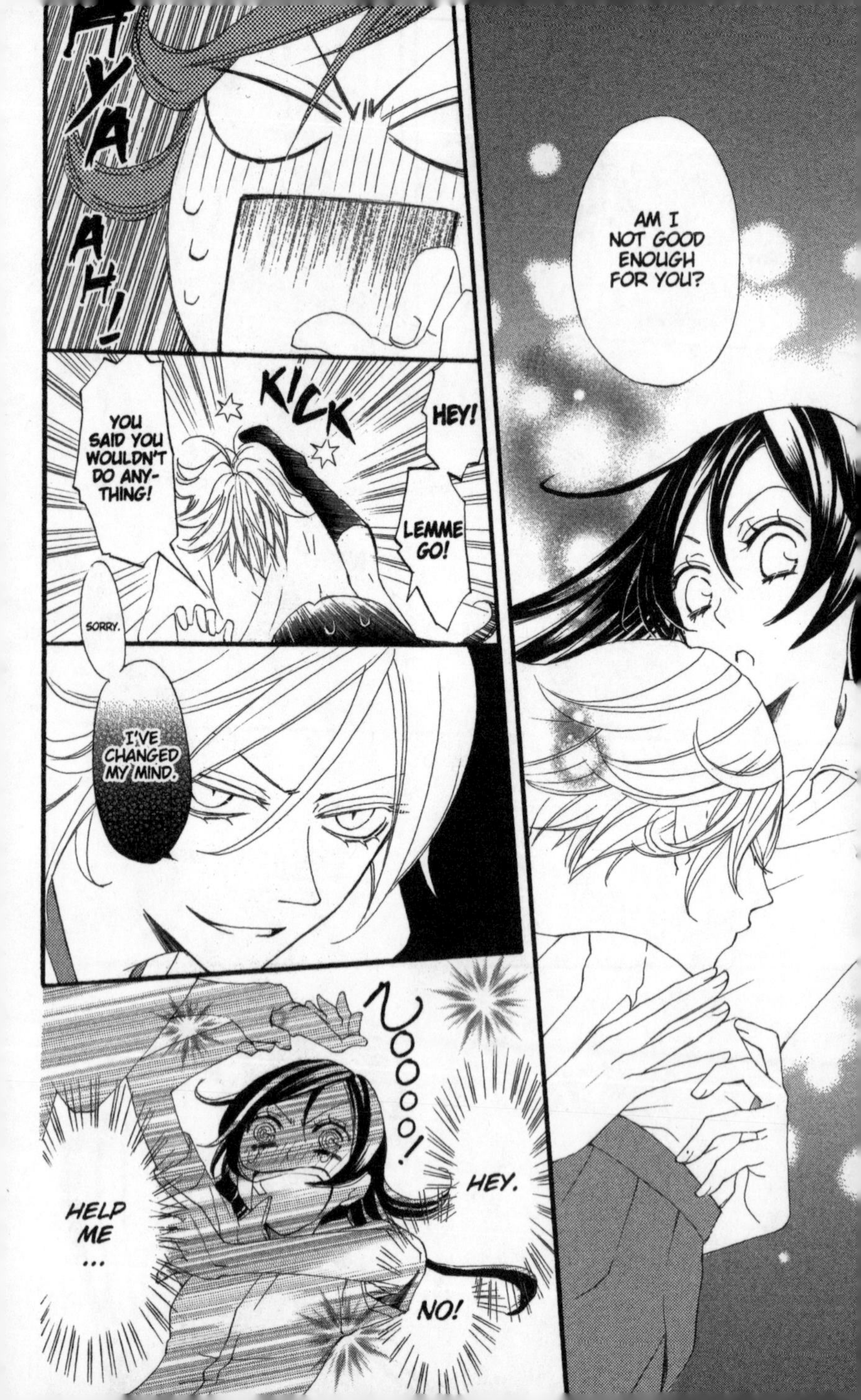
AM I NOT GOOD ENOUGH FOR YOU?
HYAAH!
HEY!
LEMME GO!
KICK
YOU SAID YOU WOULDN'T DO ANY-THING!
SORRY.
I'VE CHANGED MY MIND.
NOOOOO!
HEY.
NO!
HELP ME ...

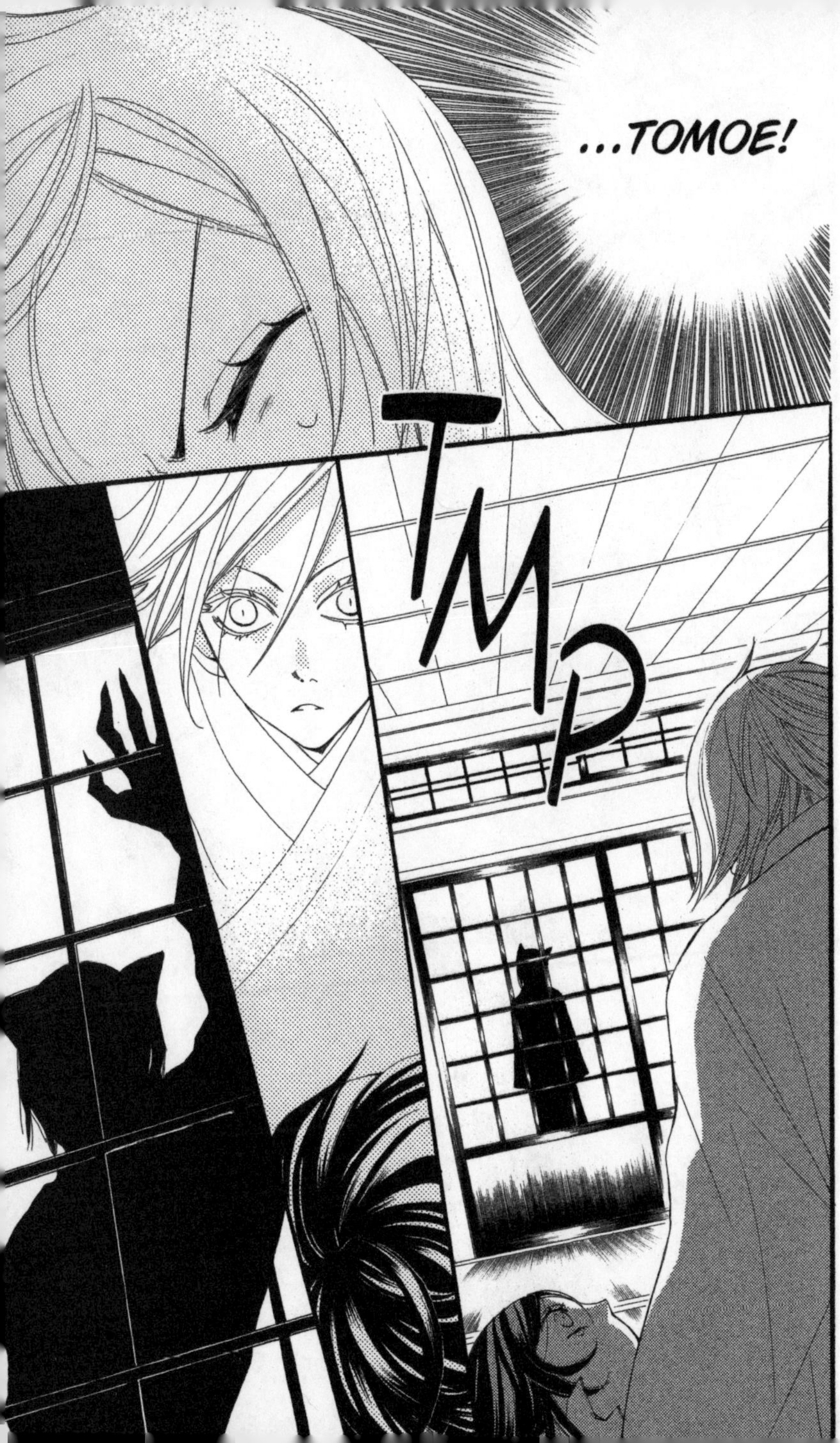
...TOMOE!
TMP

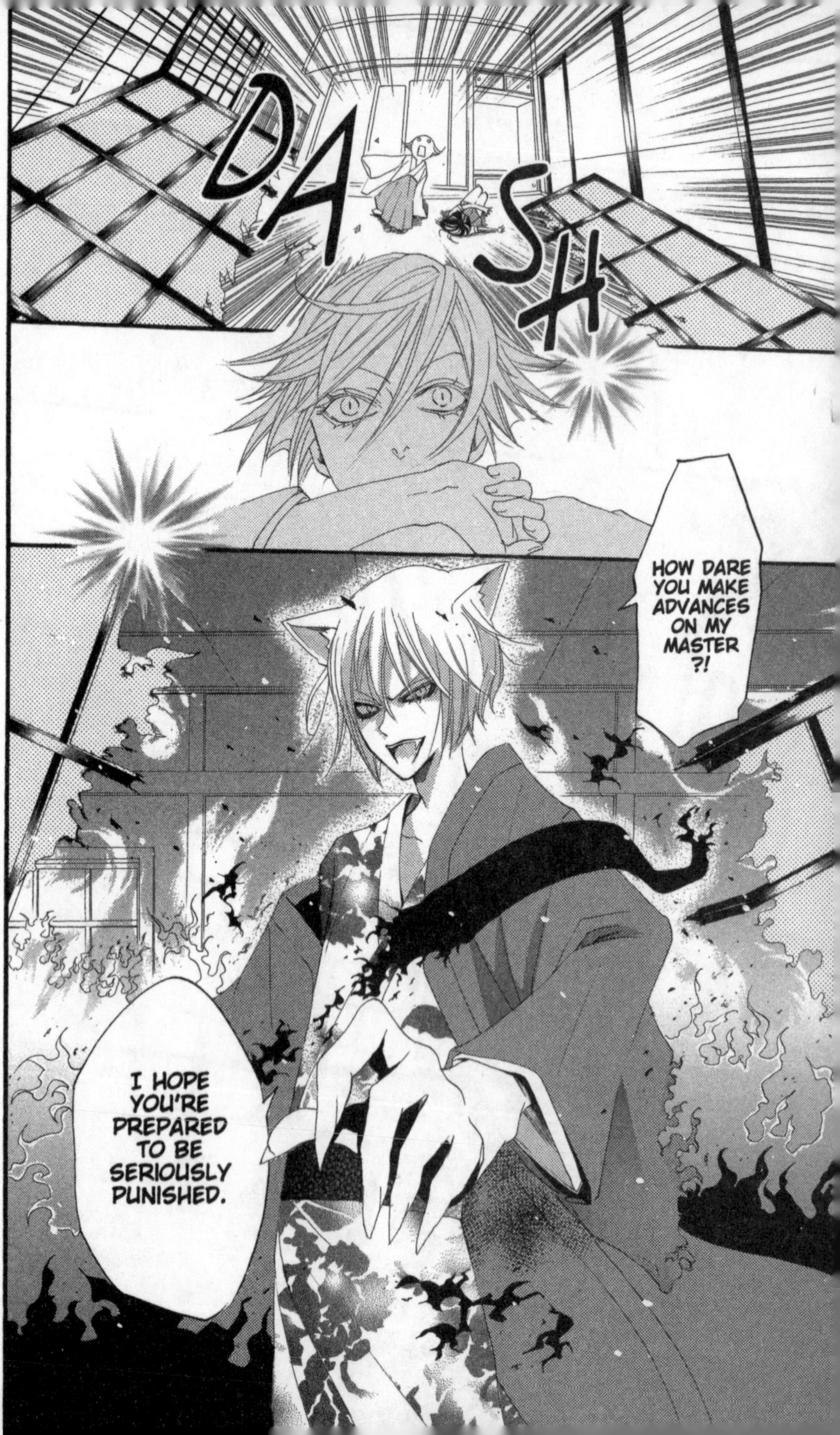
DASH
HOW DARE YOU MAKE ADVANCES ON MY MASTER?!
I HOPE YOU'RE PREPARED TO BE SERIOUSLY PUNISHED.

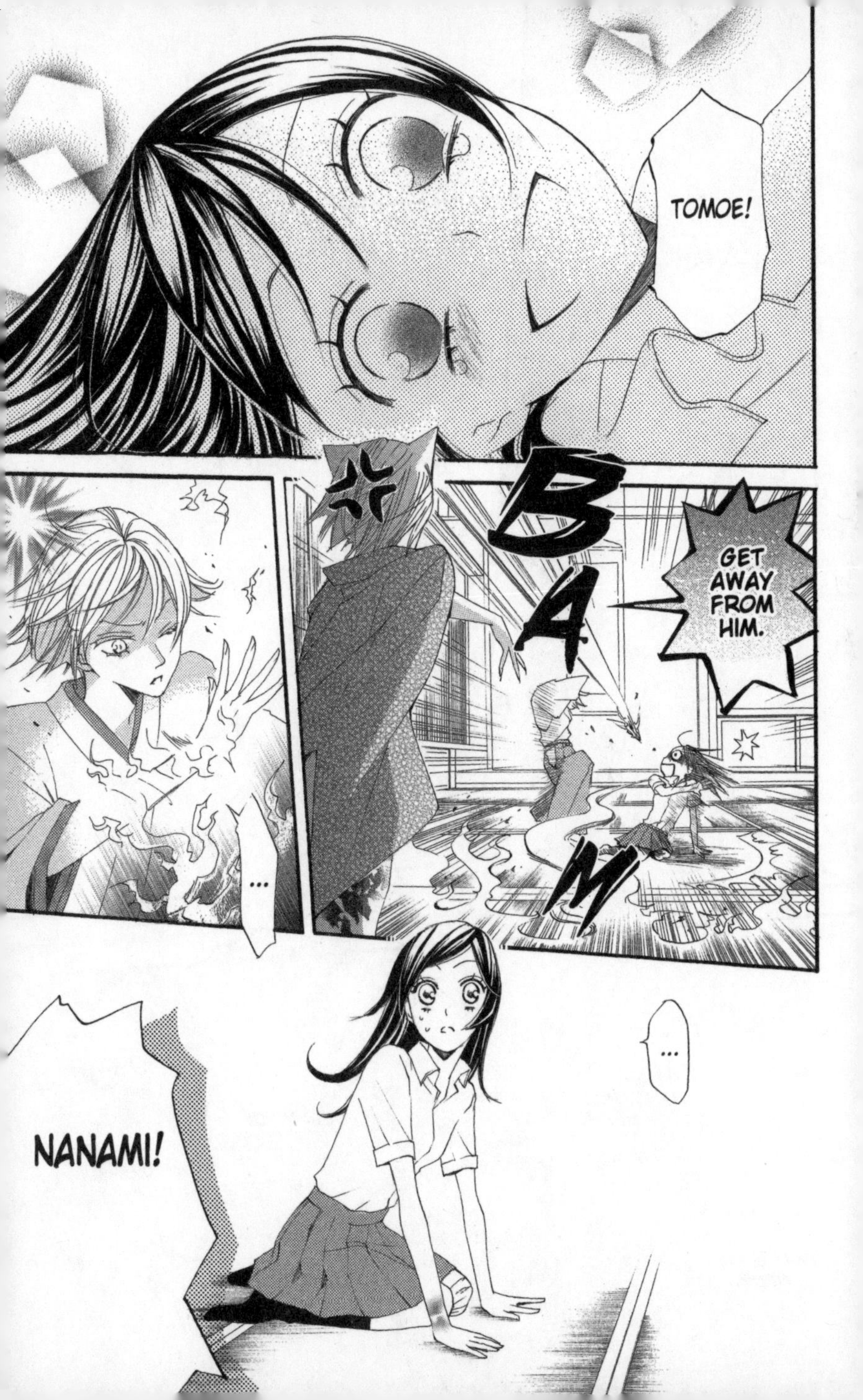
TOMOE!
GET AWAY FROM HIM.
BAM
...
...
NANAMI!

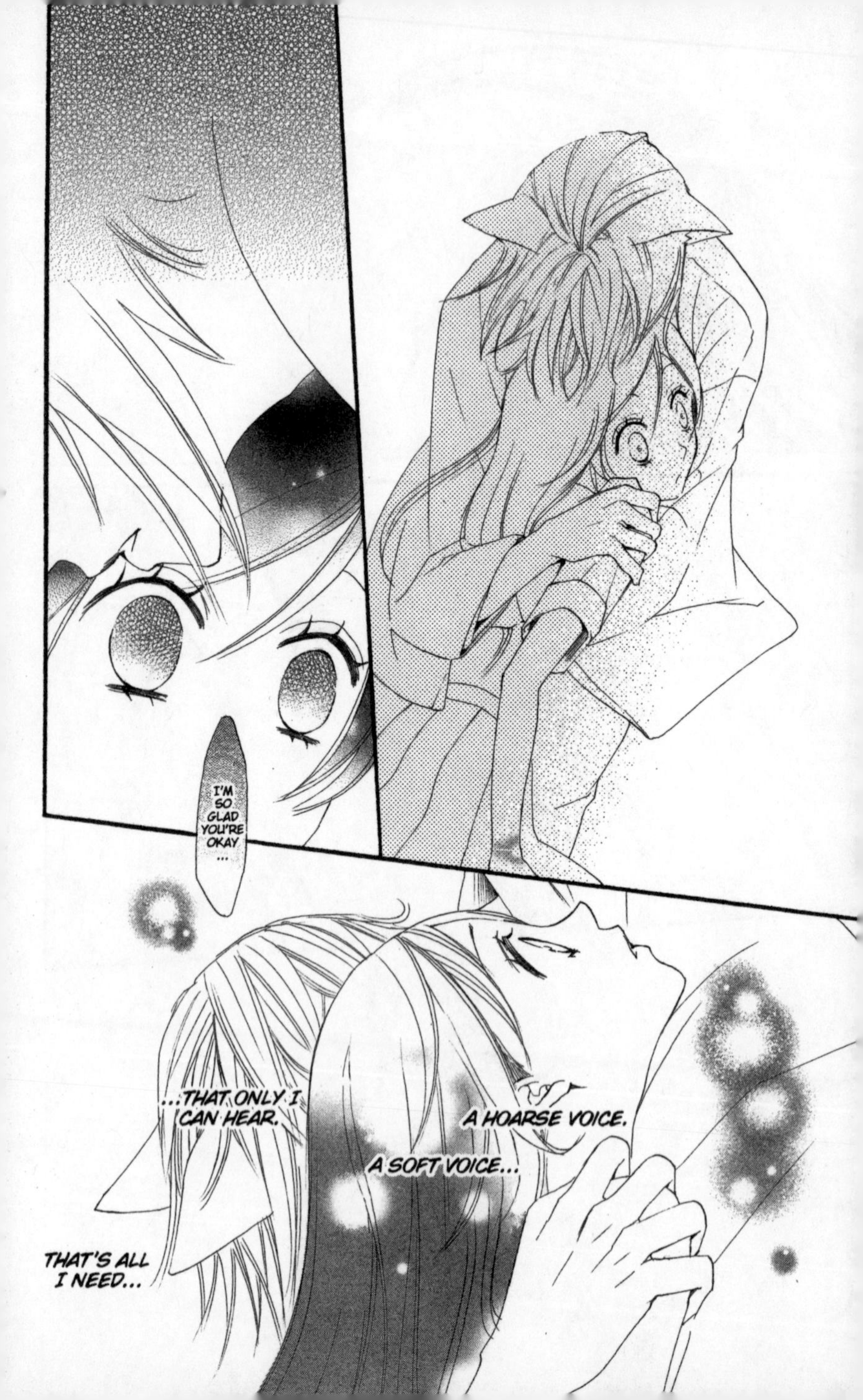
I'M SO GLAD YOU'RE OKAY ...
A HOARSE VOICE.
A SOFT VOICE...
...THAT ONLY I CAN HEAR.
THAT'S ALL I NEED...

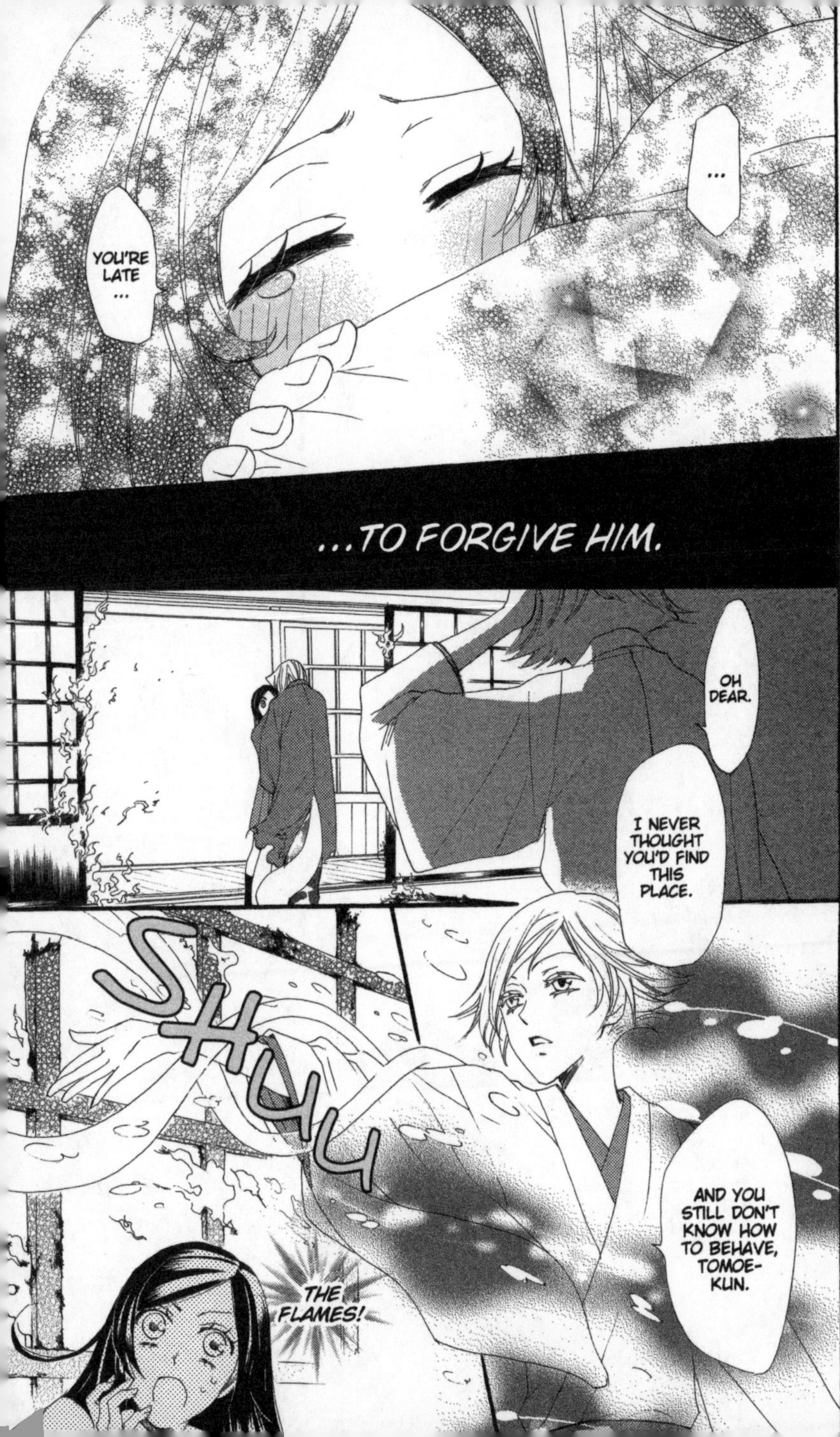
...
YOU'RE LATE ...
...TO FORGIVE HIM.
OH DEAR.
I NEVER THOUGHT YOU'D FIND THIS PLACE.
AND YOU STILL DON'T KNOW HOW TO BEHAVE, TOMOE-KUN.
SHUUU
THE FLAMES!

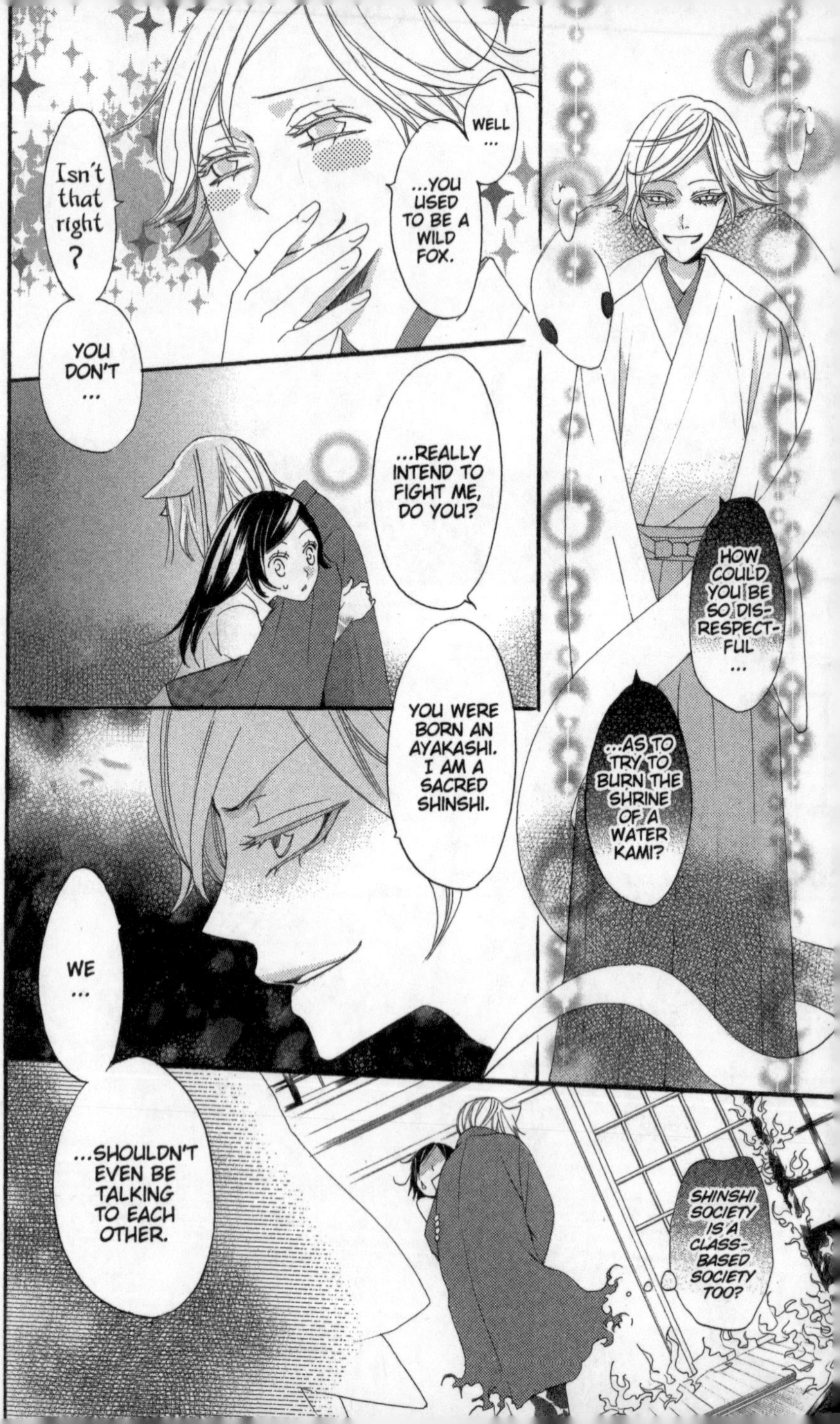
HOW COULD YOU BE SO DIS-RESPECT-FUL...
...AS TO TRY TO BURN THE SHRINE OF A WATER KAMI?
WELL...
...YOU USED TO BE A WILD FOX.
Isn't that right?
YOU DON'T...
...REALLY INTEND TO FIGHT ME, DO YOU?
YOU WERE BORN AN AYAKASHI. I AM A SACRED SHINSHI.
WE...
...SHOULDN'T EVEN BE TALKING TO EACH OTHER.
SHINSHI SOCIETY IS A CLASS-BASED SOCIETY TOO?

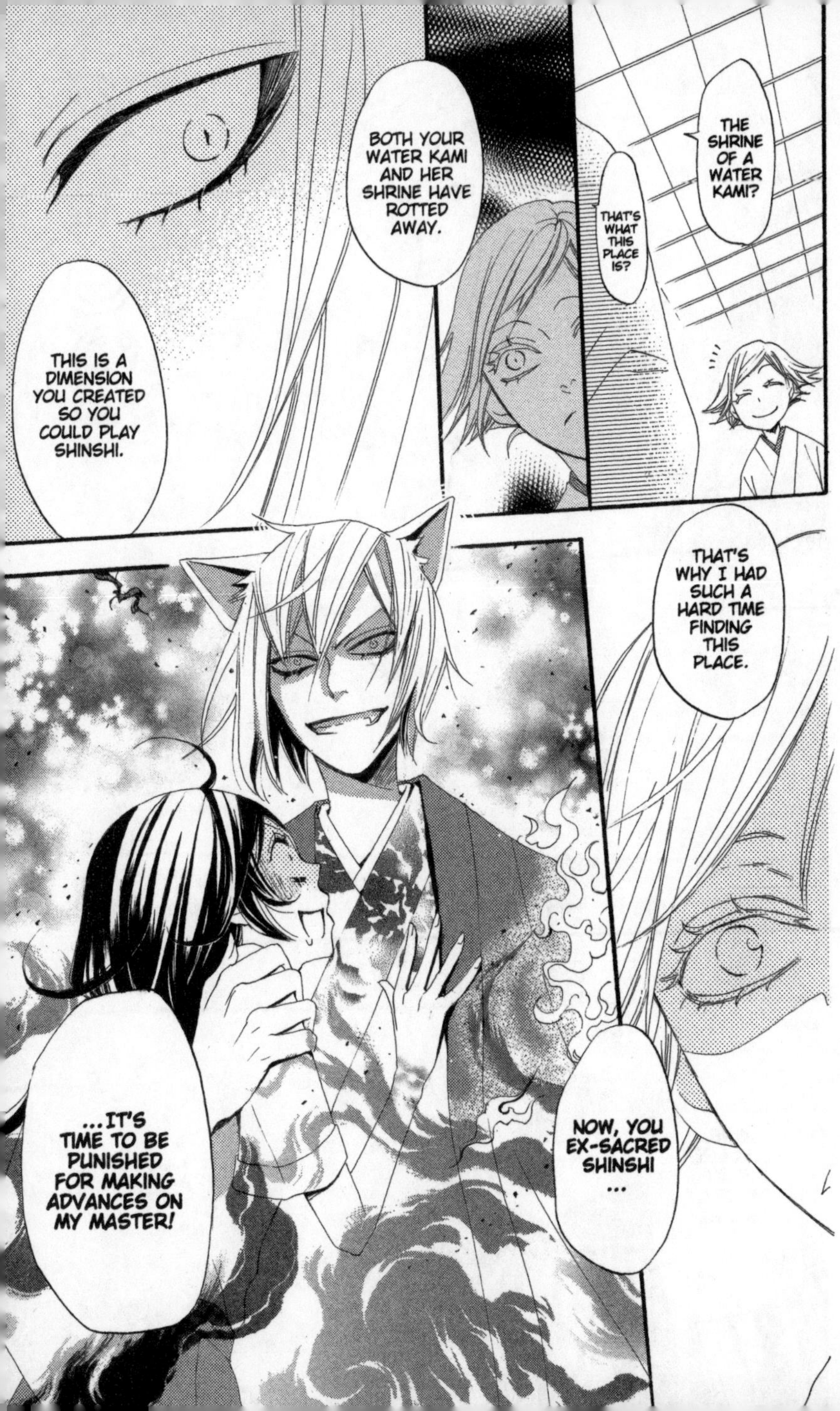
THE SHRINE OF A WATER KAMI?
THAT'S WHAT THIS PLACE IS?
BOTH YOUR WATER KAMI AND HER SHRINE HAVE ROTTED AWAY.
THIS IS A DIMENSION YOU CREATED SO YOU COULD PLAY SHINSHI.
THAT'S WHY I HAD SUCH A HARD TIME FINDING THIS PLACE.
NOW, YOU EX-SACRED SHINSHI...
...IT'S TIME TO BE PUNISHED FOR MAKING ADVANCES ON MY MASTER!

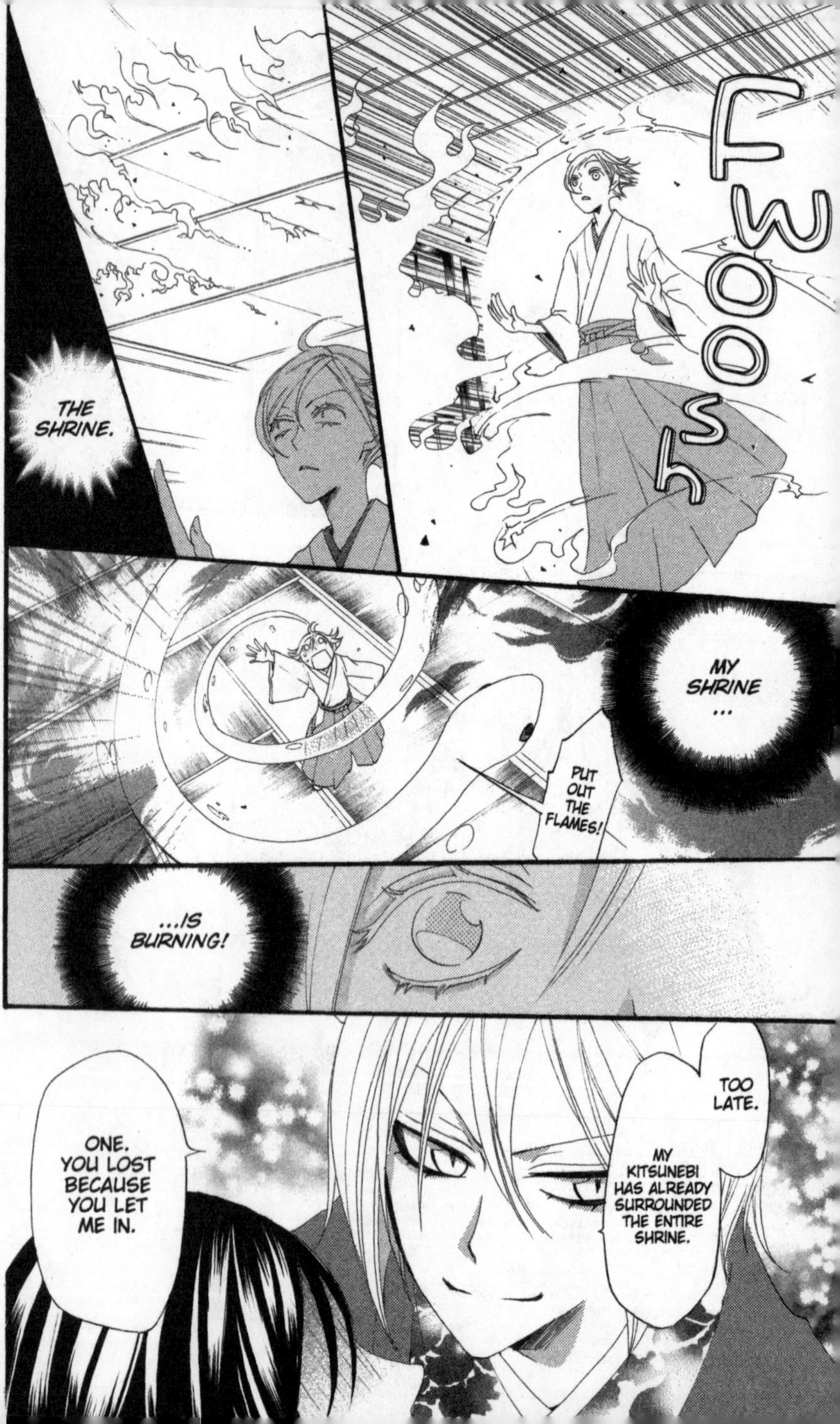
FWOOSH
THE SHRINE.
MY SHRINE...
PUT OUT THE FLAMES!
...IS BURNING!
TOO LATE.
MY KITSUNEBI HAS ALREADY SURROUNDED THE ENTIRE SHRINE.
ONE. YOU LOST BECAUSE YOU LET ME IN.

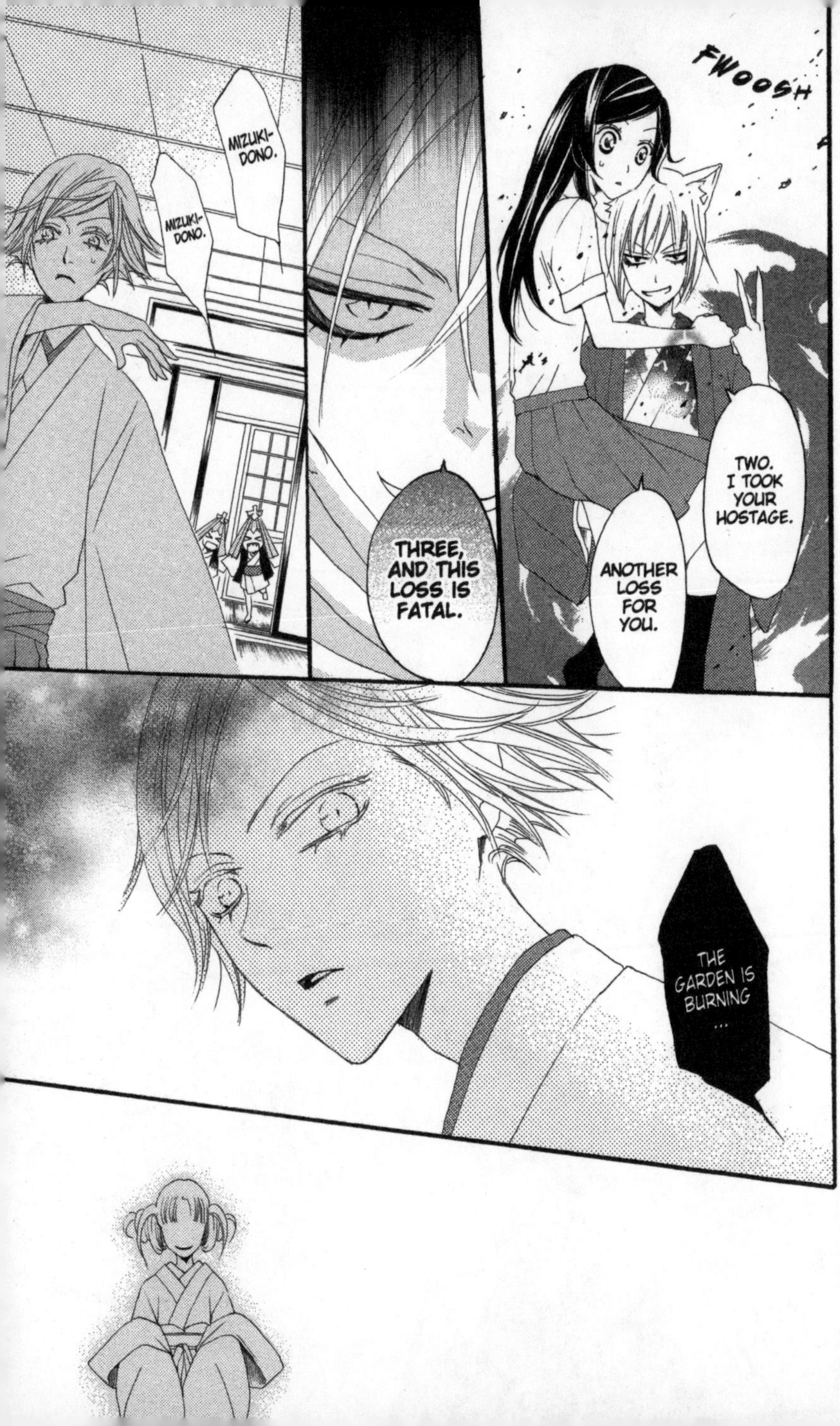
FWOOSH
TWO. I TOOK YOUR HOSTAGE.
ANOTHER LOSS FOR YOU.
THREE, AND THIS LOSS IS FATAL.
MIZUKI-DONO.
MIZUKI-DONO.
THE GARDEN IS BURNING ...

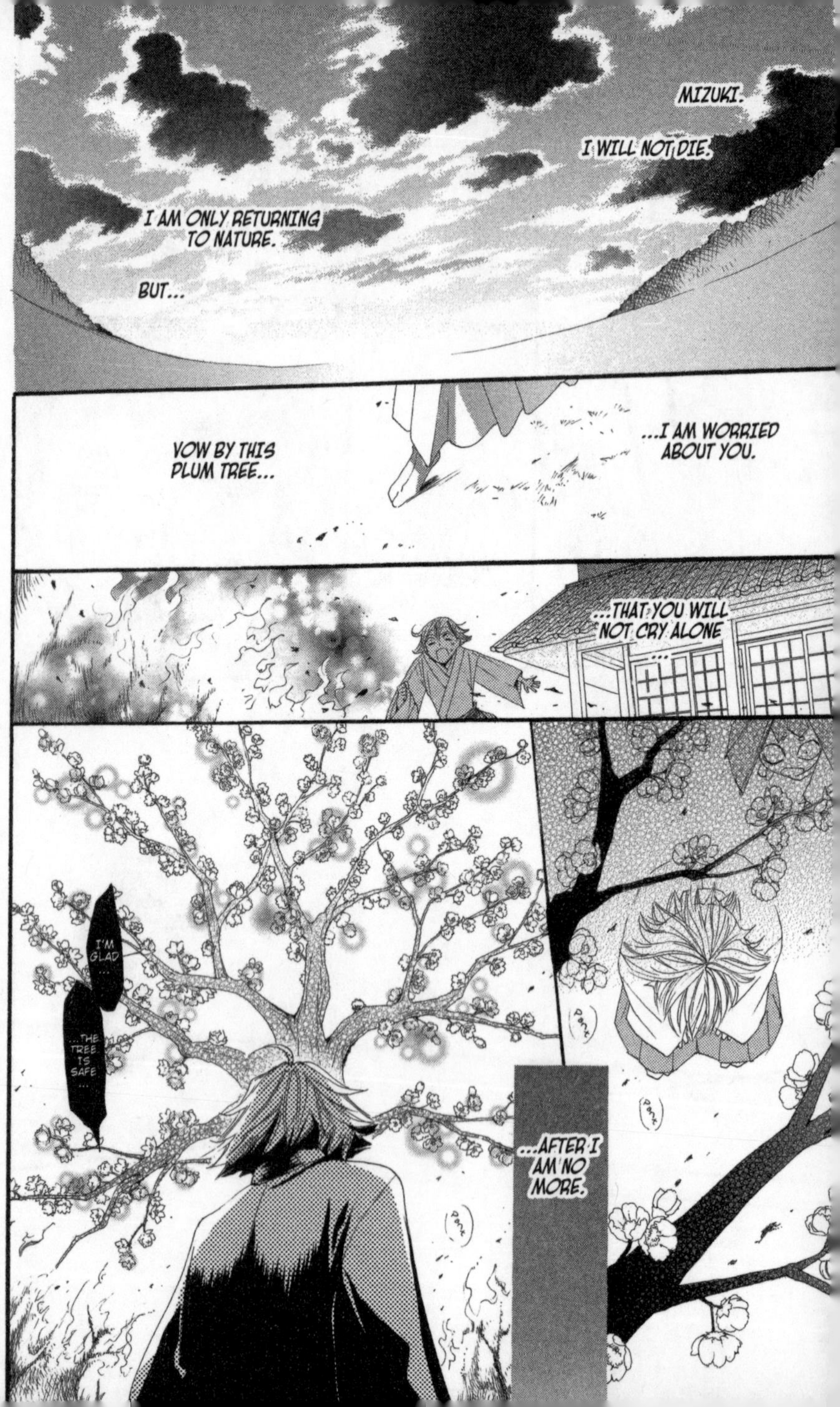
MIZUKI.
I WILL NOT DIE.
I AM ONLY RETURNING TO NATURE.
BUT...
...I AM WORRIED ABOUT YOU.
VOW BY THIS PLUM TREE...
...THAT YOU WILL NOT CRY ALONE ...
...AFTER I AM NO MORE.
I'M GLAD...
...THE TREE IS SAFE...

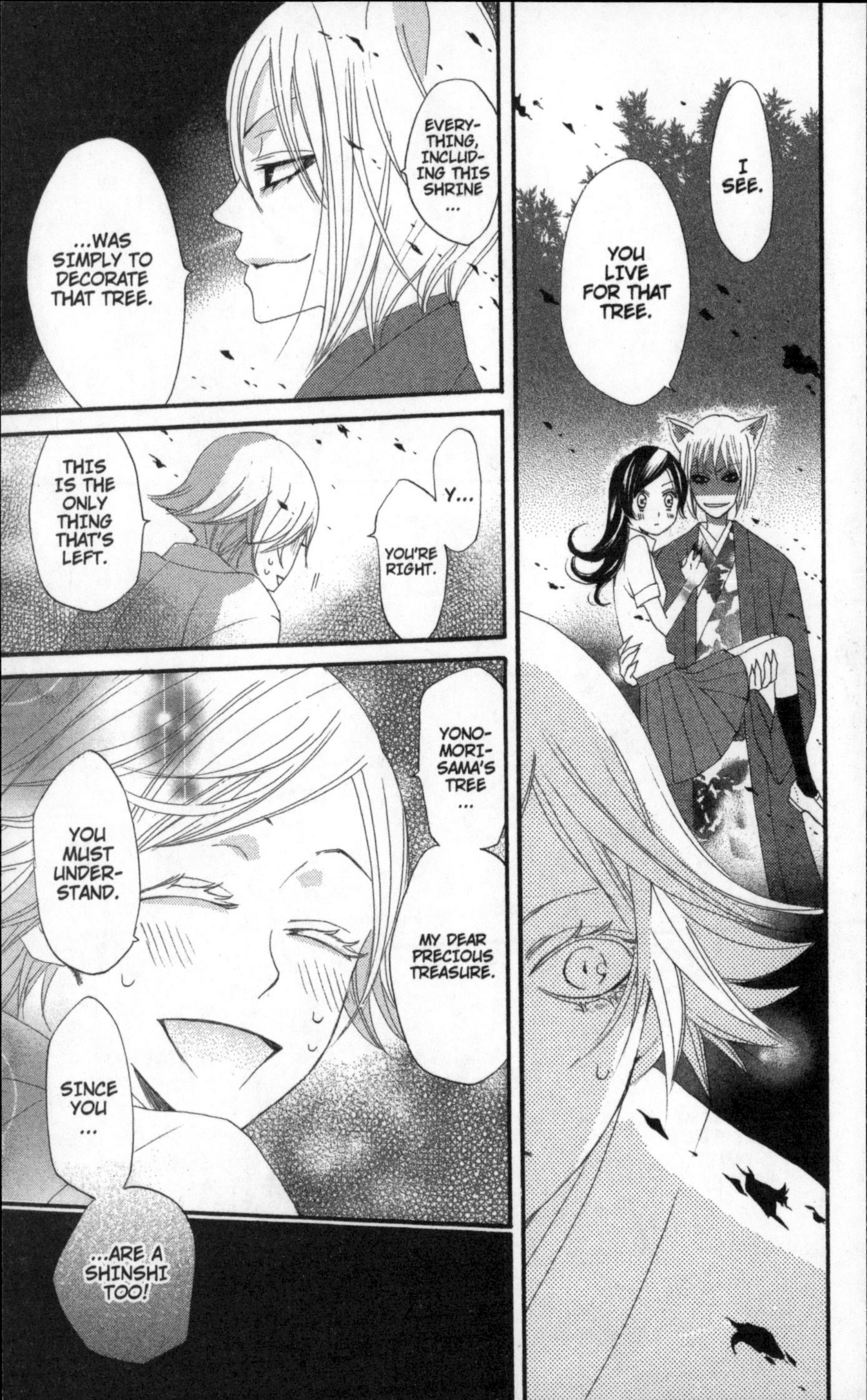
I SEE.
YOU LIVE FOR THAT TREE.
EVERY-THING, INCLUD-ING THIS SHRINE...
...WAS SIMPLY TO DECORATE THAT TREE.
Y...
YOU'RE RIGHT.
THIS IS THE ONLY THING THAT'S LEFT.
YONO-MORI-SAMA'S TREE...
MY DEAR PRECIOUS TREASURE.
YOU MUST UNDER-STAND.
SINCE YOU...
...ARE A SHINSHI TOO!

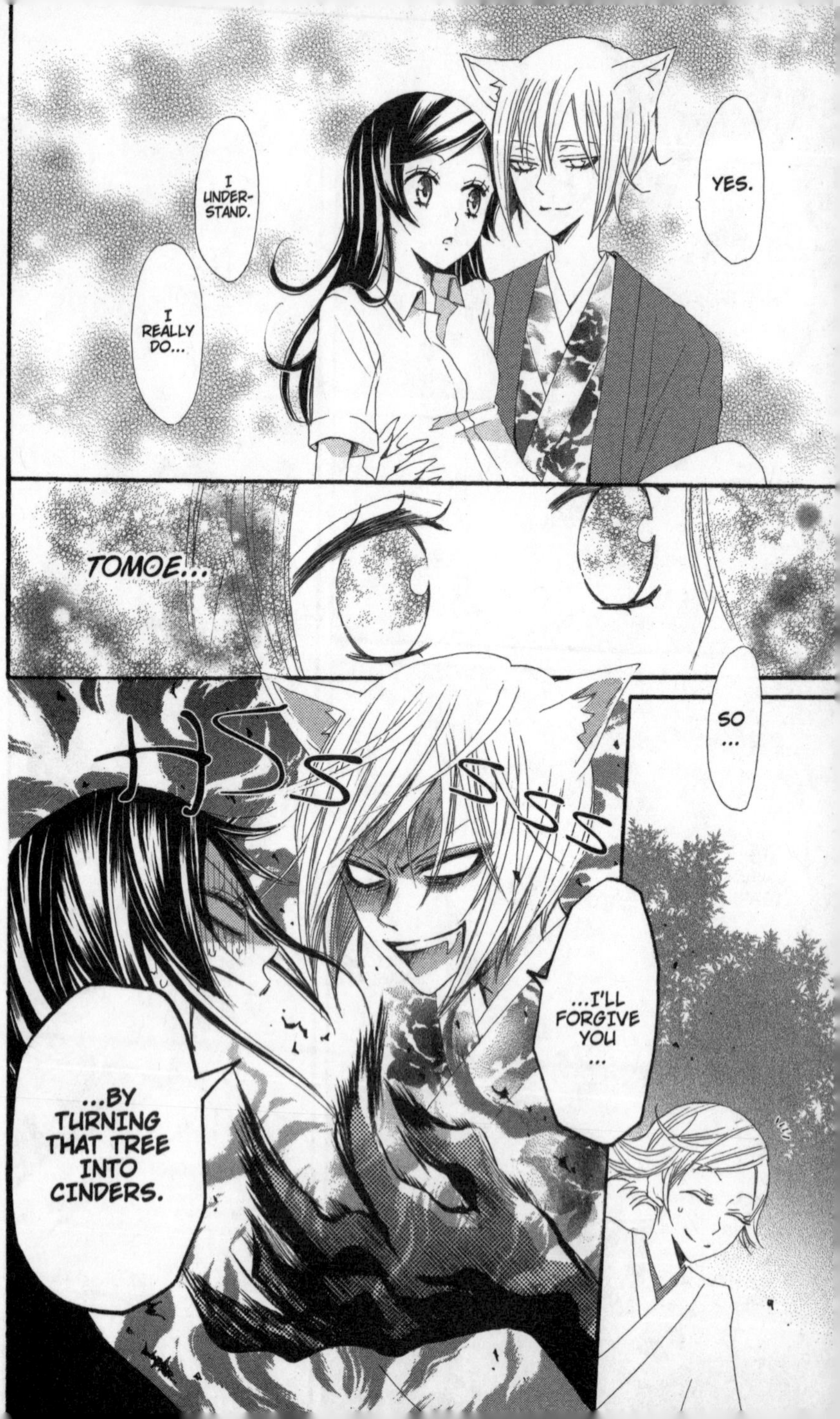
YES.
I UNDER-STAND.
I REALLY DO...
TOMOE...
SO...
HSSSS
...I'LL FORGIVE YOU...
...BY TURNING THAT TREE INTO CINDERS.

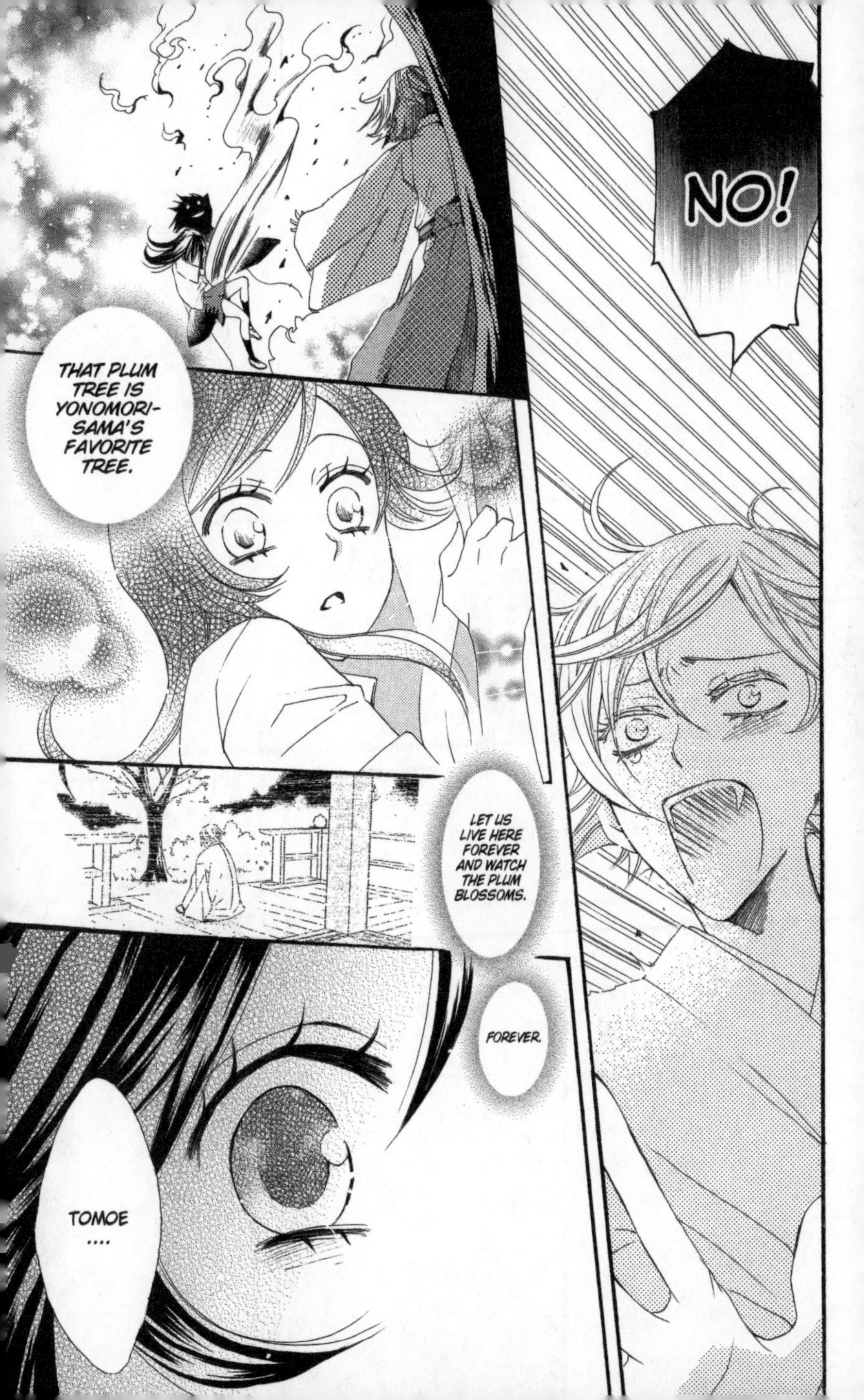
NO!
THAT PLUM TREE IS YONOMORI-SAMA'S FAVORITE TREE.
LET US LIVE HERE FOREVER AND WATCH THE PLUM BLOSSOMS.
FOREVER.
TOMOE ....

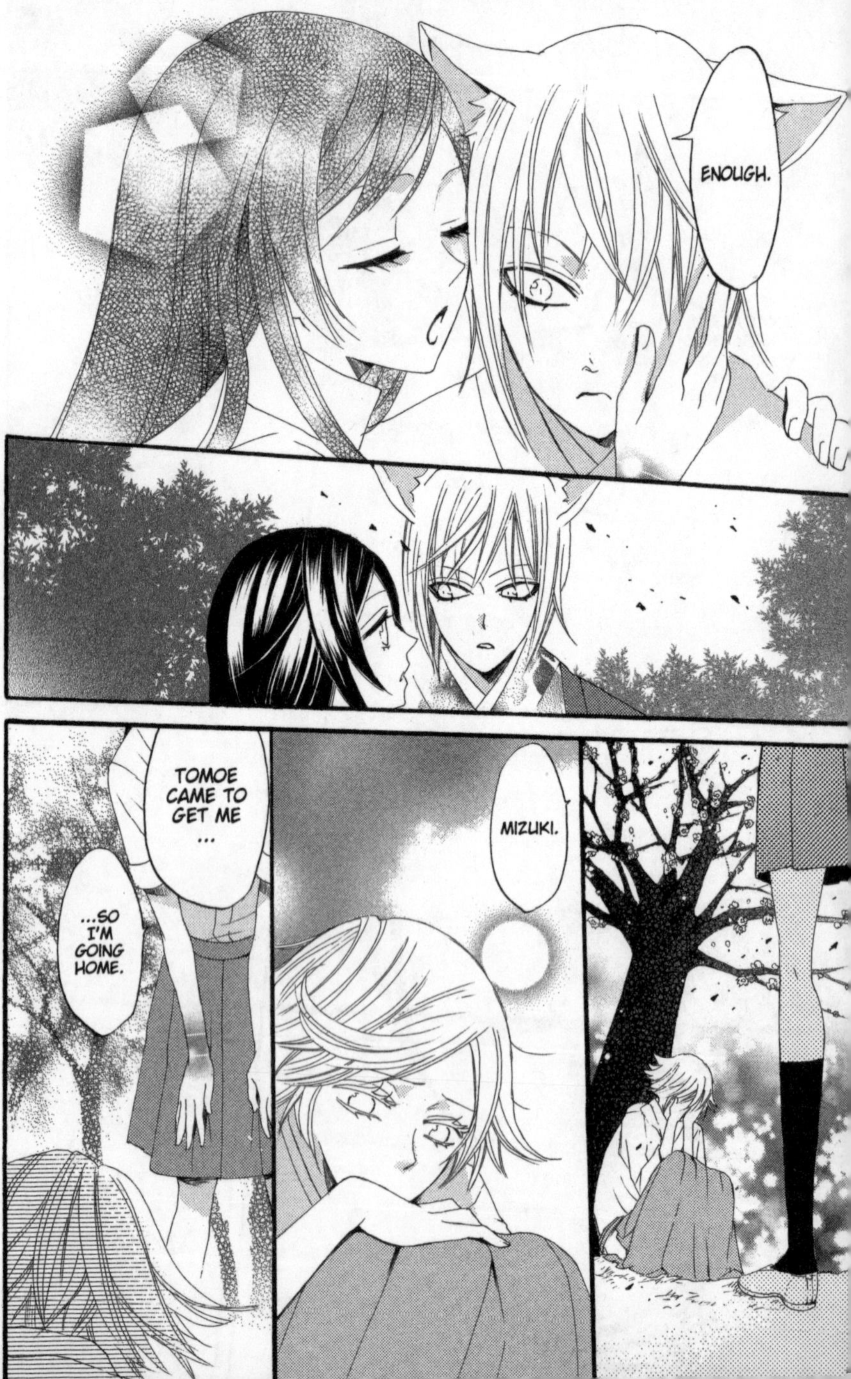
ENOUGH.
MIZUKI.
TOMOE CAME TO GET ME ...
...SO I'M GOING HOME.

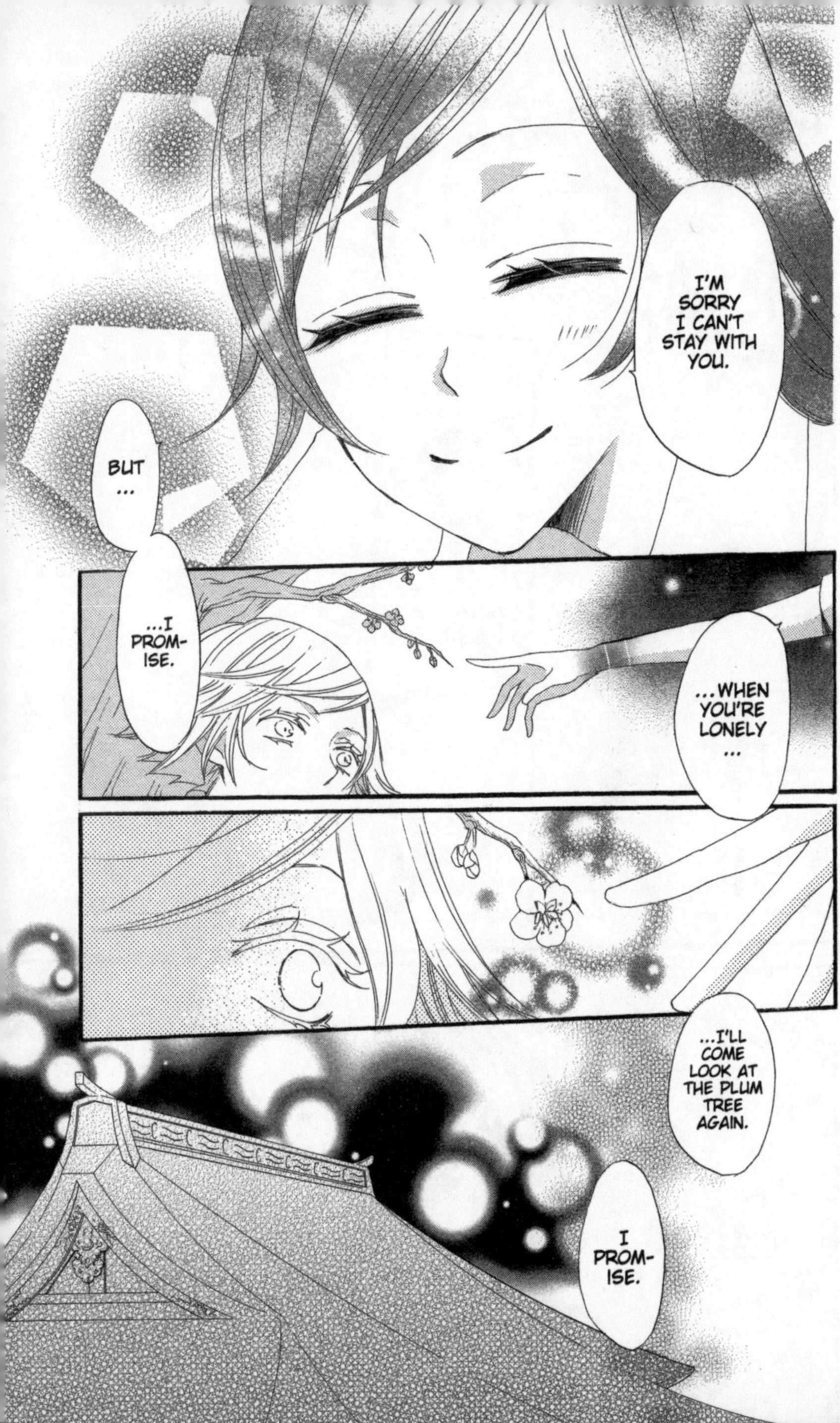
I'M SORRY I CAN'T STAY WITH YOU.
BUT ...
...WHEN YOU'RE LONELY ...
...I PROMISE.
...I'LL COME LOOK AT THE PLUM TREE AGAIN.
I PROMISE.

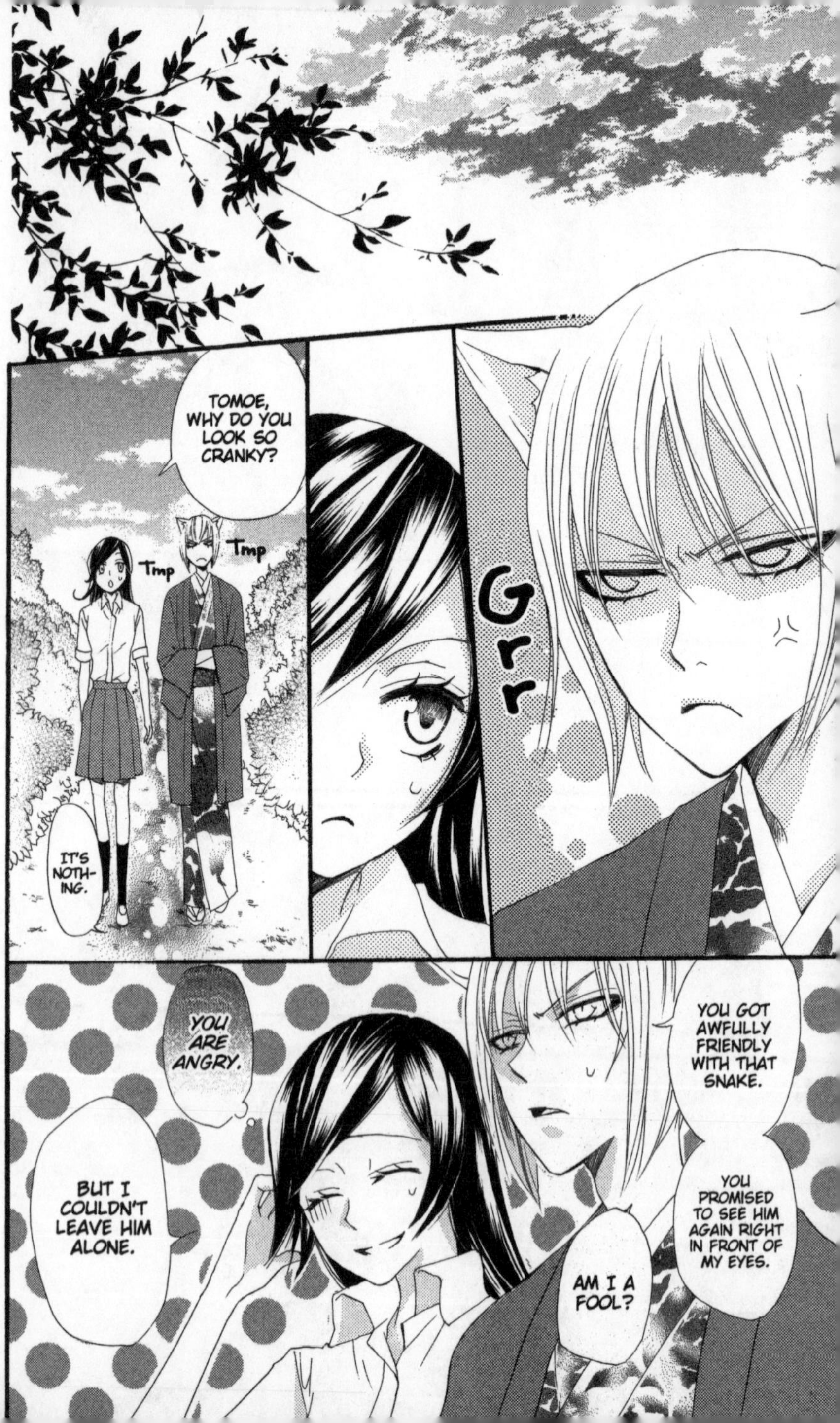
Grr
TOMOE, WHY DO YOU LOOK SO CRANKY?
Tmp
Tmp
IT'S NOTH-ING.
YOU GOT AWFULLY FRIENDLY WITH THAT SNAKE.
YOU PROMISED TO SEE HIM AGAIN RIGHT IN FRONT OF MY EYES.
YOU ARE ANGRY.
AM I A FOOL?
BUT I COULDN'T LEAVE HIM ALONE.

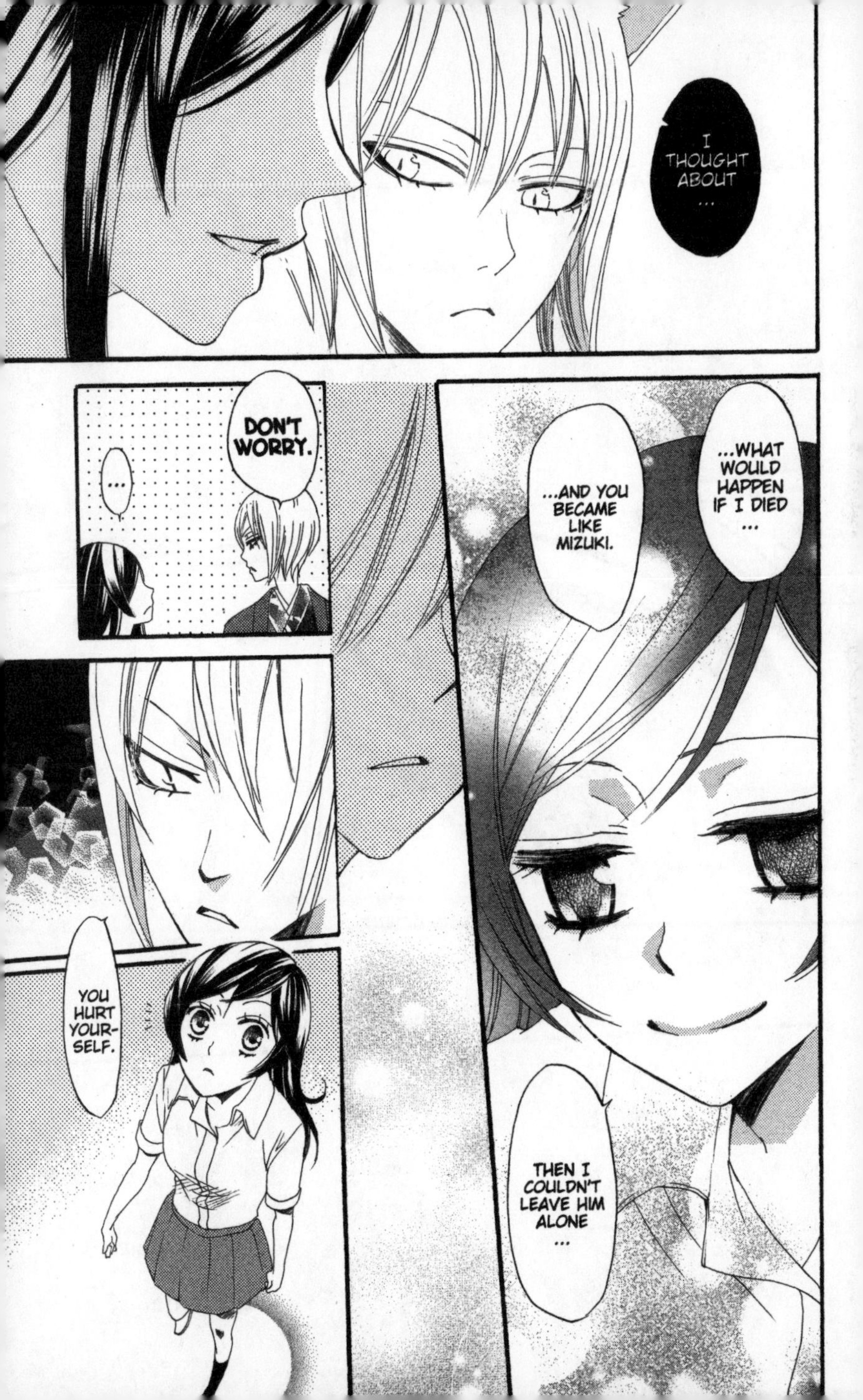
I THOUGHT ABOUT ...
...WHAT WOULD HAPPEN IF I DIED ...
...AND YOU BECAME LIKE MIZUKI.
THEN I COULDN'T LEAVE HIM ALONE ...
DON'T WORRY.
...
YOU HURT YOUR-SELF.

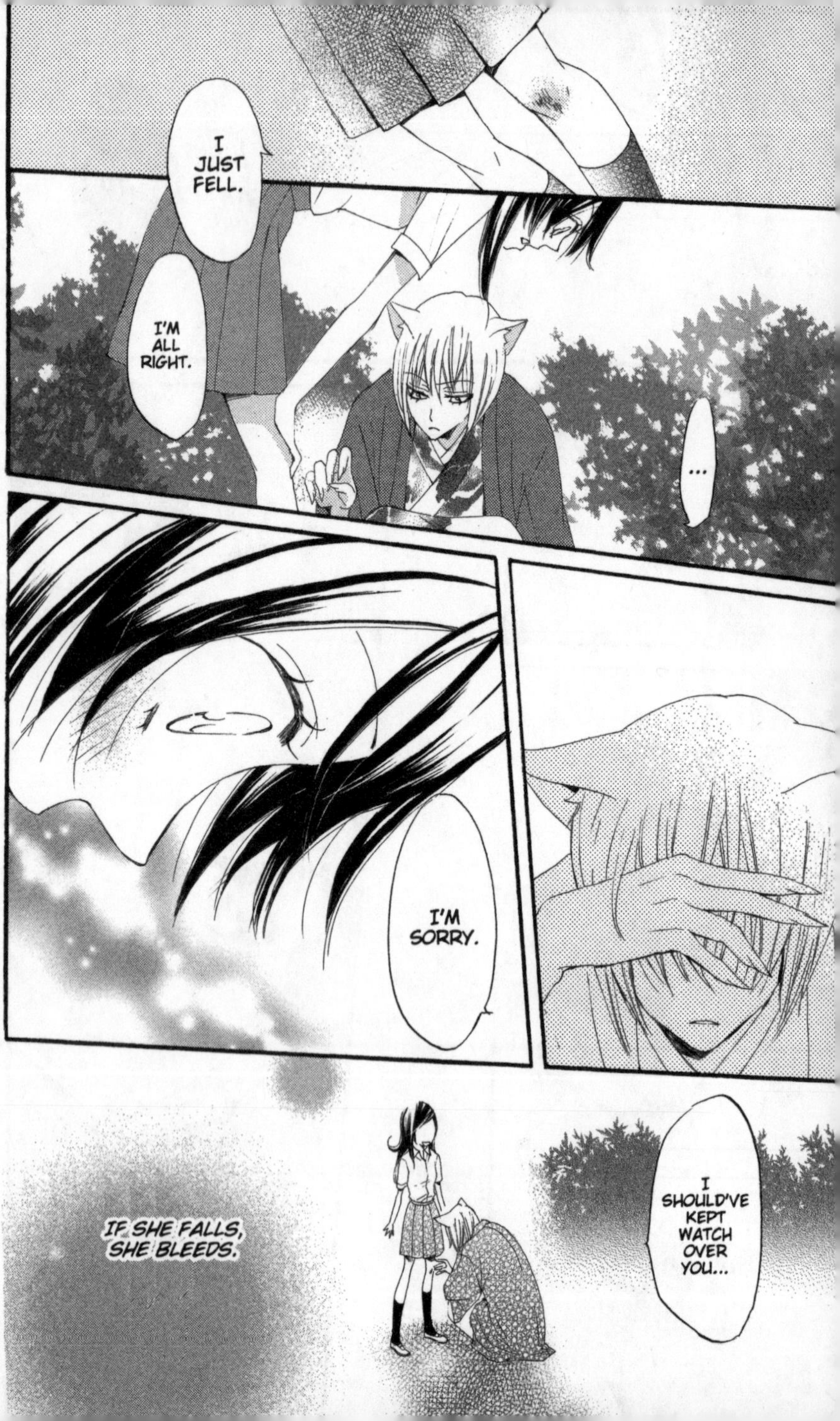

I JUST FELL.
I'M ALL RIGHT.
...
I'M SORRY.
I SHOULD'VE KEPT WATCH OVER YOU...
IF SHE FALLS, SHE BLEEDS.

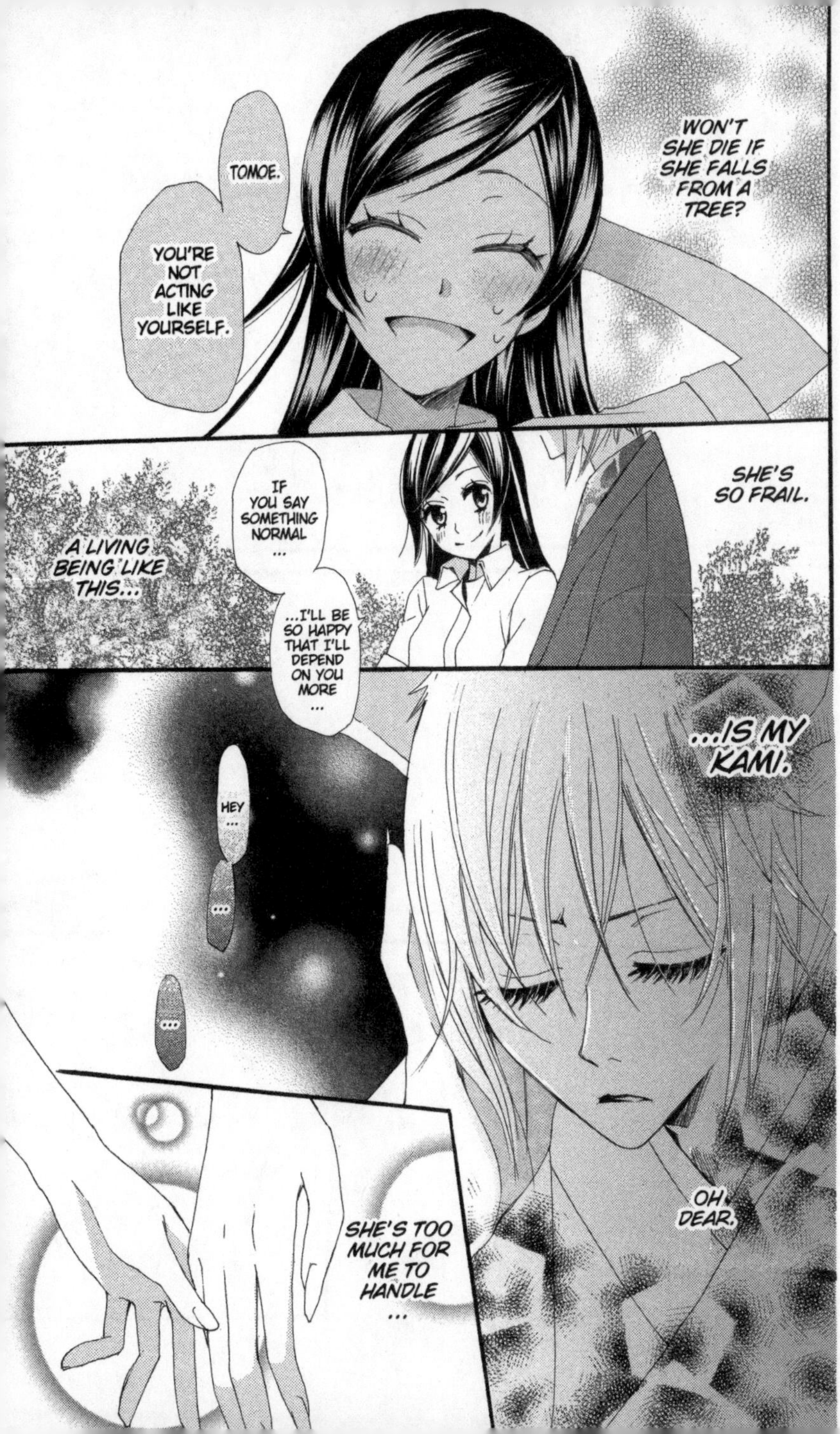
WON'T SHE DIE IF SHE FALLS FROM A TREE?
TOMOE.
YOU'RE NOT ACTING LIKE YOURSELF.
SHE'S SO FRAIL.
IF YOU SAY SOMETHING NORMAL ...
...I'LL BE SO HAPPY THAT I'LL DEPEND ON YOU MORE ...
A LIVING BEING LIKE THIS...
...IS MY KAMI.
HEY ...
...
...
OH DEAR.
SHE'S TOO MUCH FOR ME TO HANDLE ...

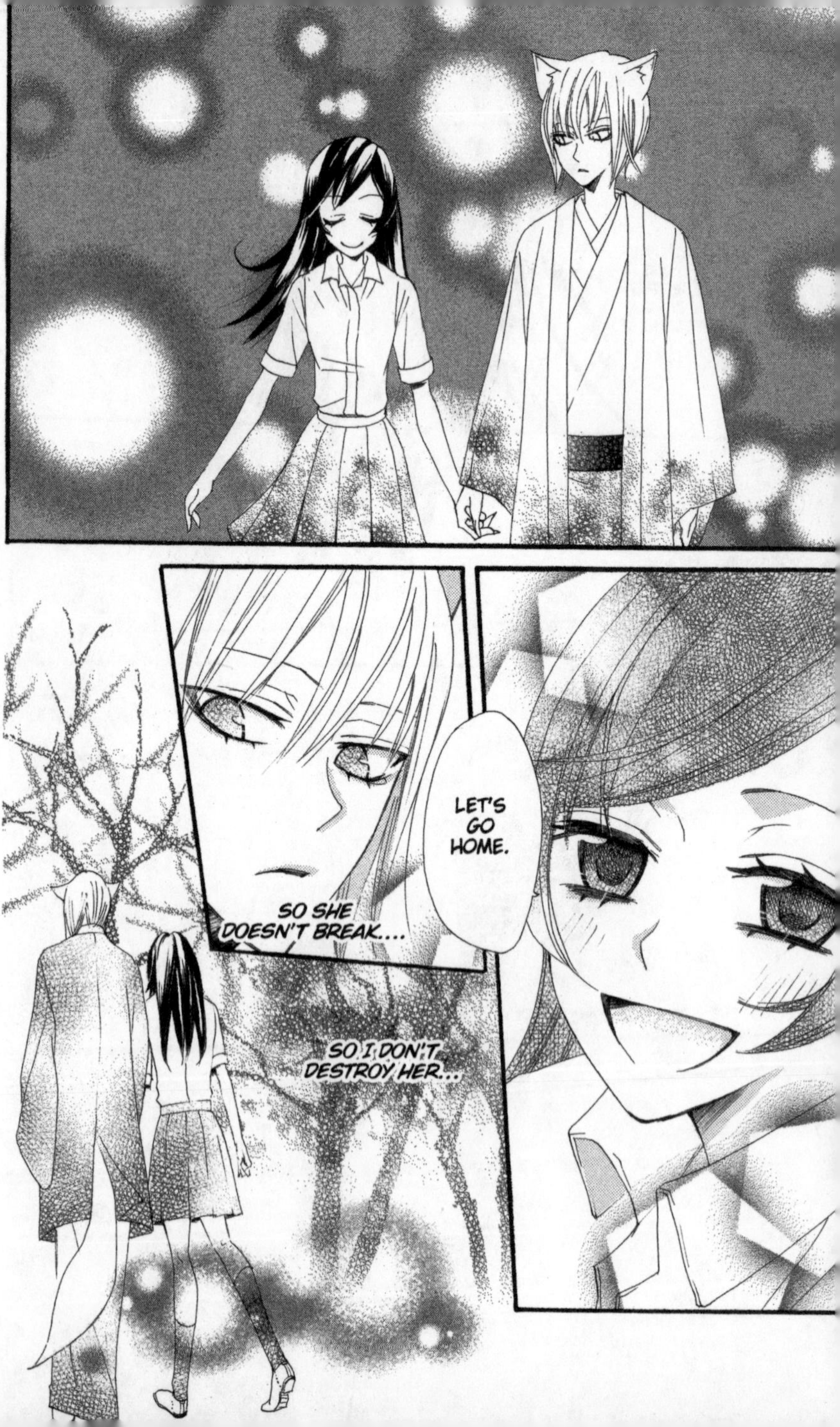
LET'S GO HOME.
SO SHE DOESN'T BREAK....
SO I DON'T DESTROY HER...

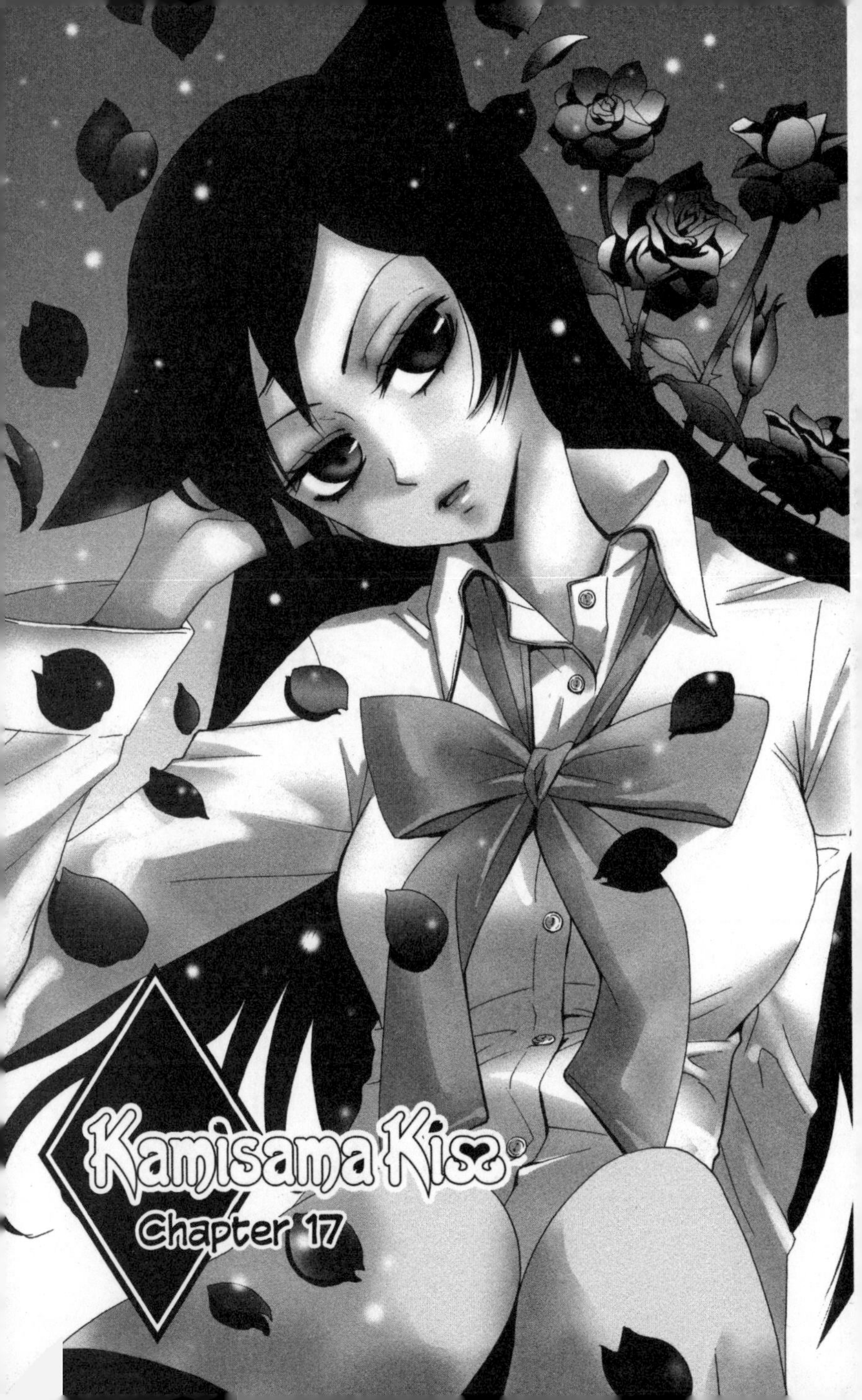
Kamisama Kiss
Chapter 17

Tomoe's Ennui Blog

I came to visit!

Month △ , Day ○

Mizuki, a fellow shinshi, came to visit the shrine.

Glug Glug

We had tea and talked about the hard life of a shinshi. It was a fun day, and I hadn't had that in a while.

See you!

Nowadays, I don't see Nanami much.

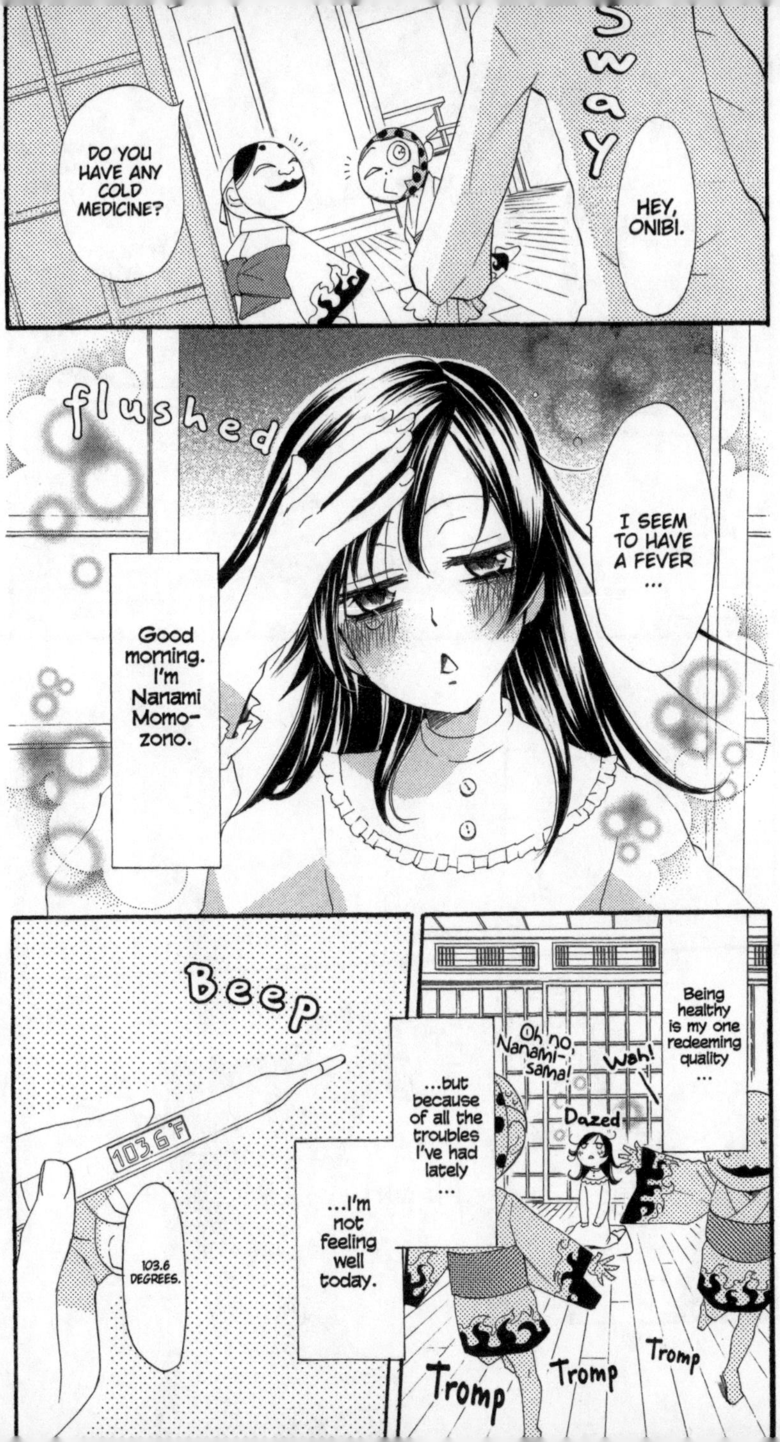
Sway
HEY, ONIBI.
DO YOU HAVE ANY COLD MEDICINE?
I SEEM TO HAVE A FEVER ...
flushed
Good morning. I'm Nanami Momo-zono.
Being healthy is my one redeeming quality ...
Wah!
Oh no, Nanami-sama!
Dazed
...but because of all the troubles I've had lately ...
...I'm not feeling well today.
Tromp
Tromp
Tromp
Beep
103.6°F
103.6 DEGREES.

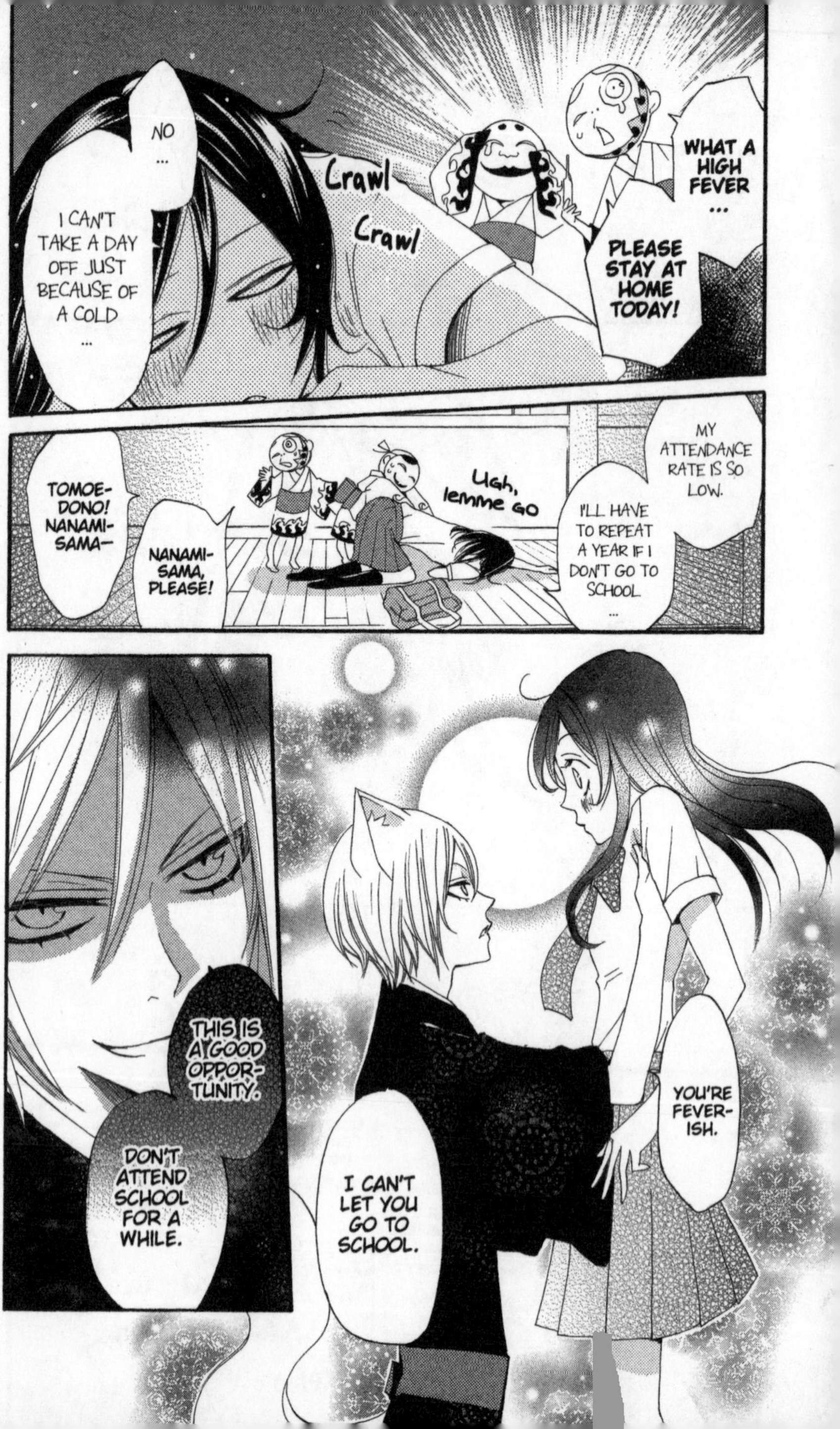
WHAT A HIGH FEVER ...
PLEASE STAY AT HOME TODAY!
Crawl
Crawl
NO ...
I CAN'T TAKE A DAY OFF JUST BECAUSE OF A COLD ...
MY ATTENDANCE RATE IS SO LOW.
I'LL HAVE TO REPEAT A YEAR IF I DON'T GO TO SCHOOL ...
Ugh, lemme go
NANAMI-SAMA, PLEASE!
TOMOE-DONO! NANAMI-SAMA—
YOU'RE FEVER-ISH.
I CAN'T LET YOU GO TO SCHOOL.
THIS IS A GOOD OPPOR-TUNITY.
DON'T ATTEND SCHOOL FOR A WHILE.

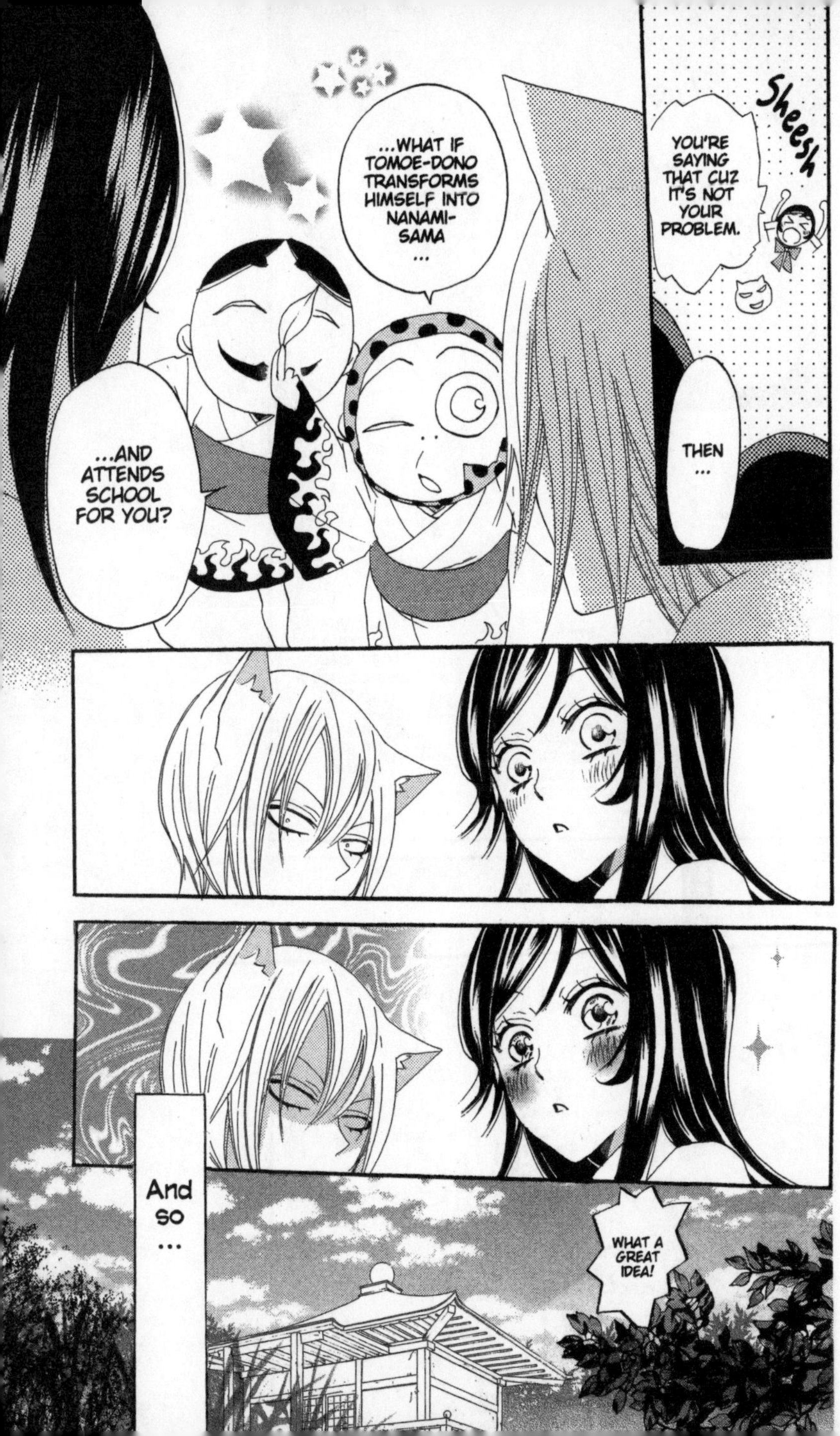
Sheesh
YOU'RE SAYING THAT CUZ IT'S NOT YOUR PROBLEM.
THEN ...
...WHAT IF TOMOE-DONO TRANSFORMS HIMSELF INTO NANAMI-SAMA ...
...AND ATTENDS SCHOOL FOR YOU?
WHAT A GREAT IDEA!
And so ...

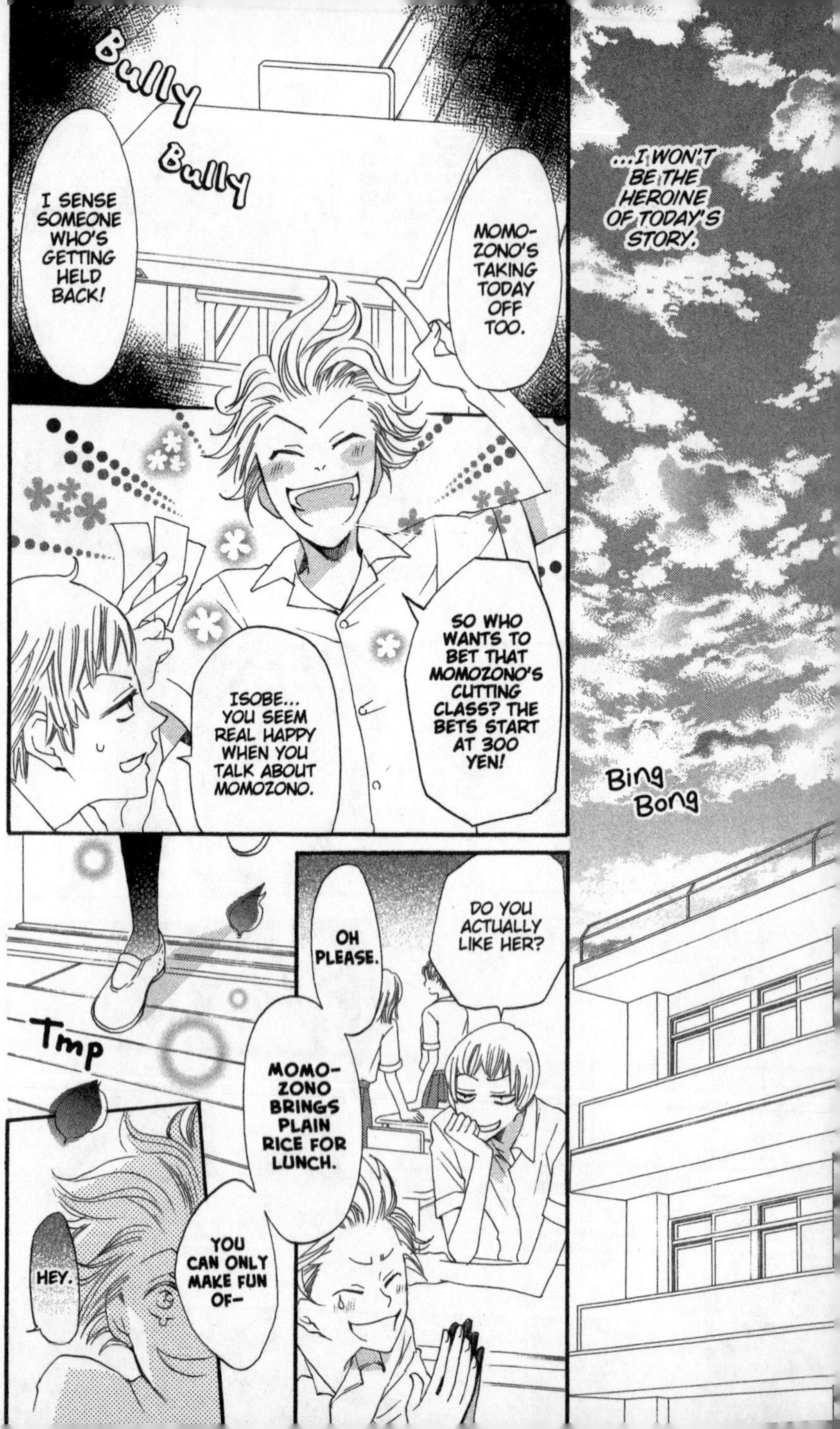

...I WON'T BE THE HEROINE OF TODAY'S STORY.
Bing Bong
MOMO-ZONO'S TAKING TODAY OFF TOO.
Bully Bully
I SENSE SOMEONE WHO'S GETTING HELD BACK!
SO WHO WANTS TO BET THAT MOMOZONO'S CUTTING CLASS? THE BETS START AT 300 YEN!
ISOBE... YOU SEEM REAL HAPPY WHEN YOU TALK ABOUT MOMOZONO.
DO YOU ACTUALLY LIKE HER?
OH PLEASE.
MOMO-ZONO BRINGS PLAIN RICE FOR LUNCH.
YOU CAN ONLY MAKE FUN OF-
Tmp
HEY.

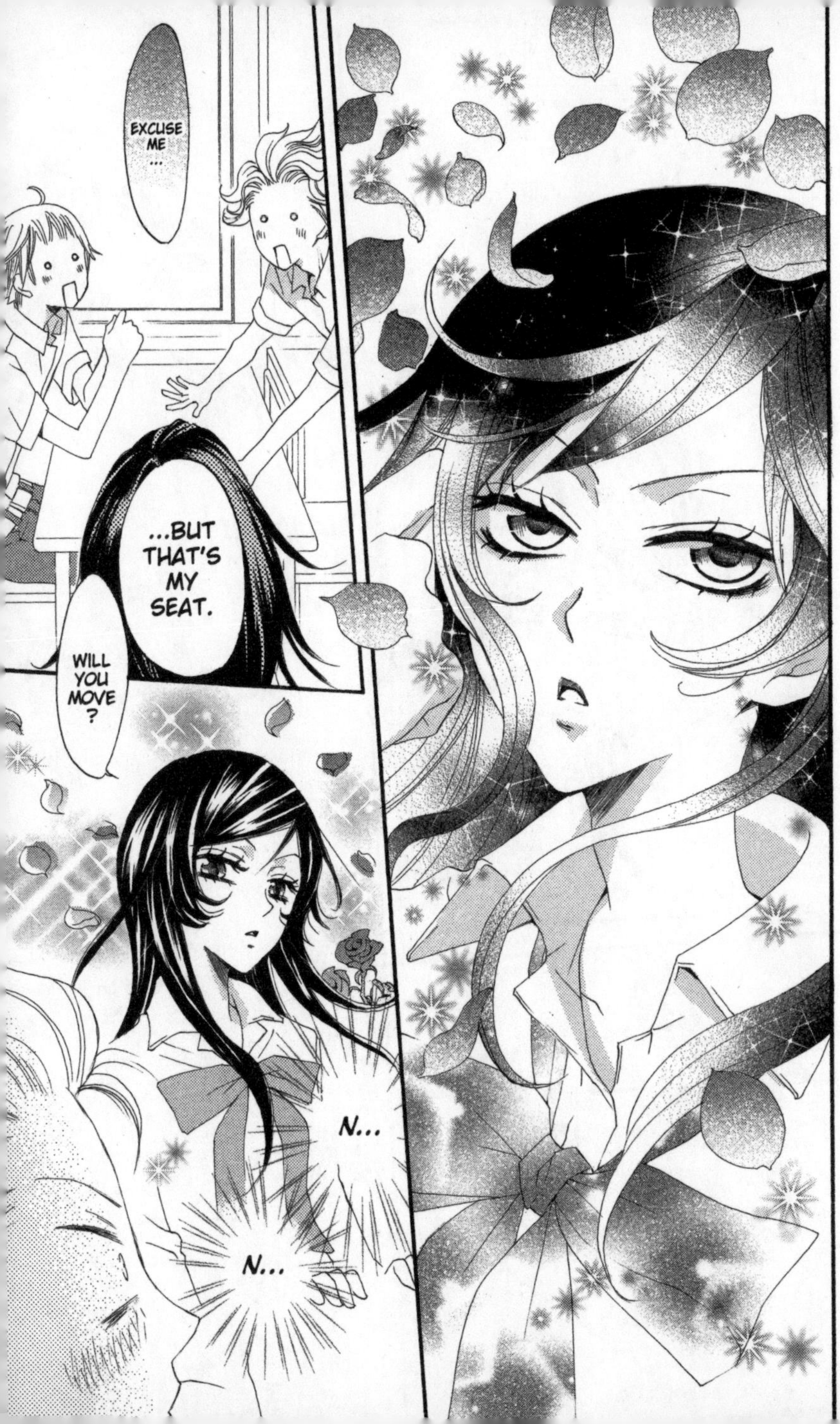
EXCUSE ME ...
...BUT THAT'S MY SEAT.
WILL YOU MOVE?
N...
N...

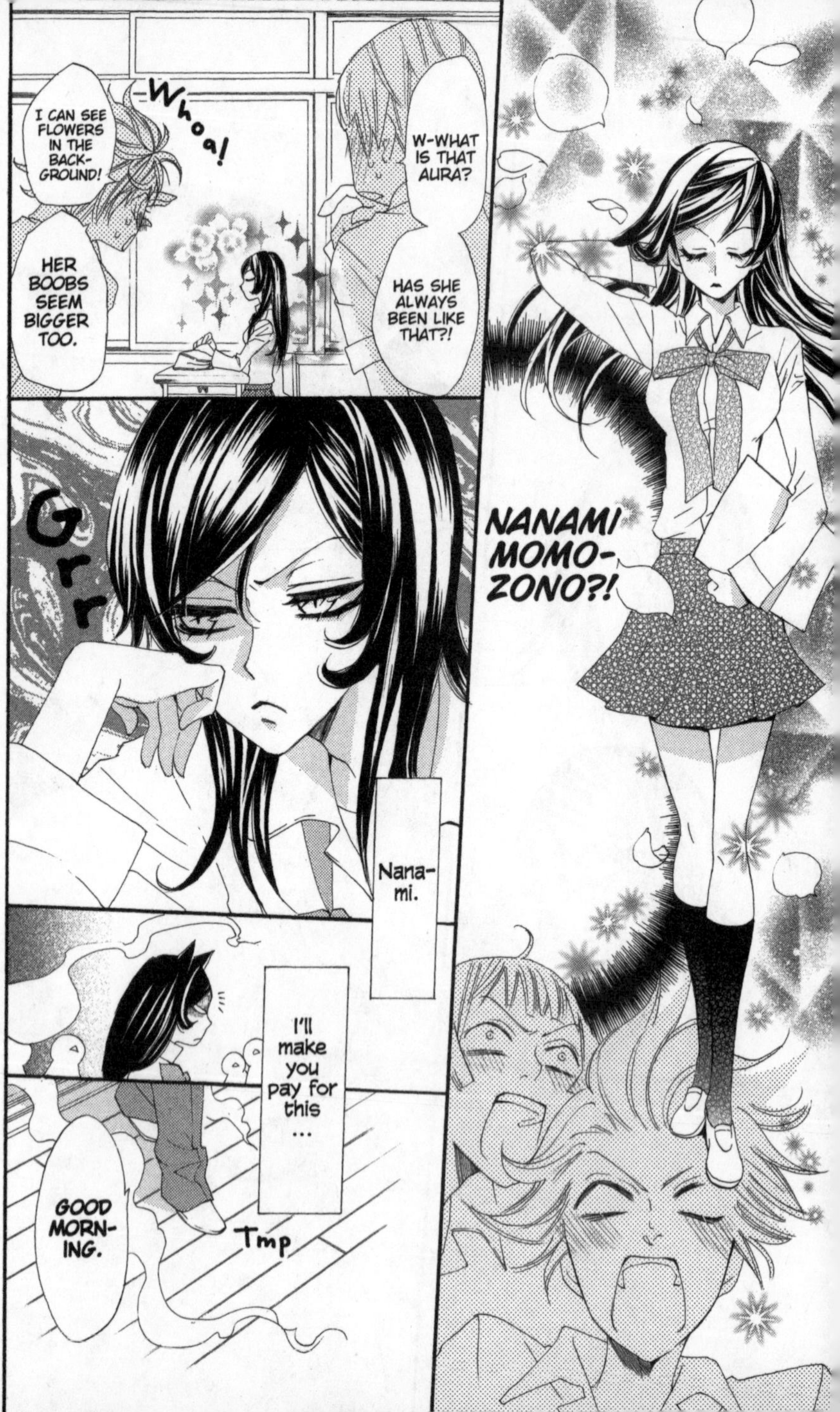
NANAMI MOMO-ZONO?!
W-WHAT IS THAT AURA?
HAS SHE ALWAYS BEEN LIKE THAT?!
Whoa!
I CAN SEE FLOWERS IN THE BACK-GROUND!
HER BOOBS SEEM BIGGER TOO.
Grr
Nana-mi.
I'll make you pay for this ...
GOOD MORN-ING.
Tmp

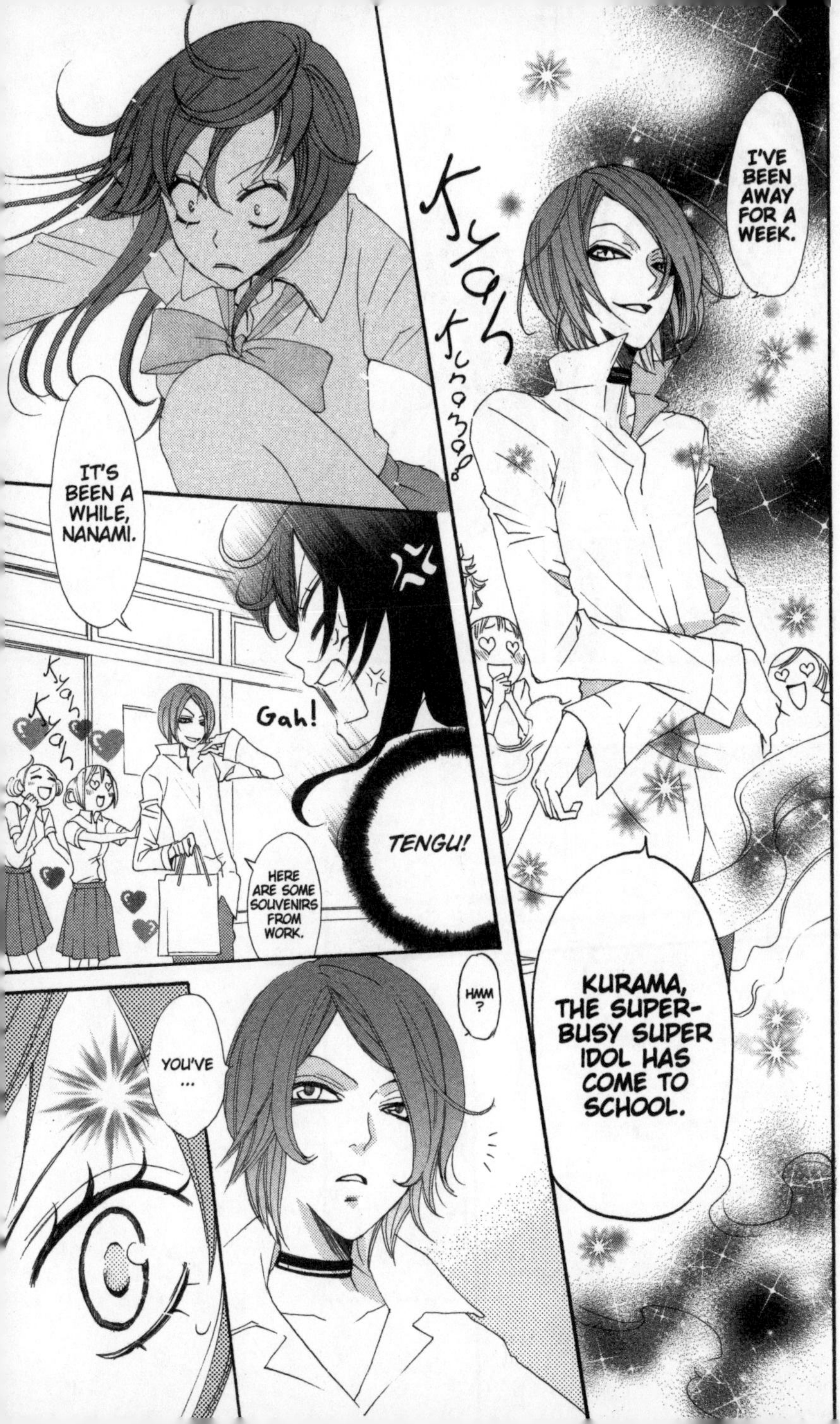
I'VE BEEN AWAY FOR A WEEK.
Kyaah
Kuramaa
KURAMA, THE SUPER-BUSY SUPER IDOL HAS COME TO SCHOOL.
IT'S BEEN A WHILE, NANAMI.
Gah!
TENGU!
Kyan
Kyan
HERE ARE SOME SOUVENIRS FROM WORK.
HMM?
YOU'VE...

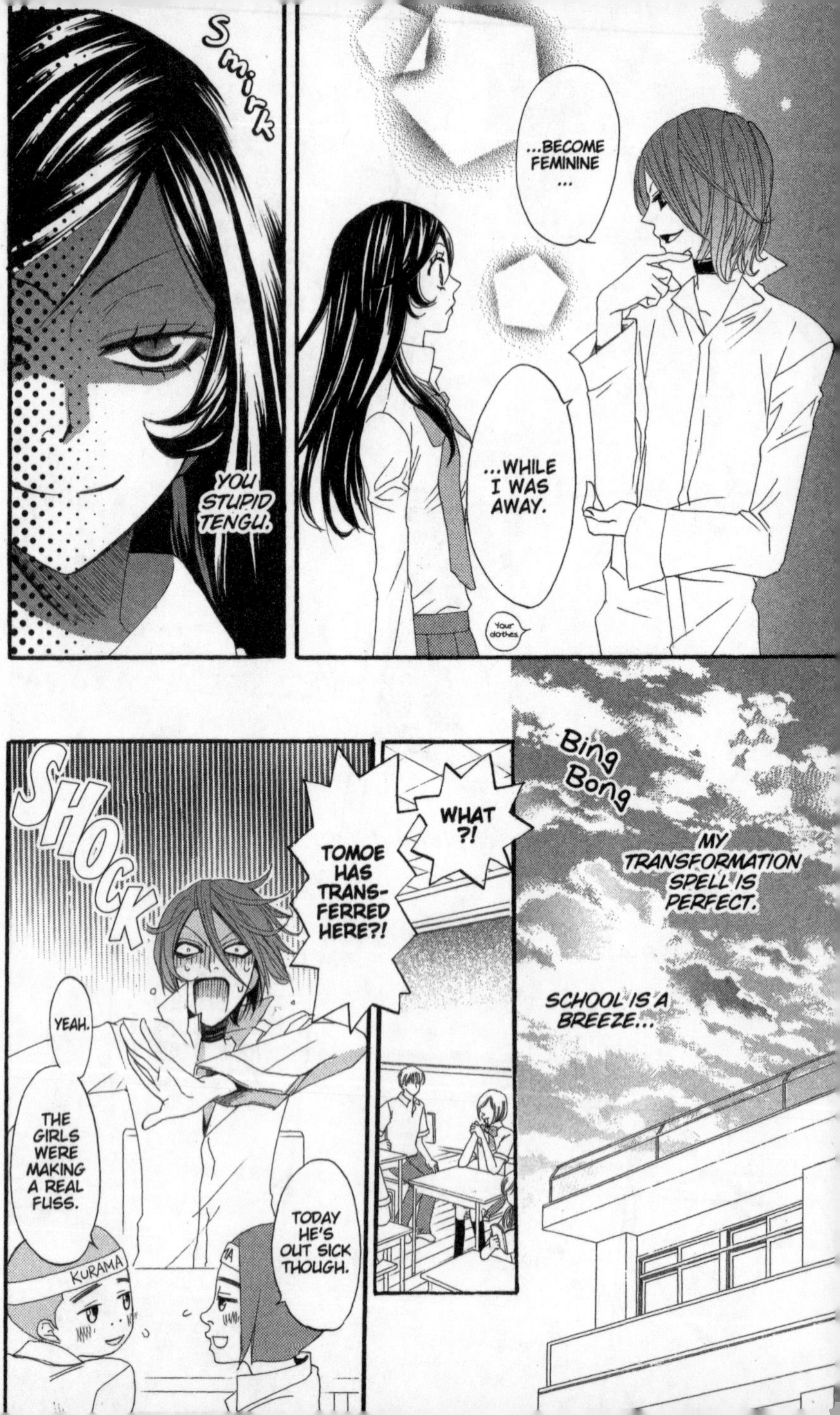
...BECOME FEMININE ...
...WHILE I WAS AWAY.
Your clothes.
Smirk
YOU STUPID TENGU.
Bing Bong
MY TRANSFORMATION SPELL IS PERFECT.
SCHOOL IS A BREEZE...
WHAT ?!
SHOCK
TOMOE HAS TRANS-FERRED HERE?!
YEAH.
THE GIRLS WERE MAKING A REAL FUSS.
TODAY HE'S OUT SICK THOUGH.
KURAMA

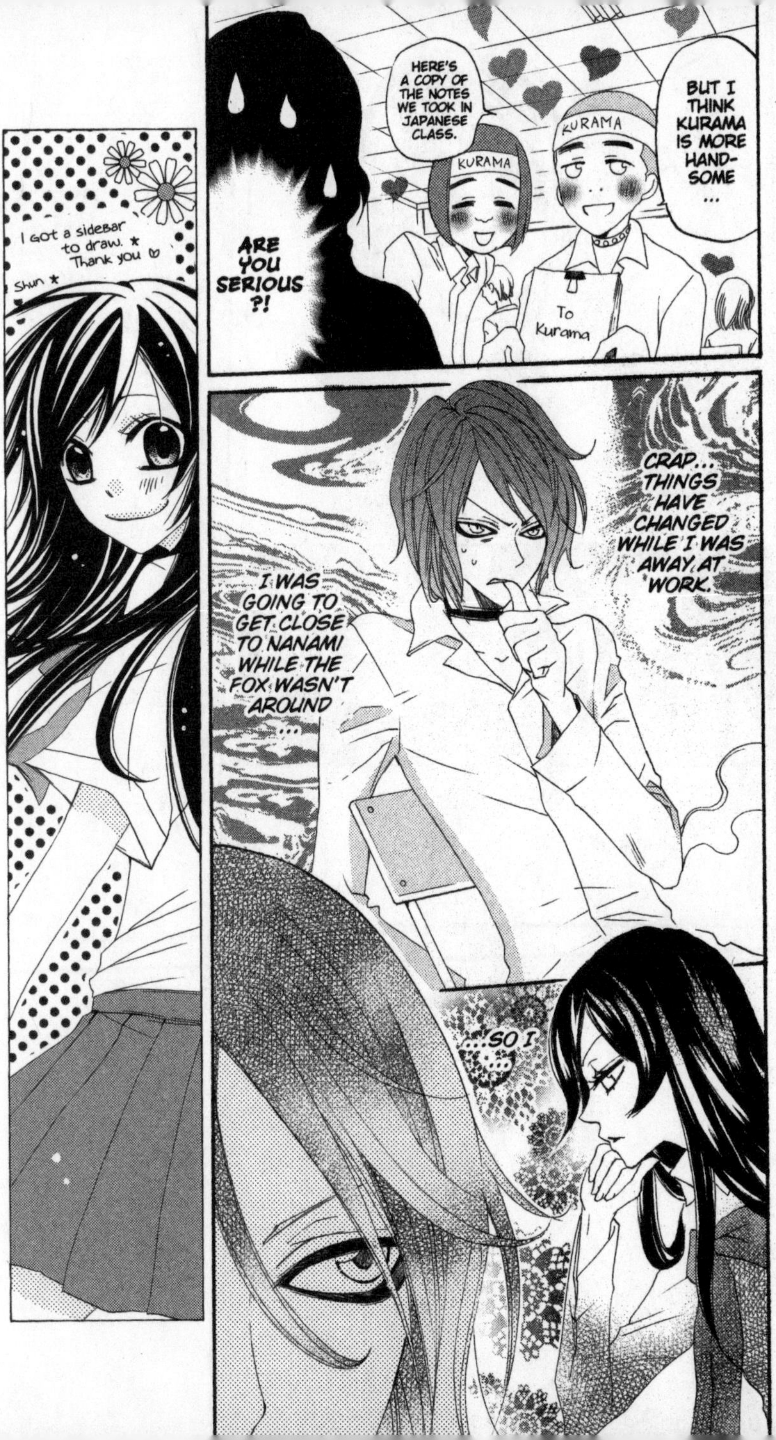
BUT I THINK KURAMA IS MORE HAND-SOME ...
KURAMA
HERE'S A COPY OF THE NOTES WE TOOK IN JAPANESE CLASS.
KURAMA
To Kurama
ARE YOU SERIOUS ?!
CRAP... THINGS HAVE CHANGED WHILE I WAS AWAY AT WORK.
I WAS GOING TO GET CLOSE TO NANAMI WHILE THE FOX WASN'T AROUND ...
...SO I ...
I got a sidebar to draw. ★ Thank you ♡
Shun ★

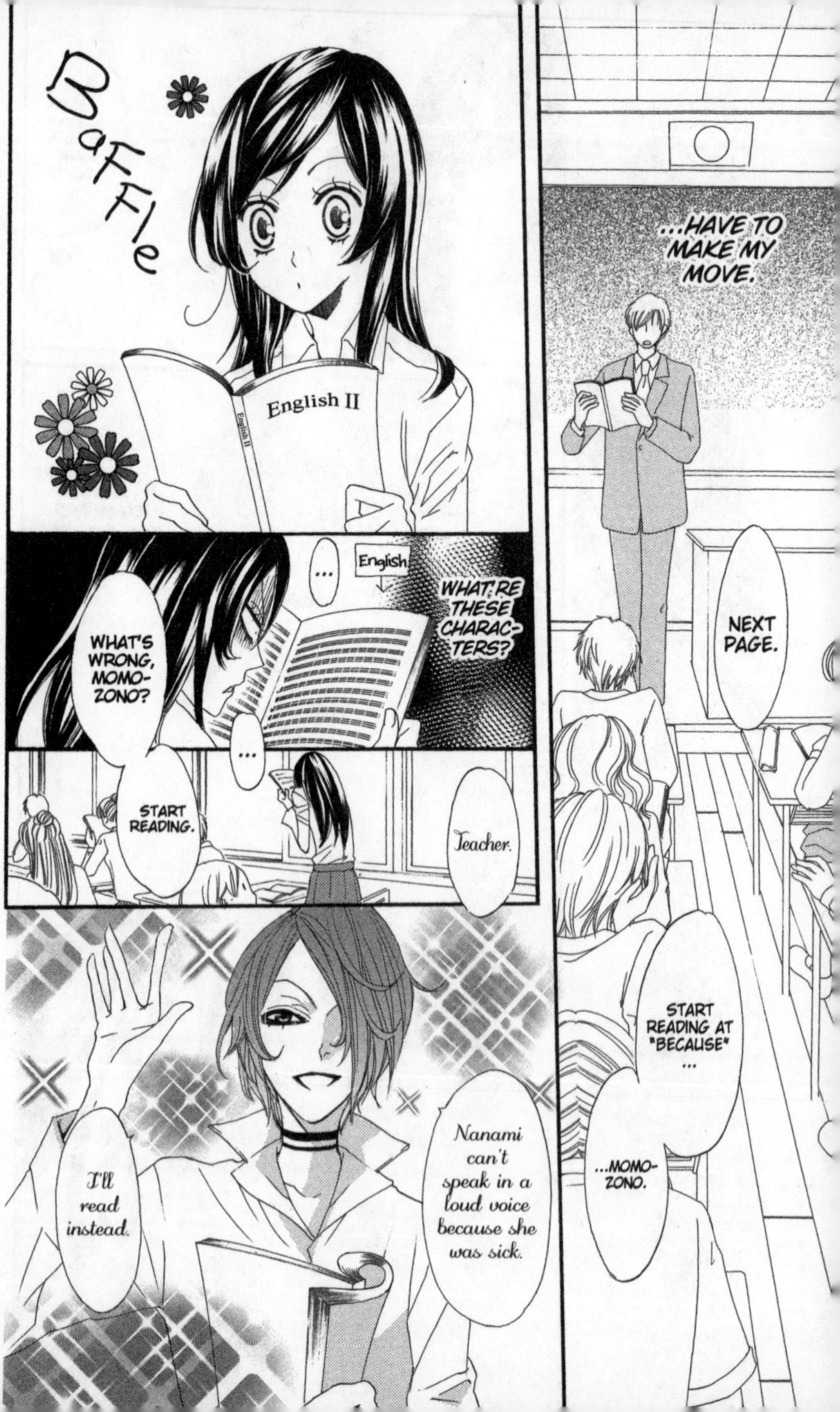
...HAVE TO MAKE MY MOVE.
NEXT PAGE.
START READING AT "BECAUSE" ...
...MOMO-ZONO.
BaFFle
English II
English II
English
...
WHAT'RE THESE CHARAC-TERS?
WHAT'S WRONG, MOMO-ZONO?
...
Teacher.
START READING.
Nanami can't speak in a loud voice because she was sick.
I'll read instead.

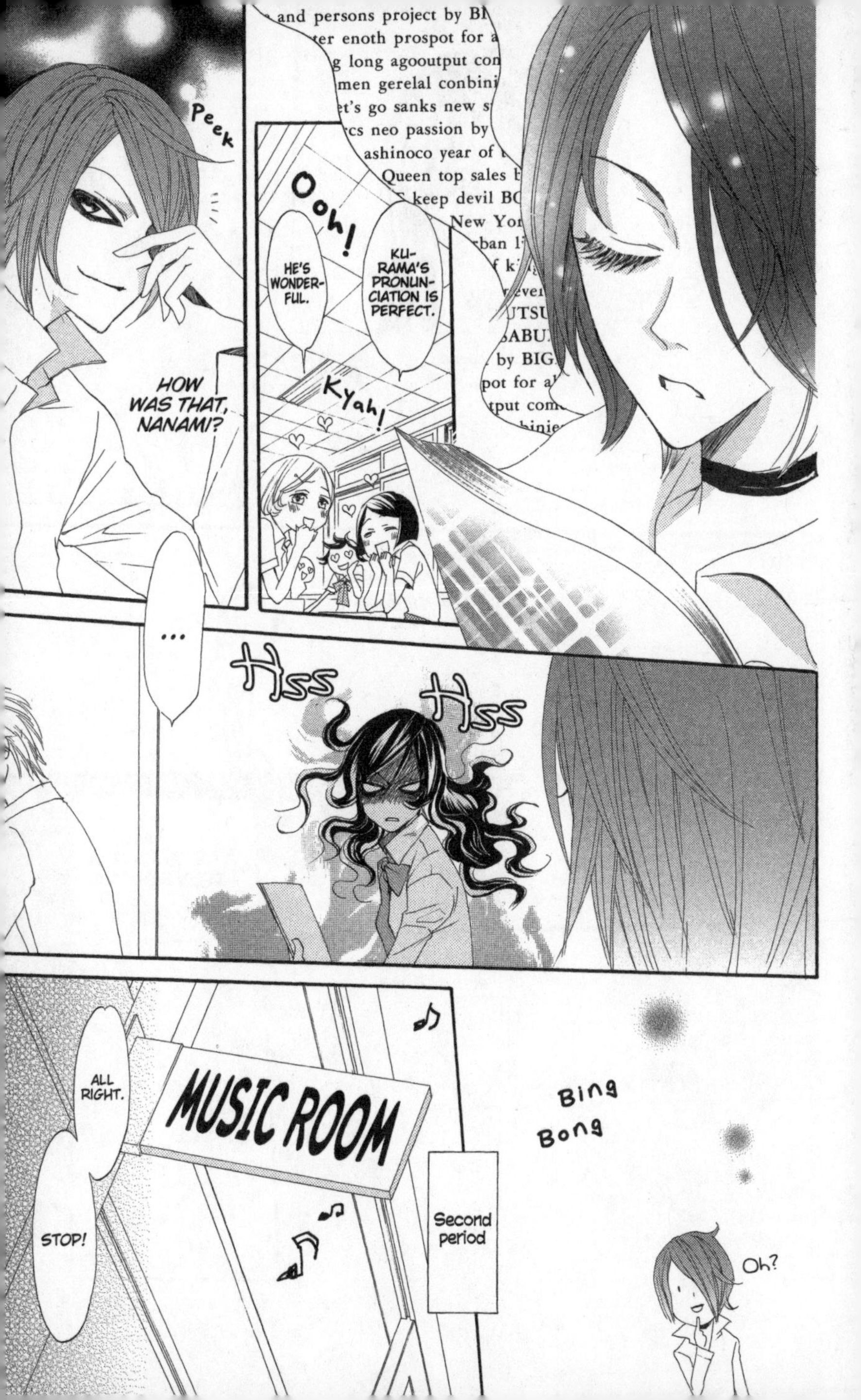

Ooh!
KURAMA'S PRONUNCIATION IS PERFECT.
HE'S WONDERFUL.
Kyah!
Peek
HOW WAS THAT, NANAMI?
Hss Hss
...
Bing Bong
Oh?
Second period
MUSIC ROOM
ALL RIGHT.
STOP!

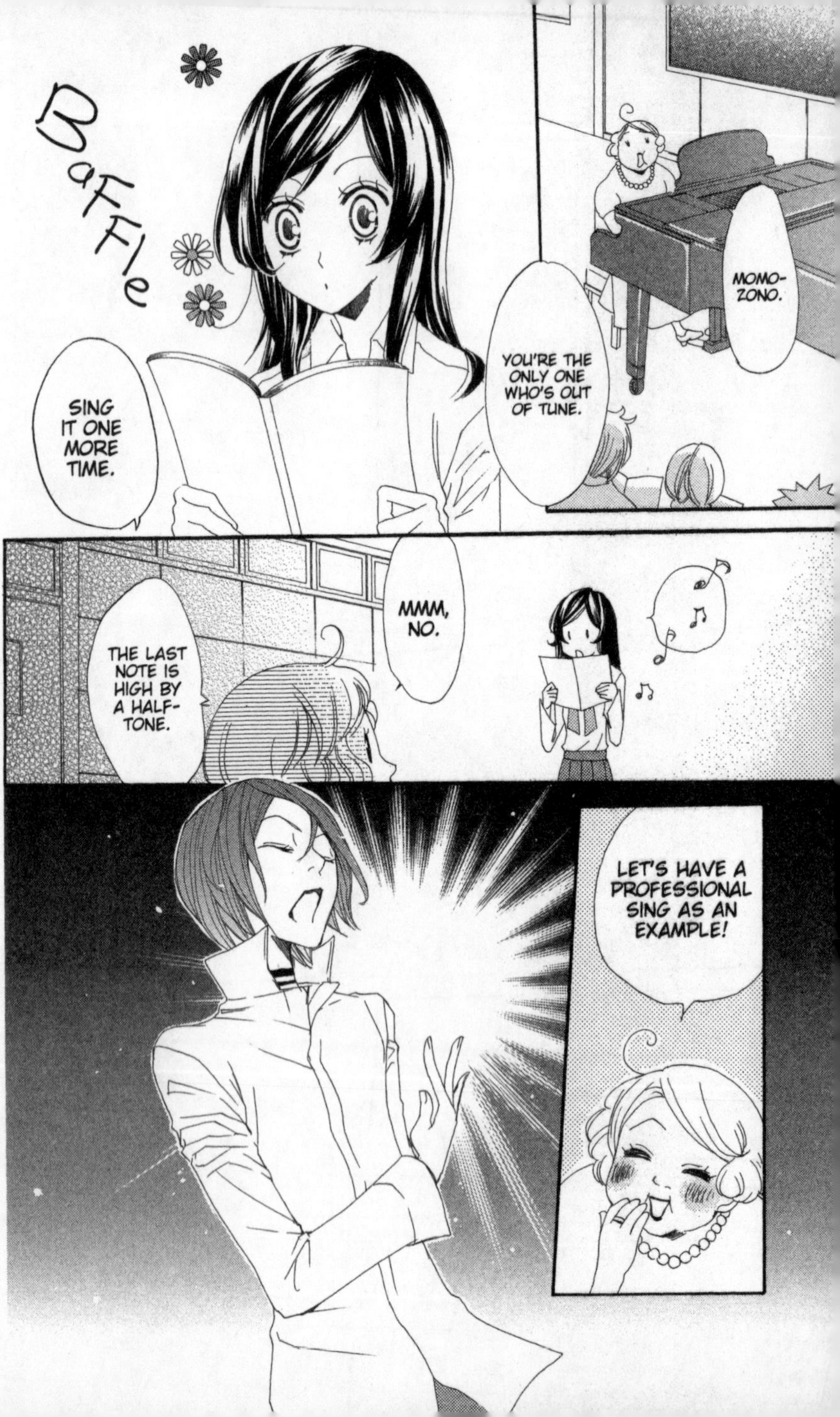
MOMO-ZONO.
YOU'RE THE ONLY ONE WHO'S OUT OF TUNE.
BaFFle
SING IT ONE MORE TIME.
MMM, NO.
THE LAST NOTE IS HIGH BY A HALF-TONE.
LET'S HAVE A PROFESSIONAL SING AS AN EXAMPLE!

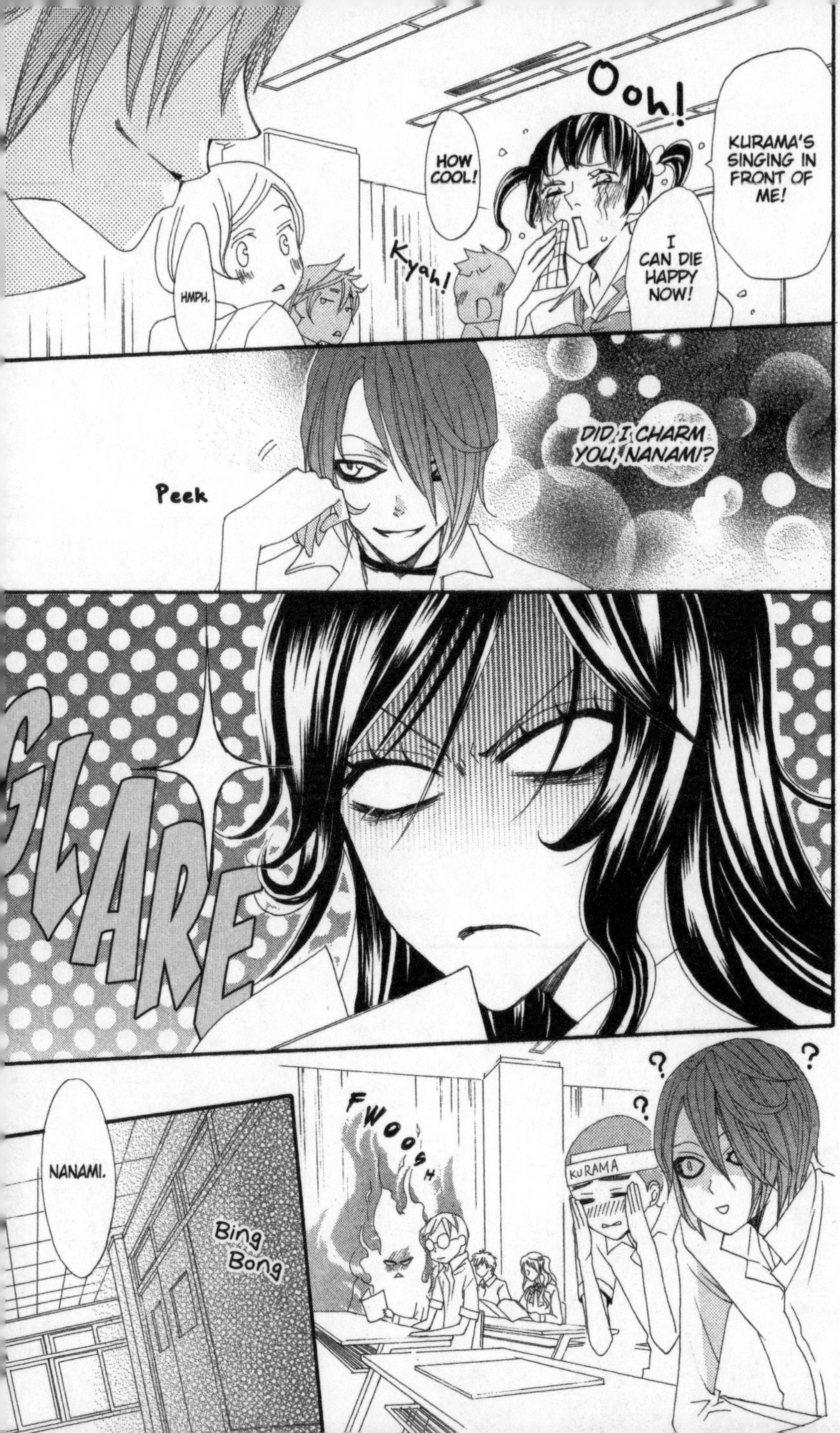
Ooh!
KURAMA'S SINGING IN FRONT OF ME!
I CAN DIE HAPPY NOW!
HOW COOL!
Kyah!
HMPH.
DID I CHARM YOU, NANAMI?
Peek
GLARE
? ? ?
KURAMA
FWOOSH
Bing Bong
NANAMI.

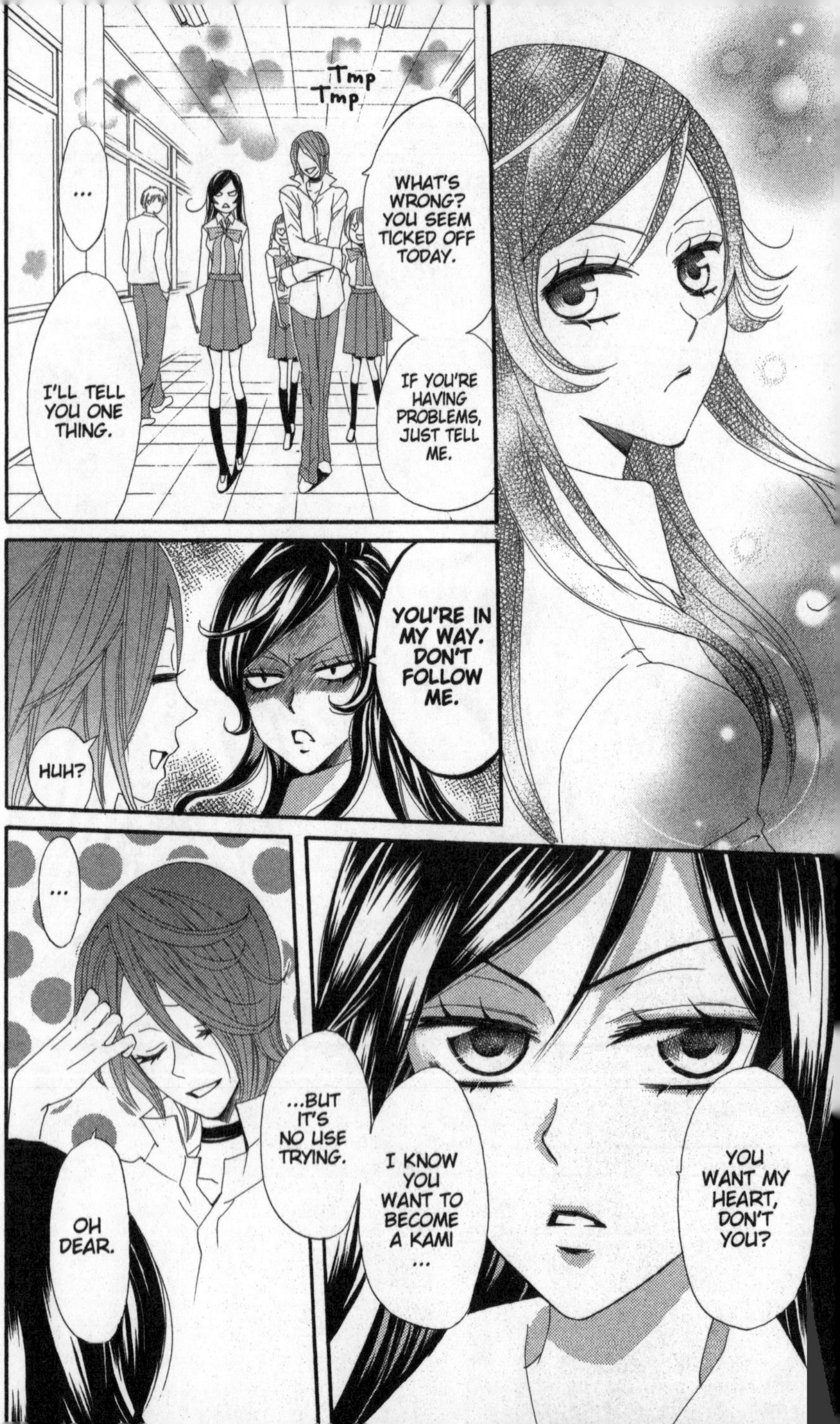
Tmp Tmp
WHAT'S WRONG? YOU SEEM TICKED OFF TODAY.
IF YOU'RE HAVING PROBLEMS, JUST TELL ME.
...
I'LL TELL YOU ONE THING.
YOU'RE IN MY WAY. DON'T FOLLOW ME.
HUH?
YOU WANT MY HEART, DON'T YOU?
I KNOW YOU WANT TO BECOME A KAMI ...
...BUT IT'S NO USE TRYING.
...
OH DEAR.

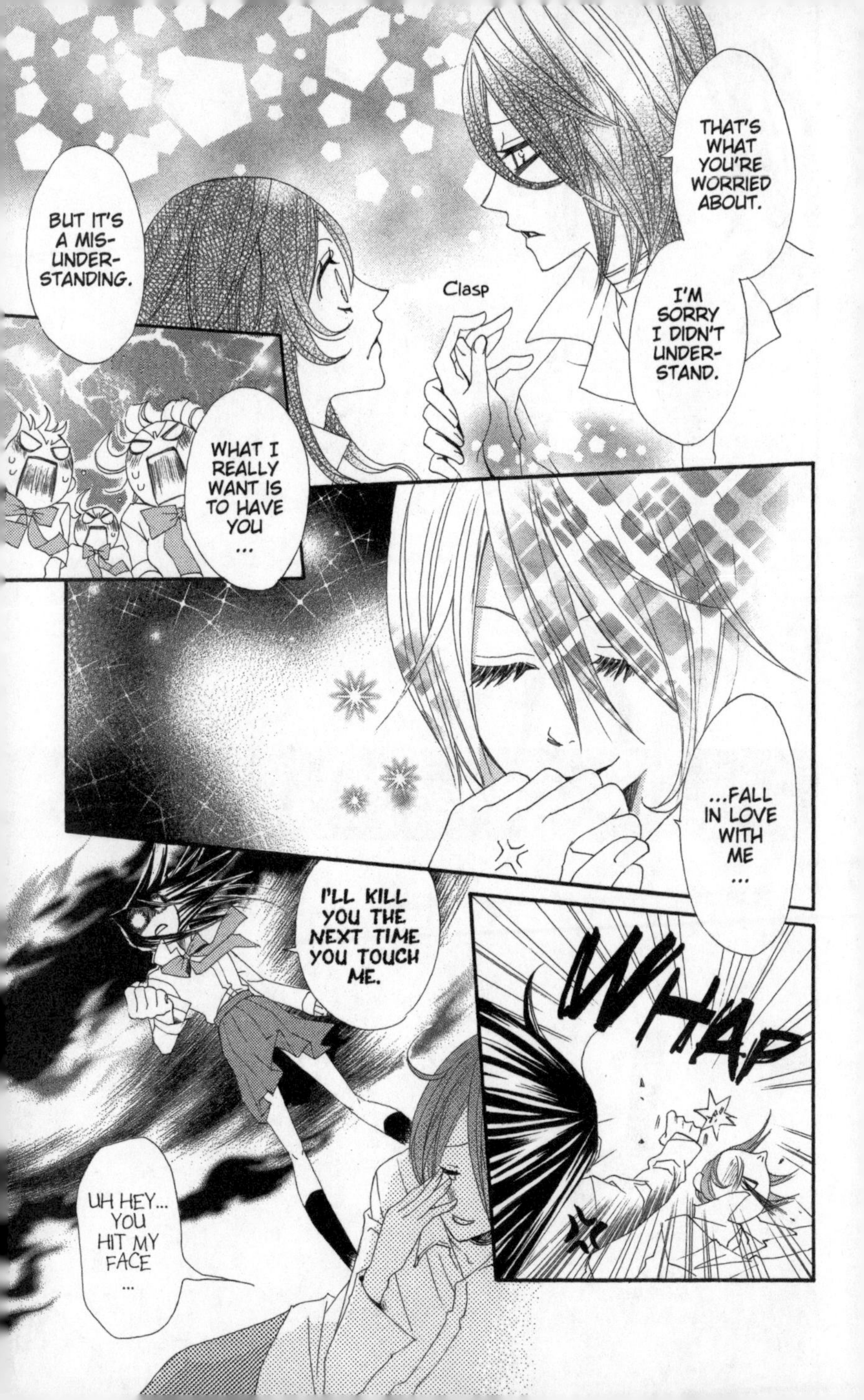
THAT'S WHAT YOU'RE WORRIED ABOUT.
BUT IT'S A MIS-UNDER-STANDING.
Clasp
I'M SORRY I DIDN'T UNDER-STAND.
WHAT I REALLY WANT IS TO HAVE YOU ...
...FALL IN LOVE WITH ME ...
WHAP
I'LL KILL YOU THE NEXT TIME YOU TOUCH ME.
UH HEY... YOU HIT MY FACE ...

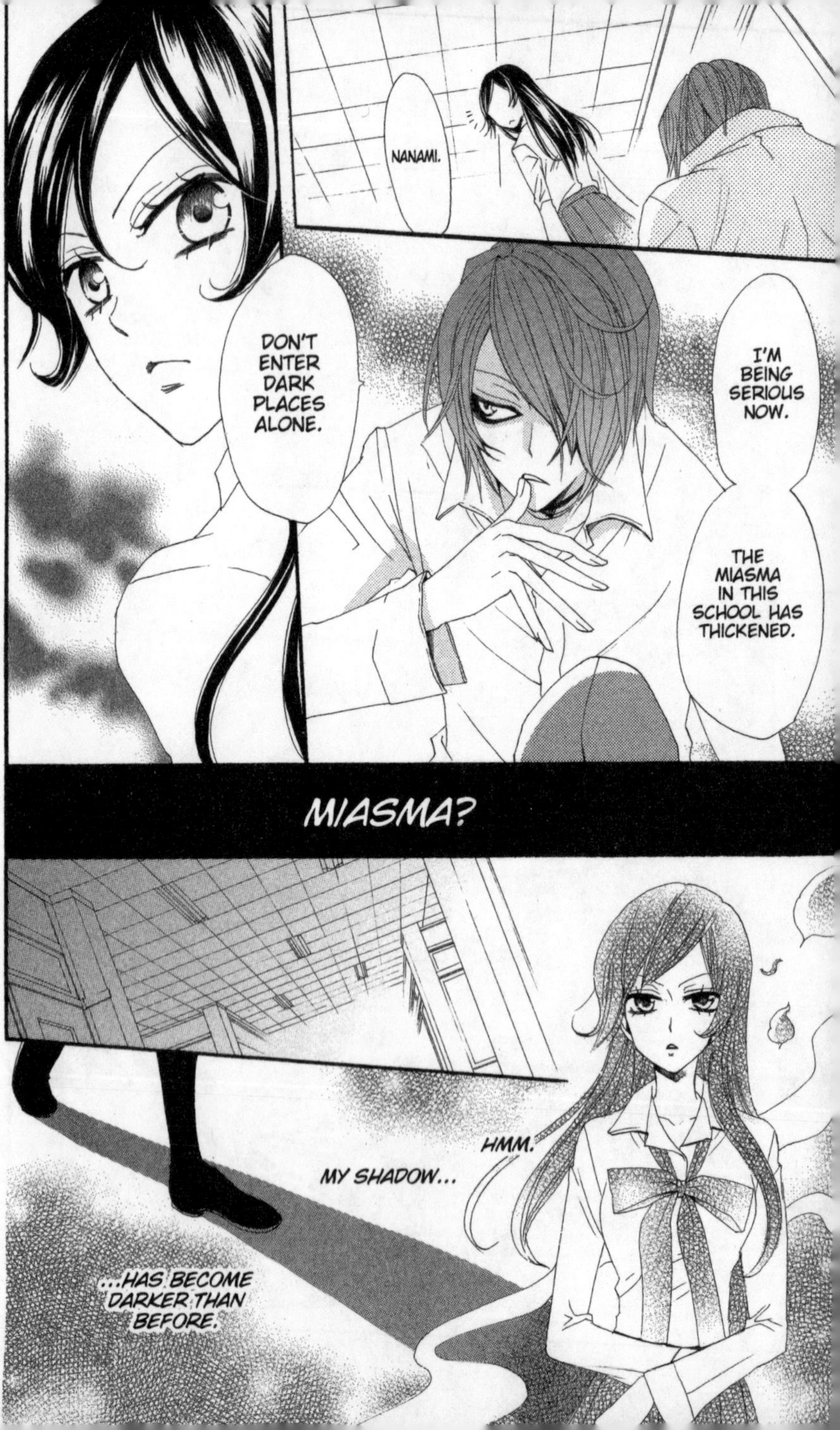
NANAMI.
I'M BEING SERIOUS NOW.
THE MIASMA IN THIS SCHOOL HAS THICKENED.
DON'T ENTER DARK PLACES ALONE.
MIASMA?
HMM.
MY SHADOW...
...HAS BECOME DARKER THAN BEFORE.

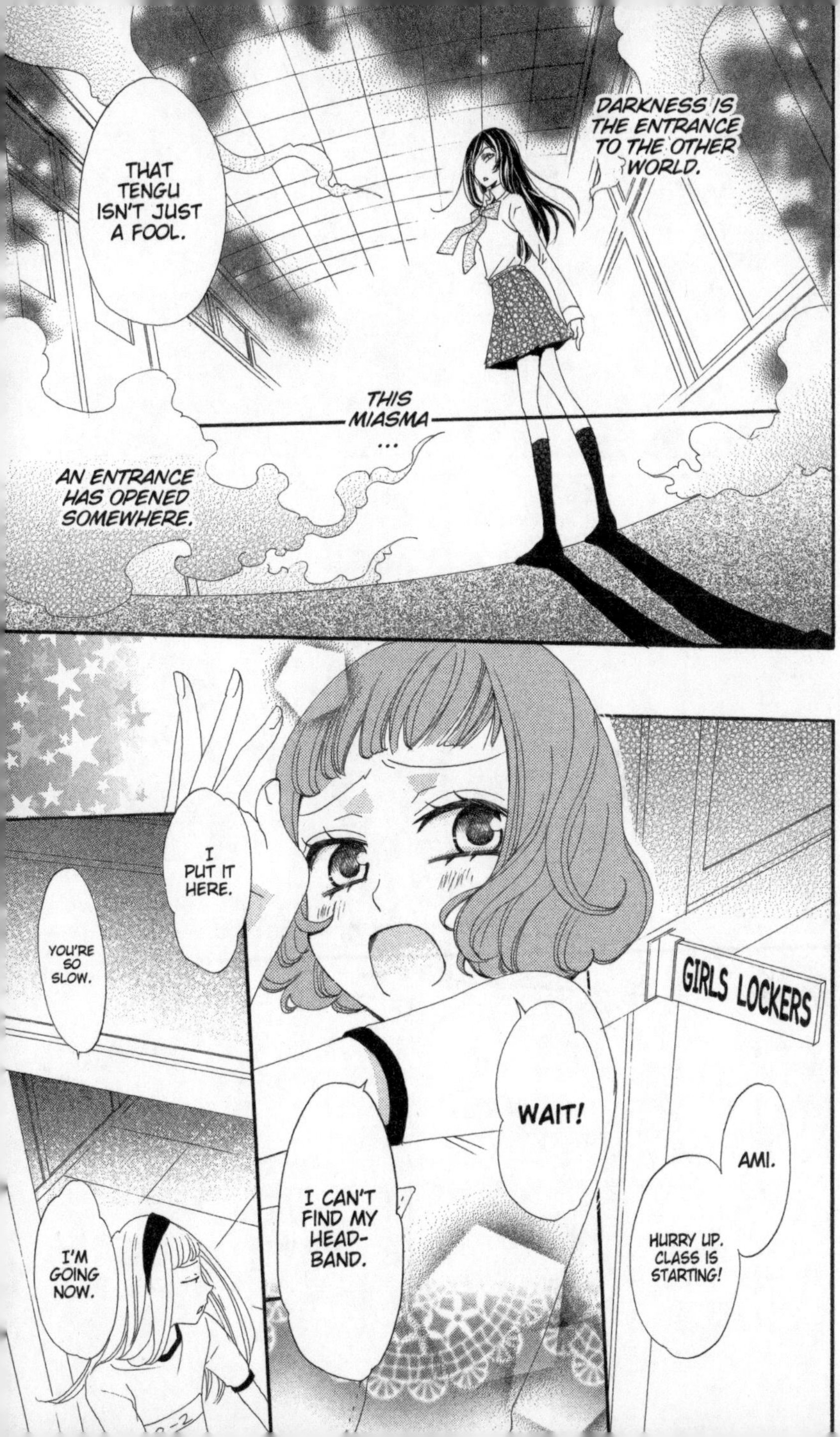
DARKNESS IS THE ENTRANCE TO THE OTHER WORLD.
THAT TENGU ISN'T JUST A FOOL.
THIS MIASMA...
AN ENTRANCE HAS OPENED SOMEWHERE.
GIRLS LOCKERS
AMI.
HURRY UP. CLASS IS STARTING!
WAIT!
I CAN'T FIND MY HEAD-BAND.
I PUT IT HERE.
YOU'RE SO SLOW.
I'M GOING NOW.

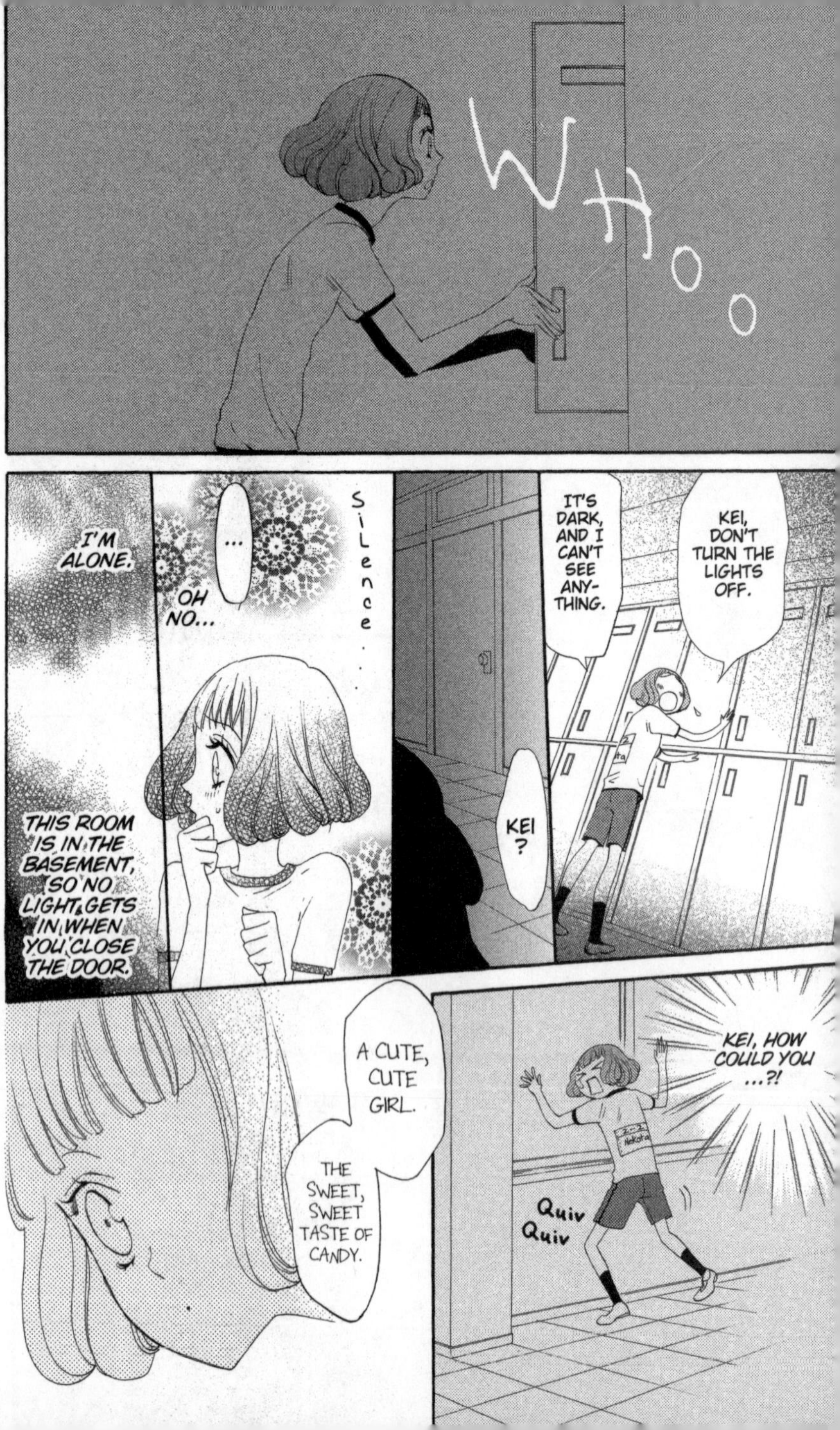
WHOO
KEI, DON'T TURN THE LIGHTS OFF.
IT'S DARK, AND I CAN'T SEE ANYTHING.
KEI?
Silence...
...
OH NO...
I'M ALONE.
THIS ROOM IS IN THE BASEMENT, SO NO LIGHT GETS IN WHEN YOU CLOSE THE DOOR.
KEI, HOW COULD YOU ...?!
Quiv Quiv
A CUTE, CUTE GIRL.
THE SWEET, SWEET TASTE OF CANDY.

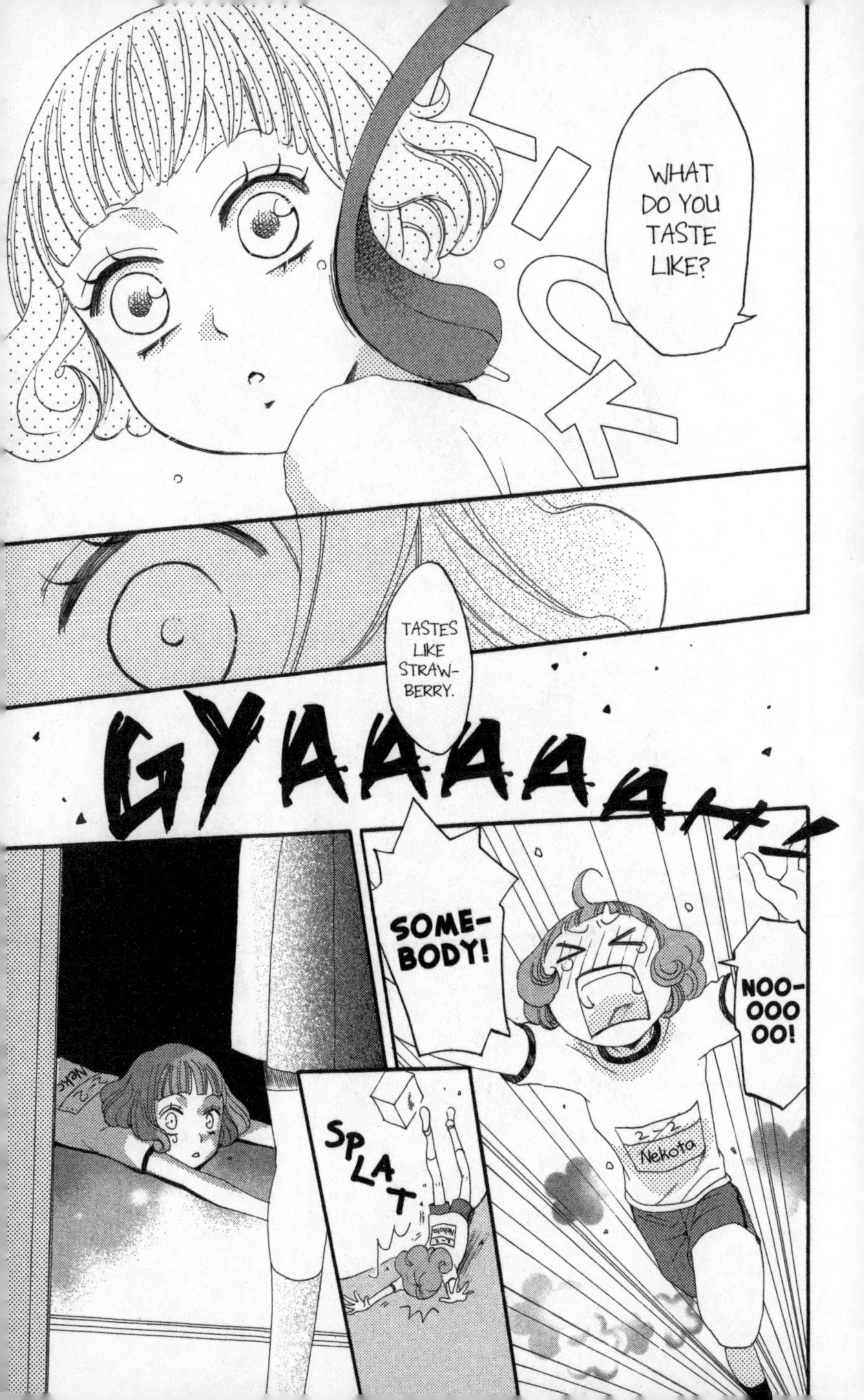
WHAT DO YOU TASTE LIKE?
LICK
TASTES LIKE STRAW-BERRY.
GYAAAAAH!!
NOO-OOO OO!
2-2
Nekota
SOME-BODY!
SPLAT

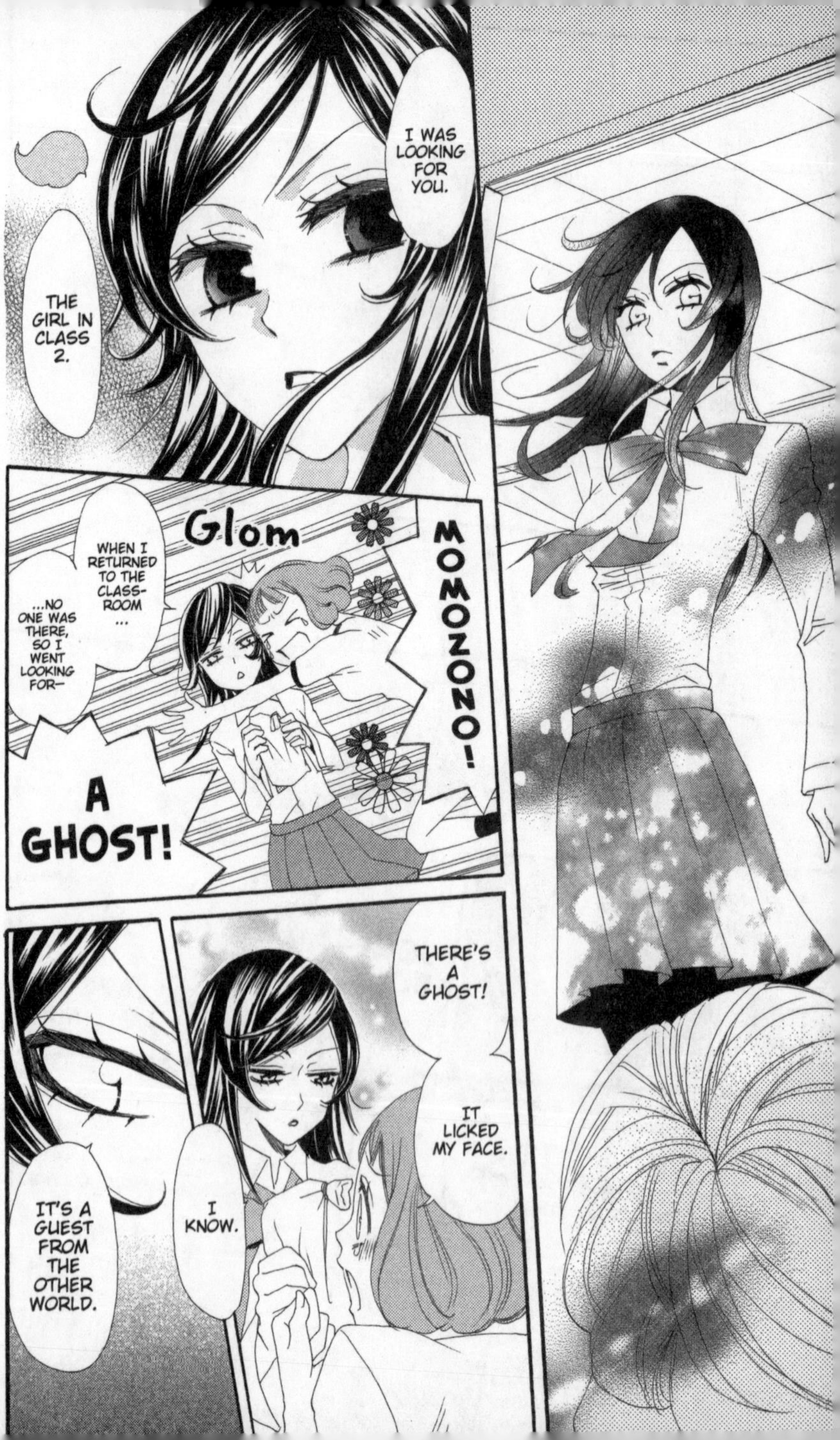
I WAS LOOKING FOR YOU.
THE GIRL IN CLASS 2.
MOMOZONO!
Glom
WHEN I RETURNED TO THE CLASS-ROOM ...
...NO ONE WAS THERE, SO I WENT LOOKING FOR—
A GHOST!
THERE'S A GHOST!
IT LICKED MY FACE.
I KNOW.
IT'S A GUEST FROM THE OTHER WORLD.

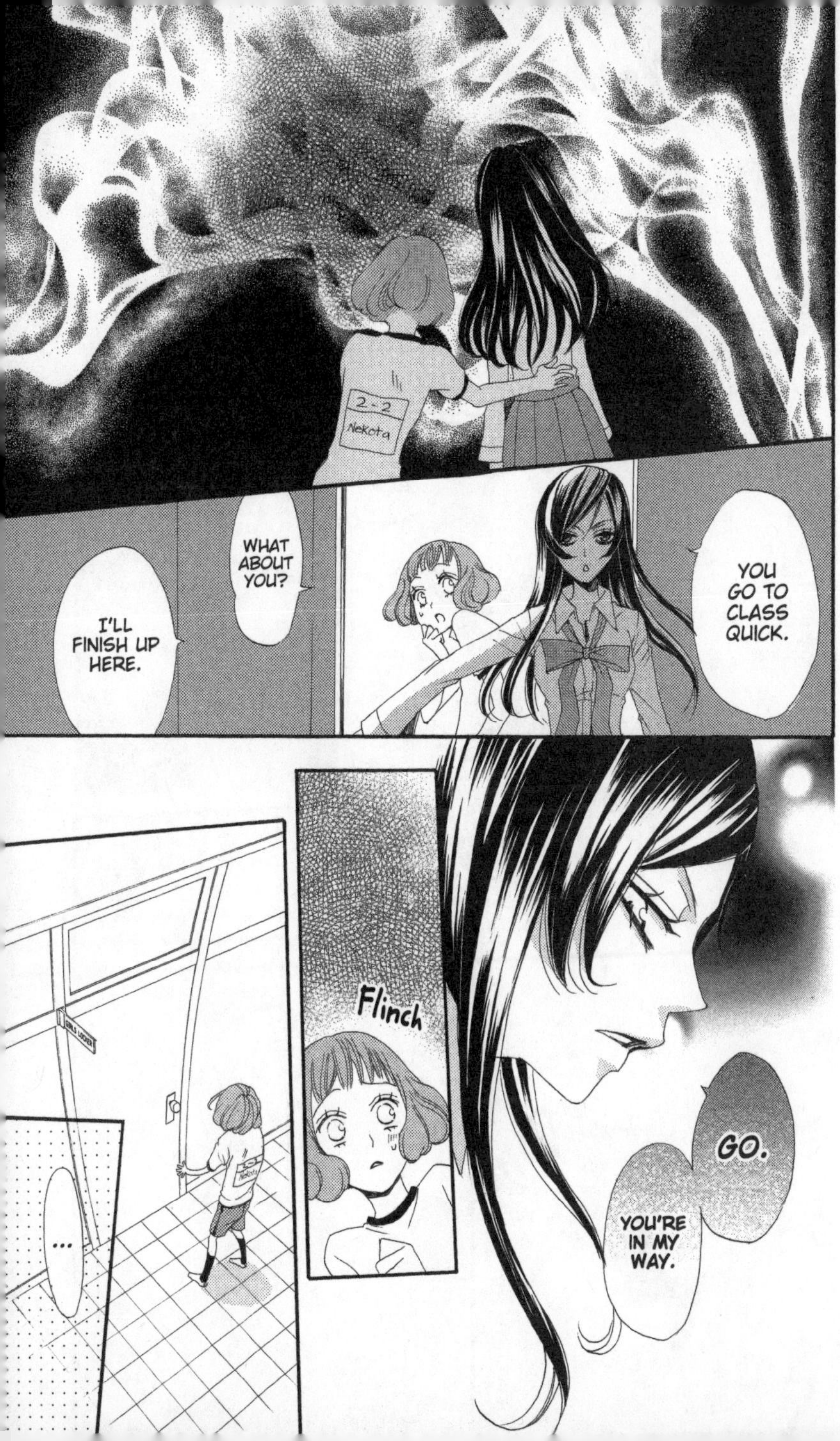
2-2
Nekota
YOU GO TO CLASS QUICK.
WHAT ABOUT YOU?
I'LL FINISH UP HERE.
GO.
YOU'RE IN MY WAY.
Flinch
...

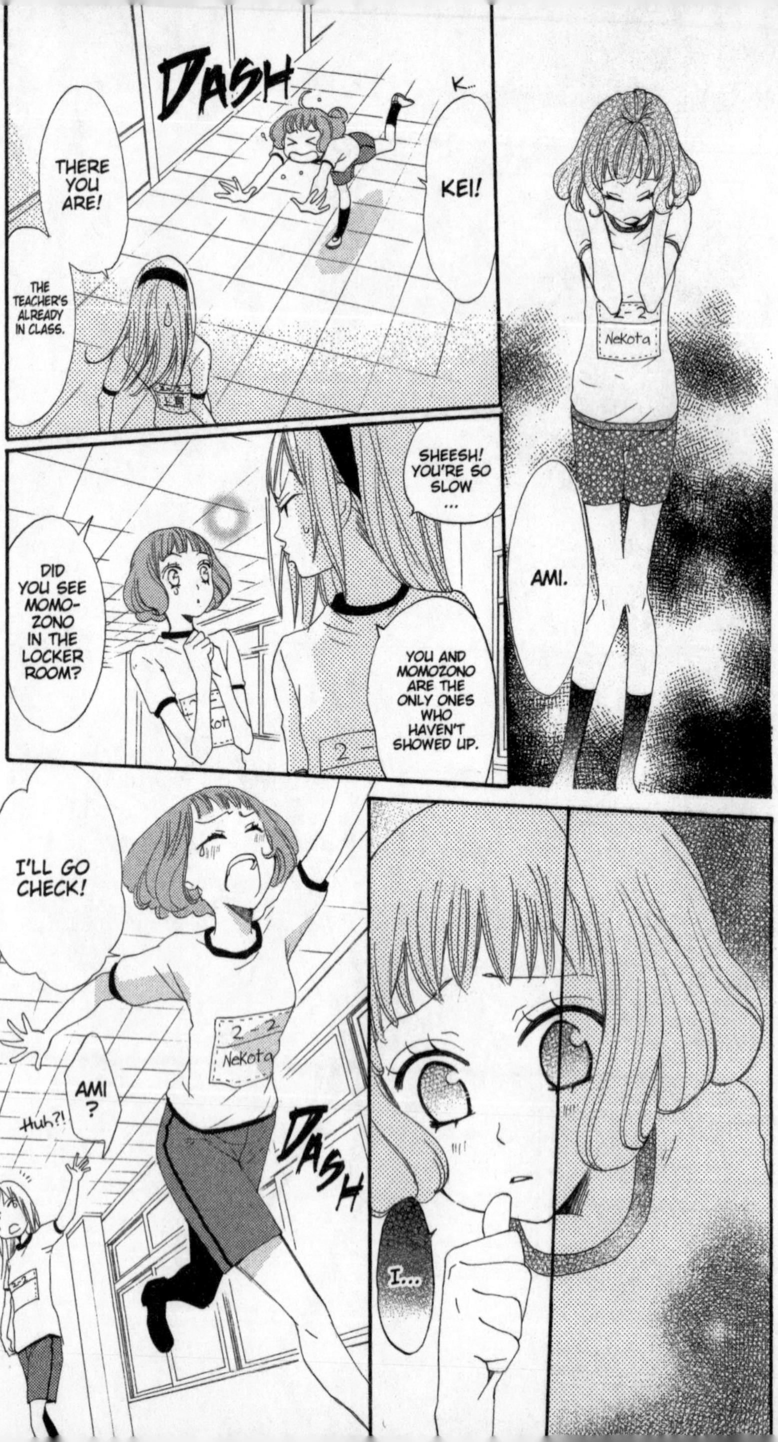
AMI.
K...
KEI!
DASH
THERE YOU ARE!
THE TEACHER'S ALREADY IN CLASS.
SHEESH! YOU'RE SO SLOW ...
YOU AND MOMOZONO ARE THE ONLY ONES WHO HAVEN'T SHOWED UP.
DID YOU SEE MOMOZONO IN THE LOCKER ROOM?
Nekota
I...
I'LL GO CHECK!
DASH
AMI ?
Huh?!
2-2
Nekota

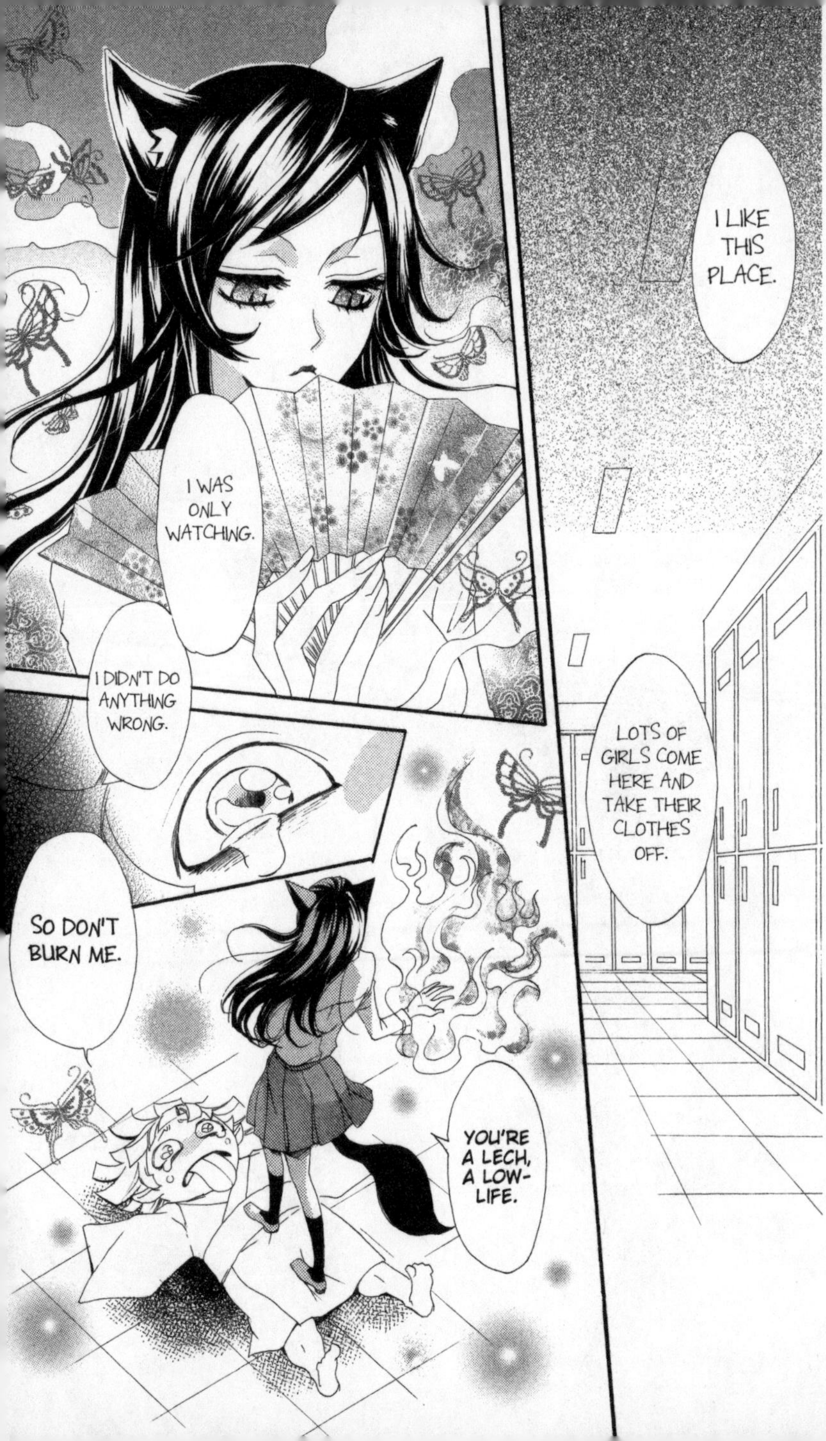
I LIKE THIS PLACE.
LOTS OF GIRLS COME HERE AND TAKE THEIR CLOTHES OFF.
I WAS ONLY WATCHING.
I DIDN'T DO ANYTHING WRONG.
YOU'RE A LECH, A LOW-LIFE.
SO DON'T BURN ME.

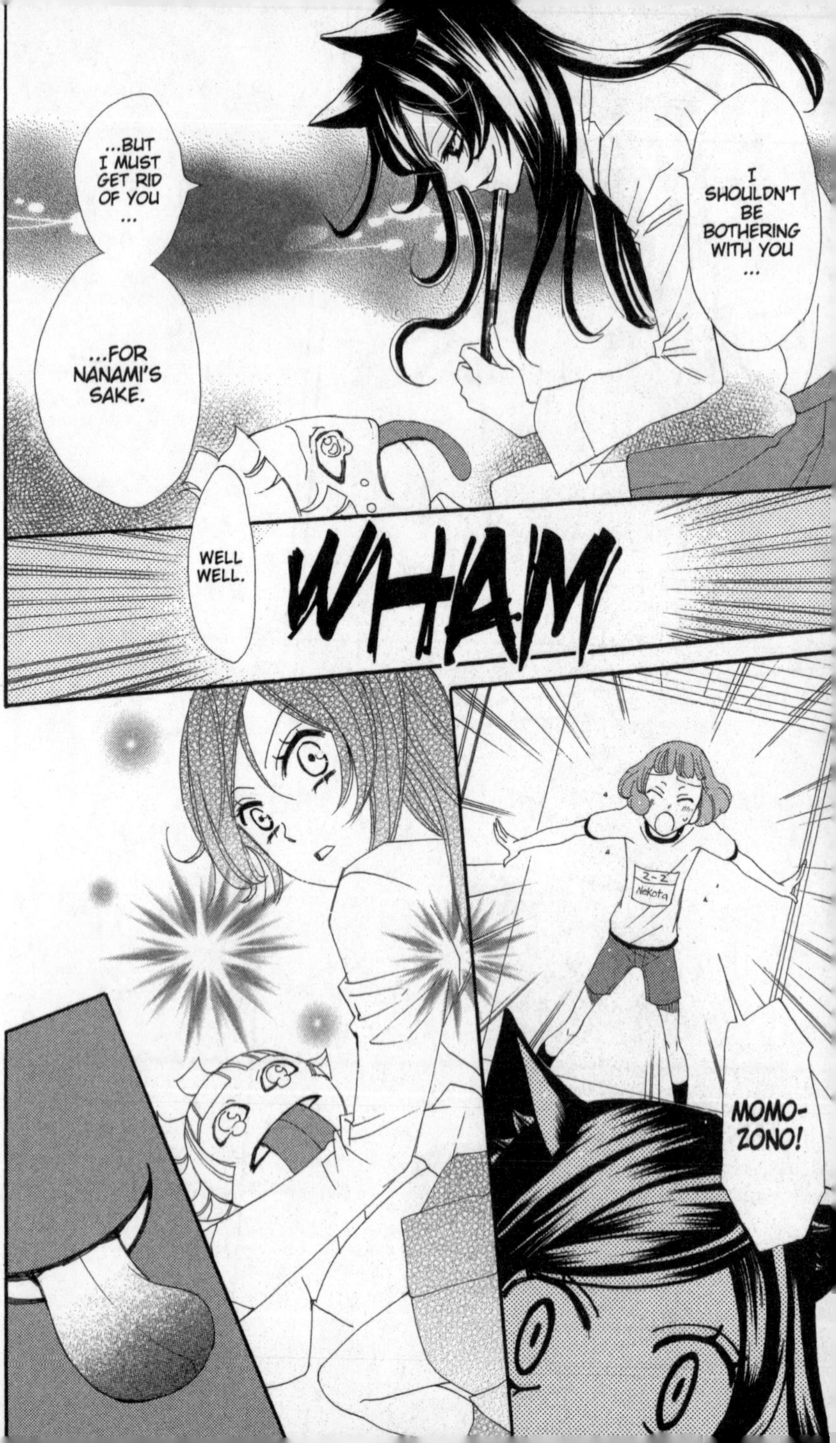
I SHOULDN'T BE BOTHERING WITH YOU ...
...BUT I MUST GET RID OF YOU ...
...FOR NANAMI'S SAKE.
WHAM
WELL WELL.
MOMO-ZONO!
2-2 Nekota

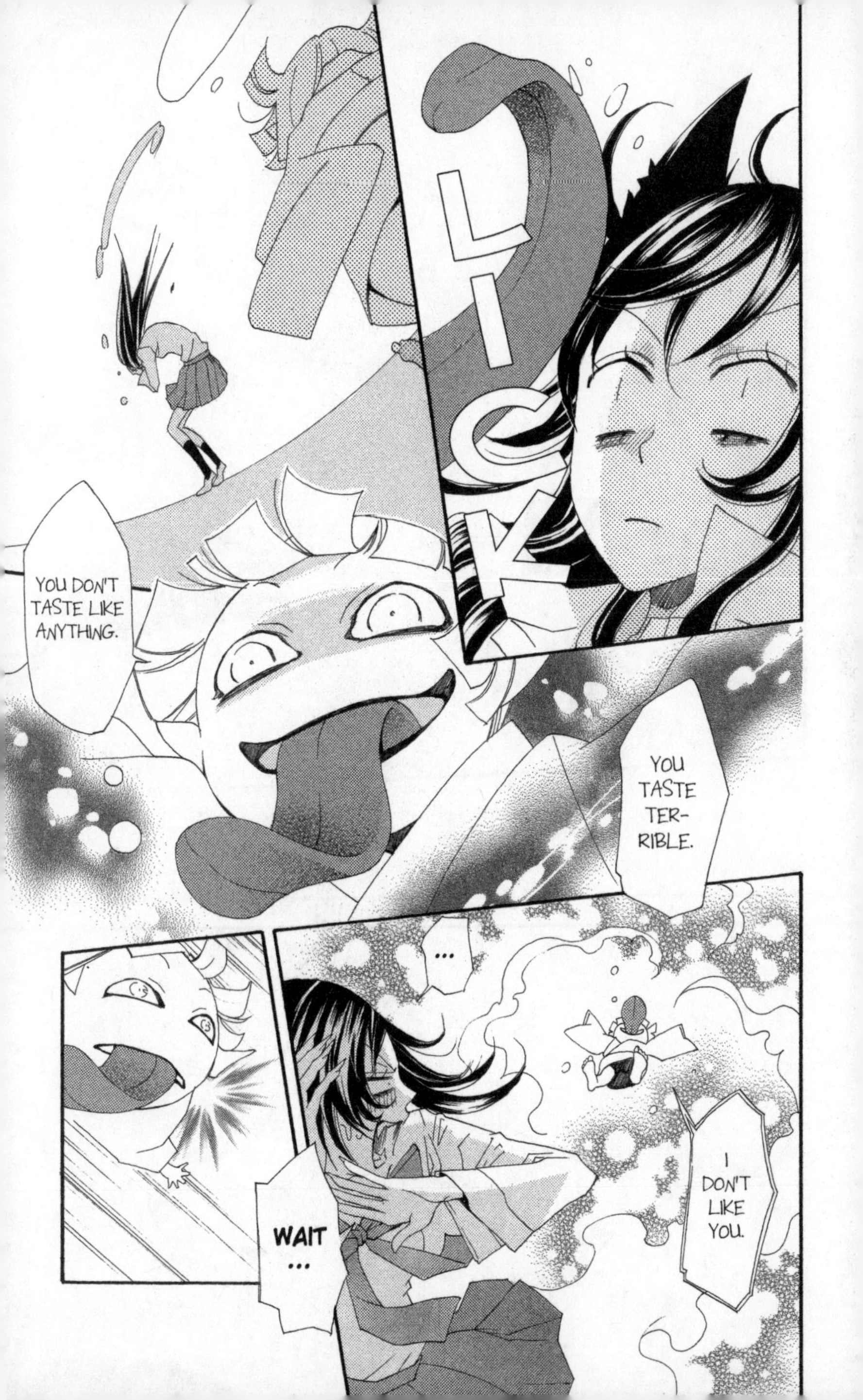
LICK
YOU DON'T TASTE LIKE ANYTHING.
YOU TASTE TER-RIBLE.
...
I DON'T LIKE YOU.
WAIT ...

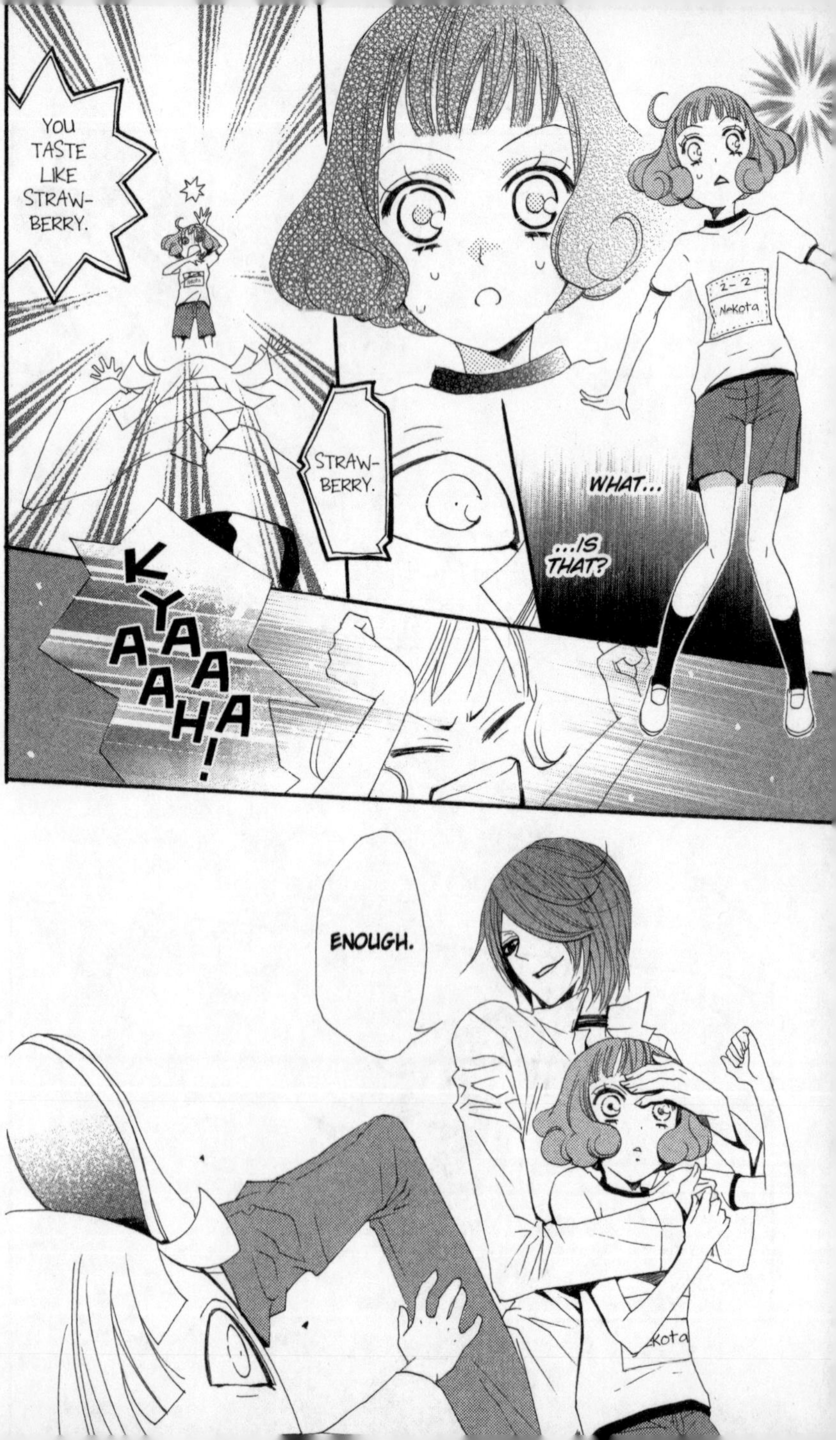
STRAW-BERRY.
WHAT...
...IS THAT?
YOU TASTE LIKE STRAW-BERRY.
KYAAAAAH!
ENOUGH.
2-2
Nekota

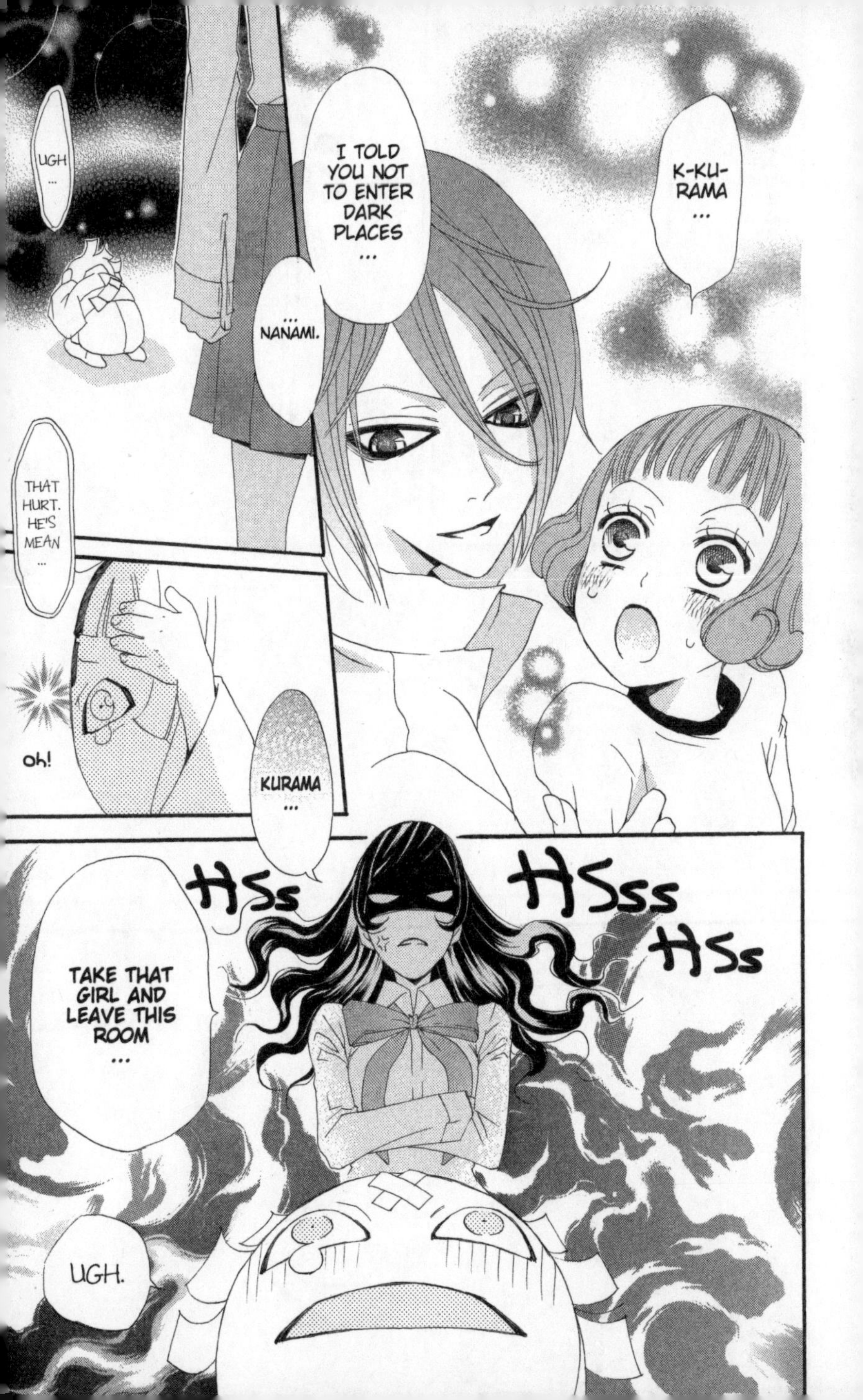
K-KU-RAMA ...
I TOLD YOU NOT TO ENTER DARK PLACES ...
... NANAMI.
KURAMA ...
UGH ...
THAT HURT. HE'S MEAN ...
oh!
HSsss
HSs
HSs
TAKE THAT GIRL AND LEAVE THIS ROOM ...
UGH.

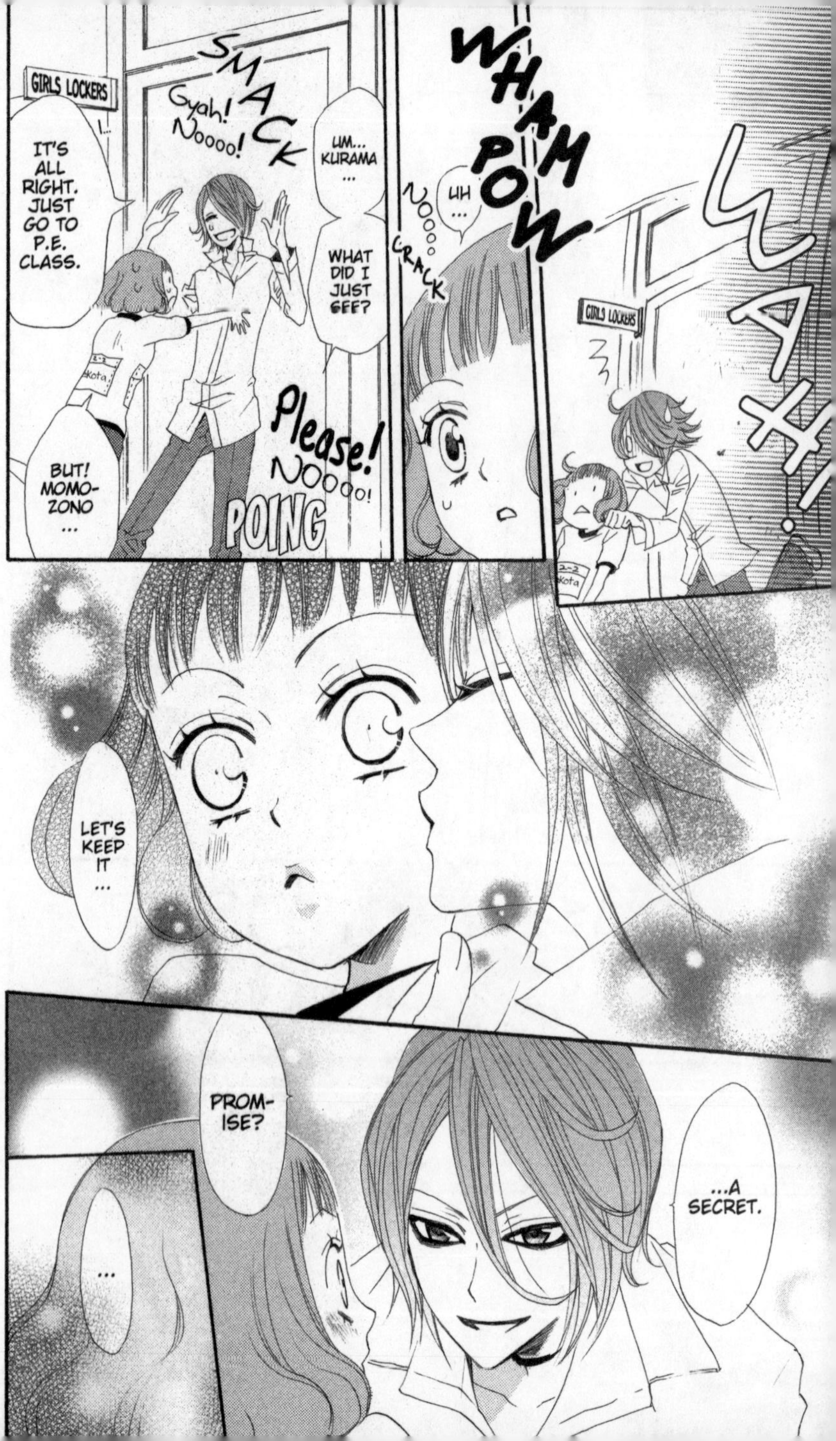
WAAH!
GIRLS LOCKERS
WHAM
POW
UH ...
NOOOOO
CRACK
SMACK
GIRLS LOCKERS
Gyah! Noooo!
UM... KURAMA ...
WHAT DID I JUST SEE?
I...
IT'S ALL RIGHT. JUST GO TO P.E. CLASS.
BUT! MOMO-ZONO ...
Please! Noooo!
POING
LET'S KEEP IT ...
...A SECRET.
PROMISE?
...

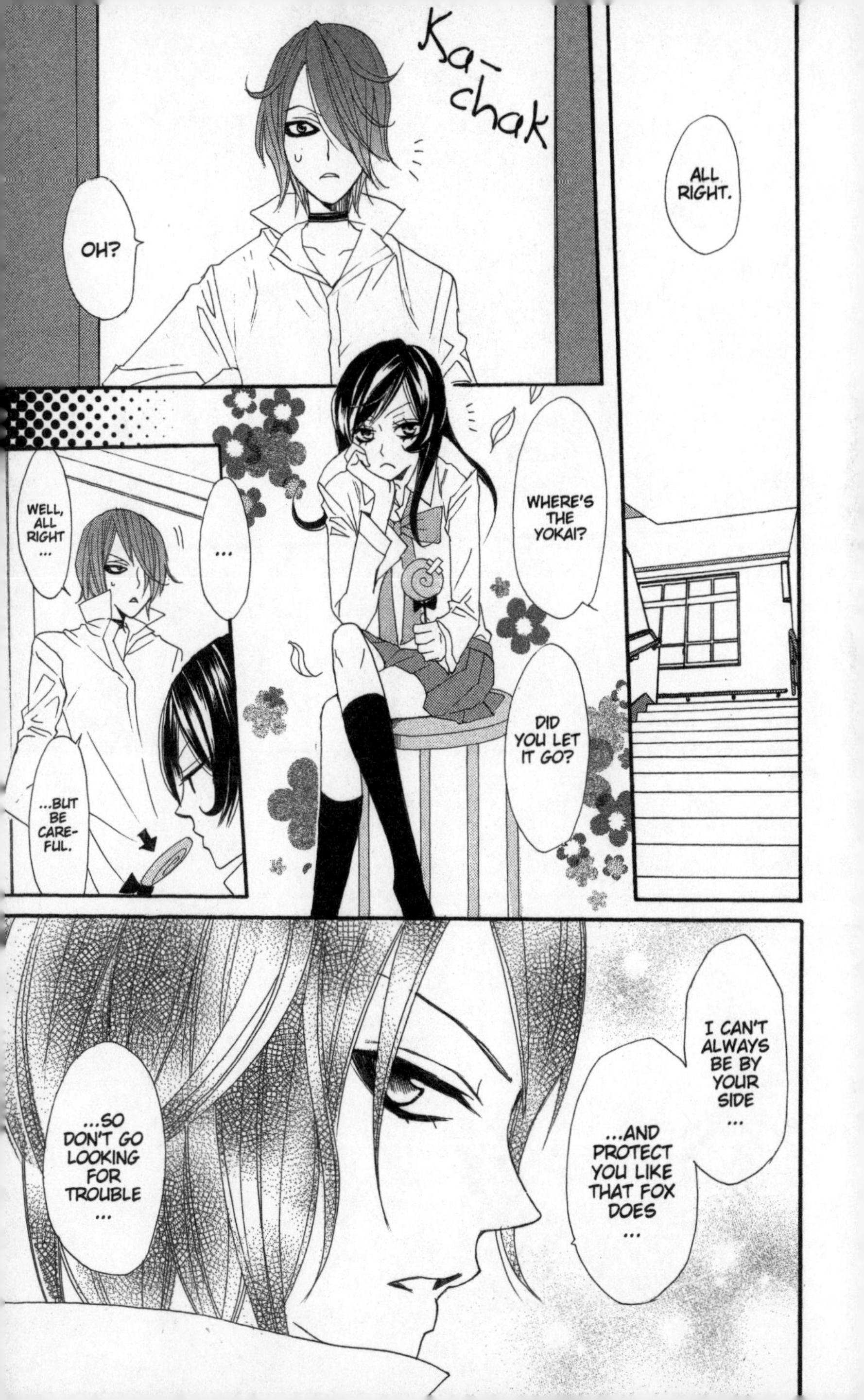
ALL RIGHT.
Ka-chak
OH?
WHERE'S THE YOKAI?
DID YOU LET IT GO?
...
WELL, ALL RIGHT...
...BUT BE CAREFUL.
I CAN'T ALWAYS BE BY YOUR SIDE...
...AND PROTECT YOU LIKE THAT FOX DOES...
...SO DON'T GO LOOKING FOR TROUBLE...

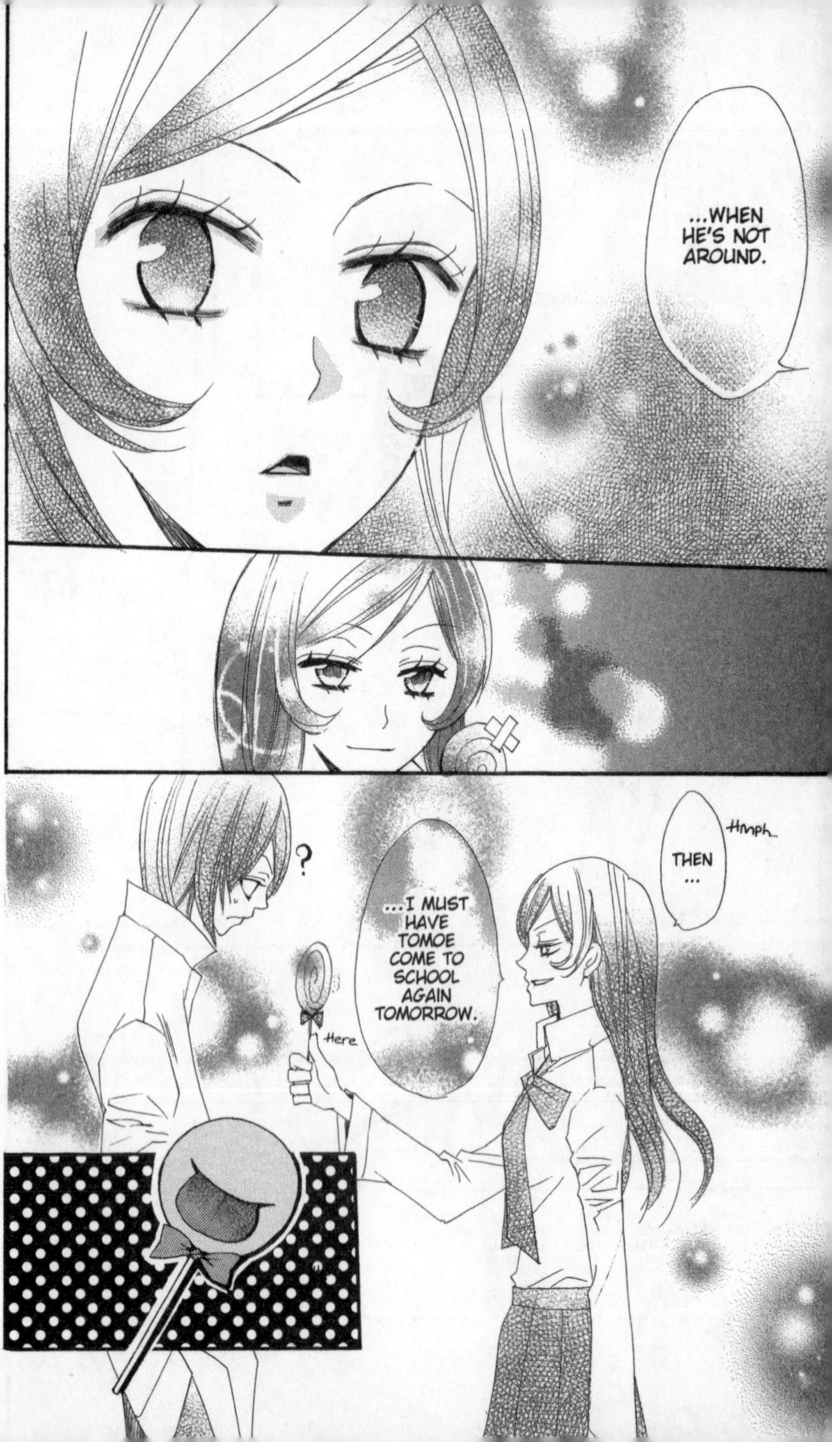
...WHEN HE'S NOT AROUND.
Hmph..
THEN ...
...I MUST HAVE TOMOE COME TO SCHOOL AGAIN TOMORROW.
?
Here

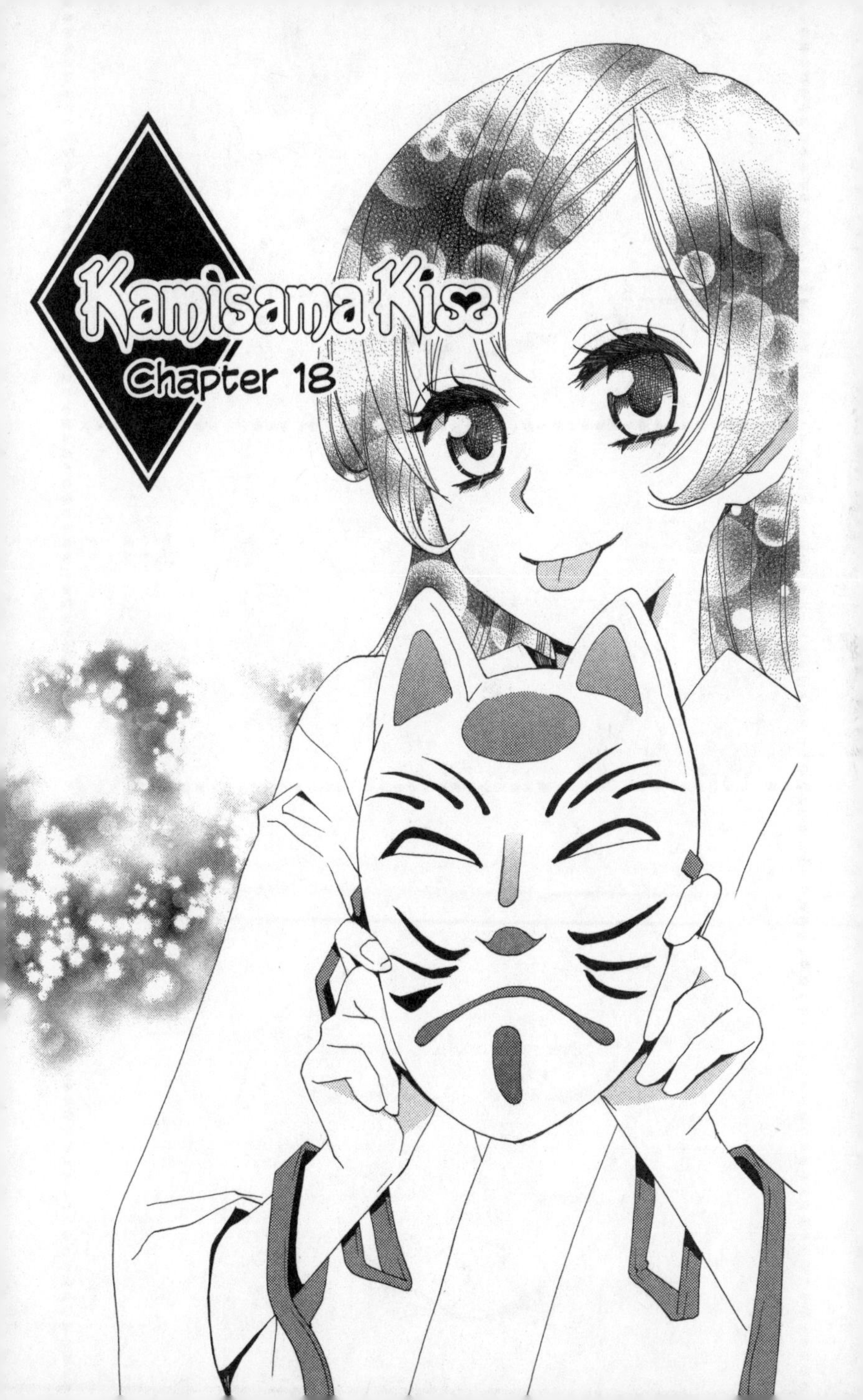
Kamisama Kiss
Chapter 18

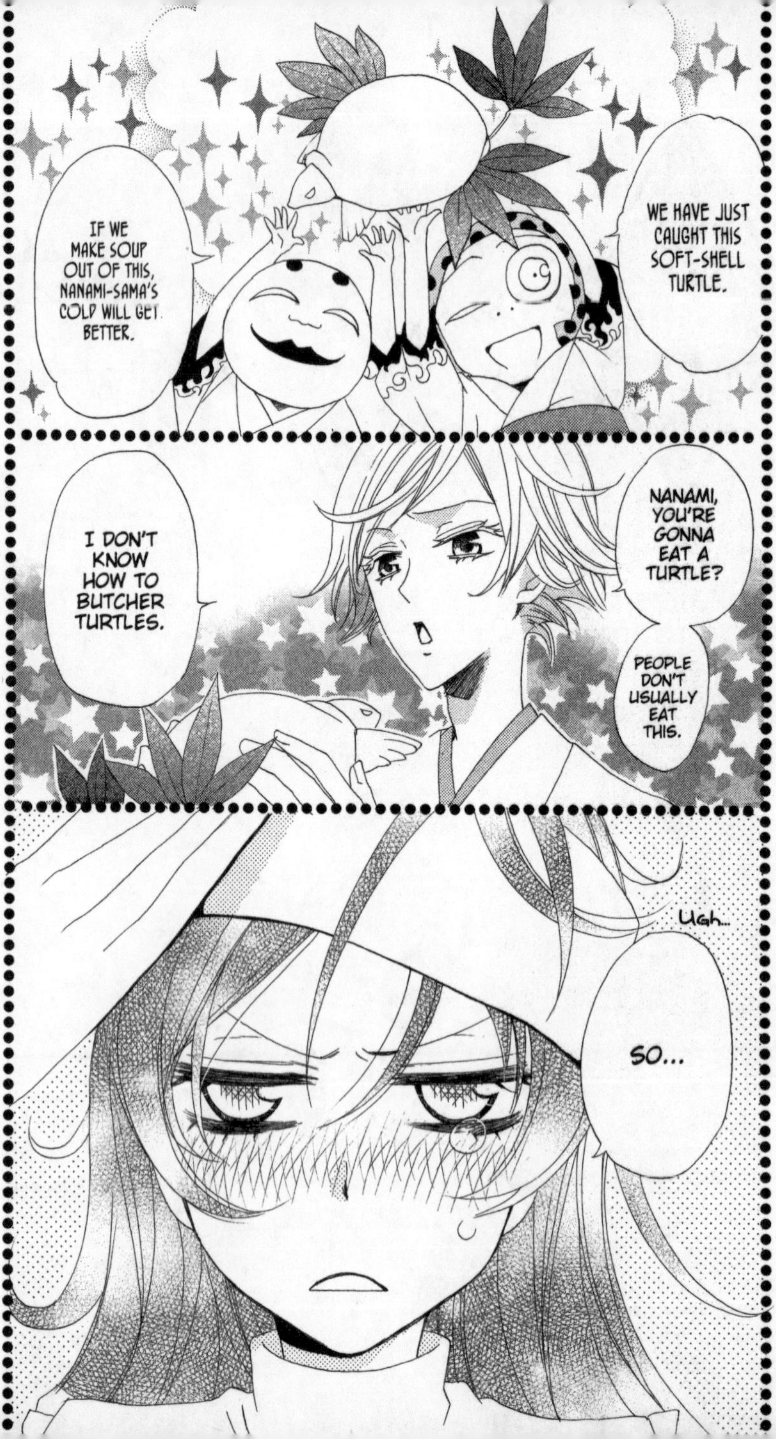
WE HAVE JUST CAUGHT THIS SOFT-SHELL TURTLE.
IF WE MAKE SOUP OUT OF THIS, NANAMI-SAMA'S COLD WILL GET BETTER.
NANAMI, YOU'RE GONNA EAT A TURTLE?
PEOPLE DON'T USUALLY EAT THIS.
I DON'T KNOW HOW TO BUTCHER TURTLES.
Ugh...
SO...

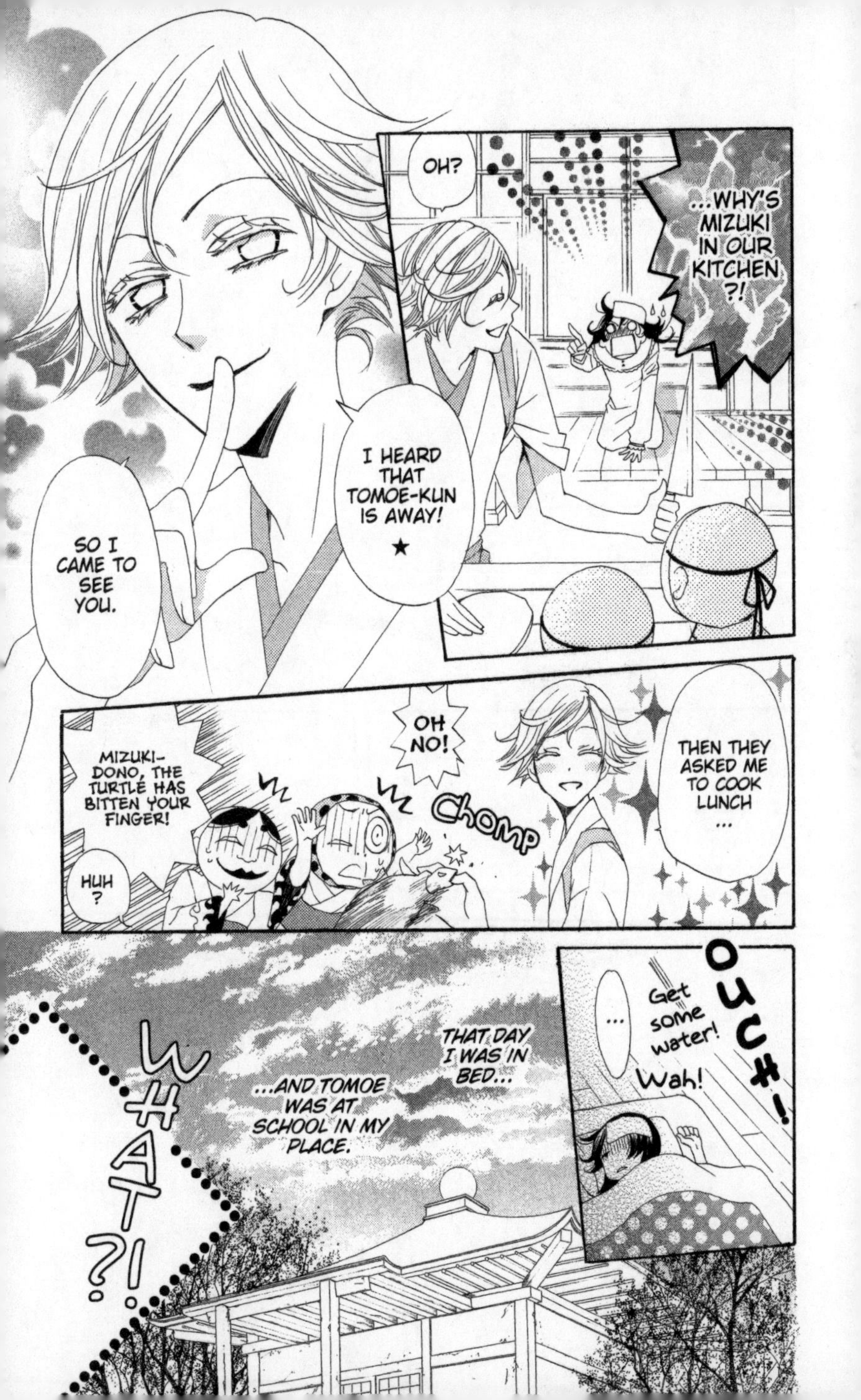
...WHY'S MIZUKI IN OUR KITCHEN?!
OH?
I HEARD THAT TOMOE-KUN IS AWAY! ★
SO I CAME TO SEE YOU.
THEN THEY ASKED ME TO COOK LUNCH...
CHOMP
OH NO!
MIZUKI-DONO, THE TURTLE HAS BITTEN YOUR FINGER!
HUH?
OUCH!
Get some water!
Wah!
...
THAT DAY I WAS IN BED...
...AND TOMOE WAS AT SCHOOL IN MY PLACE.
WHAT?!

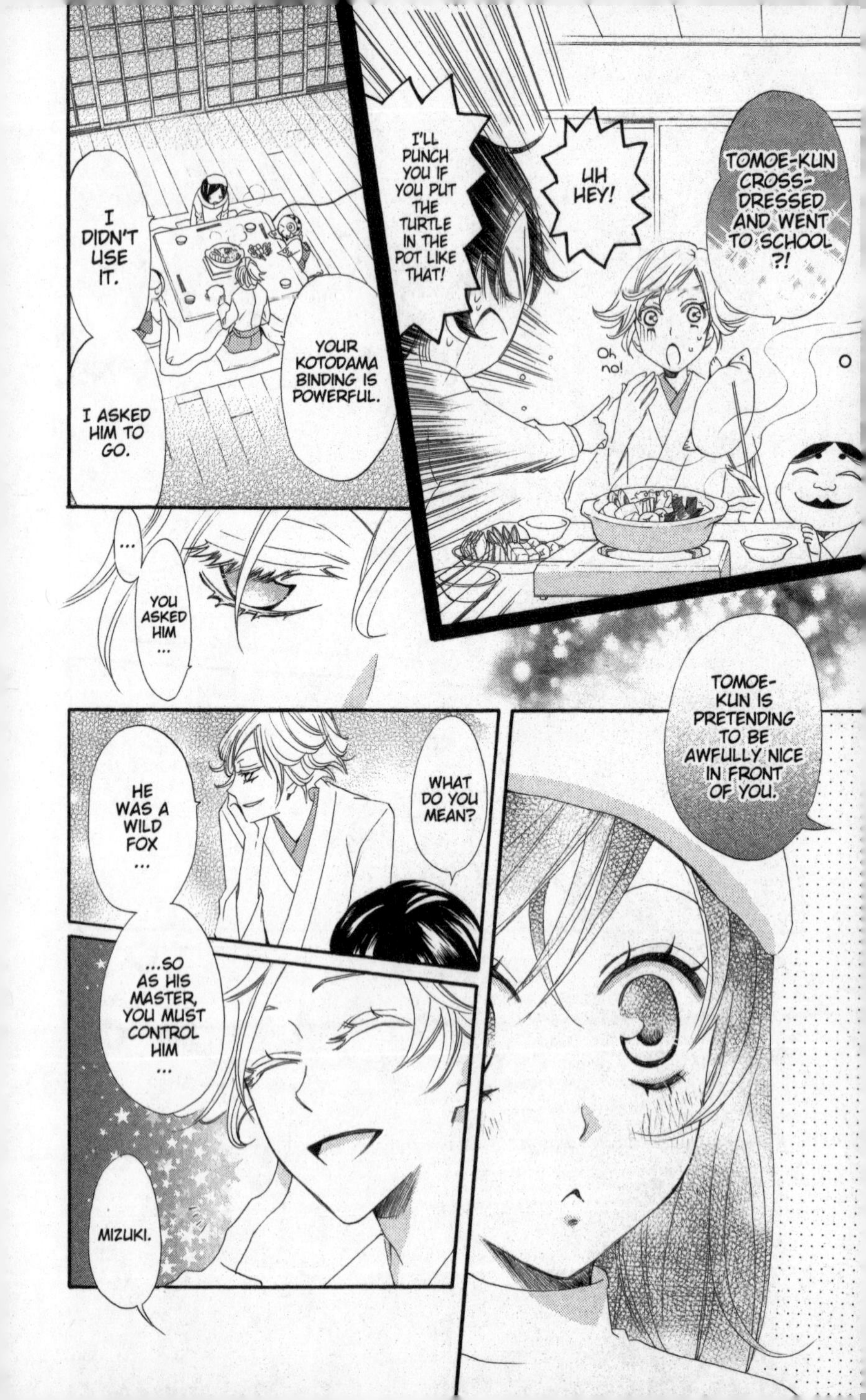
TOMOE-KUN CROSS-DRESSED AND WENT TO SCHOOL ?!
UH HEY!
I'LL PUNCH YOU IF YOU PUT THE TURTLE IN THE POT LIKE THAT!
Oh no!
YOUR KOTODAMA BINDING IS POWERFUL.
I DIDN'T USE IT.
I ASKED HIM TO GO.
TOMOE-KUN IS PRETENDING TO BE AWFULLY NICE IN FRONT OF YOU.
YOU ASKED HIM ...
...
WHAT DO YOU MEAN?
HE WAS A WILD FOX ...
...SO AS HIS MASTER, YOU MUST CONTROL HIM ...
MIZUKI.

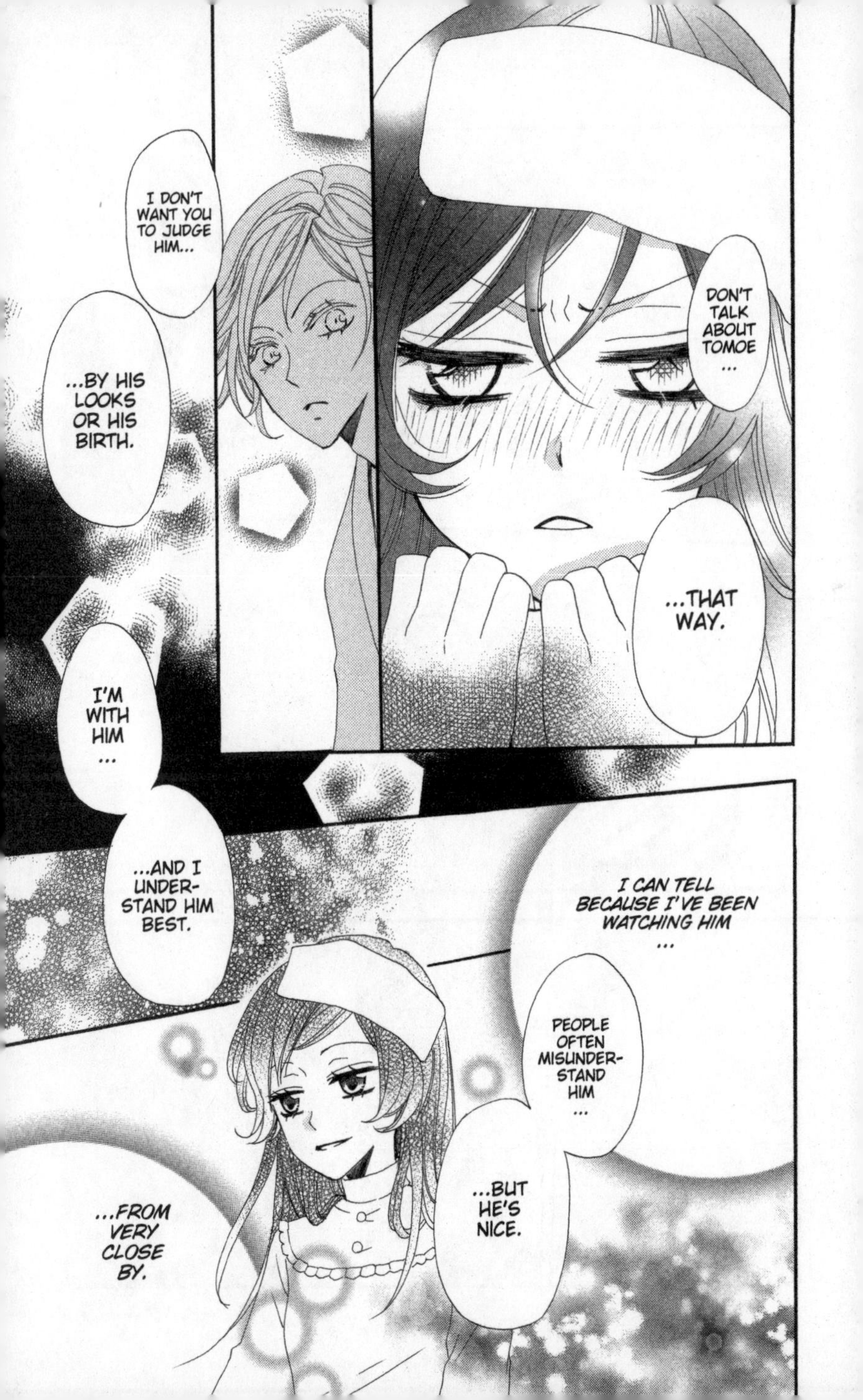

DON'T TALK ABOUT TOMOE ...
...THAT WAY.
I DON'T WANT YOU TO JUDGE HIM...
...BY HIS LOOKS OR HIS BIRTH.
I'M WITH HIM ...
...AND I UNDER-STAND HIM BEST.
I CAN TELL BECAUSE I'VE BEEN WATCHING HIM ...
PEOPLE OFTEN MISUNDER-STAND HIM ...
...BUT HE'S NICE.
...FROM VERY CLOSE BY.

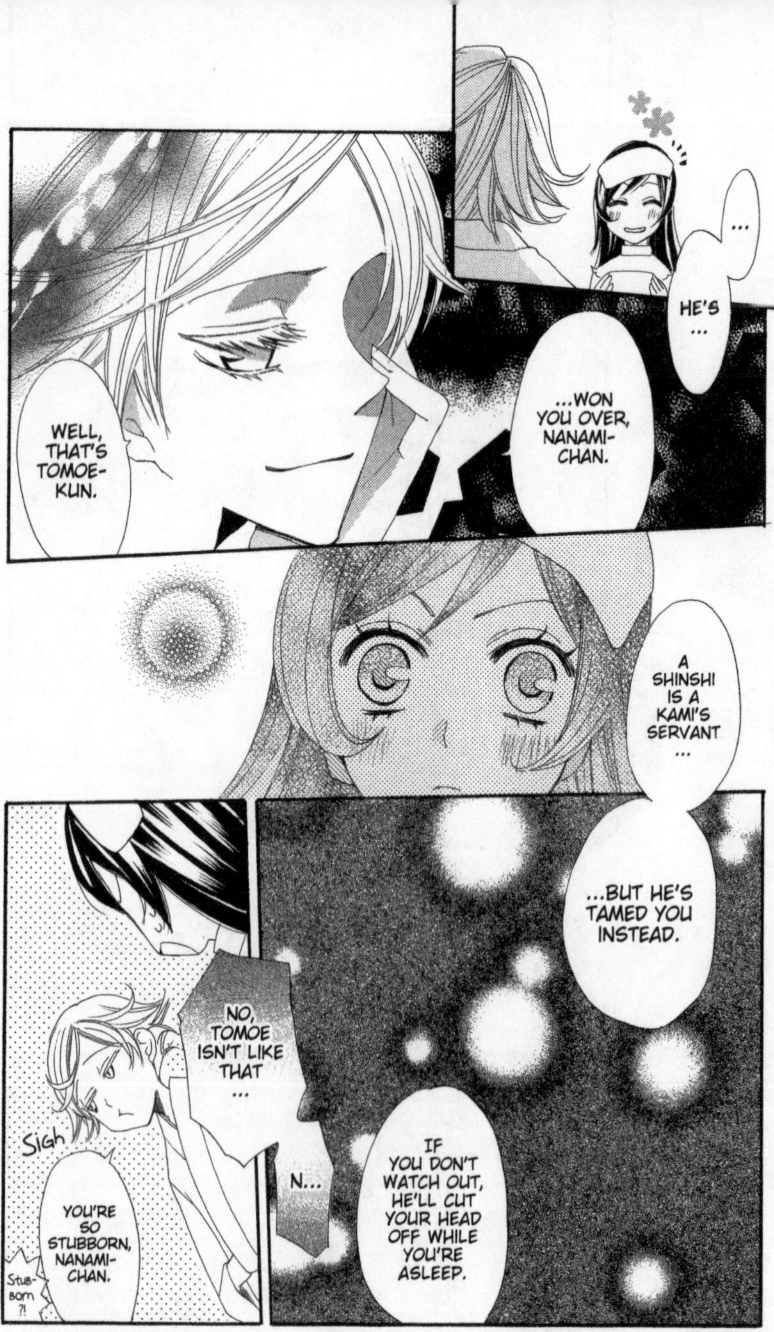
...
HE'S ...
...WON YOU OVER, NANAMI-CHAN.
WELL, THAT'S TOMOE-KUN.
A SHINSHI IS A KAMI'S SERVANT ...
...BUT HE'S TAMED YOU INSTEAD.
IF YOU DON'T WATCH OUT, HE'LL CUT YOUR HEAD OFF WHILE YOU'RE ASLEEP.
N...
NO, TOMOE ISN'T LIKE THAT ...
Sigh
YOU'RE SO STUBBORN, NANAMI-CHAN.
Stubborn?!

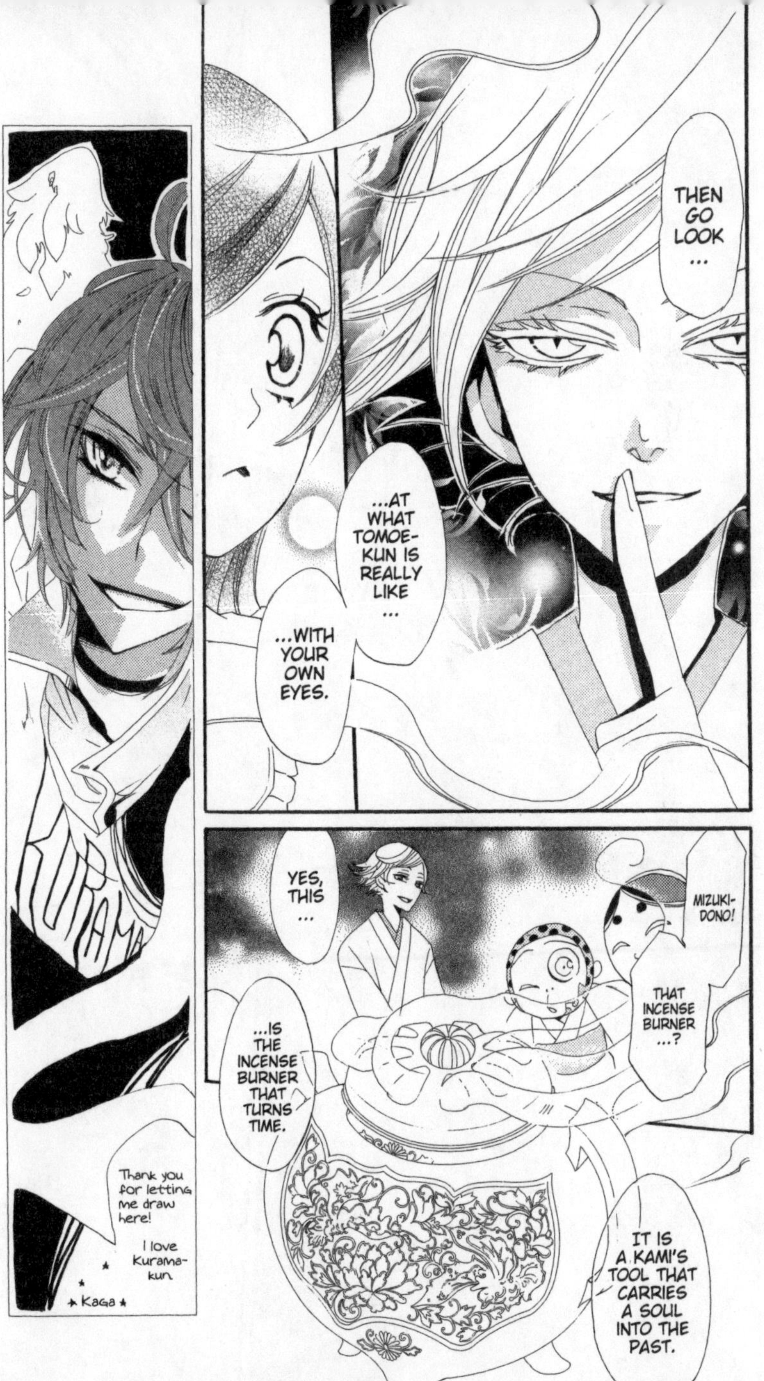
THEN GO LOOK ...
...AT WHAT TOMOE-KUN IS REALLY LIKE ...
...WITH YOUR OWN EYES.
MIZUKI-DONO!
THAT INCENSE BURNER ...?
YES, THIS ...
...IS THE INCENSE BURNER THAT TURNS TIME.
IT IS A KAMI'S TOOL THAT CARRIES A SOUL INTO THE PAST.
KURAMA
Thank you for letting me draw here!
I love Kurama-kun.
Kaga

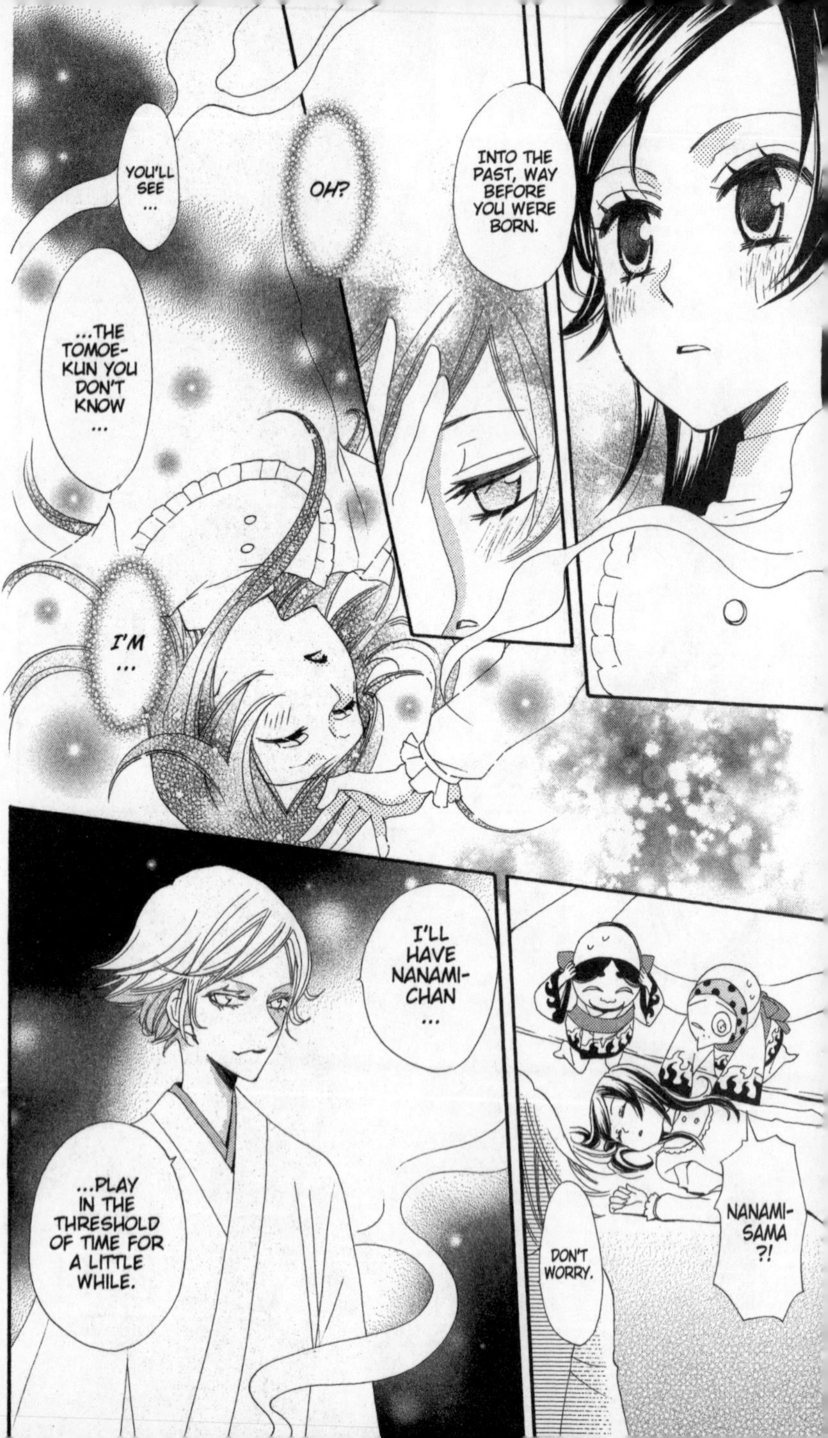
INTO THE PAST, WAY BEFORE YOU WERE BORN.
OH?
YOU'LL SEE ...
...THE TOMOE-KUN YOU DON'T KNOW ...
I'M ...
NANAMI-SAMA ?!
DON'T WORRY.
I'LL HAVE NANAMI-CHAN ...
...PLAY IN THE THRESHOLD OF TIME FOR A LITTLE WHILE.

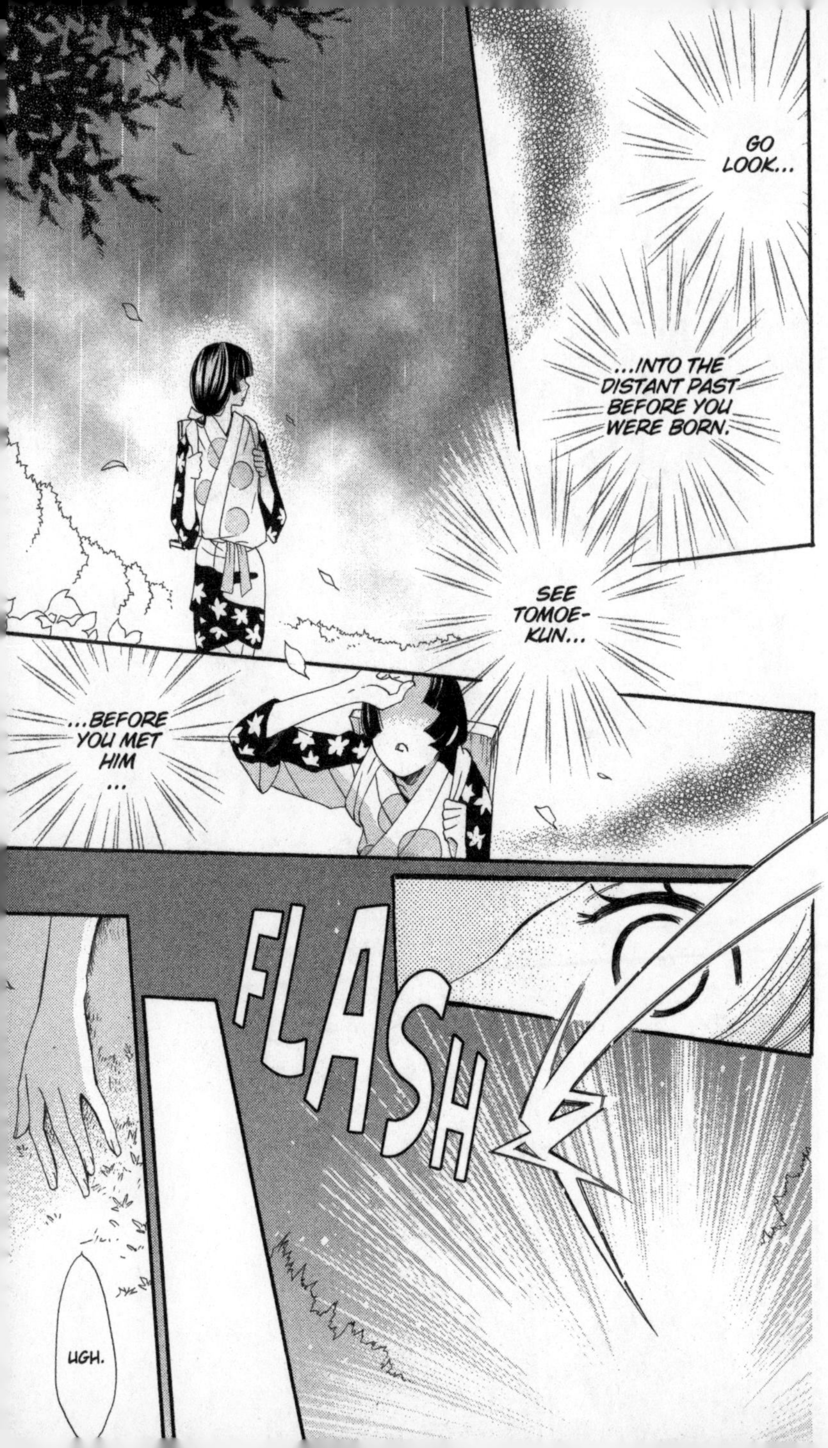
GO LOOK...
...INTO THE DISTANT PAST BEFORE YOU WERE BORN.
SEE TOMOE-KUN...
...BEFORE YOU MET HIM ...
FLASH
UGH.

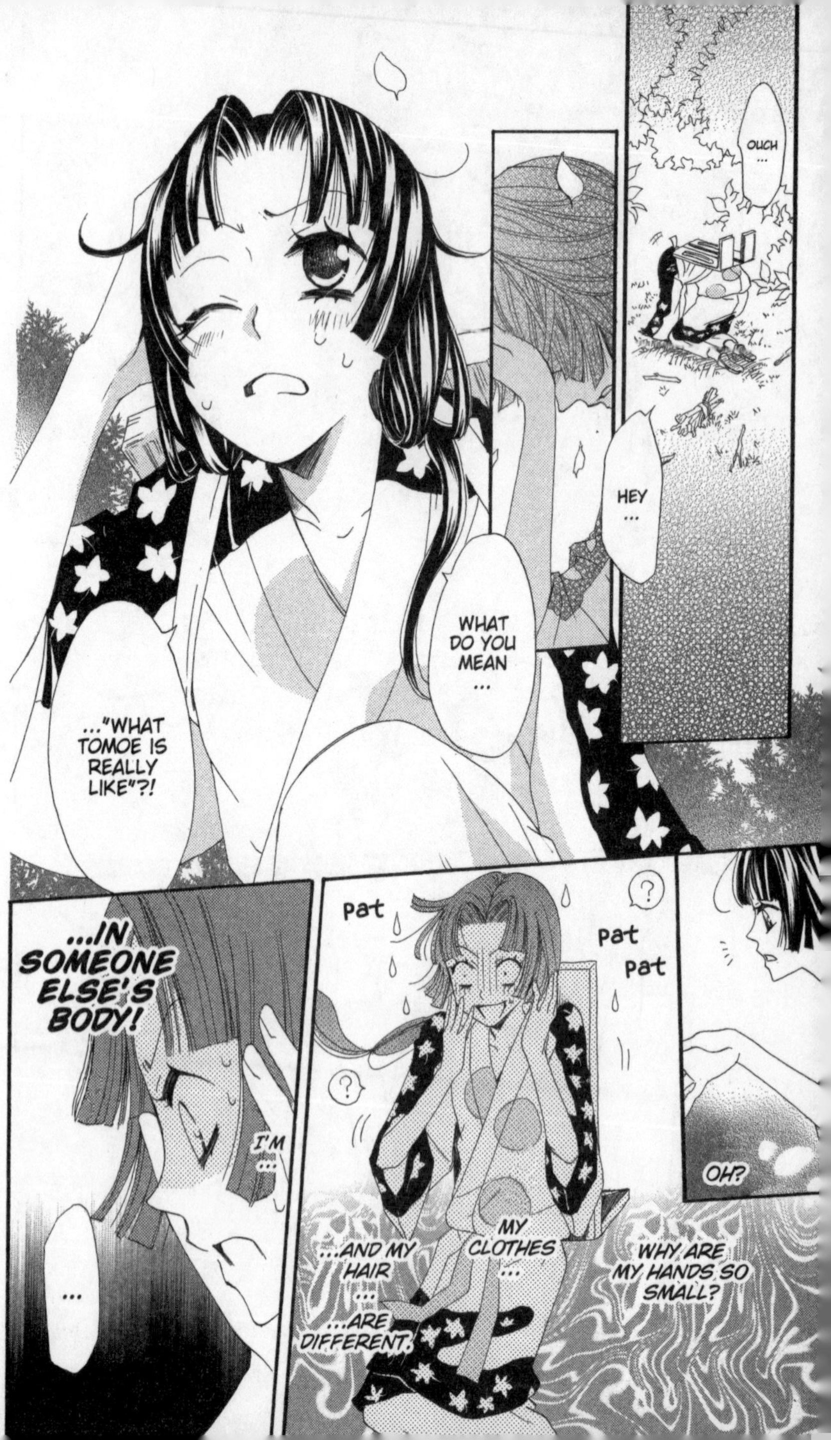
OUCH ...
HEY ...
WHAT DO YOU MEAN ...
..."WHAT TOMOE IS REALLY LIKE"?!
OH?
pat
pat
pat
?
?
WHY ARE MY HANDS SO SMALL?
MY CLOTHES ...
...AND MY HAIR ...
...ARE DIFFERENT.
I'M ...
...
...IN SOMEONE ELSE'S BODY!

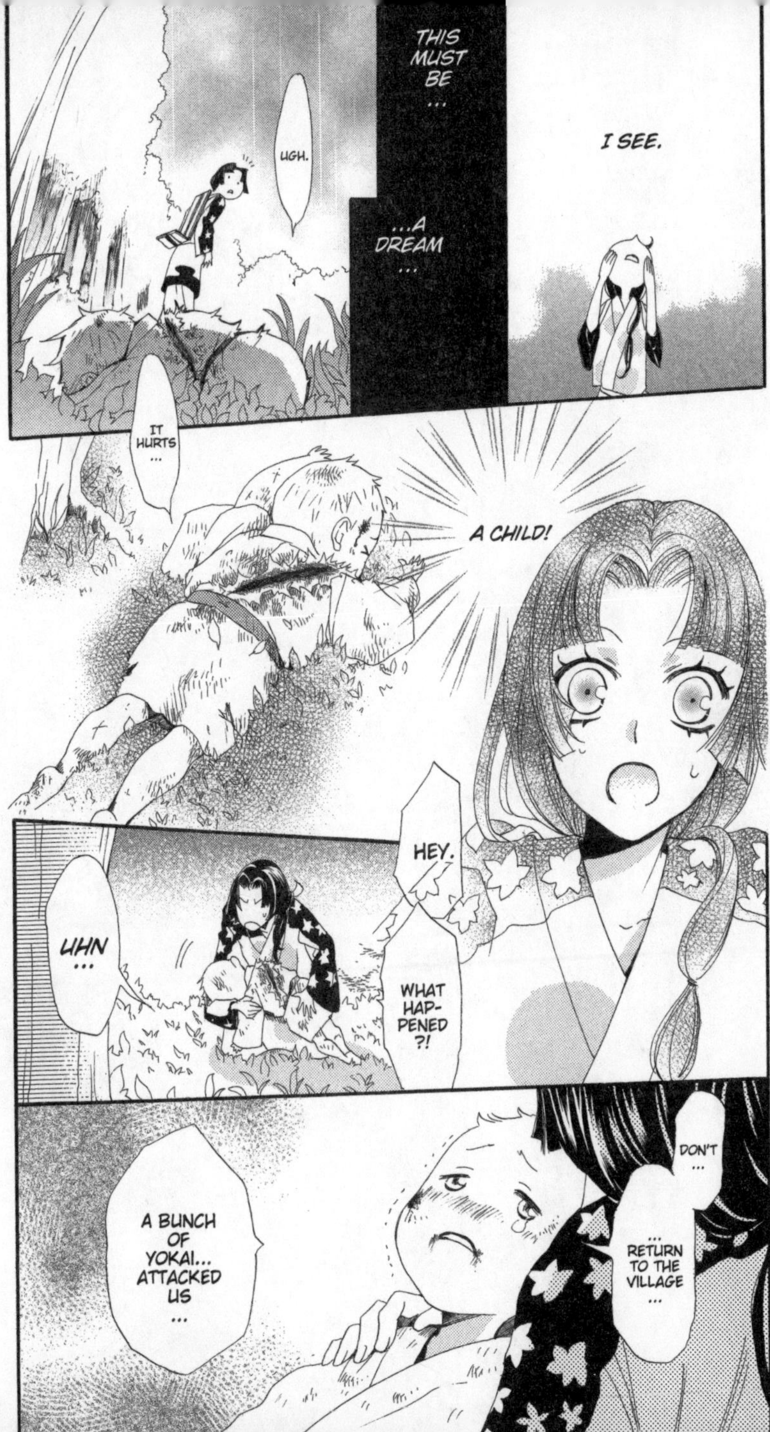
I SEE.
THIS MUST BE ...
...A DREAM ...
UGH.
IT HURTS ...
A CHILD!
HEY.
WHAT HAP-PENED ?!
UHN ...
DON'T ...
... RETURN TO THE VILLAGE ...
A BUNCH OF YOKAI... ATTACKED US ...

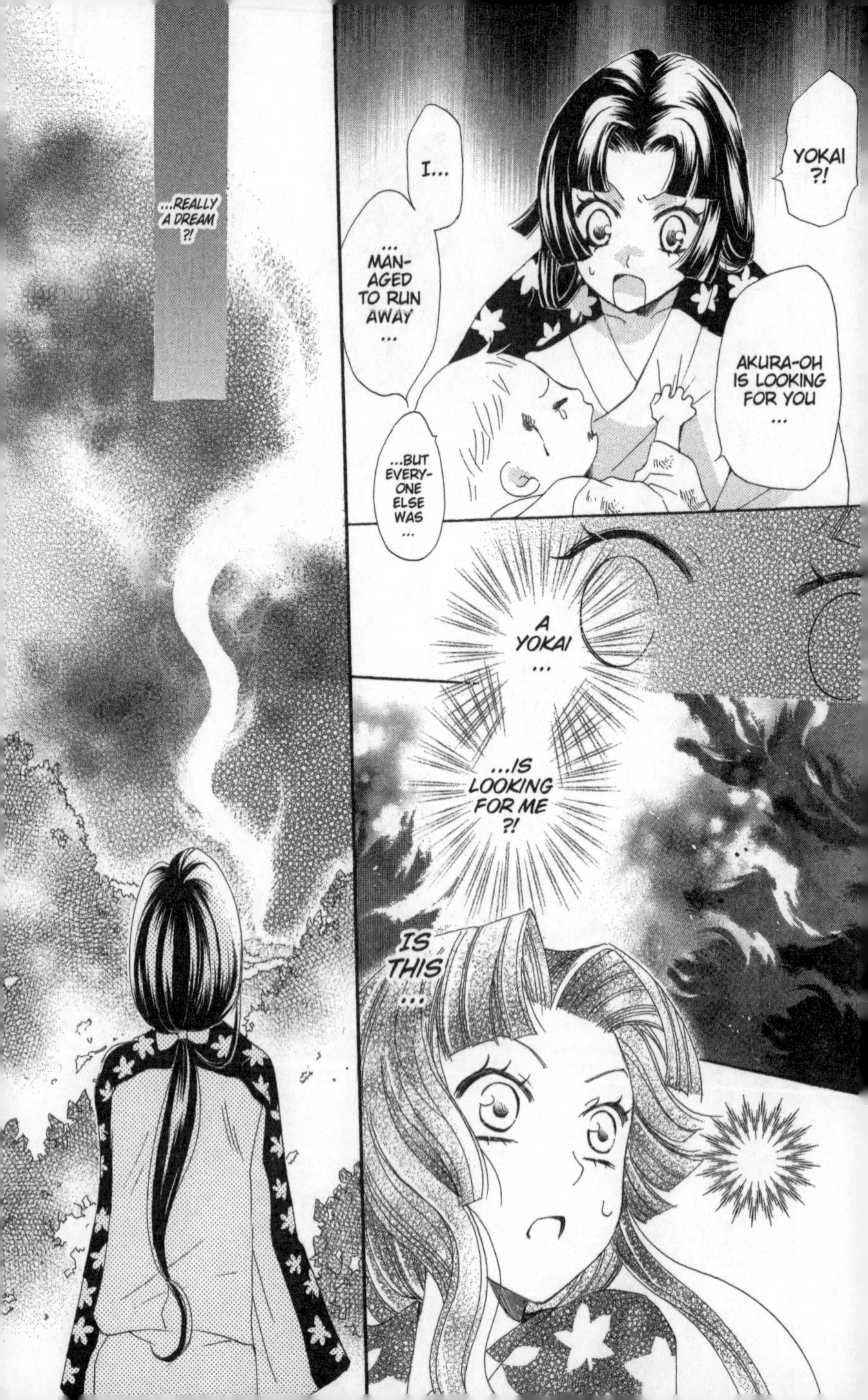
YOKAI ?!
AKURA-OH IS LOOKING FOR YOU ...
I...
...MAN-AGED TO RUN AWAY ...
...BUT EVERY-ONE ELSE WAS ...
A YOKAI ...
...IS LOOKING FOR ME ?!
IS THIS ...
...REALLY A DREAM ?!

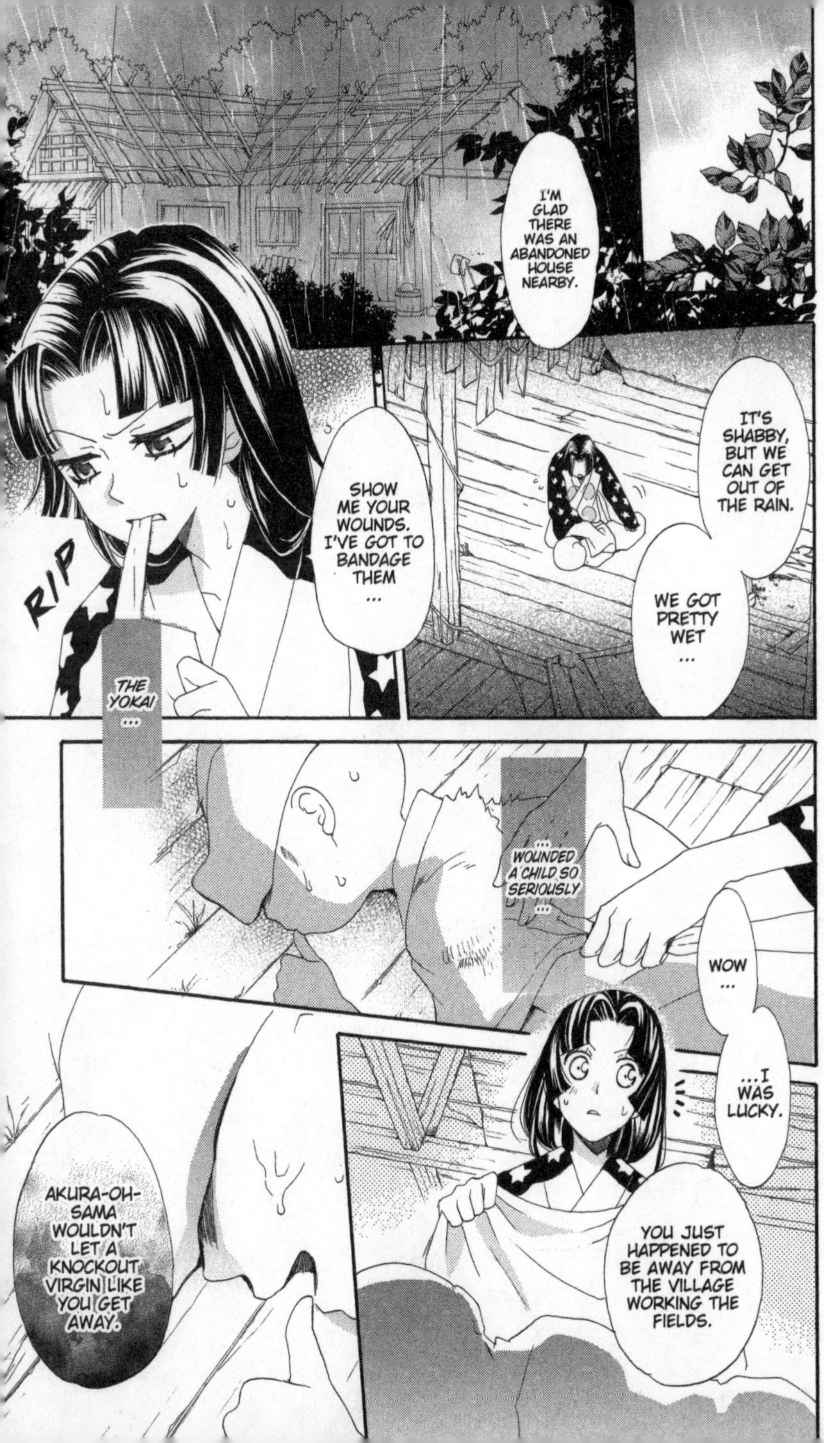
I'M GLAD THERE WAS AN ABANDONED HOUSE NEARBY.
IT'S SHABBY, BUT WE CAN GET OUT OF THE RAIN.
WE GOT PRETTY WET ...
SHOW ME YOUR WOUNDS. I'VE GOT TO BANDAGE THEM ...
RIP
THE YOKAI ...
... WOUNDED A CHILD SO SERIOUSLY ...
WOW ...
...I WAS LUCKY.
YOU JUST HAPPENED TO BE AWAY FROM THE VILLAGE WORKING THE FIELDS.
AKURA-OH-SAMA WOULDN'T LET A KNOCKOUT VIRGIN LIKE YOU GET AWAY.

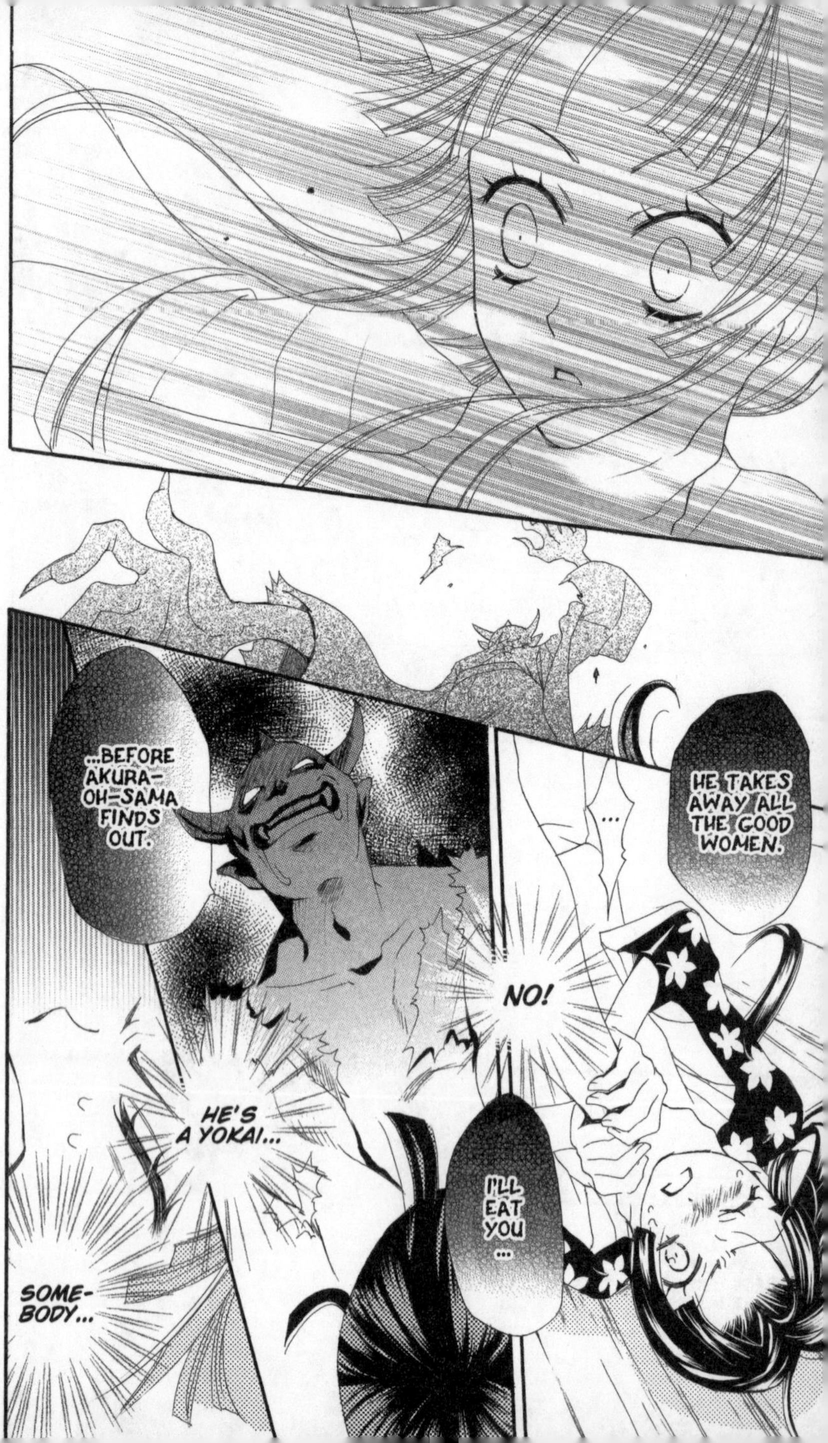
HE TAKES AWAY ALL THE GOOD WOMEN.
...
...BEFORE AKURA-OH-SAMA FINDS OUT.
NO!
I'LL EAT YOU...
HE'S A YOKAI...
SOME-BODY...

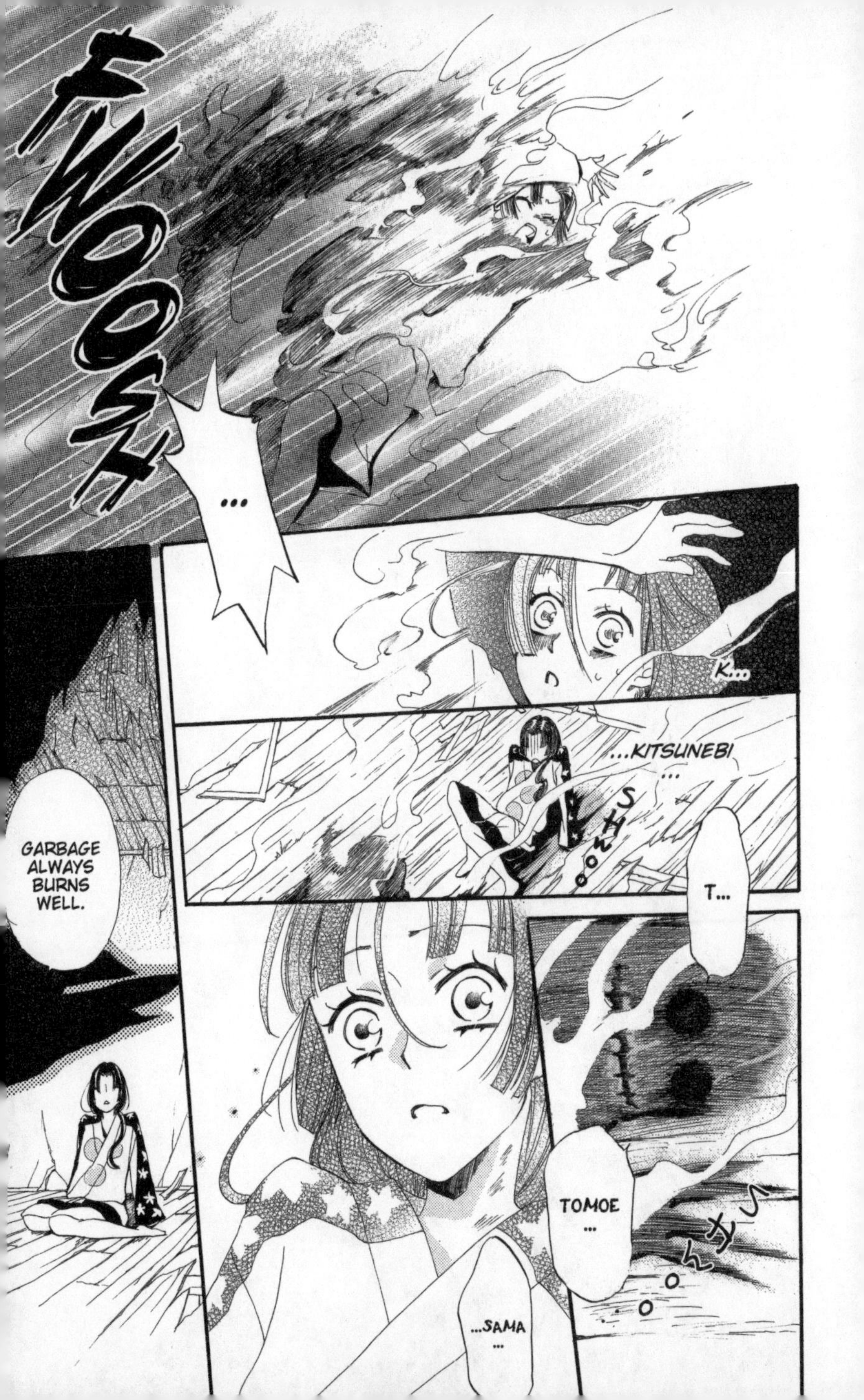
WHOOSH
...
K...
...KITSUNEBI ...
SHWOO
T...
TOMOE ...
...SAMA ...
GARBAGE ALWAYS BURNS WELL.

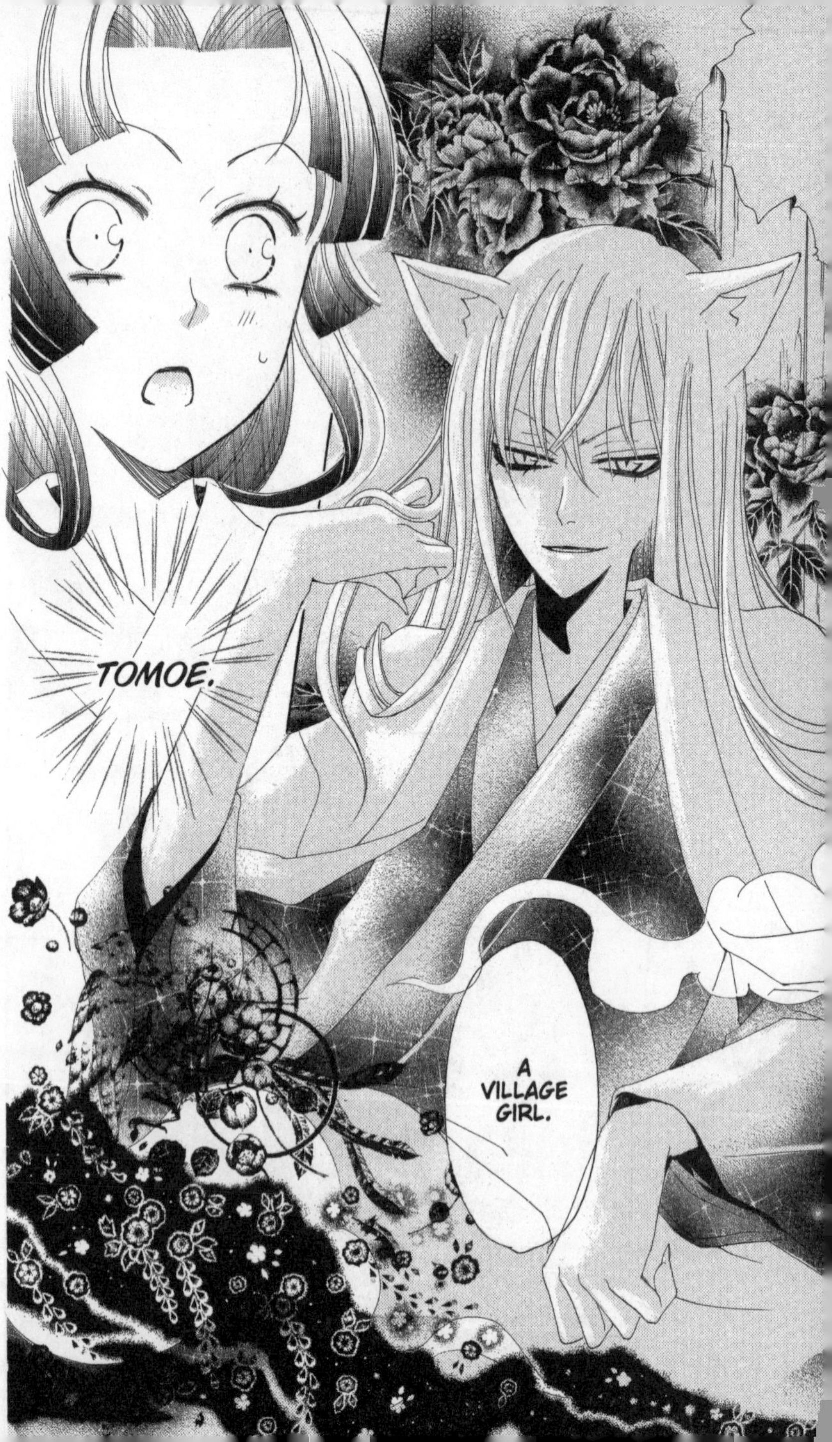
A VILLAGE GIRL.
TOMOE.

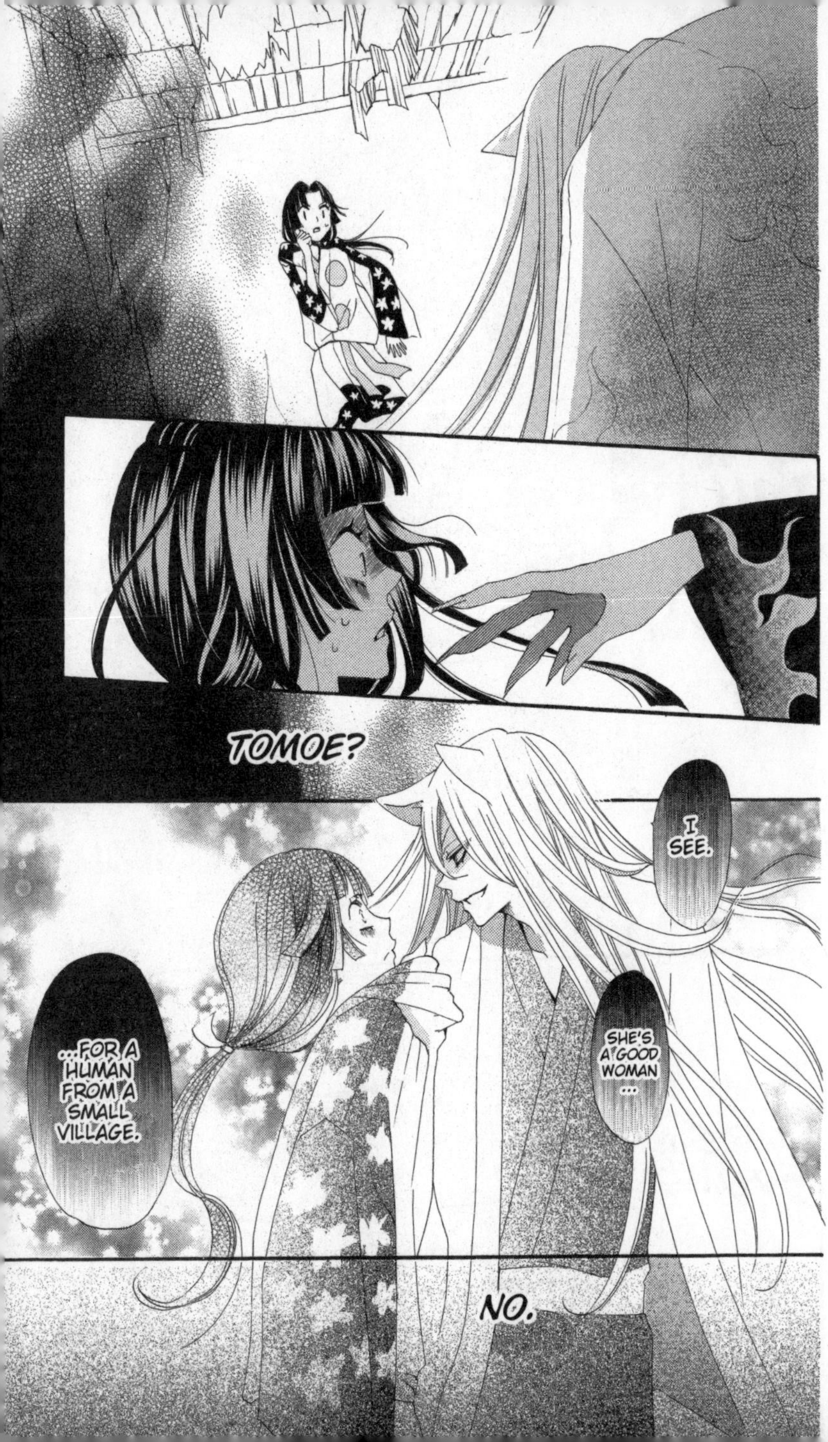
TOMOE?
I SEE.
SHE'S A GOOD WOMAN...
...FOR A HUMAN FROM A SMALL VILLAGE.
NO.

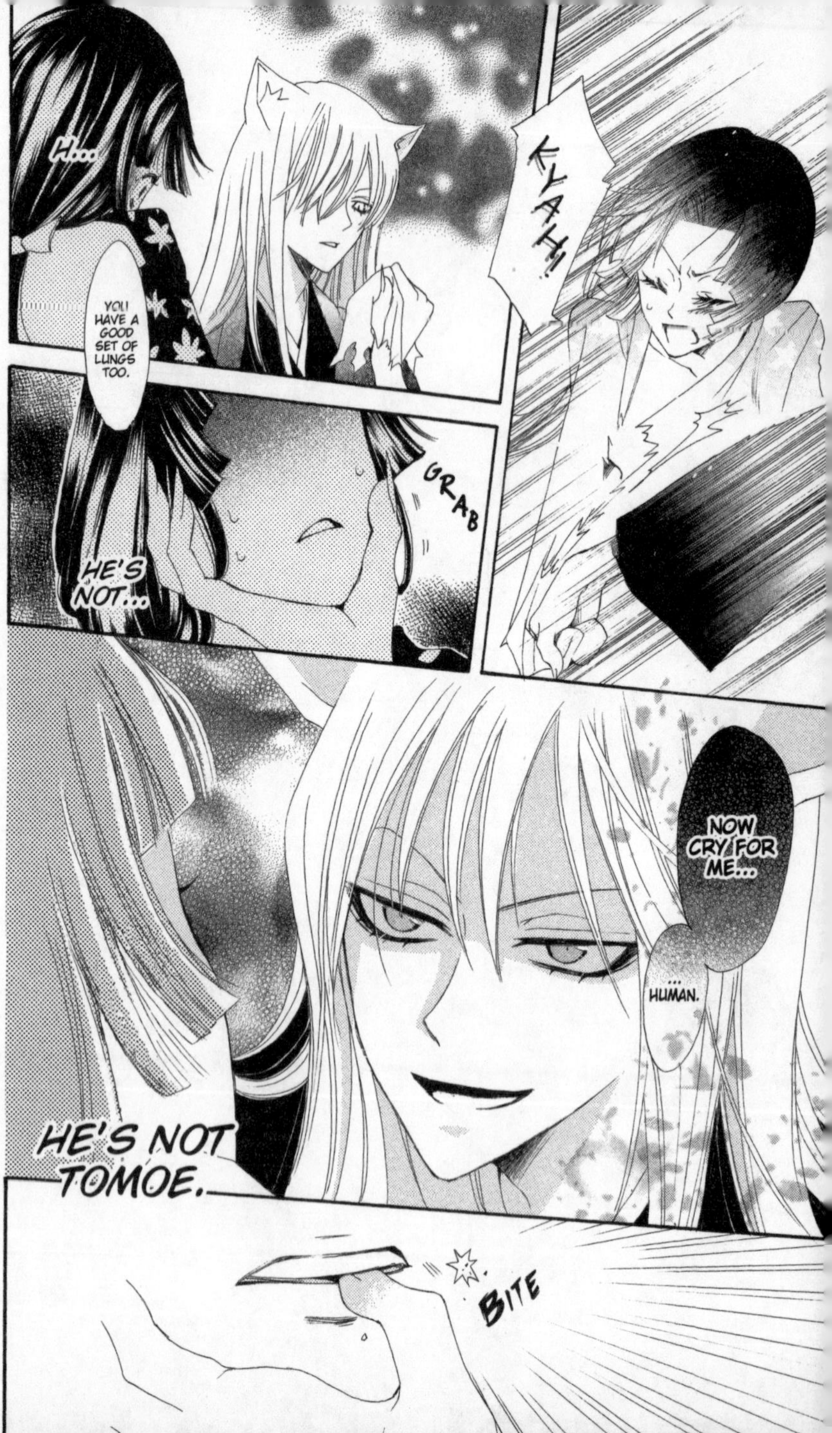

KYAH!!
H...
YOU HAVE A GOOD SET OF LUNGS TOO.
GRAB
HE'S NOT...
NOW CRY FOR ME...
...HUMAN.
HE'S NOT TOMOE.
BITE

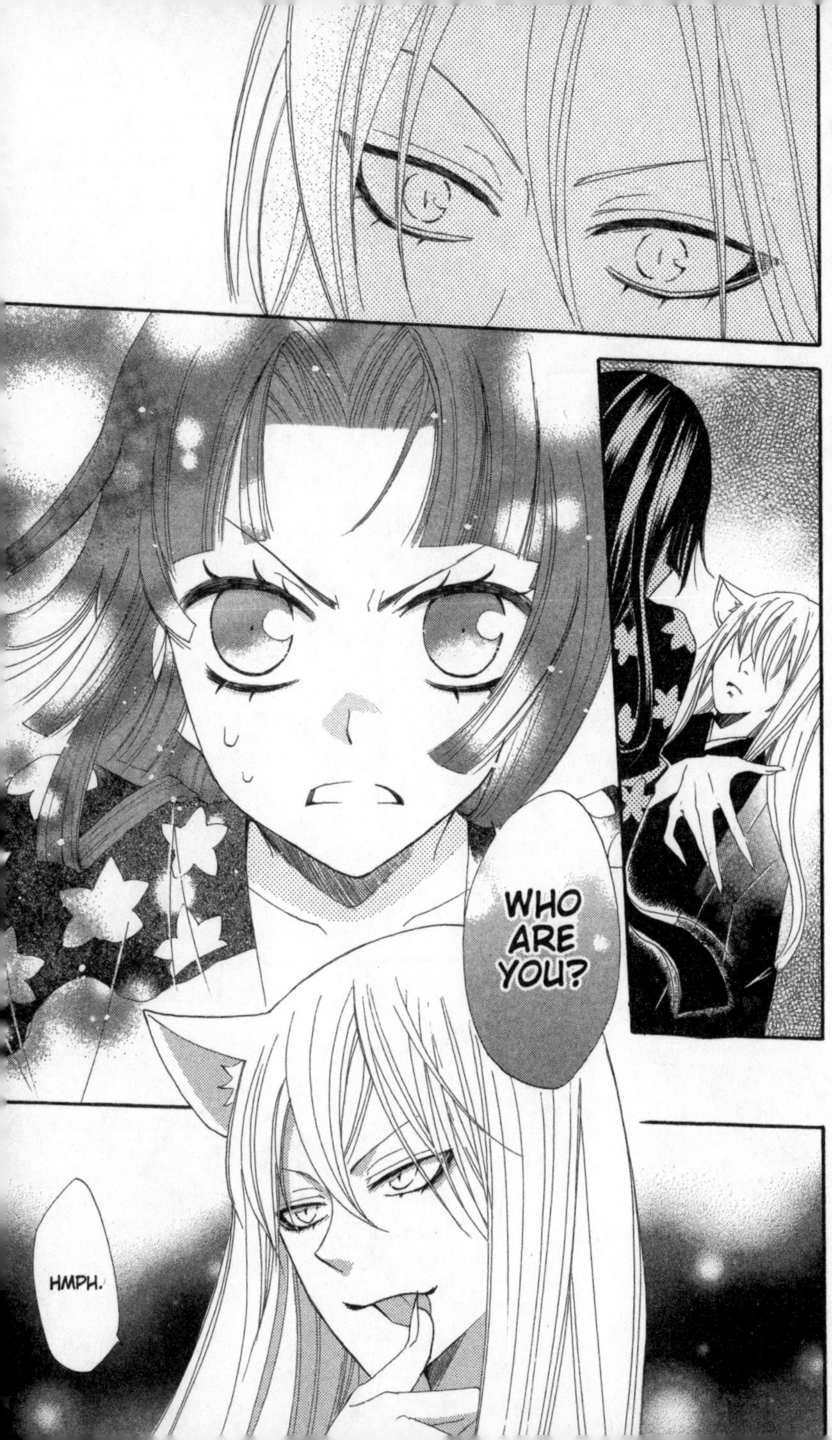
WHO ARE YOU?
HMPH.

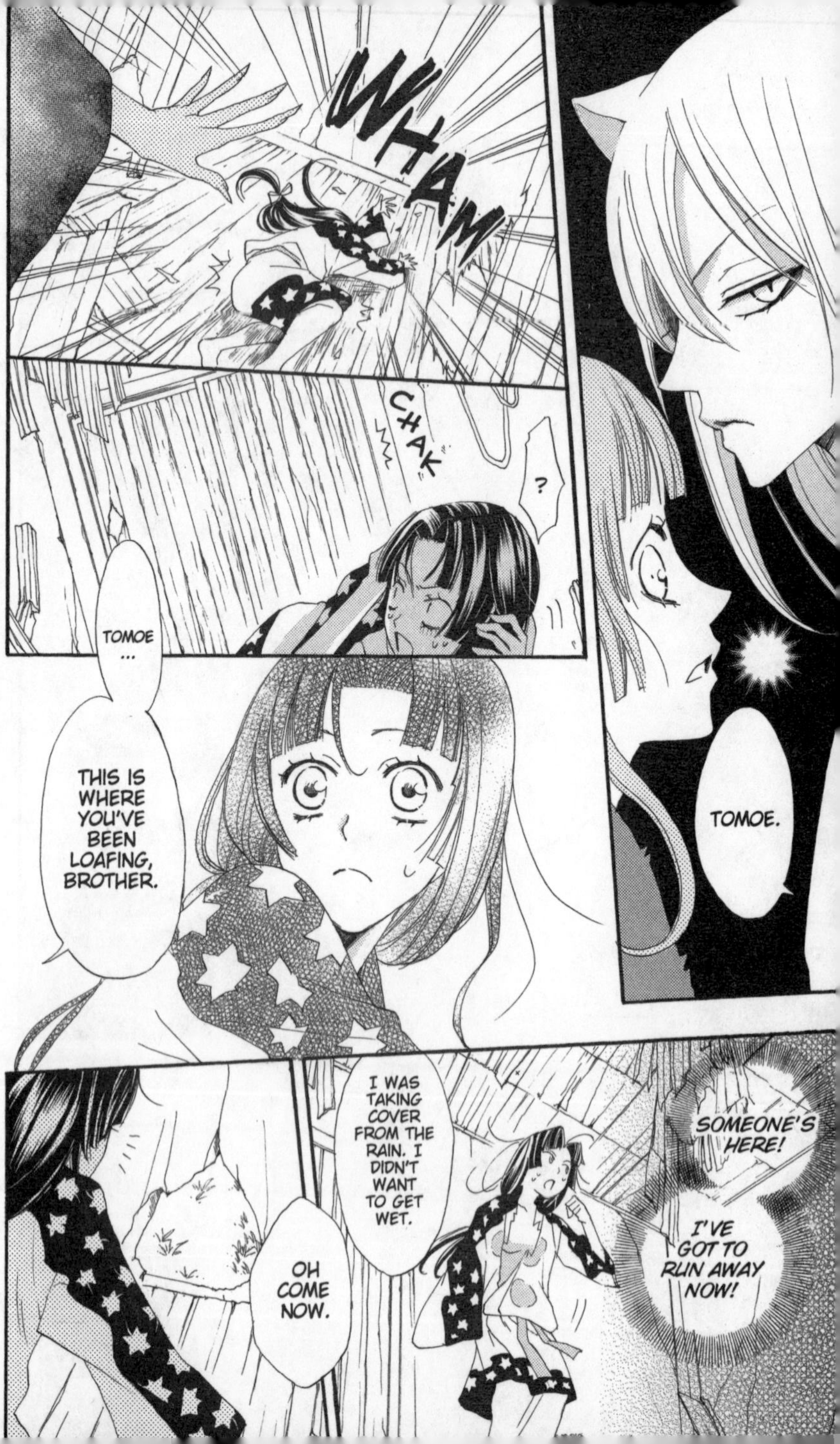
TOMOE.
WHAM
CHAK
?
TOMOE ...
THIS IS WHERE YOU'VE BEEN LOAFING, BROTHER.
SOMEONE'S HERE!
I'VE GOT TO RUN AWAY NOW!
I WAS TAKING COVER FROM THE RAIN. I DIDN'T WANT TO GET WET.
OH COME NOW.

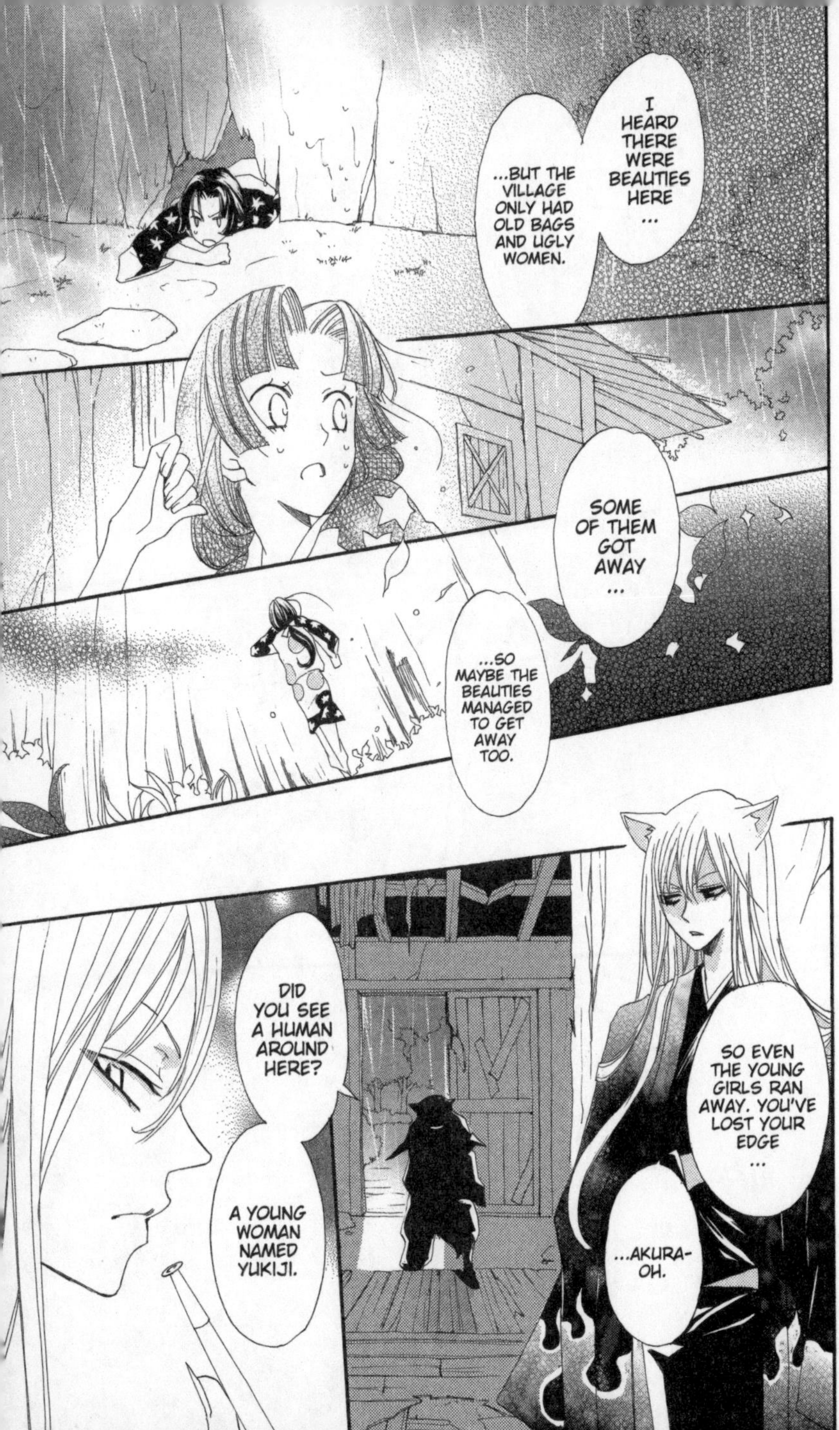
I HEARD THERE WERE BEAUTIES HERE ...
...BUT THE VILLAGE ONLY HAD OLD BAGS AND UGLY WOMEN.
SOME OF THEM GOT AWAY ...
...SO MAYBE THE BEAUTIES MANAGED TO GET AWAY TOO.
SO EVEN THE YOUNG GIRLS RAN AWAY. YOU'VE LOST YOUR EDGE ...
...AKURA-OH.
DID YOU SEE A HUMAN AROUND HERE?
A YOUNG WOMAN NAMED YUKIJI.

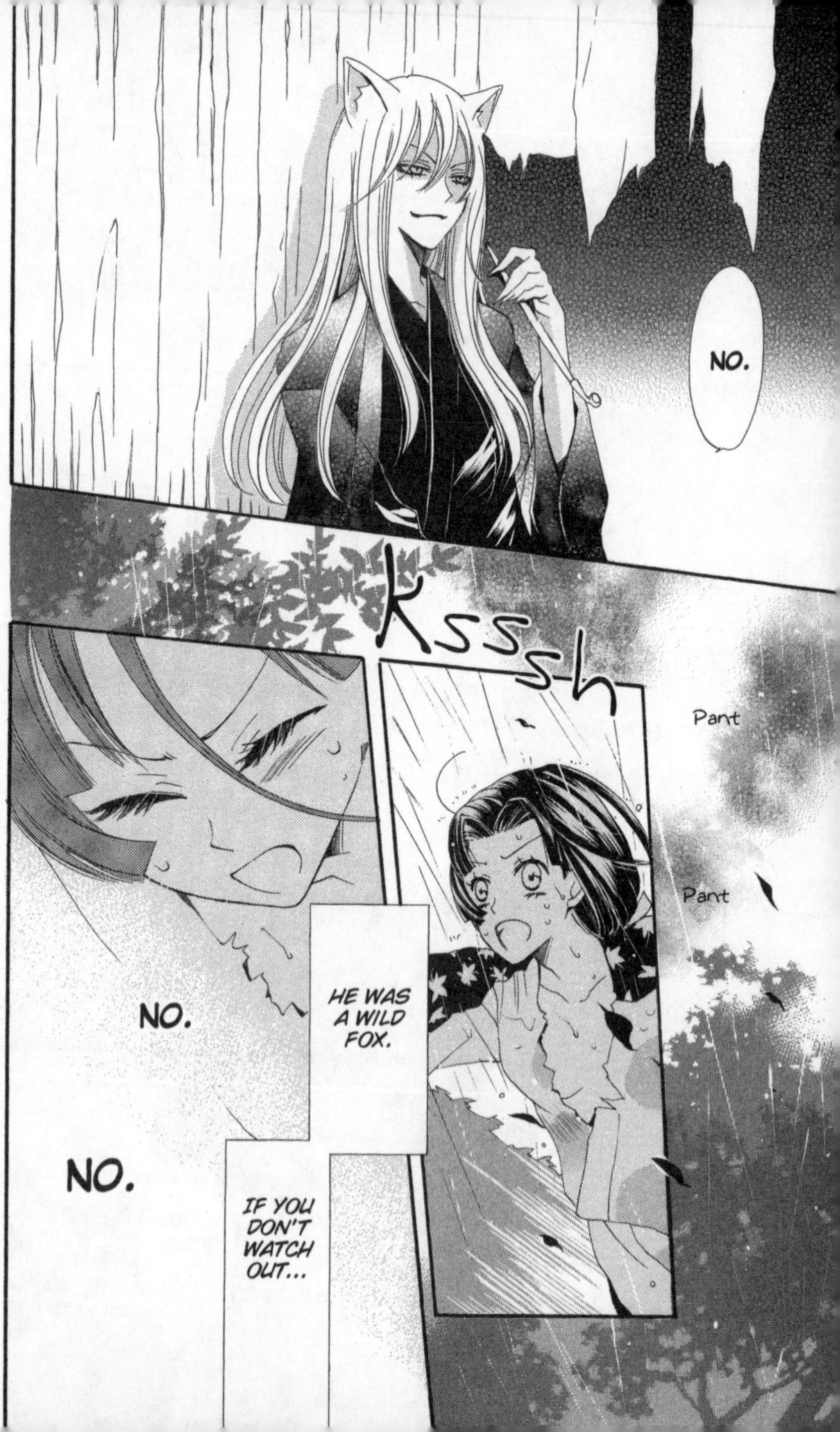
NO.
Ksssh
Pant
Pant
HE WAS A WILD FOX.
NO.
NO.
IF YOU DON'T WATCH OUT...

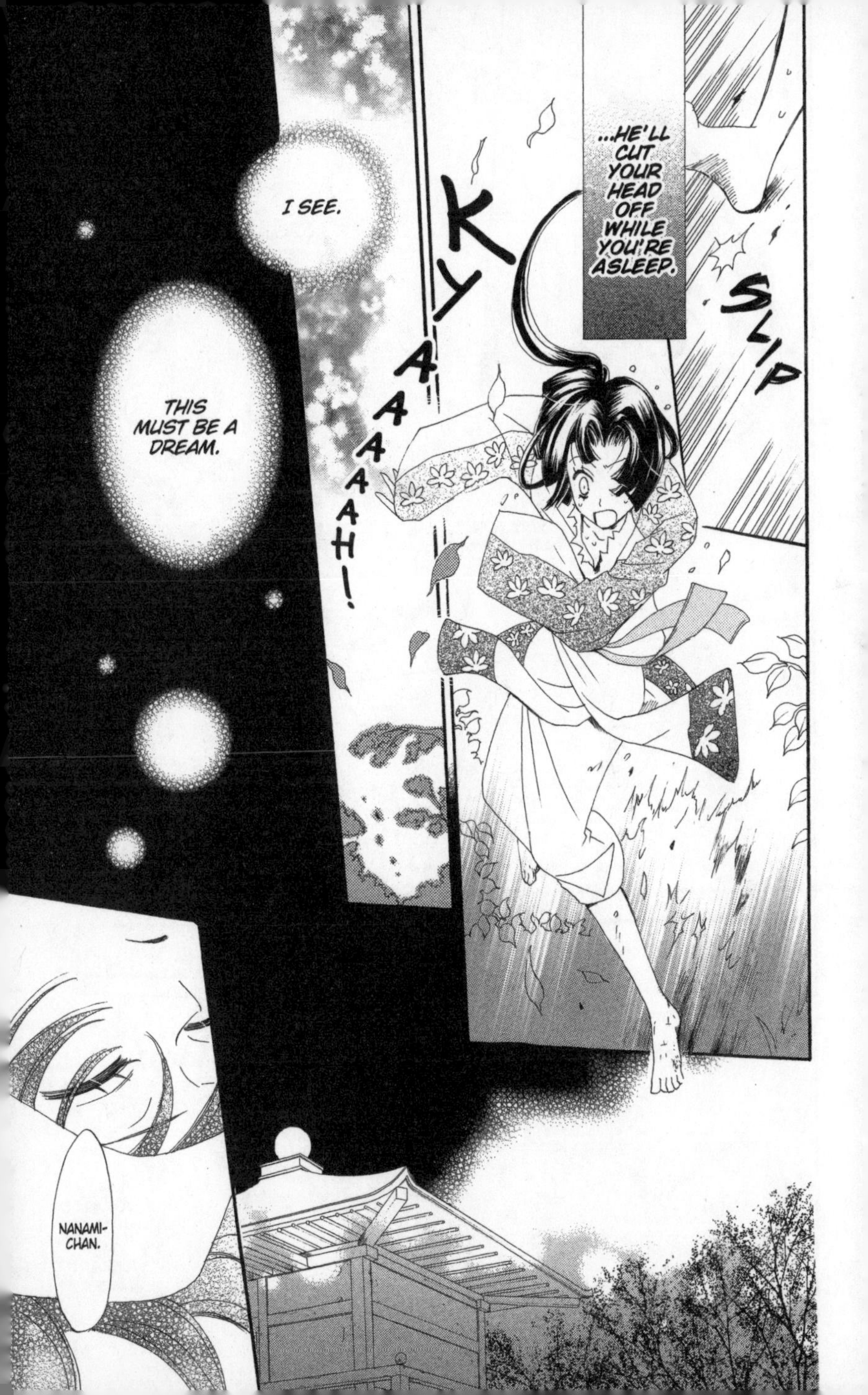
...HE'LL CUT YOUR HEAD OFF WHILE YOU'RE ASLEEP.
SLIP
KYAAAAAH!
I SEE.
THIS MUST BE A DREAM.
NANAMI-CHAN.

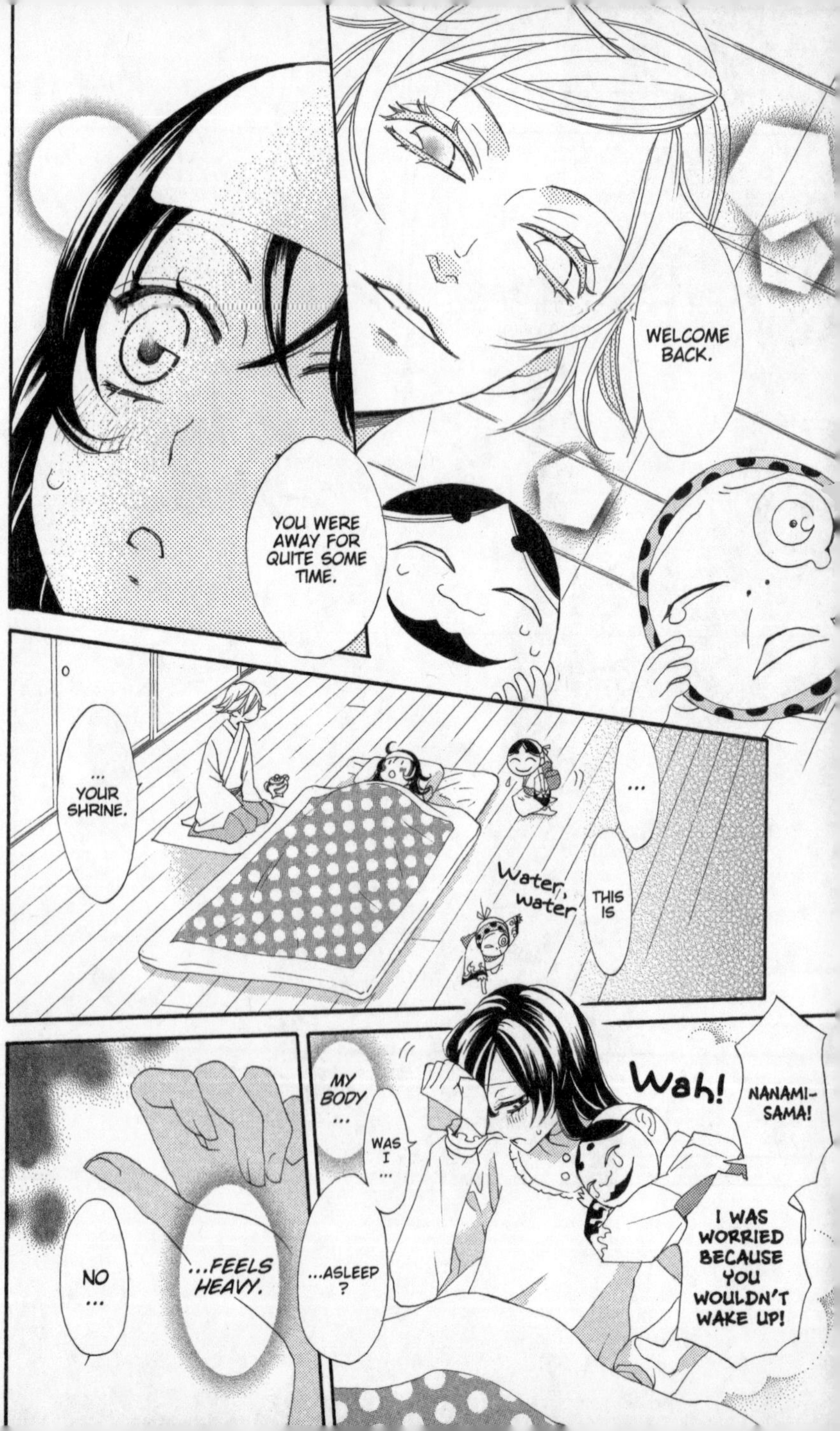
WELCOME BACK.
YOU WERE AWAY FOR QUITE SOME TIME.
...
THIS IS
Water, water
... YOUR SHRINE.
Wah!
NANAMI-SAMA!
I WAS WORRIED BECAUSE YOU WOULDN'T WAKE UP!
MY BODY ...
WAS I ...
...ASLEEP ?
...FEELS HEAVY.
NO ...

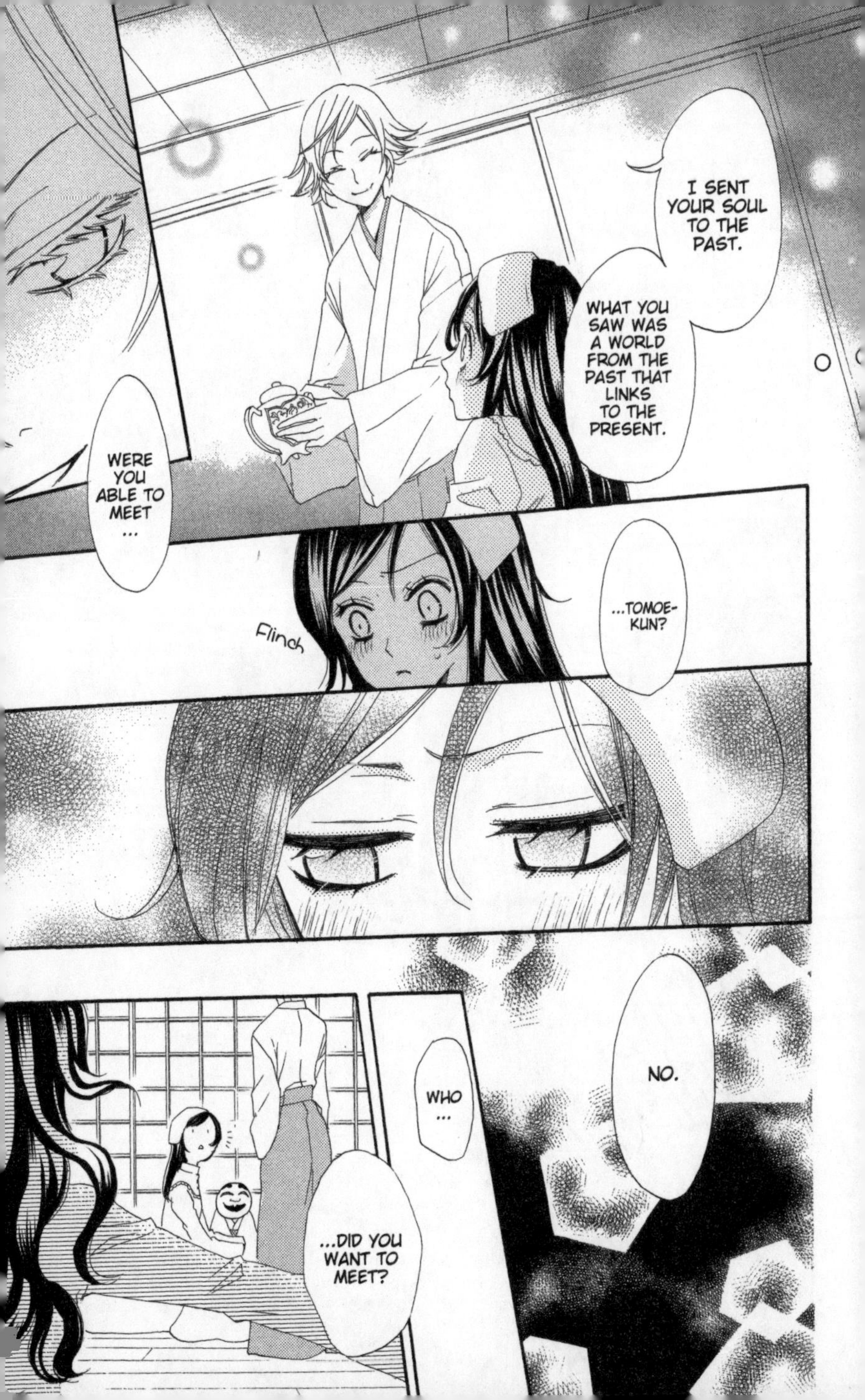
I SENT YOUR SOUL TO THE PAST.
WHAT YOU SAW WAS A WORLD FROM THE PAST THAT LINKS TO THE PRESENT.
WERE YOU ABLE TO MEET ...
...TOMOE-KUN?
Flinch
NO.
WHO ...
...DID YOU WANT TO MEET?

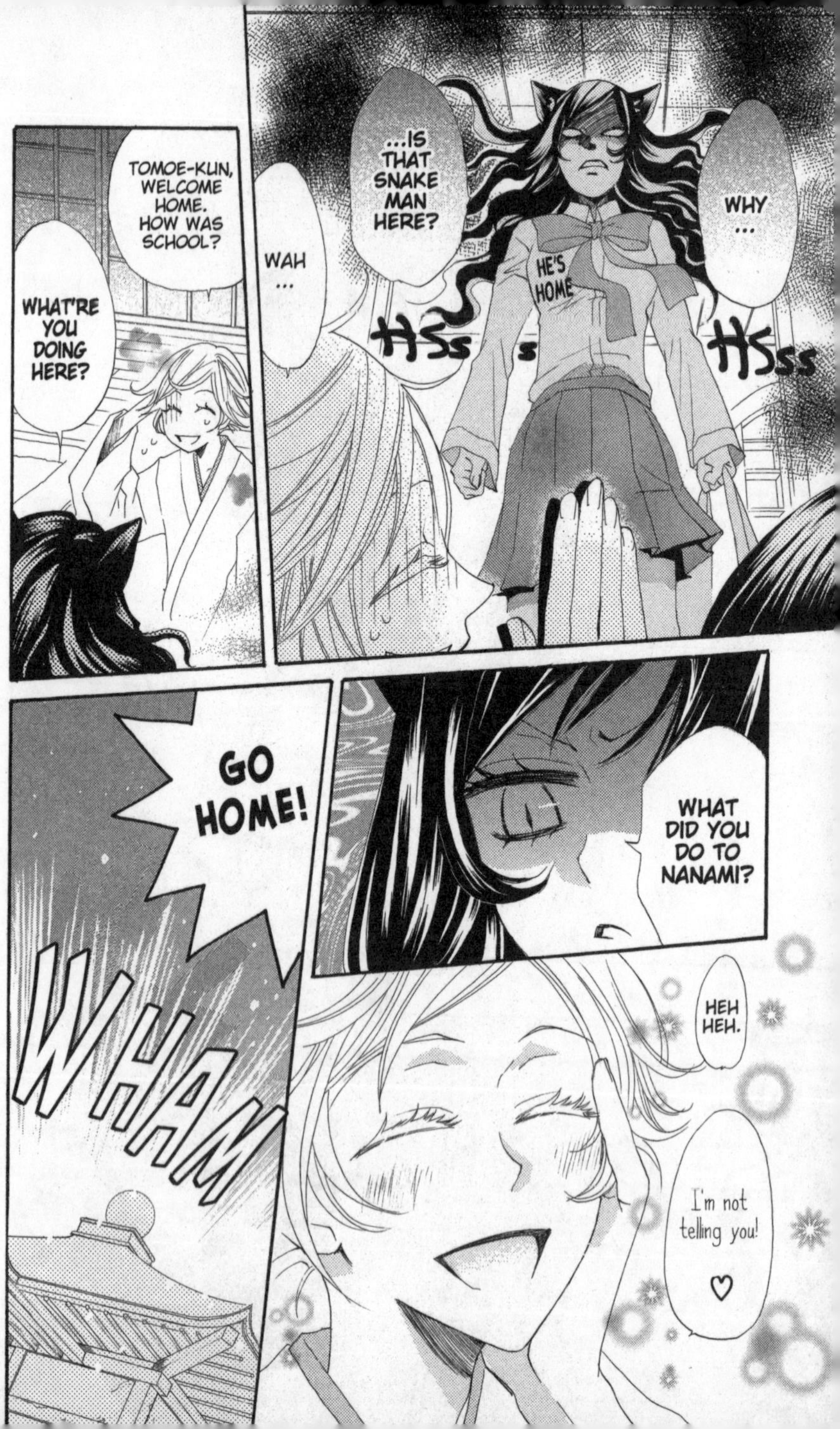
WHY ...
...IS THAT SNAKE MAN HERE?
HE'S HOME
HSss
s
HSss
WAH ...
TOMOE-KUN, WELCOME HOME. HOW WAS SCHOOL?
WHAT'RE YOU DOING HERE?
WHAT DID YOU DO TO NANAMI?
HEH HEH.
I'm not telling you! ♡
GO HOME!
WHAM

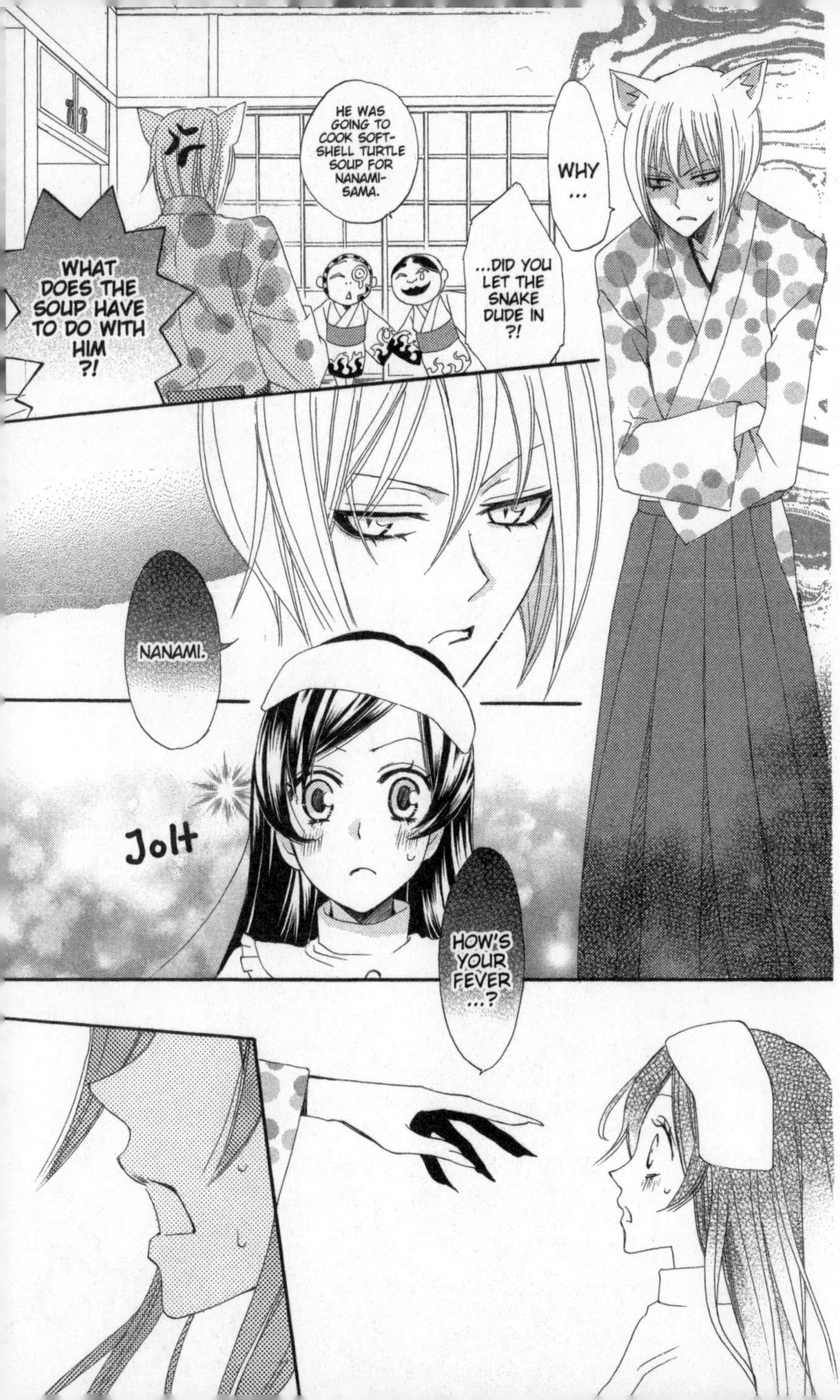
WHY ...
...DID YOU LET THE SNAKE DUDE IN ?!
HE WAS GOING TO COOK SOFT-SHELL TURTLE SOUP FOR NANAMI-SAMA.
WHAT DOES THE SOUP HAVE TO DO WITH HIM ?!
NANAMI.
Jolt
HOW'S YOUR FEVER ...?

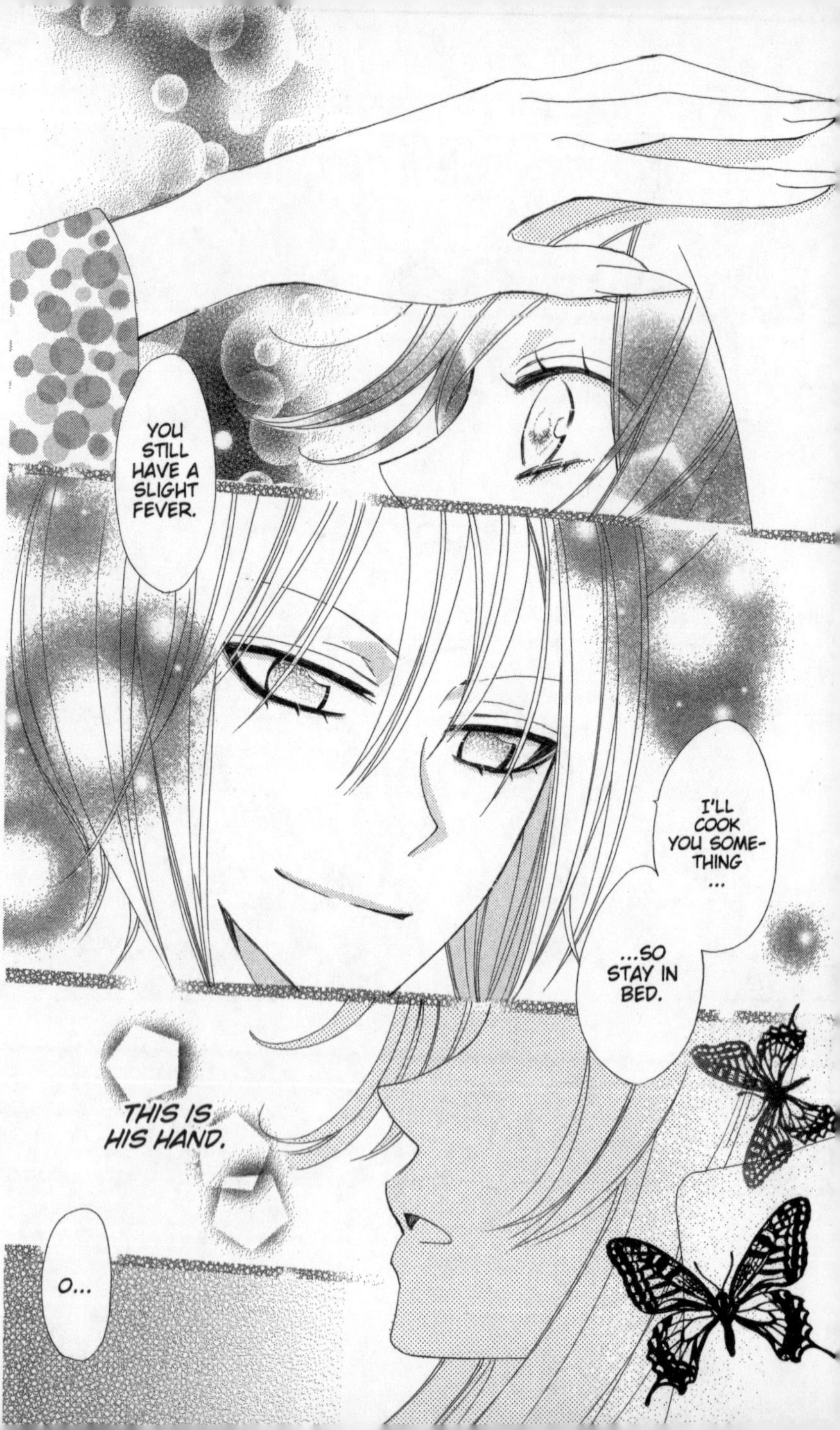
YOU STILL HAVE A SLIGHT FEVER.
I'LL COOK YOU SOME-THING...
...SO STAY IN BED.
THIS IS HIS HAND.
O...

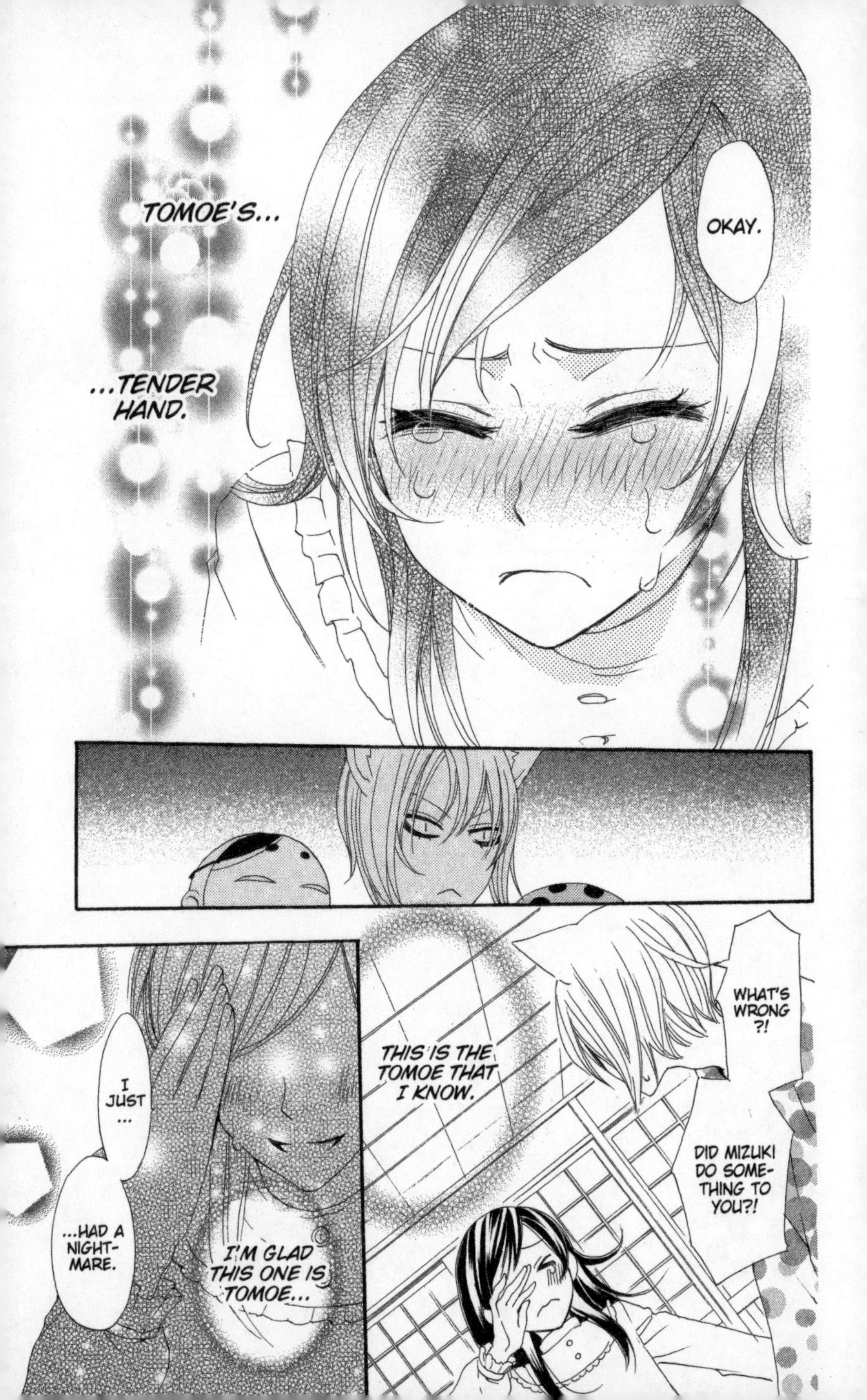
OKAY.
TOMOE'S...
...TENDER HAND.
WHAT'S WRONG ?!
DID MIZUKI DO SOME-THING TO YOU?!
THIS IS THE TOMOE THAT I KNOW.
I JUST ...
...HAD A NIGHT-MARE.
I'M GLAD THIS ONE IS TOMOE...

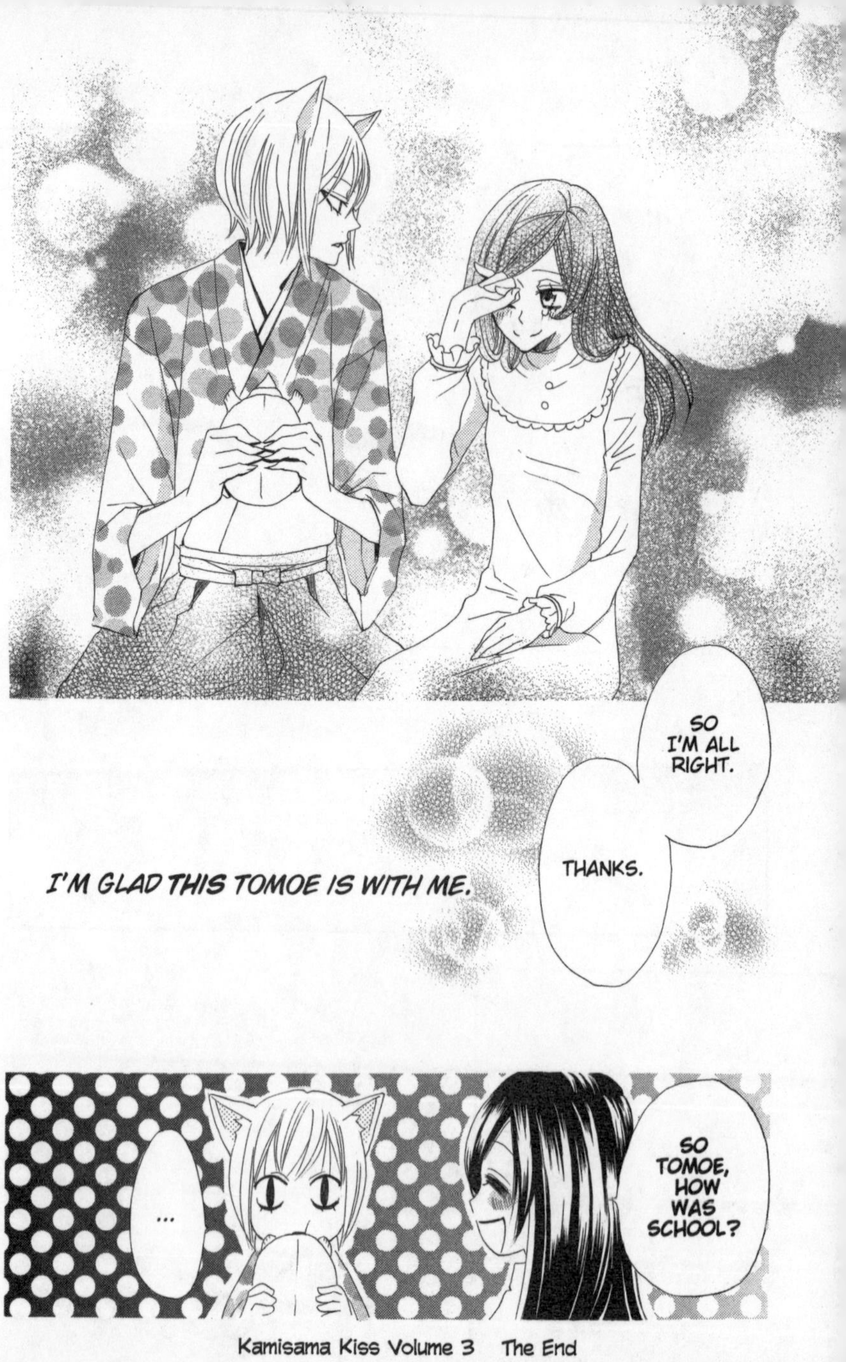
SO I'M ALL RIGHT.
THANKS.
I'M GLAD THIS TOMOE IS WITH ME.
SO TOMOE, HOW WAS SCHOOL?
...

Kamisama Kiss Volume 3 The End

The Otherworld

Ayakashi is an archaic term for yokai.

Kami are Shinto deities or spirits. The word can be used for a range of creatures, from nature spirits to strong and dangerous gods.

Kitsunebi literally means "fox fire" and are the flames controlled by fox spirits.

Onibi-warashi are like will-o'-the-wisps.

Shinshi are birds, beasts, insects or fish that have a special relationship with a kami.

Shirohebi means "white snake" and is a type of yokai.

Tengu are a type of yokai. They are sometimes associated with excess pride.

Honorifics

-chan is a diminutive most often used with babies, children or teenage girls.

-dono roughly means "my lord," although not in the aristocratic sense.

-himemiko is a title that means "Imperial princess."

-kun is used by persons of superior rank to their juniors. It can sometimes have a familiar connotation.

-sama is used with people of much higher rank.

-san is a standard honorific similar to Mr., Mrs., Miss or Ms.

Notes

Page 10, panel 2: Kosode
A basic Japanese robe worn by both women and men, as either an inner or outer garment. The name means "small sleeves."

Page 11, panel 4: Obi
The wrapped sash worn with kimono.

Page 23, sidebar: Takachiho
Many Japanese myths are located in Takachiho, including that of Ninigi, the grandson of the sun goddess Amaterasu, who descended from heaven.

Page 40, panel 3: Tomoe's white too
Many white animals are considered lucky or holy in Japan.

Page 59, panel 2: Day duty, daybook
In Japan, students take turns recording what occurs in the classroom in a daybook.

Page 68, panel 1: PIA magazine
This Japanese magazine specializes in write-ups of culture and entertainment.

Page 75, sidebar: Kendo
Japanese sword fighting. *Kendo* means "way of the sword."

Page 102, panel 4: Went into hiding
A euphemism for dying. This is the expression used when the emperor passes away.

Page 162, panel 1: Softshell turtle
Said to purify the blood and increase stamina (and male virility).

Page 164, panel 2: Kotodama
Literally "word spirit," the spiritual power believed to dwell in words. In Shinto, the words you speak are believed to affect reality.

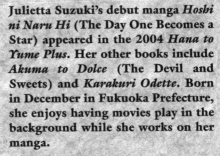

Julietta Suzuki's debut manga *Hoshi ni Naru Hi* (The Day One Becomes a Star) appeared in the 2004 *Hana to Yume Plus*. Her other books include *Akuma to Dolce* (The Devil and Sweets) and *Karakuri Odette*. Born in December in Fukuoka Prefecture, she enjoys having movies play in the background while she works on her manga.

KAMISAMA KISS
VOL. 3
Shojo Beat Edition

STORY AND ART BY
Julietta Suzuki

English Translation & Adaptation/Tomo Kimura
Touch-up Art & Lettering/Joanna Estep
Cover Design/Hidemi Dunn
Interior Design/Yukiko Whitley
Editor/Pancha Diaz

KAMISAMA HAJIMEMASHITA by Julietta Suzuki
© Julietta Suzuki 2009
All rights reserved.
First published in Japan in 2009 by HAKUSENSHA, Inc., Tokyo.
English language translation rights arranged with
HAKUSENSHA, Inc., Tokyo.

Printed in Italy

Published by VIZ Media, LLC
P.O. Box 77010
San Francisco, CA 94107

13
First printing, June 2011
Thirteenth printing, May 2024

viz.com   shojobeat.com

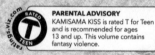

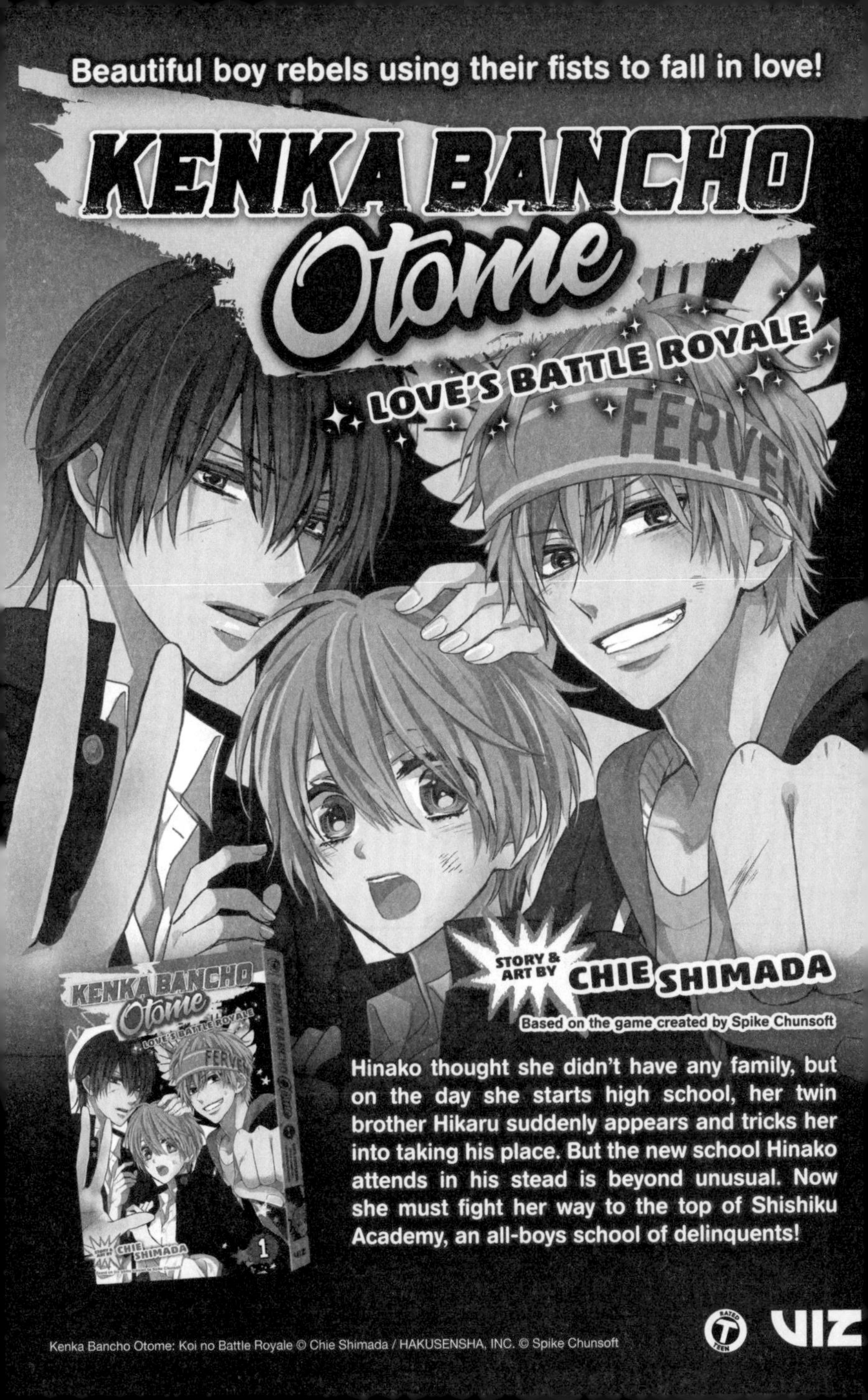
Beautiful boy rebels using their fists to fall in love!
KENKA BANCHO
Otome
LOVE'S BATTLE ROYALE
STORY & ART BY CHIE SHIMADA
Based on the game created by Spike Chunsoft
Hinako thought she didn't have any family, but on the day she starts high school, her twin brother Hikaru suddenly appears and tricks her into taking his place. But the new school Hinako attends in his stead is beyond unusual. Now she must fight her way to the top of Shishiku Academy, an all-boys school of delinquents!
RATED T TEEN
VIZ
Kenka Bancho Otome: Koi no Battle Royale © Chie Shimada / HAKUSENSHA, INC. © Spike Chunsoft

This is the last page.

In keeping with the original Japanese comic format, this book reads from right to left—so action, sound effects, and word balloons are completely reversed. This preserves the orientation of the original artwork—plus, it's fun! Check out the diagram shown here to get the hang of things, and then turn to the other side of the book to get started!